ASIA'S FINANCIAL MARKETS

CAPITALISING ON REFORM

EAAU

East Asia Analytical Unit

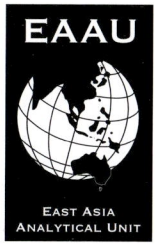

DEPARTMENT OF FOREIGN AFFAIRS AND TRADE

PACIFIC POWER

BHP

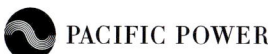

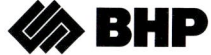

www.dfat.gov.au/eaau

© Commonwealth of Australia 1999

This work is copyright. Apart from any use permitted under the *Copyright Act 1968*, no part may be reproduced by any process without prior written permission from the East Asia Analytical Unit. Requests and inquiries concerning reproduction and rights should be addressed to the Executive Director, East Asia Analytical Unit, Department of Foreign Affairs and Trade, RG Casey Building, John McEwen Crescent, Barton ACT 0221.

The Australian Agency for International Development and Department of Industry, Science and Resources contributed to the cost of producing this report.

National Library of Australia Cataloguing-in-Publication data: 26 October 1999

Asia's financial markets: capitalising on reform

Bibliography.

Includes index.

ISBN 0 642 56561 9.

ISBN 0 642 56560 0 (CD-ROM)

1. Markets – Asia. 2. Banks and banking – Asia. 3. Financial crises – Asia. 4. Financial institutions – Asia. 5. Asia – Economic conditions. I. Australia. East Asia Analytical Unit.

332.095

Design, typesetting and printing by Green Advertising #12034

ACKNOWLEDGMENTS

This report was designed and managed by William Brummitt, Director, East Asia Analytical Unit. Dr Frances Perkins, Executive Director, provided advice and oversight; Chris Elstoft, Deputy Director, made up the remainder of the research team; and Edward Sulikowski, Director, was responsible for the Korea chapter. Susan Prosser and Katrina Sargent provided research and administrative assistance.

Australian missions in Asia provided invaluable assistance in producing this report. In particular, thanks are due to those overseas missions which helped to coordinate EAAU visits to the region and provided data and analysis: Manila (Nicholas Coppel, Jeremy Kruse, Jane Carangal); Kuala Lumpur (Steve Scott), Singapore (Michaela Browning), Bangkok (David Grabau and Pornthida Thongplengsri); Beijing (Mick Shadwick and Jason Fitts); Shanghai (Nancy Gordon); Hong Kong (Alan Atchison); Jakarta (Tony Urbanski, Kate Duff and Mike Waslin); Seoul (David Garner and Liza Chong); Taipei (Christopher Smith and Jill Collins); and Tokyo (Trevor Wilson, Walter Goode, Sally Anne Watts and Margaret Bowen).

The EAAU wishes to acknowledge the valuable contributions provided by the following consultants: Professor Michael Aitken, Dr Alex Frino, Dr Michael Briers, Dr Roland Winn and Dr Carole Comerton-Forde, all of the Securities Industry Research Centre of Asia-Pacific; Professor Tony Naughton, Griffith University; Dr Jian-Xin Wang and Vic Edwards, Asia Pacific Financial Research Centre; Dr Luke Gower, Dr Heather Smith, and Dr Ross McLeod, Australian National University; Dr Jenny Corbett, Nissan Institute for Japanese Studies, Oxford University; Professor Kui-Wai Li, City University of Hong Kong; Professor Michael Skully and Dr Mohammed Ariff, Monash University; and Patrick de Fontenay and Dr Suiwah Leung, National Centre for Development Studies, Australian National University.

Within the Department of Foreign Affairs and Trade in Canberra, Joanna Hewitt, Deputy Secretary, Colin Heseltine, First Assistant Secretary, North Asia Division; Mark Pierce, Assistant Secretary, Services and Intellectual Property Branch; Michael Wood, Director and Paul Wojciechowski, Executive Officer, International Economics and Finance Section; Les Humphries and Greta Nielsen, Hong Kong, Macau and Taiwan Section provided useful comments. The International Economy, Financial Institutions and International Finance Divisions within The Australian Treasury all provided valuable comments as did Andrew Lumsden from the Australian Centre for Global Finance, Dr Gordon de Brouwer and Dr Robert Rankin from the Reserve Bank of Australia; Robert McKinnon and Anthony Krieg from AusAID; Jan Coggan from Austrade; and Karl Brennan from the Department of Industry, Science and Resources.

Others who provided valuable assistance in Australia, include Ken Waller, Senior Economic Adviser, CMG Asia; James Fennessy, Anthony Gill and Glenn Goddard of Macquarie Bank; Steven Chambers, of the Sydney Futures Exchange; Michael Roche, Executive General Manager, and Dimitri Burshtein, Australian Stock Exchange; Julie Newman, First Data Corporation; Penny Hewitt, AXA National Mutual Holdings; and Professor Ian Harper, Melbourne Business School.

Thanks are due also to the participants in the AusAID funded workshop organised by the East Asia Analytical Unit and the National Centre for Development Studies at the Australian National University. In particular the following participants provided papers which were valuable contributions: Diwa Guinigundo, Bangko Sentral ng Pilipinas; Gill Beltran, the Philippine Ministry of Finance; and Dr Somchai Sujjapongse, Thai Ministry of Finance.

Special thanks also are due to the following people in Asia who gave time to be interviewed by the East Asia Analytical Unit, or supplied material, information and insights.

In the Philippines we thank: Michael La Brooy, General Manager, ANZ Philippines; Dr Johnny Noe E. Ravalo, Chief Economist, Bankers Association of the Philippines; Joven T. Balbosa W.I. Carr Securities; Henri Lorie, IMF representative in Manila; Diwa Guinigundo, Director, Department of Economic Research, Banko Sentral Pilipinas; Dr Cayetano Paderanga, Member of the Monetary Board, Bangko Sentral ng Pilipinas; Dr Vaughn Montes, Vice President, Citibank; Professor Ben Diokno, Budget Secretary; and Dr Ghon Rhee, Asian Development Bank resident scholar.

In Hong Kong we thank: David T.R. Carse, Deputy Chief Executive, Hong Kong Monetary Authority; John Hobson, Head of Asian Banking Research, Credit Suisse First Boston; Peter Cutler, Director, Fitch IBCA; Henny Sender, Finance Editor, *Far Eastern Economic Review*; Ken Davies, Chief Economist, Economist Intelligence Unit; Peter Murray, Managing Director, Stephen Yun-Li Jen, Principal, Andy Xie, Executive Director, Morgan Stanley Asia Limited; Dr Andrew Freris, Chief Economist, Bank of America; Andrew Proctor, Member of the Commission and Executive Director, Securities and Futures Commission; Dr Guonan Ma, Co-head of economic research, Asia-Pacific region, Salomon Smith Barney; Peter Richardson, General Manager and Guy Beale, Head Of Markets, Foreign Exchange, ANZ Bank; Ian Perkin, Chief Economist, HK Chamber Of Commerce; Joe Zhang, W.I. Carr Securities; Louis Quinn, US Treasury Representative, US Consulate; K.Y. Tang, Financial Services Bureau, HK Government; and Harry Wu, Research Fellow, Hong Kong Polytechnic University.

In Thailand we thank: Steve Sloman, Associate Director, PricewaterhouseCoopers Financial Advisory Services; Dr Pakorn Vichyanondh, Thailand Development Research Institute; Glen Collins, General Manager, National Australia Bank; Sub. Lt. Yodchai Choosri, Office of the Corporate Debt Restructuring Advisory Committee; Siritida Panomwon, Bank of Thailand; Dr Somchai Sujjapongse, Ministry of Finance; Gary White, Chief Representative, Westpac and head of Australian-Thai Chamber of Commerce; Patareeya Benjapolchai, Senior Vice President, Securities and Exchange Commission; Yothin Koo-Smith, Stock Exchange of Thailand; Ian Pascoe, Partner, Grant Thornton Thailand; Michael Markels and Jacques Bussieres, Senior Advisers, World Bank; John Hancock, Baker and McKenzie; Desmond Holmes, ANZ Bank; David Took, counsel; Alan Wood and Alan Fieldus, Krungthai AXA Insurance (NML); and Thanomsri Fongarun-Rung, Phatra Research Institute, Phatra Securities Company.

In Indonesia we thank: Harry Wiguna, Director, Jakarta Stock Exchange; Dasa Sutantio, Senior Vice President, Indonesian Bank Restructuring Agency; Yves Guerard, Chairman, Ernst and Young (Canada); Freddy Saragih, Indra Surya and Gonthor Aziz, Capital Market Supervisory Agency (BAPEPAM); Anthony Kuek,

Asian Development Bank; Indromen Saragih, Director of Insurance, Ministry of Finance; Dr Muliaman Hadad, Office of the Governor, Bank Indonesia; Anton Gunawan, Faculty of Economics, University of Indonesia; and David Cain and Zaki Mansoer, The Jakarta Initiative.

In Singapore we thank: Dr Tan Lin Yeok and Dr Amina Tyalbji, National University of Singapore; Koh Foong Yin, Vice President and Chief Manager, Economics Department, Overseas Union Bank; Ang Swee Tian, President, and Jeffrey Tan, Vice President, Business Planning, SIMEX; Neil Saker, Director, Head Of Research, and Manu Bhaskaran, Managing Director, Group Head of Research, SG Securities; Ronald Chong, Manager Public Affairs, Central Provident Fund Board; Andrew Tulloch, Manager, Investment Attraction, Invest Australia; and Kostas Panagiotou, Senior Economist, Kim Eng Securities.

In Malaysia we thank: Ranjit Ajit Singh, General Manager, Economic Analysis and Financial Policy, Securities Commission; Associate Professor Mahani Zainal Abidin, Associate Professor of Economics, University of Malaya and National Economic Action Council; Shariffuddin Khalid, General Manager, Communications and Human Resources and Liew Willip, Head, Research Unit, Corporate Services Division, Danaharta; Nasaruddin Arshad, Director, Economics Division, Public Bank; Wilson Wong, Assistant Vice President, Malaysian Rating Corporation Limited; Christopher Gee, Head of Research, Ing Barings; Dr Yeah Kim Leng, Manager, Economics and Marketing Research, Jeffrey Tan Cheong Chai, Manager and Shahina Azura, Deputy Manager, Financial Institution Ratings, Rating Agency Malaysia; Andrew Wong Yee Kong, Manager, Operations, and Mohamed Hazem Abd Rahman, Senior Executive Operations, Danamodal; Abdul Rashid Ghafur, Bank Regulations Department, Nor Aslaini Bte Mohd Nasir, Senior Executive and Chew Hock Poon, Senior Executive, Bank Negara Malaysia; and Khairussaleh Ramli, Senior Manager, International Affairs Department, Ong Li Lee, Manager, Strategic Planning and International Affairs Division, Kuala Lumpur Stock Exchange.

In Korea we thank: Dr Ji Dong-hyun, Director of Research, Korea Institute of Finance; Professor Un-Chan Chung, Economics Department, Seoul University; John Dodsworth, Senior Resident Repesentative, IMF, Seoul; Dr Buhmsoo Choi, Standing Counsellor to the Chairman, Financial Supervisory Commission; Hyung-Gu Shin, Director, Office of International Relations, Securities Supervisory Board; Dr Moon-Suk Oh, LG Economic Research Institute; Professor Phil Sang Lee, Institute for Business Research and Education, Korea University; Yoon Je-Chul, Deputy General Manager, Corporate Management Department, Korea Asset Management Corporation; Dr Yun Jong-mo, Chief Economist, Research Team, Korea Exchange Bank; Dr Hahn Sangsub, Dr Kim Ilhwan and Sung-Rai Cho, Bank of Korea; Dr Park Jae Hu, Chief Financial Policy Division, Korea Institute of Finance; Dr Choi Joong-Kyung, Director, Financial Cooperation Division and Dr Park Young-Chung, Deputy Director, International Financial Institutions Division, MOFE; Dr Shim Sang-dal, Head, Macroeconomic Division and Dr Duk-Hoon Lee, Senior Fellow, Financial Division, Korea Development Institute; Professor Sang-Woo Nam, Korea Development Institute School of International Policy and Management; Dr Lee Young-Ki, Senior Fellow, Korea Development Institute; Dr Mun Kun Cheong, Executive Director, Economic Research Division, Samsung Research Institute; and Kim Joe-Il, Director International Division, Korea Stock Exchange.

In China we thank: Lance Brown, Chief Executive, Standard Chartered Bank, Shanghai; Yan Xu, Shanghai Securities and Futures Regulatory Office; Zhu Congjui, Executive Vice President, Shanghai Stock Exchange; Phil Parton, General Manager, ANZ Bank Shanghai; Frank Xing Zhang, People's Bank of China (PBOC), Shanghai Branch; John Beeman, Country Corporate Officer, Citibank; Dr Geng Qun, Director, Institute of International Finance, Bank of China; Dominic Ziegler, Chief Correspondent, *The Economist*; Professor Huang Da, Member of the Monetary Policy Committee, PBOC; Malachy McAllister, Hong Kong Shanghai Bank, China; Dr Shawn Xu, China International Capital Corporation; Phil Lucas, General Manager, ANZ Bank; Paul Au, General Manager, China Chief Representative, Commonwealth Bank; Charles Brent, Chief Representative, CMG Asia, Beijing; David Kier, Deloitte Touche Tohmatsu; Davin Mackenzie, Chief of Mission, International Finance Corporation, Beijing; Kathy Krumm, Lead Economist, World Bank; Paul Heytens, Acting International Monetary Fund Representative; Cai Zhiwei, China Development Bank; and Dr Wang Haijun, Xinda Asset Management Company.

In Taiwan we thank: Hsien-Nung Kuei, Secretary General, Bureau of Monetary Affairs, Ministry of Finance.

The Australian Agency for International Development, AusAID, and the Department of Industry, Science and Resources provided substantial financial assistance for this report.

We would also like to thank BHP and Pacific Power for their invaluable corporate sponsorship.

Editorial assistance for the report was provided by Ann Duffy, with typesetting by Lyn Lalor.

EAST ASIA ANALYTICAL UNIT

The East Asia Analytical Unit was established in 1990 as the main agency within the Australian Government responsible for publishing analyses of major economic and political issues in Asia.

Located within the Department of Foreign Affairs and Trade, the Unit has to date undertaken and commissioned 22 studies on a range of topics related to Australia's trade policy interests in the region.

Staffed with six professionals, the EAAU also contracts a range of consultants with specific areas of expertise. It draws on a wide range of data and information sources, including reports from Australia's diplomatic and trade missions in Asia.

Reports and briefing papers produced by the unit are intended to assist analysts and decision makers in business, the Australian Government and the academic community.

Full copies of previous reports and briefing papers and executive summaries of reports can now be downloaded from the Internet. See access details below.

Contact details:

East Asia Analytical Unit
Department of Foreign Affairs and Trade
RG Casey Building
John McEwen Crescent
Barton ACT 0221
Australia

Executive Director of the Unit:
Dr Frances Perkins

Directors:
Edward Sulikowski
William Brummitt

Deputy Directors:
Chris Elstoft
James Bloomfield

Administration:
Susan Prosser

Telephone: 61 2 6261 2237
Facsimile: 61 2 6261 3493
Email: eastasia.analytical@dfat.gov.au
Internet site: www.dfat.gov.au/eaau

CONTENTS

Executive Summary		**1**
	Capital Flows and the Crisis	2
	Prudential Reforms	2
	Banking Reforms and Developments	3
	Capital Market Developments	4
	Non-bank Financial Institutions	6
	Indonesia	6
	Thailand, Malaysia and the Philippines	7
	Hong Kong and Singapore	8
	Taiwan	9
	Japan	9
	China	10
	Korea	11
	Implications for Australia	12
Chapter 1	**Setting the Scene**	**13**
	Post-crisis Financial Market Prospects	14
	Key Issues in Asian Financial Sector Reform	15
	Economy Level Financial Market Developments	16
	References	19
Chapter 2	**Capital Flows and the Crisis**	**21**
	Role of Capital Flows in the Financial Crisis	21
	The Causes of Capital Inflows	24
	Capital Inflow Composition and the Crisis	27
	International Bank Lending in East Asia	32
	Reforming International Financial Architecture	34
	Financial Restructuring, Capital Inflows and Recovery	36
	Post-crisis Exchange Rate and Monetary Policy Trends	37
	Conclusions	39
	Appendix 2.1 - Maturity and Sector Distribution of International Bank Lending to Asia-5 and China	40
	Appendix 2.2 - Financial Restructuring Measures Agreed with IMF	42
	References	44
Chapter 3	**Prudential and Financial Infrastructure Reform**	**47**
	Prudential Failures and the Crisis	47
	Prudential Regulation	49
	Prudential Supervision	54
	Market Regulation through Disclosure	61

	Corporate Governance Reforms	63
	Financial Market Infrastructure	65
	The Payments System	67
	Deposit Insurance Schemes	69
	Future Prospects	72
	References	73
Chapter 4	**Banking in Post-crisis Asia**	**75**
	Banks' Importance in East Asia	75
	NPL Problems in East Asian Banks	77
	Approaches to Banking Reform	81
	Global Trends in Financial Services Industries	87
	East Asian Financial Market Trends	88
	Foreign Banks in East Asia	93
	Opportunities for Foreign Banks	95
	Conclusions	97
	Appendix Table 4.1 - Bank Mergers and Acquisitions in East Asia Involving Foreign Financial Institutions, January 1998 to September 1999	98
	References	100
Chapter 5	**Capital Markets**	**103**
	The Importance of Capital Markets	103
	East Asian Equity Markets	**104**
	Post-crisis Stock Exchange Reforms	108
	Stock Market Consolidation	114
	Asian Bond Markets	**116**
	Trends in the Size and Role of Bond Markets	116
	Major Constraints on East Asian Bond Markets	119
	Outlook for Asia's Bond Markets	124
	Risk Management Instruments	**125**
	Derivatives and Financial Risk Reduction	125
	Derivatives Use in East Asian Markets	126
	Derivatives Regulation	131
	Moves to Automated Exchanges	133
	Foreign Traders in Derivative Markets	133
	Likely Future Trends in East Asian Derivatives Markets	134
	Conclusions	135
	References	136

Chapter 6	Non-bank Financial Institutions	139
	The Nature and Role of NBFIs	139
	Poorly Regulated NBFIs and the Crisis	140
	Insurance Companies	143
	Pension Funds	149
	Challenges in the NBFI Sector	154
	Conclusions	155
	References	156
Chapter 7	Indonesia	159
	Impact of the Crisis	159
	Banking Growth and Crisis	162
	Bank Restructuring	164
	Foreign Participation in Bank Restructuring	168
	Corporate Debt Restructuring	169
	Stock Market Development	170
	The Bond Market	171
	The Insurance Sector	173
	Reforming the Financial and Legal Infrastructure	174
	Future Challenges for Financial System Recovery	179
	References	180
Chapter 8	Thailand, Malaysia and the Philippines	183
	Thailand	**183**
	Prelude to the Crisis	184
	Impact of the Crisis on Financial Markets	185
	Major Post-crisis Reforms	185
	Improving Financial and Legal Infrastructure	187
	Recapitalising the Banking System	188
	Resolving NPLs	190
	Disposing of Nationalised Banks and Finance Companies	191
	Prudential Control Prospects	193
	Financial System Prospects and Opportunities	194
	Malaysia	**195**
	Impact of the Crisis	196
	Prudential Regulation and Supervision Reforms	197
	Capital Market Reforms	198
	Capital Controls	199
	Resolving NPLs and Recapitalising the Banking System	200
	Consolidating the Financial Sector	203
	Foreign Participation	203
	Future Trends and Challenges	204

The Philippines — 205

- Pre-crisis Experiences — 205
- Financial System Structure — 206
- Impact of the Crisis on Financial Markets — 207
- Pre-crisis Financial Sector Reforms — 209
- Post-crisis Banking Reforms — 209
- Prudential Supervision Reforms — 212
- Mergers — 213
- Foreign Financial Institution Entry — 213
- Capital Market Developments — 214
- Future Challenges — 215
- Prospects for Thailand, Malaysia and the Philippines — 216
- References — 218

Chapter 9 Hong Kong and Singapore — 221

Hong Kong — 221

- Prudential Regulation — 221
- Banking System Structure — 222
- Hong Kong's Banking Reforms — 223
- Hong Kong's Capital Market and Pension Reforms — 224
- Hong Kong's Currency Board and the Peg — 227

Singapore — 230

- Financial System Structure — 230
- Singapore's Financial Market Reforms — 231
- Singapore's Banking Sector Foreign Investment Reforms — 233
- Central Provident Fund Reforms — 234
- Singapore's Future Trends and Opportunities — 235
- Implications for Hong Kong and Singapore — 236
- References — 237

Chapter 10 Taiwan — 239

- Financial Sector Performance in the Crisis — 239
- The Regulatory System — 242
- The Banking System — 243
- Taiwan's Banks during the Crisis — 245
- Banks' Wider Business Scope — 246
- Bank Rationalisation — 247
- Foreign Bank Operations — 247
- Non-bank Financial Institutions — 249
- The Informal Financial Sector — 251
- Capital Markets — 252
- Future Challenges — 256
- Conclusions — 257
- References — 258

Chapter 11	Japan	261
	Financial Sector Developments	261
	Major Financial Sector Reforms	263
	Non-performing Loans	265
	Scale of NPLs	266
	Structural Change in Banking and Insurance	270
	The Growing Foreign Presence	273
	Industry Level Foreign Participation Trends	274
	Australia's presence in Japan's Financial Sector	277
	Factors Promoting Foreign Financial Institutions	277
	Likely Future Trends	279
	Future Challenges	280
	Conclusions	281
	References	282
Chapter 12	China	285
	Structure of China's Financial Sector	286
	The People's Bank of China	289
	The Four State Owned Commercial Banks	291
	Key Commercial Bank Weaknesses	293
	Bank Management Reforms	295
	Non-performing Loans	295
	Asset Management Companies	297
	Deposit Insurance Scheme	299
	The State Policy Banks	299
	Other Commercial Banks	300
	Foreign Banks	302
	Non-bank Financial Institutions	305
	Insurance Companies	305
	Trust and Investment Companies	308
	Credit Cooperatives	310
	Capital Markets	310
	Stock Markets	311
	Bond Markets	313
	Prospects for Foreign Financial Institutions	315
	Conclusions	315
	References	316
Chapter 13	Korea	319
	Pre-crisis Financial Market Management	319
	Post-crisis Financial Sector Reform	320
	Bank Restructuring	321
	Non-bank Financial Institution Restructuring	322
	Cost of Financial Sector Restructuring	323
	Prudential Regulation and Supervision Reform	324

	Capital Market Developments	325
	Stock Market Developments	326
	Futures and Options Markets	327
	Bond Markets	328
	Financial Sector Consolidation	331
	Prospects for Foreign Financial Institutions	332
	Financial Sector's Long Term Recovery Prospects	334
	References	336
Chapter 14	**Implications For Australia**	**339**
	Implications for Government	339
	Implications for Australian Business	341
	Implications of Australia's Financial Market Performance	343
	Australia as a Regional Financial Centre	344
	Future Prospects	345
	References	347
Index		**349**
Also by the East Asia Analytical Unit		**357**

GLOSSARY

A-share	An 'A-share' is a Chinese share which only local residents can buy and sell, in renminbi.
APEC	Asia Pacific Economic Cooperation, a cooperative grouping of Asian, North American, Latin American economies and Australia and New Zealand.
ATM	Automatic Teller Machine.
B-share	A 'B-share' is a Chinese share which only foreigners can buy and sell, in foreign currency.
BIS	Bank for International Settlements.
Capital account liberalisation	A process of removing capital controls and restrictions on the convertability of currency.
Capital adequacy	A risk management concept requiring financial institutions to have sufficient capital to protect their counterparties and depositors from on and off-balance sheet risks, including non-performing loans. Capital adequacy requirements tend to be simple mechanical rules.
	Ability to provide banking services to the public while maintaining the legally required ratio of capital to assets.
Capital adequacy ratio	A ratio of capital to a financial institution's risk weighted assets, used in financial sector regulation.
	The minimum Bank for International Settlements' capital adequacy ratio is 8 per cent of risk weighted assets.
Capital markets	Markets for longer term capital largely consisting of equity and bond markets.
Chapter 11 provision	A provision in US bankruptcy laws that gives firms a respite from their creditors while they try to resolve their financial difficulties.
Convertible bond	Corporate loan stock that can be converted into the issuer's common or preferred stock at a stipulated price over a designated time.
Demutualisation	Mutual organisations are owned by members and generally only members can receive services provided. Demutualisation involves moving from ownership by members to another ownership structure, generally a limited liability public company, where there is no link between ownership and access to services.
Derivative	A financial product where the payoff depends on changes in the value of an underlying asset.

Disintermediation	A process whereby companies borrow money directly from institutions such as capital markets, and depositors put their money directly into institutions such as the stock market and cash management funds rather than into banks.
Futures and forwards	Derivative transactions in underlying assets taking place at a future date whose terms, such as price and quantity, are determined today.
GDP	Gross domestic product, the total net value added in an economy.
IBRA	Indonesia Bank Restructuring Agency.
IMF	International Monetary Fund.
Interbank market	Market between banks for foreign exchange, eurodeposits or domestic funds.
Intermediation	The process of banks accepting deposits, pooling them and making loans.
Internationalisation of financial services	Eliminates discrimination in treatment between foreign and domestic financial service providers.
Investment, or merchant, banking	The business of raising debt and equity financing for companies from sources other than deposits.
Market capitalisation	The total shares on issue multiplied by the market price of the shares.
Market infrastructure	Trading facilities, payment systems, trading personnel and communications facilities, which form the basic operational support for market activities.
Market maker	Any dealer who regularly quotes both bids and offers and is ready to make a two-sided market.
	A trader on the floor of an exchange who enjoys certain trading privileges in exchange for accepting an obligation to help maintain a fair and orderly market.
Marking to market	An accounting adjustment to reflect unrealised gains or losses on book values at the end of a particular period.
Moral hazard	Moral hazard arises when uncertainty, incomplete contracts or government intervention prevent the assignment of full damages or benefits to the agent responsible. When unchecked it can create incentives to repeat behaviour that is detrimental to society as a whole.
Non-performing loans, NPLs	The emerging international standard is to consider loans as non-performing when they are three months or more in arrears on interest payments.
OECD	Organisation for Economic Cooperation and Development.

Operating expense ratio	Shows the percentage of insurance premiums spent on operating expenses.
Options	Contracts which give the holder a right to buy (or sell) an underlying asset at a fixed price.
Over-the-counter markets	Financial markets in which contracts are not traded on exchanges.
Real effective exchange rate	An exchange rate measure showing changes in trade competitiveness by adjusting the official exchange rate against a single currency (such as the US dollar) for exchange rate and inflation movements in an economy's trading partners, on a trade weighted basis.
Real time gross settlement (RTGS)	Systems which settle, in full, individual fund transfers continually during the processing day, helping to reduce two major sources of risk in the payment system: the time lag between the execution of the transaction and its final completion, and the lag between the payment and delivery of a transaction.
Reinsurance	The spreading of insurance risk between insurers. In return for a premium, an insurer may pass all or part of the insurance risk to another insurer.
Securitisation	A financial technique that repackages assets or receivables that have a predictable and regular cashflow into tradeable securities.
Trade finance	The generic term covering many types of trade related banking activity, ranging from simply issuing letters of credit to structuring complex countertrade transactions.
Underwriting of securities	The process by which an underwriting syndicate of securities firms or, less frequently a single security firm, guarantees the sale of an issue of securities by purchasing it at a stated price from the issuing enterprise for resale to public customers at a slightly higher price.
WTO	World Trade Organisation.
Yield curve	Shows the relationship between bond yields and maturity length. A risk free yield curve, ideally based on government bond yields, is important in pricing non-government bonds.

EXECUTIVE SUMMARY

As 2000 approaches, East Asia's financial markets are reforming, consolidating and restructuring. These systemic changes are driven by the Asian financial crisis, intense market positioning to secure lucrative regional financial centre business, and global technological and regulatory changes.

The financial crisis forced a major overhaul of regional prudential regulations, supervisory mechanisms and legal frameworks including bankruptcy laws. Governments of the Republic of Korea,[1] Thailand and Indonesia responded to the crisis by opening financial markets to international competition, potentially enhancing long term efficiency and transparency. However, global trends also are driving enormous changes in world financial markets, including universal banking (the removal of regulatory barriers between different financial sectors); greater segmentation of banking into deposit taking, lending and funds management; new products like securitisation; and rapidly developing electronic commerce, especially Internet banking and stockbroking. Many of these changes increasingly affect East Asian financial markets; at the same time, these markets are absorbing the systemic shocks of the financial crisis. This report analyses the likely long term impact on regional financial markets of the crisis and these global competitive, technological and regulatory changes. It assesses the response of regional policy makers to these challenges and the resulting opportunities for international, particularly Australian, financial sector institutions and service providers.

Serious structural weakness in East Asian financial markets and prudential controls substantially caused the financial crisis. Consequently, financial sector reform, restructuring and refinancing is essential to sustain regional economic recovery. While most regional economies can further improve prudential supervision and competition, the better supervised, provisioned and capitalised financial sectors emerging from the crisis will be significantly more open and efficient, and support more sustainable growth. By late 1999, of the most seriously affected regional economies, Korea, Japan and Malaysia had progressed considerably in resolving banks' non-performing loans, refinancing financial institutions and strengthening prudential controls. Thailand's progress is slower but still significant, while Indonesia's attempts to address its serious systemic problems have been impeded by political uncertainty and controversy.

In the long term, major competitive, technological and global regulatory changes could affect East Asian financial markets as much as the crisis has in the short term. As Sydney, Tokyo, Hong Kong, Singapore and Shanghai position themselves to attract regional and global financial centre business, their governments are streamlining regulatory and taxation frameworks to increase their competitive advantage. Falling regulatory barriers between financial sectors are driving mergers and acquisitions, increasing competition and encouraging the development of financial conglomerates. Internet and electronic banking are changing the viability

---

[1] The Republic of Korea is referred to as Korea in the remainder of this report.

of bank branching, and encouraging the segmentation of previously integrated banks into specialist deposit taking, funds management and lending institutions. New products like securitisation hasten this process by allowing banks to package and on-sell mortgages and other loans, freeing balance sheets for new lending activities.

Currently these developments are most prevalent in Japan, Australia, Hong Kong and Singapore. However, eventually these trends will affect all regional financial markets, particularly those in Korea, the Philippines, Taiwan and Malaysia, which are being strengthened by crisis induced reforms.

CAPITAL FLOWS AND THE CRISIS

Large capital inflows to the region were central to the crisis; thus regional and foreign governments have incentives to reduce the volatility and misuse of international capital flows. Pre-crisis capital flows often caused significant exchange rate appreciation. Where capital inflows exceeded productive investment opportunities, resources were wasted through excessive expansion of real estate and industrial capacity. Korea, Thailand and Indonesia were particularly vulnerable because their high levels of short term foreign debt exceeded their foreign exchange reserves, and most foreign debt was unhedged.

However, the region's long term economic health depends on the resumption of more stable, well invested capital flows, particularly foreign direct investment. Thailand, Malaysia and the Philippines need to attract foreign capital because they relied heavily on capital inflows before the crisis and Indonesia, Korea and Thailand need inflows because they are incurring huge foreign and domestic liabilities refinancing their banking systems.

Immediate crisis induced changes affecting regional capital flows include more freely floating exchange rates, rapid financial sector consolidation, increased international participation in regional financial markets and reduced regional lending by international, particularly Japanese, banks. In the longer term, other crisis induced changes should include improved financial sector and possibly corporate transparency, and streamlined bankruptcy procedures. Also, in the medium to long term, reform of international financial architecture to improve system stability should complement domestic reform efforts. International working groups are according priority to: adopting international standards and codes on a range of prudential and corporate governance issues; increasing transparency in both the public and private sectors; examining the volatility of capital flows; assessing the role of offshore financial centres and highly leveraged institutions, including hedge funds; and increasing private sector involvement in crisis prevention and management.

PRUDENTIAL REFORMS

In Indonesia, Thailand and Korea, poor prudential regulation and supervision contributed to the financial crisis. Consequently, their strengthening is central to IMF-endorsed recovery programs. Across East Asia, though to varying degrees, central banks are becoming more independent and supervisors require better bank capitalisation and provisioning for non-performing loans. Even non-crisis economies learned lessons from the crisis and are upgrading prudential standards. For example,

China has adopted the international standard, five category loan classification system, and is strengthening bank management control, prudential regulations and payment systems to reduce systemic risk.

Before the crisis, many regional banks were poorly capitalised. In Indonesia and Thailand, reported average capital adequacy ratios were adequate, but many individual banks were well below the Basle Bank for International Settlements' standard levels. Regulators often failed to enforce controls on lending to bank owners and related companies. Limits on credit to volatile sectors like real estate and advances of foreign exchange to unhedged borrowers were largely ineffective.

While all regional economies aim to upgrade their financial market regulation and supervision, Indonesia and Thailand will take some years to build supervisory skills and effectively implement new laws and regulations. Major prudential control reforms in regional economies include:

- strengthening prudential regulations like capital adequacy ratios, loan loss provisioning and non-performing loan classifications
- introducing legal reforms, including upgraded bankruptcy laws
- increasing supervisors' independence and expecting better performance, as in Korea, Japan, China, Thailand and Indonesia
- moving supervision from central banks to new, integrated supervisors to facilitate consolidated supervision, as in Australia, Japan, Indonesia and Korea
- replacing blanket government deposit guarantees issued during the crisis with limited deposit insurance schemes, as in Korea and Japan, and possibly in China, Indonesia and Malaysia
- introducing market based regulation and raising disclosure standards, as in Singapore, the Philippines, Korea and Malaysia.

The new international capital accord, currently being negotiated to replace the 1988 Basle Capital Accord in late 2000, will reduce reliance on rules based regulation by emphasising better disclosure, stronger internal risk management systems and greater use of credit rating agency assessments.

BANKING REFORMS AND DEVELOPMENTS

The financial crisis severely affected banks in Indonesia, Thailand, Malaysia and Korea, and exacerbated serious Japanese banking problems evident since the early 1990s. Banking systems, which dominate regional financial markets, now are undergoing major consolidations, refinancing and often, temporary nationalisation. Governments of many of the most severely affected economies have recapitalised banks with public funds and established asset management companies to purchase non-performing loans.

Among these, Korea and Malaysia are most successful. By late 1999, Korea almost had completed its purchase of non-performing loans in the banking sector and disposal of assets was well underway. Malaysia's asset management company also quickly purchased non-performing loans but its disposal strategy emphasises restructuring failing businesses and waiting for market recovery. Thailand allows banks to dispose of most non-performing loans and refinance themselves; this approach may reduce the short term public cost of bank restructuring but slows recovery and could increase long term economic costs.

Executive Summary

Structural changes to the global financial services industry will reinforce the crisis driven restructuring of East Asia's financial markets. The spread of new financial products and electronic banking, and growing competition from non-bank financial institutions and capital markets should increase:

- competition for traditional bank business as large foreign financial institutions purchase parts of distressed financial institutions and asset portfolios from asset management companies

- securitisation as East Asia's post-crisis environment stresses capital adequacy; securitisation enables banks and other institutions to originate loans, then shift them off balance sheets by selling them to firms who package them for securitisation

- the importance of bank profitability as banks repair capital bases and compete for equity funds; banks will emphasise lower cost approaches such as electronic banking, higher fee incomes and fewer cross subsidies.

Since the crisis began, many regional governments have raised allowable foreign equity levels in local banks. Indonesia, Korea and Thailand have liberalised significantly to allow virtually 100 per cent foreign ownership of existing banks; the Philippines has similar legislation before Congress. Since January 1998, foreign financial institutions have acquired all or part of 18 East Asian banks. Standard Chartered, ABN Amro and the Development Bank of Singapore are particularly active, and Thailand, the Philippines and Korea are among the most attractive economies for acquisitions.

Other opportunities for foreign financial institutions include purchasing discrete financial sector activities, forming partnerships and strategic alliances in specific areas, supplying outsourced services and assisting local banks to reform. Australian financial institutions are actively pursuing these opportunities. For example, Macquarie Bank formed partnerships with China Construction Bank in housing loan securitisation and Industrial Bank of Japan in derivatives trading. The Colonial Mutual Group, CMG Asia, formed joint ventures in Thailand, Indonesia, Malaysia and China. As part of its acquisition of equity in Panin Bank, ANZ is transferring its experience of Australian banking industry restructuring.

CAPITAL MARKET DEVELOPMENTS

Since the crisis, Japanese and Korean corporate bond markets have been most resilient, although bond markets in Hong Kong, Singapore, Taiwan and Malaysia also are promising. However, in many East Asian economies, underdeveloped capital markets increase reliance on short term, often volatile domestic and international bank lending. Deeper primary and secondary bond and equity markets allow corporates to raise more stable long term finance. However, lack of secondary capital markets inhibits primary markets, as investors are reluctant to buy if they cannot readily sell. More developed derivative markets also would help corporates hedge risk.

While all East Asian equity markets except Japan remain small in world terms, contrary to worldwide trends, consolidation is not on the agenda. As trading on larger exchanges is cheaper, in the US and European markets, the second and fourth largest US stock exchanges are merging, and the London and German stock exchanges are leading the move to a single European stock market. Although most East Asian equity markets had recovered much of their financial crisis losses by late 1999, capitalisation of the Tokyo and Osaka exchanges remains over three times that of all other East Asian exchanges combined. However most East Asian (and even provincial) governments see their stock and futures exchanges in nationalistic terms and are unwilling to merge with other exchanges even if this is commercially viable. If large European and US exchanges extend their electronic networks to the region and attract top East Asian stocks, they could marginalise smaller East Asian exchanges.

Since the financial crisis, East Asian equity markets have reformed across a broad front, strengthening information disclosure, accounting standards, brokerage provisioning, market surveillance and enforcement. Exchanges in Korea, Malaysia and Taiwan are progressing significantly to improve information disclosure, often using Internet based systems. Equity markets in Thailand, Malaysia, China, Hong Kong, Singapore and the Philippines require listed companies to adopt international accounting standards. However, compliance remains a major concern. For example, despite recent reports that around 80 per cent of Indonesian listed companies are technically insolvent, the number of listed Indonesian companies actually grew in 1998.

Key constraints on East Asian bond markets include inadequate prudential frameworks, poor corporate governance, unsympathetic taxation regimes, an absence of benchmark yield curves and credible local rating agencies, and poor settlement and liquidity support systems. The Hong Kong, Singapore and Malaysian governments strongly support bond market development, but other economies need to strengthen transparency and corporate governance before their markets can expand significantly. With widespread computerised trading, market surveillance must improve to keep pace with faster trading. Exchanges in Hong Kong and Indonesia use an Australian-made real time surveillance system to assist in surveillance. As most East Asian governments issue more bonds to finance bank recapitalisation and stimulate economic activity, they will help to establish benchmark yield curves, thereby developing corporate bond markets.

Greater use before the crisis of financial derivatives, particularly foreign exchange and interest rate hedging, would have protected corporates during the crisis. However, use of derivatives should expand post-crisis as exchange rates float more freely and the need to manage risks is better understood. While many East Asian economies have exchange traded and over-the-counter futures markets, liquidity often is thin. Also, in many regional economies, the opportunities to hedge domestic interest rates and currency risk offshore are limited. Official permission for offshore based derivative markets therefore is important to expand regional corporates' hedging options.

Regulation is critical for derivative market development. Regulations should protect market integrity while minimising the impact on market liquidity and efficiency. As many East Asian futures exchanges were established after the Barings incident, most strongly regulate dual trading and trade reporting. However, controls on daily price movements are likely to be counter-productive, as they prevent traders from trading when they most want to. The Sydney Futures Exchange is the only regional exchange that does not limit price movements.

Executive Summary

NON-BANK FINANCIAL INSTITUTIONS

In Thailand, Korea and Malaysia, poorly regulated non-bank financial institutions, NBFIs, such as finance companies and merchant banks, helped trigger the financial crisis. Consequently, regional governments have strengthened NBFI regulations, introducing risk based capital requirements for merchant banks, finance companies and insurers, and consolidating NBFI supervisory responsibility. As economic growth resumes, NBFIs should become increasingly important players in regional financial markets; consequently, further regulatory framework refinement will be critical. Expected growth in these markets will create significant opportunities for foreign and domestic financial institutions.

While badly regulated NBFIs can cause systemic risk, well supervised institutions can contribute significantly to regional economic development. Life insurance and pension funds provide important stores of long term savings to fund long lived investments, and promote capital market development and financial product innovation. These benefits are amplified if funds are managed competitively rather than by monopoly institutions, which usually achieve low returns and do not trade bonds or develop new products.

Until 1998, life insurance premiums grew rapidly throughout East Asia. However, the financial crisis hit premium growth, particularly in Malaysia, Indonesia and Thailand; the Philippines and China were less affected. The crisis has left many life insurers severely undercapitalised; in Korea and Japan, several have closed, and throughout the region, more closures are likely. Many insurers now seek foreign capital. However, once economic growth recovers, strong premium growth should resume, boosted by higher incomes, population aging and, in Korea, Indonesia, Thailand, China and the Philippines, lack of universal pension schemes. This growth should occur as foreign access to regional insurance markets is liberalised further, significantly expanding opportunities for foreign financial institutions.

Pension fund development varies enormously depending on the economy's development. Singapore and Malaysia have comprehensive schemes, although most funds are centrally managed and generate low returns; China and Hong Kong are establishing comprehensive pension schemes. Hong Kong's Mandatory Provident Fund should set the benchmark for funds management, offering employers a choice of providers and employees a choice of funds. The regional trend is to ease restrictions on what asset classes are investable and who manages pension assets. This trend also opens major new opportunities for foreign financial institutions.

INDONESIA

From late 1997, Indonesia suffered the world's worst banking crisis since the 1970s. Its cost could reach 80 per cent of GDP and quadruple the country's public debt. By the end of 1999, the Indonesian Government will own banks holding 85 per cent of banking system deposits. Moreover, 75 to 85 per cent of bank loans are non-performing, so the task to recapitalise, restructure and eventually re-privatise banks is massive. With international financial institution assistance, the Government has established the institutional mechanisms to restructure bank and corporate debt, and after long delays, achieved limited progress. Unfortunately, the Bank Bali scandal undermined market confidence in the Indonesian Bank Restructuring Agency, delaying insolvent bank restructuring.

While the Government has removed most restrictions on foreign ownership of banks and insurers, international investors have been cautious; ANZ and Standard Chartered bought sizeable stakes in strong Indonesian banks, but many potential investors consider most local banks too risky.

The financial crisis set Indonesia's capital market development back several years, but by late 1999, these markets were recovering. The insurance industry is underdeveloped, dominated by state enterprises and monopolistic practices. It requires widespread consolidation as its many players have inadequate capital.

While new laws foreshadow the long term tightening of prudential regulations and supervision, the severity of the crisis forced the Government to loosen prudential regulations in the short to medium term. To date, the new bankruptcy framework has been only partly successful and courts will need strong decisions to convince creditors that their loans are secure. Consequently, increased scrutiny of the judiciary is a positive sign. However, strengthening the accounting profession, corporate governance and government transparency remain major challenges.

THAILAND, MALAYSIA AND THE PHILIPPINES

In 1997 and 1998, Thailand, Malaysia and the Philippines all experienced similar currency depreciations, stock market falls and interest rate rises as a result of the Asian crisis. Thailand and Malaysia also suffered serious financial market and economic turmoil; as a result, both are undergoing significant programs to refinance and restructure their financial sectors, and improve prudential controls. The Philippines' stronger prudential system and extensive foreign currency deposits cushioned it during the crisis. Nevertheless, the Philippine Government is using the opportunity to upgrade its prudential system.

Since the crisis began, half of Thailand's banks and most of its finance companies have been closed, nationalised or taken over by foreign companies. The overall cost of repaying depositors and restructuring and refinancing financial institutions could reach Baht 2 trillion (US$54 billion) or 35 to 40 per cent of 1999 GDP. Slow corporate and financial restructuring, including by bank owners loath to lose control over their banks, has lengthened and deepened the crisis. However, as foreign banks purchase nationalised banks and form strategic alliances they should increase competition and change banking practices over time. Prudential reforms are a high priority, but Thailand's supervisors may take some time to establish credibility with market analysts.

In 1997-99, the Malaysian Government led its banking system rescue using two restructuring agencies, Danaharta, to purchase non-performing loans, and Danamodal, to recapitalise banks. However, following banking crises in 1985-86 and 1997-99, the Malaysian Government has signalled it cannot tolerate further bank bailouts and wants bigger, stronger banks. Consequently, in mid 1999, it announced it wants all domestic banks to merge into six or more major banking groups by the end of 2000. Owners can chose their partners on the basis of commercial criteria.

The Malaysian Government generally has addressed financial system weaknesses rapidly and effectively. Bank Negara Malaysia, the central bank, is strict and transparent, and is pushing ahead with consolidated and risk based supervision. Malaysia continues to recapitalise and restructure its banking system; however, unlike the Philippines, Indonesia, Korea and Thailand, it is unlikely to further open financial markets to international competition in the short term. While capital controls give Malaysia greater policy flexibility, they may deter foreign investors, and are not giving a clear boost to economic performance relative to Malaysia's neighbours with open capital accounts. Pre-crisis Malaysian capital markets were better developed than those of Thailand or the Philippines, and with the large volumes of new government bonds issued during the crisis, they will grow significantly.

The Philippines escaped the financial crisis without a systemic banking crisis, partly because it learned the lessons of previous crises, and partly because its asset boom was less advanced than Thailand's or Malaysia's. Over the past 30 years, the Philippine central bank has received extensive IMF assistance, and before the crisis, it had begun many of the central bank independence and prudential control reforms Thailand and Indonesia now are undertaking. Nevertheless, its uncompetitive banking system needs considerable consolidation and competitive pressure, and less onerous taxation and reserve requirements would reduce the large gap between borrowing and lending rates. Bank mergers already are underway, and likely future regulatory changes promise greater market opening and competition. The insurance industry is one of the most open in East Asia, and capital markets are developing with the merger of the two stock exchanges, and improved transparency and regulation.

HONG KONG AND SINGAPORE

Since the Asian financial crisis, Hong Kong has implemented some significant financial market reforms, including announcing banking sector liberalisation and a stock and futures exchange merger. However, during the crisis, the Government significantly intervened in the stock market and tightened regulations to deter currency speculators; these actions concern some analysts.

While the Hong Kong dollar peg is not central to Hong Kong's future as a regional financial centre, the Government remains strongly committed to it. However, the peg caused Hong Kong's economy to fare badly during the crisis, compared to economies like Singapore, which have a flexible exchange rate. The peg needed high interest rates to defend it; these severely restricted local economic activity. However, recent reforms should reduce interest rate rises from speculative attacks on the Hong Kong dollar. While Hong Kong's markets are relatively flexible, they could not compensate for the pegged exchange rate's real appreciation resulting from major regional devaluations in 1997-98, and Hong Kong lost international competitiveness.

Singapore has implemented comprehensive financial market reforms since the financial crisis began. The speed of liberalisation indicates the Monetary Authority of Singapore now sees Singapore's status as a regional financial centre as a more important policy goal than the survival of individual financial institutions. Singapore's securities market regulation is moving towards a disclosure based system. Important banking reforms include introducing a new class of foreign bank licence with fewer restrictions on branching, and abolishing foreign equity limits on new banks. While full foreign takeovers of domestically-owned banks remain unlikely, decisions to abolish foreign equity limits and permit financial holding companies should stimulate mergers and alliances.

Executive Summary

TAIWAN

Taiwan's economy was strong throughout the crisis. Strong macroeconomic management, prudent bank lending policies and much lower foreign borrowing exposure largely explain this good performance. Taiwan was less dependent on foreign borrowing because it is a large net exporter of capital, it has generally sound prudential controls and has a relatively small divergence between US and domestic Taiwanese interest rates.

However, Taiwan's financial system faces several important challenges. With a population of 22 million and around 470 deposit taking institutions, Taiwan is over-banked. Consequently Taiwan's financial institution consolidation process is ongoing, moving towards universal banking and stimulated by reforms to remove barriers between financial sectors. Conglomerate ownership of banks and connected lending also present challenges for Taiwan's regulators. Since 1990, Taiwan's equity market capitalisation has more than tripled and the number of listed firms has doubled. However, around 500 major firms chose not to list, preferring to retain family control. While corporate bond issues are growing strongly, secondary market trading is negligible, largely because of taxation barriers.

Reforms in 1994 and 1999 further opened Taiwan's financial sectors to foreign financial institutions. This trend is likely to continue as part of Taiwan's bid for World Trade Organisation membership. The stock exchange offers attractive opportunities for international participation, including custodial business managing foreign capital, and work on the rapidly growing initial public offers market. Taiwan's new derivatives market also may provide attractive opportunities, as volumes and product range grow. The Government currently is considering a proposal to allow foreign banks to acquire a 50 per cent share in local banks.

JAPAN

Although it is too early to be certain, major reforms in Japan's financial sector may well reinforce the fiscal stimulus and underpin the nascent economic recovery evident in late 1999. The Japanese Government was very slow to react to the severe financial sector problems, which had been evident since the early 1990s. However, since 1996, the Government has improved significantly the financial supervisory system and addressed major banks' non-performing loan, provisioning and capital adequacy problems.

Recent government capital injections helped major banks write off and provide for non-performing loans; in March 1999, these were 8 per cent of loans. However, smaller local Japanese banks' non-performing loans were still 12 per cent of loans. Preliminary estimates of investment losses in Japan's life insurance companies range from 10 to 18 per cent of assets, with problems compounded by gaps between returns received on funds and yields guaranteed to many policy holders. These problems must be resolved urgently, as after banks, life insurers are the most important store of Japanese wealth.

Lower regulatory barriers between financial sectors, increased international participation, low profitability and high levels of non-performing loans are transforming Japan's financial sector. Consolidation is underway with mergers and alliances occurring among domestic institutions. However, some mergers driven by public funds injections may not be commercially based.

Executive Summary

Despite stagnant economic growth, expanding opportunities stimulated foreign financial sector investment approvals worth US$3.5 billion in 1998; this was more than in the previous six years combined. Many foreign financial institutions, including Macquarie Bank, are forming alliances with local firms. Fewer firewalls between financial markets allow foreign financial institutions entering Japan to access the many opportunities the restructuring process provides. For example, many Japanese banks now undertake trust business by forming strategic alliances with international banks and insurance companies.

Other major trends also are shaping Japan's financial system. Financial institutions' poor stock market performance, government's reduced willingness to rescue failing institutions and several major bankruptcies are driving a growing preoccupation with profitability. The focus on profits is straining some main bank relationships (cross-shareholding patterns and exclusive business relationships between local banks and corporates). These relationships often inhibit foreign financial institutions from expanding business with Japanese corporates. In addition, life insurers are becoming more proactive institutional investors, taking a more direct interest in their investment firms. Finally, the Government is liberalising rules on pension fund management, and even government pension funds employ some international fund managers. These developments, along with major transparency and 1996 'big bang' regulatory reforms, systematically are changing Japan's financial sector.

CHINA

While China's financial sector has many features that caused financial crises in other East Asian economies, the Asian financial crisis only modestly affected China. Nevertheless, economic growth slowed during 1998 and 1999, due to poor export performance, relatively tight monetary policy and structural problems, including an inefficient financial sector. Throughout the crisis the Government maintained the renminbi's peg to the US dollar; it is unlikely to free capital controls or move to a floating exchange rate until it completes essential financial sector and state enterprise reforms. Government-directed lending to state owned enterprises, a weak prudential and legal framework, limited financial sector disclosure and restricted foreign competition have generated serious non-performing loan problems in the dominant state owned banking sector.

Since the Asian financial crisis began, the Government has accorded top priority to financial sector reform, and is making good progress. Although the financial sector will take many years to become efficient and commercially oriented, most analysts anticipate that if reforms announced since late 1997 are implemented successfully, the Government should avert a financial sector crisis. In any case, the almost total state ownership of China's financial institutions makes serious bank runs unlikely. Over the next two to three years, financial sector and state owned enterprise reform needs continued high priority to stop banks accumulating new non-performing loans.

The significant financial sector reform program announced in early 1998 tightened bank loan classifications, raised bank and non-bank financial institution capital adequacy ratios to 8 per cent and required financial institutions to upgrade their accounting standards. The Government also is upgrading the prudential supervision of banks, the stock market, insurers, pension schemes and credit cooperatives.

Most importantly, the Chinese Government acknowledged it must tackle the banks' non-performing loan problem; at over 30 per cent of outstanding loans, these are significant. In April 1999, the Government established four new asset management companies at the four major commercial banks to dispose of non-performing loans. While the Government has not yet announced who will fund this write-off, the lesson from Japan is that covering up these problems within the banking system slows growth; eventually the taxpayer will have to pay most of the cost.

The Government is slowly increasing domestic and foreign competition in Chinese financial markets. By late 1999, it had issued 17 limited domestic currency banking licences and nine joint-venture insurance licences. Because of operating restrictions, foreign financial institutions still have only 3 per cent of the local banking and 1 per cent of the local life insurance market. However, foreign financial institutions' role should expand after China enters the World Trade Organisation.

KOREA

By late 1997, Korea's foreign exchange reserves equalled only two weeks of imports and 8 per cent of foreign debt. As Korea faced the prospect of defaulting on its foreign trade and borrowing obligations, the Government made an emergency arrangement with the IMF. In early 1998, to avert a potential collapse of the financial system, the Government guaranteed bank deposits, tightened capital adequacy ratios and established mechanisms for purchasing banks' non-performing loans and recapitalising banks. These policies were implemented effectively and rapidly, although the Daewoo collapse and related difficulties of investment trust companies introduced new uncertainty regarding the total cost. The Korean Government significantly improved financial market prudential regulations, approaching Bank for International Settlements' standards, and strengthened enforcement. It also strengthened corporate and bank transparency, introduced new international accounting standards and strengthened minority shareholder rights.

To strengthen equity, bond and money markets, the Korean Government liberalised virtually all international capital movements, foreign participation in bond and equity markets and funds management, and foreign takeovers of domestic companies. It also has consolidated and strengthened capital market regulation and supervision.

Crisis related bankruptcies and reform, technological change and foreign competition are stimulating significant financial sector consolidation. In a reshaped Korean financial industry, foreign investors should play a prominent role. As a result of recent reforms, foreign investors are participating in several bank takeovers and joint ventures, including of First Korea Bank, Korea Housing Bank and Korea Exchange Bank. Foreign financial institutions also are entering broking, insurance and funds management sectors, introducing competition and modern, profit oriented business and management practices. In line with global trends, the Government is removing divisions between Korean banks, securities companies, insurers and other financial institutions.

IMPLICATIONS FOR AUSTRALIA

Major reforms and restructuring in East Asian financial markets significantly affect Australian business and government.

The Australian economy and financial sectors performed strongly during the financial crisis, partly because over the past two decades, Australia has reformed prudential controls and liberalised its financial market. These moves strengthen Australia's position as a regional and global financial centre, as do skilled, competitively priced financial market human resources. Recent taxation reforms enhance this competitiveness; consequently major foreign financial institutions including Citibank, Deutsche Bank and Hong Kong Shanghai Bank are relocating regional functions to Australia.

Australian financial service providers and institutions are well placed to compete for emerging business opportunities in East Asia. Opportunities are occurring in banking, capital markets and non-bank financial institutions. Australian financial institutions have actively formed joint ventures in specific business areas, including derivatives, securitisation and credit card business. Other opportunities include acquisitions, business outsourcing, funds management, software provision to improve financial institution management, risk management and regulatory enforcement. However, in most parts of the world, significant barriers remain to financial service providers; consequently the World Trade Organisation mandated negotiations on financial services, starting January 2000, are important to both Australia and the region.

The financial crisis highlighted the importance of economic governance in bilateral development assistance programs. Augmenting its ongoing economic governance assistance, AusAID is implementing the major new economic governance initiative for East Asia announced by the Australian Prime Minister at the 1998 APEC Leaders' Meeting. This is funding a broad range of assistance programs, including skills transfer to East Asian governments from many Australian regulatory and economic management institutions, such as the Reserve Bank of Australia, the Australian Prudential Regulation Authority, the Australian Attorney General's Department and the Bureau of Statistics. Scope may exist to expand such programs and to provide other economic management training courses.

If regional governments maintain reform momentum, their generally effective responses eventually should underpin stronger, more sustainable regional growth. Reforms and market opening, as well as global technological developments will provide opportunities for Australian financial institutions and service providers.

Chapter 1

SETTING THE SCENE

Before the 1997-98 Asian financial crisis, East Asia enjoyed enormous economic success. Since the 1960s, East Asian economies had grown faster than any other region's, and absolute poverty had declined significantly.[1] However, in many regional economies, financial sectors formed the weak link in development strategies. Because many financial sectors were protected from foreign and domestic competition, regulated poorly or subjected to government credit allocation and interest rate intervention, they often were inefficient, poorly capitalised and weak in managing risk. Private and state owned banks dominated financial activity at the expense of capital markets and non-bank financial institutions. Banks often made capital available to favoured sectors and borrowers; lending was based on connections rather than sound credit risk analyses. Consequently, many financial institutions were highly leveraged after lending to risky private and public projects. Heavy, often undiscriminating, international capital flows into these financial sectors exacerbated risks.

The financial crisis seriously challenged Asia's spectacular growth and socio-economic development. In six months from mid 1997, the currencies of Indonesia, Korea, Malaysia, the Philippines and Thailand, hereafter called the Asia-5, almost halved in value against the US dollar.

Net private capital inflows to the Asia-5 of US$63 billion in 1996 turned to outflows of US$20 billion in 1997, then US$45 billion in 1998, and a further US$26 billion in 1999; this credit contraction equalled 16 per cent of the Asia-5's US$935 billion combined, pre-crisis gross domestic product, GDP (Figure 2.6). This capital flight and unhedged foreign debt held by domestic corporates, helped escalate the currency crisis into a major financial crisis that threatened financial systems in Indonesia, Thailand and Korea. By mid 1998, the crisis was affecting emerging markets from Russia to Venezuela, undermining growth in Japan and China, and even threatening international financial system stability.

By late 1999, the region's macroeconomic variables had recovered substantially. Growth was positive; exchange rates were more stable; nominal interest rates had fallen, often to below pre-crisis levels; and current accounts had moved into surplus. However, at the microeconomic level, enormous work remains in Indonesia, Thailand, and to a lesser extent, Malaysia and Korea to restructure financial sectors, write off non-performing loans, NPLs, recapitalise banks and restructure corporate debt. In addition, to protect economies from future crises, all regional governments are undertaking significant structural reforms, strengthening financial market regulation and supervision, opening financial sectors to competition, upgrading bankruptcy procedures and improving financial sector infrastructure. Progress in all these areas is crucial to sustain the region's economic recovery. Moreover, it opens many opportunities for foreign financial institutions.

....

1   Between 1975 and 1995, the poverty rate dropped 95 per cent in Malaysia, 90 per cent in Thailand, 82 per cent in Indonesia, and 63 per cent in China (World Bank, 1998).

Major global regulatory, technological and structural trends also are shaping East Asia's financial markets. Together, with crisis induced developments, they will drive consolidation, competition from new service providers and use of technology based delivery including Internet and electronic banking.

This report analyses the role of capital inflows and poorly regulated financial markets in triggering the crisis, assesses regional governments' reform responses and explores the evolution of regional financial markets since the crisis. Finally, it highlights challenges and opportunities for domestic economic managers and foreign financial institutions resulting from crisis induced and global financial developments.

The report has three main parts:

- the first six chapters examine the role of capital flows in creating the financial crisis, and a range of key, region-wide financial market reforms and global financial market developments in prudential controls, banking, capital markets and non-bank financial institutions
- the next seven chapters examine significant financial sector reforms, challenges and opportunities in major regional economies
- the final chapter draws out implications for Australian business and government.

POST-CRISIS FINANCIAL MARKET PROSPECTS

Structural changes currently underway in regional financial sectors should enhance East Asia's ability to generate sustainable economic growth. However, post-crisis growth may be slower than in the mid 1990s when large short term capital inflows artificially boosted output and currencies (East Asia Analytical Unit, 1998). Furthermore, in the post-crisis environment, regional economies' uneven progress in resolving NPLs, refinancing banks, restructuring corporate debt, opening financial markets and implementing financial market and other reforms could cause economic performance to diverge more than it did pre-crisis.

The financial market reform underway since the crisis is profoundly changing Asian financial markets, upgrading supervision arrangements, lowering barriers between different financial activities, increasing foreign financial institutions' presence and increasing competition for financial service provision. Despite current problems, over the decade to 2010, financial services will be a major growth industry in Asia. Asia's financial services industry will be worth US$450 billion by 2010, more than double its 1998 level, according to a McKinsey estimate. Real growth of 10 per cent per year is projected for non-Japan Asia (Casserly and Gibb, 1999). Tapping into this growth represents a major opportunity for Australia financial service exporters.

Australian Exports of Financial and Insurance Services to Asia

Between 1987 and 1998, Australia's financial and insurance service exports to East Asia rose by an average annual rate of 14 per cent to reach A$183 million; this is 12 per cent of Australia's total exports of these services (Figure 1.1). Furthermore, financial consultancy service exports are not included in this figure. Driven largely by reinsurance business, exports of insurance services grew at 25 per cent per year after 1987, reaching A$69 million in 1998; financial service exports grew 9 per cent per year over this period, reaching $A114 million in 1998.

Setting the Scene

Figure 1.1

Exports of Financial Services Go to Developed East Asian Markets
Australian Financial Service Exports, 1998, A$ million, Per cent

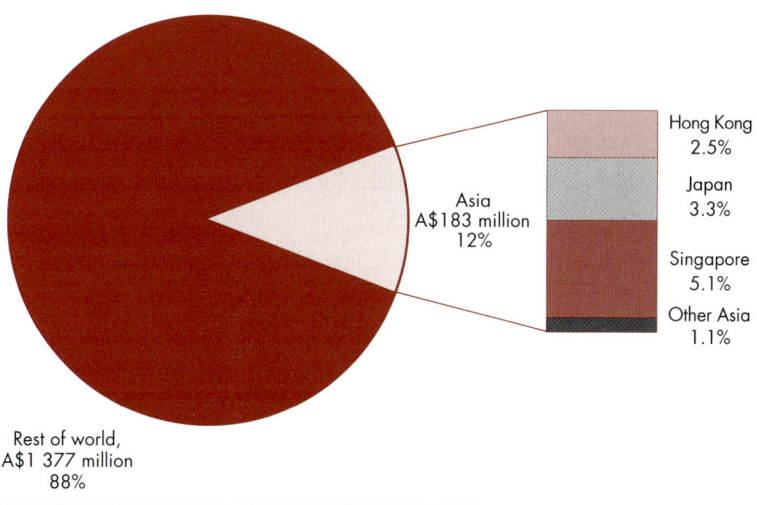

Source: Australian Bureau of Statistics, 1999.

Exports to developed Asian economies dominate Australia's Asian financial service exports (Figure 1.1), confirming that these service exports have considerable potential in the rest of East Asia as incomes rise. Exports of financial services to Singapore and Hong Kong are growing steadily but those to Japan fluctuate considerably.

KEY ISSUES IN ASIAN FINANCIAL SECTOR REFORM

International capital flows are 60 times greater than trade flows (Sutherland, 1998). At the macroeconomic level, international capital flows were at the root of the Asian financial crisis. They also remain critical to Asia's future. How these capital flows helped precipitate the financial crisis, why they occurred and where they went is examined in Chapter 2 - *Capital and the Crisis*. This chapter also examines proposed international financial architecture reforms and the nexus between financial sector reform and growth.

To prevent a recurrence of the financial crisis, restore domestic and foreign investors' faith in regional financial institutions and keep long term savings in Asia, regional governments recognise they must significantly improve prudential regulation and supervision, and develop their financial infrastructure. Several regional governments also are adopting new prudential approaches, including consolidated supervision and disclosure based regulatory regimes, to better supervise open capital markets and universal banks. Chapter 3 - *Prudential Reform* discusses these developments, reforms achieved to date and those still required.

East Asian developing economies, like most other emerging markets, rely heavily on bank finance; in 1994, banking sector assets accounted for 70 per cent of non-Japan East Asia's financial sector assets (World Bank, 1997). In contrast to the United States, banks in Japan, Hong Kong and Singapore are relatively important. Restoring banking sector health therefore is crucial to the economic prospects of East Asian economies. Moreover, as in many western economies, regulatory reforms, new financial products and technological developments will transform banking in East Asia. This process is likely to involve considerable consolidation, the continued growth of financial conglomerates and growing opportunities for foreign financial institutions. Chapter 4 - *Banking* examines major banking reforms, refinancing developments, market opening initiatives, technological developments and future prospects for this sector.

Heavy corporate exposure to short term foreign and domestic bank borrowing was a major cause of the financial crisis. Asian corporates need more liquid domestic stock and corporate bond markets to deliver more stable, less risky and longer term sources of investment finance. While governments in Hong Kong, Singapore and Malaysia are helping to develop corporate bond markets, most regional economies need stronger capital market regulation and supervision, higher corporate governance standards and taxation reforms to encourage capital market growth. Recent developments and reforms are analysed in Chapter 5 - *Capital Markets*.

To date, East Asia has failed to effectively intermediate its enormous savings to meet long term investment needs. As East Asian incomes grow and populations age, consumers will demand more insurance and pension products which should help address this problem. However, their funds will not stay in local financial institutions unless savers have confidence in domestic regulatory frameworks and institutions. This provides an important challenge for governments to strengthen prudential oversight and open domestic financial markets more widely to domestic and international competition. Chapter 6 - *Non-bank Financial Institutions* discusses recent reforms and developments.

ECONOMY LEVEL FINANCIAL MARKET DEVELOPMENTS

Japan is the world's largest capital exporter and second largest economy. Consequently, Japan's financial sector health not only is critical to the Japanese economy but also to the regional and world economies. Japan is Asia's financial market giant; the capitalisation of the Tokyo and Osaka Stock Exchanges is three times greater than that of all other Asian exchanges combined (Federation of International Stock Exchanges, 1999). Furthermore, Japan is in the midst of major reforms, which are transforming its financial sector. Its financial markets now have few formal entry barriers; foreign financial institutions are making major acquisitions and increasingly, are welcome business partners. Chapter 11 - *Japan* analyses the significant progress in Japan's financial market reforms; its achievements in refinancing financial institutions and resolving NPLs, the dramatic financial sector restructuring underway and major emerging opportunities for foreign financial institutions.

Increasingly, the health of China's economy also has region-wide implications. Its financial markets have tremendous potential and slowly are opening to foreign participation. Moreover, a major new round of market opening will occur with

China's anticipated accession to the World Trade Organisation. China's major financial sector problems include high levels of NPLs in the state owned banking sector, massive debts owed by insolvent state owned enterprises, weak and inefficient state owned financial institutions, uneven prudential control and financial sector overcrowding. However, since the crisis, the Chinese Government has launched wide-ranging financial system reforms to strengthen prudential controls and tackle NPLs. Chapter 12 - *China* examines these and other recent financial market developments.

Since 1997, Indonesia has experienced widespread economic, social and political disruption, and the world's worst banking crisis since the 1970s. However, the Indonesian Government also has undertaken major reforms, lifting many restrictions on foreign ownership in banking and insurance, and planning to raise prudential standards over time. It has begun the long process of bank and corporate restructuring but political uncertainty and corruption have slowed progress. The IMF's emergency support program remains a key driver of reform. Chapter 7 - *Indonesia* analyses these issues.

Thailand, Malaysia and the Philippines all experienced major interest rate, exchange rate and stock market shocks during the crisis. However, the Thai and Malaysian financial sectors encountered more severe structural problems than did the Philippines. Malaysia is resolving its financial sector problems quite rapidly; it has largely finished carving NPLs from its banks' balance sheets. Thailand's progress is slower but still significant. The Philippines is using this opportunity to further strengthen prudential controls. In all three economies, future growth hinges on ongoing financial sector reform. Chapter 8 - *Thailand, Malaysia and the Philippines* explores reform progress and future prospects.

Hong Kong and Singapore are developed regional financial centres. Hong Kong is a natural capital source for mainland China while Singapore mainly intermediates capital into South East Asia. The desire to maintain and expand these economies' role as regional financial centres drives their reforms. In many cases, these reforms create new opportunities for Australian financial institutions. In other cases, such as the stock and futures exchange mergers, recent reforms may challenge Australian institutions. Chapter 9 - *Hong Kong and Singapore* examines these issues.

The Taiwanese economy was relatively unaffected by the Asian crisis. However, in 1999, its NPLs rose, many of its conglomerates own banks, and its financial markets are oversupplied, all symptoms of the need for further financial sector strengthening. Taiwan is continuing significant financial market reform, including privatising the large state owned banks, consolidating private banks and cooperatives, and opening its stock exchange to foreign investment. Chapter 10 - *Taiwan* analyses recent reforms and market opportunities.

Since nearly defaulting on short term foreign loans in late 1997, Korea has aggressively implemented financial sector reform: it has opened its financial sectors to foreign competition and takeovers, strengthened prudential control, and rationalised and refinanced banks. As a result, Korea has reaped significant rewards: investor sentiment has improved and rapid economic growth has resumed. Combined with technological change, reforms also are stimulating major financial sector consolidation. Chapter 13 - *Korea* analyses these developments.

Setting the Scene

The Asian financial crisis and its aftermath have important implications for Australian business and government.[2] Chapter 14 - *Implications* discusses these. With its world class regulatory framework and highly developed banking, equity, bond, insurance and superannuation markets, Australia recognises it could become a more important regional and global financial centre. Hence, it is building on its long standing financial reform program and its strong financial sector skills and legal framework, and implementing specific measures to attract foreign financial sector institutions. Major financial institutions like Citibank, Deutsche Bank and the Hong Kong Shanghai Banking Corporation already have located some regional functions in Australia.

The financial crisis highlights the importance of economic governance assistance to support regional financial regulators and build market infrastructure. The Australian Government already provides much ongoing assistance of this type. However, as regional governments and donors identify more specific needs, further Australian assistance may be possible and beneficial.

This report demonstrates East Asia's financial market reforms offer significant opportunities to Australian business. Recent market opening goes beyond anything seriously contemplated before 1997. Key competencies for Australian financial institutions include strong skills in using and customising computer software, a track record of experience in growth areas such as debt restructuring, derivatives and securitisation, and strong skills in risk management. While risks as well as rewards are high, many foreign financial institutions now are actively expanding their presence in East Asia. As the interaction of financial market reform, global technological and regulatory trends, and competition for regional financial business continues, many further opportunities will emerge for Australian financial sector institutions and service providers.

---

[2] Australia, along with the United States and the United Kingdom, is occasionally mentioned in other chapters as a point of reference. However, apart from in Chapter 14 - *Implications*, Australia is not specifically a subject of analysis.

REFERENCES

Australian Bureau of Statistics, ABS, 1999, *Balance of Payments - Regional Series 1997-98*, ABS cat no 5338.0, Canberra.

Casserly, D. and Gibb, G., 1999, *Banking in Asia: the End of Entitlement*, John Wiley and Sons, Singapore.

East Asia Analytical Unit, 1998, *Asia's Infrastructure in the Crisis: Harnessing Private Enterprise*, Department of Foreign Affairs and Trade, Canberra.

Federation of International Stock Exchanges, 1999, 'Annual Statistics on Market Capitalisation', www.fibv.com/statistics, accessed on 28 September.

Sutherland, P., 1998, 'Managing the International Economy in an Age of Globalisation,' The 1998 Per Jacobsson Lecture, the annual meeting of the IMF and the World Bank, October, Washington DC.

World Bank, 1998, *East Asia: The Road to Recovery*, September.

___ 1997, *Private Capital Flows to Developing Countries: the Road to Financial Integration*, Oxford University Press, New York.

Setting the Scene

Chapter 2

CAPITAL FLOWS AND THE CRISIS

World capital flows now outweigh trade flows by a factor of about 60 to 1 (Sutherland, 1998) exerting tremendous influence on world economies. Capital inflows to regional markets were central in creating the 'East Asian miracle' and remain critical to post-crisis recovery. However, large pre-crisis inflows also created vulnerability and abrupt capital outflows precipitated the Asian financial crisis. This volatility generated considerable debate about the adequacy of regional economies' prudential regulation and supervision, and international financial architecture. Reforms to international financial architecture to increase disclosure by highly leveraged institutions, improve the operation of offshore financial centres, reduce capital flow volatility and increase the private sector's role in crisis prevention and management, should complement country level financial market reforms. However, to resume sustainable growth, domestic financial market reforms have the highest priority.

Heavy pre-crisis reliance on short term foreign borrowing was a central cause of the financial crisis. In 1998, by necessity, most regional economies reduced their reliance on short term capital flows after creditors refused to roll over short term loans and the Korean and Indonesian Governments renegotiated the maturity of their private sectors' foreign borrowing. To increase the stability of foreign capital inflows, Thailand, Korea, Indonesia, the Philippines and Malaysia would benefit from increasing their reliance on foreign direct investment relative to foreign borrowing. Recognising this, Korea and Indonesia have significantly liberalised their foreign investment regimes.

This chapter first explores the role of capital flows in precipitating the financial crisis. It examines the nature and impact on various East Asian economies of international capital flows, including short term bank lending, and the causes of capital flow volatility before and since the crisis. The chapter then assesses efforts to reform international financial architecture. Finally, it examines links between financial sector restructuring and growth, and analyses broad trends in post-crisis exchange rate and monetary policy.

ROLE OF CAPITAL FLOWS IN THE FINANCIAL CRISIS

Capital inflows were crucial to the rapid, sustained growth experienced in East Asia over the last 30 years. These inflows financed high investment rates and current account deficits, raising sustainable growth rates and living standards. However, large pre-crisis capital inflows also inflated regional economies' real exchange rates, undermining export competitiveness and encouraging excessive resource allocation to non-traded sectors. In 1996, high real exchange rates slowed export and economic growth, undermining foreign creditor confidence and ultimately contributing to the crisis.

Capital and the Crisis

Exchange Rate Appreciation and Export Slowdown

Until 1995, the strong yen offset pressures for appreciation of the real, trade weighted value of East Asian currencies caused by high capital inflows. However, from mid 1995, the yen depreciated sharply against the US dollar and capital inflows continued; the real effective exchange rates of Indonesia, Thailand, Malaysia, the Philippines and Korea appreciated steeply (Figure 2.1).[1] These five economies, which the financial crisis affected most severely, hereafter are called the Asia-5.

In 1996, these exchange rate appreciations undermined export competitiveness, particularly as the electronic components market also slumped, sharply reducing export and overall economic growth in the export oriented East Asian economies, especially Thailand, Malaysia and Korea (Figure 2.2).

Figure 2.1

Currencies in Crisis Economies Appreciate after 1995
Asia-5 Real Effective Exchange Rates, 1990-99

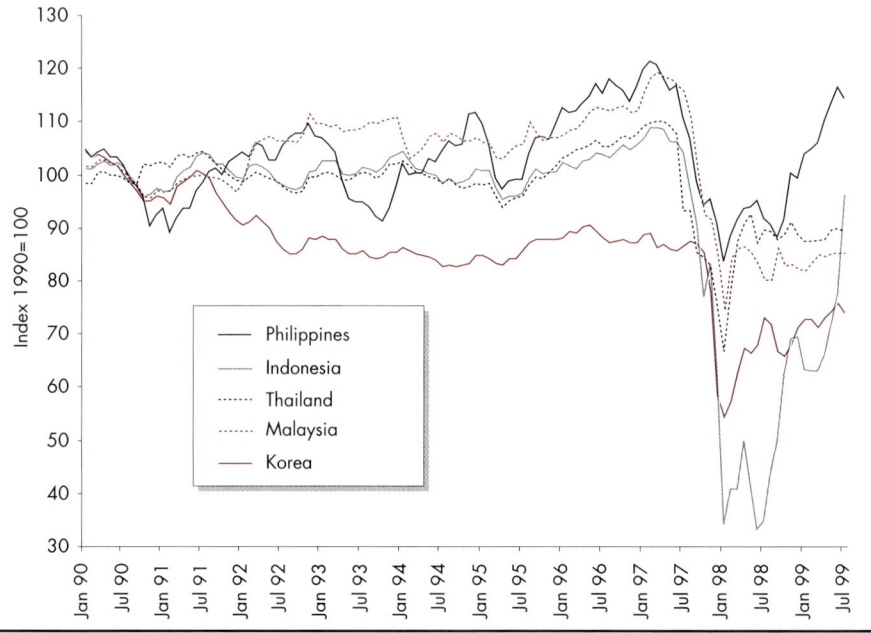

Source: JP Morgan, 1999.

---

[1] Real effective exchange rates show changes in trade competitiveness by adjusting for inflation and exchange rate movements of economies' trading partners, on a trade weighted basis. Between June 1995 and January 1997, real effective exchange rates appreciated by 21 per cent in the Philippines, 14 per cent in Thailand, 11 per cent in Indonesia, 10 per cent in Malaysia and 5 per cent in Korea.

Figure 2.2

Asia-5 Export Growth Drops Sharply after 1995
Growth in US$ Exports, 1995-98

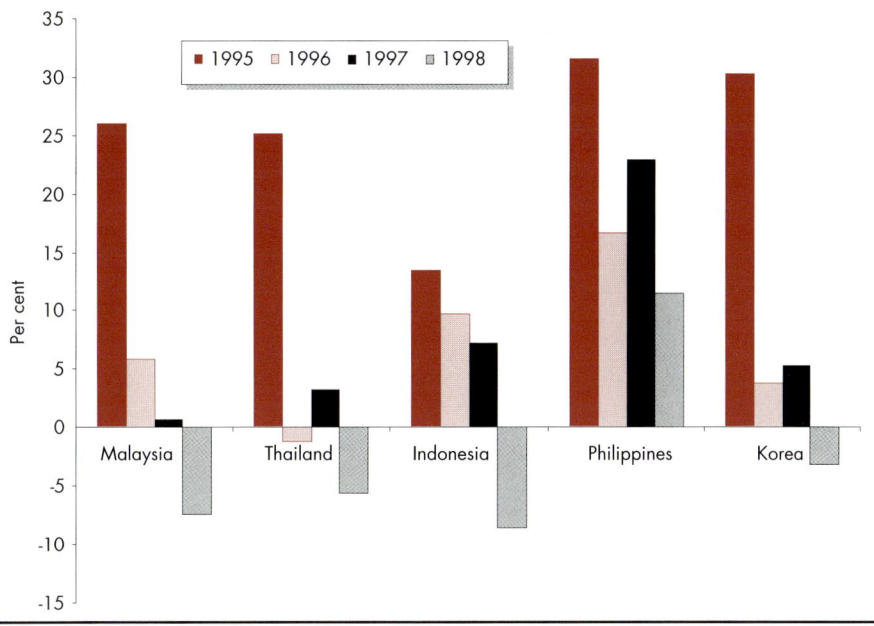

Source: International Monetary Fund, 1998a and 1999a.

Capital Flows and Resource Misallocation

Large capital inflows also distorted resource allocation. In many regional economies, real exchange rate appreciation made investments in non-traded sectors (domestic service sectors, retailing and real estate) appear more attractive than investments in export and import competing sectors. This drove excessive real estate investment in Hong Kong, Singapore, Thailand, Malaysia and Indonesia, and investment efficiency declined.[2]

Capital inflows also inflated equity prices, contributing to booms on most regional equity markets (Figure 2.3).[3] When capital flows reversed, equity and real estate prices fell sharply. As many asset buyers had financed their purchases with highly leveraged loans, plummeting asset prices left many borrowers with negative equity and consequently, banks' non-performing loans, NPLs, rose sharply.

---

[2] For example, poorly allocated investment probably contributed to Thailand's rising incremental capital to output ratio, the amount of capital investment required to produce an extra baht of output, from 3.5 in the 1980s to 4.5 in 1990-96 (International Monetary Fund, 1997).

[3] Stock markets in Korea and Indonesia were more subdued, due partly to constraints on foreign ownership of Korean shares, and foreign institutional investors' long standing view that the Indonesian stock exchange was not for 'outsiders'. (See Chapter 5 - *Capital Markets*.)

Figure 2.3

Stock Prices Boom in Mid 1990s
Regional Stock Market Indices (March Quarter 1990=100)

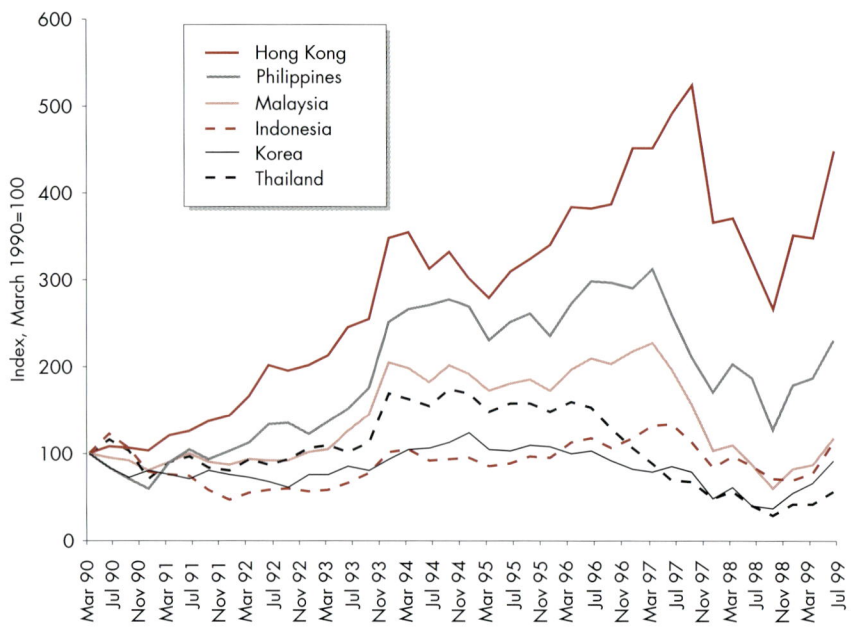

Note: These indexes are rebased versions of the flagship index for each country.
Source: CEIC, 1999.

Regional and international banks also extended unhedged foreign currency loans to local corporates and banks. Repayment costs escalated dramatically with sharp currency depreciations in 1997, also precipitating a rise in NPLs and insolvencies. (See Chapter 4 - *Banking* and relevant country chapters.)

THE CAUSES OF CAPITAL INFLOWS

Persistent pre-crisis current account deficits, generated by heavy investment in excess of local savings, drove Asia's dependence on foreign capital inflows (Figure 2.4). However, high domestic interest rates, inappropriate sequencing of financial market liberalisation, government incentives for foreign borrowing, market sentiment, and corporate governance and supervisory problems all stimulated capital inflows.

Interest Rate Differentials

Throughout the 1990s, interest rate differentials relative to the United States have been high in Korea, Thailand, Indonesia and the Philippines due to a range of factors including high intermediation costs, strong economic growth, and in the mid 1990s, efforts to sterilise (neutralise) inflationary effects of capital inflows in an

Capital and the Crisis

Figure 2.4

Current Account Deficits High before the Crisis
Current Account Balance as a Proportion of GDP, 1990-99

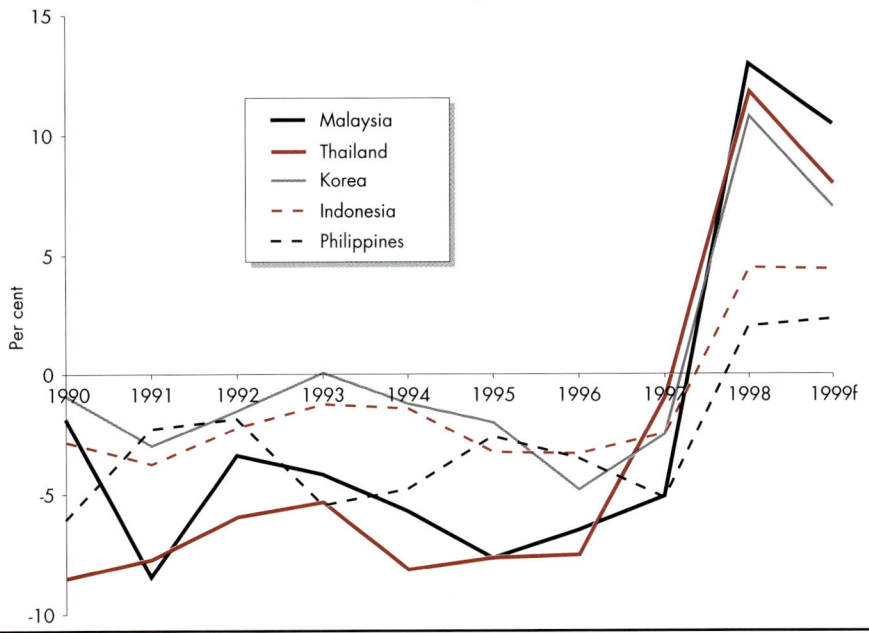

Note: Asia-5 economies are Indonesia, Malaysia, the Philippines, Thailand and Korea. A negative current account as a per cent of GDP represents a deficit. The forecasts for 1999 are from Bank of America.

Source: Department of Foreign Affairs and Trade, 1998; and Bank of America, 1999.

environment of pegged exchange rates (Figure 2.5).[4] These positive interest rate differentials generated increased willingness of foreign banks and investors to supply capital to East Asia. Pegged exchange rates and high interest rate differentials also increased demand by regional corporations and banks for unhedged foreign funds.

Sequencing of Financial Market Liberalisation

Poor sequencing of financial market reforms also increased the magnitude of capital inflows and distorted their composition. For example, in 1991, Indonesia reintroduced controls on domestic banks' foreign borrowing because of concerns about excessive foreign debt build up. However, the Government continued to liberalise borrowing abroad by corporates; by 1997, the non-bank private sector accounted for 68 per cent of Indonesia's foreign debt (Appendix Table 2.1). In 1994, Korean authorities liberalised restrictions on short term foreign borrowing by financial institutions and corporates, but retained controls on long term borrowing. Subsequently, the time profile of Korea's foreign debt shortened significantly (Appendix Table 2.1). As part of Thailand's financial liberalisation, authorities provided tax concessions on short term borrowing, again encouraging a dangerous shortening of foreign borrowing maturity.

---

4   The inflationary effects were neutralised by selling government bonds, thus reducing their price and raising interest rates.

Figure 2.5

Asian Interest Rates Higher than Industrial Economy Rates
Asian, US and German Short Term Interest Rates, 1990-99

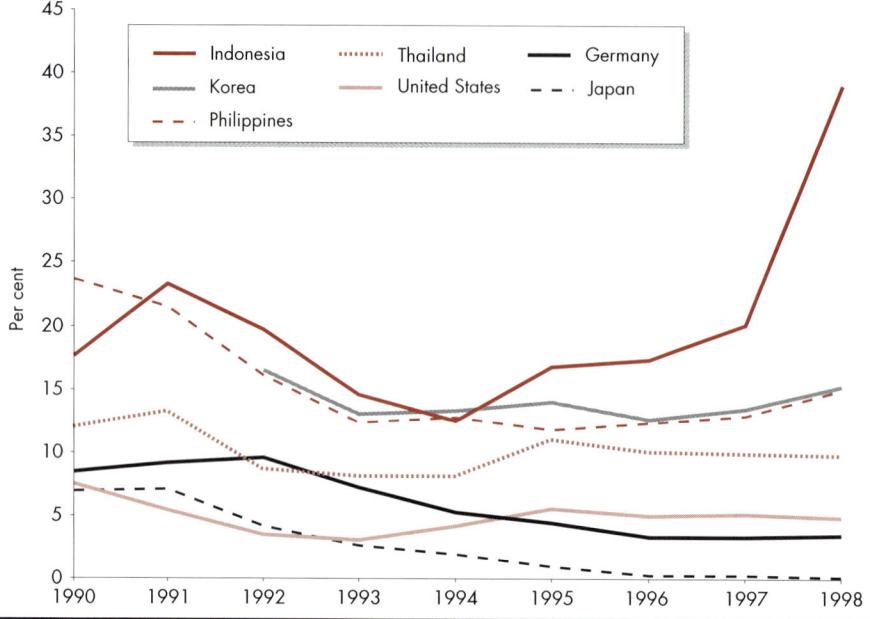

Note: Interest rates are three month certificates of deposit for the United States, Korea, Japan and Indonesia; three month interbank deposits for Germany; and three to six month commercial bank time deposits for Thailand.

Source: International Monetary Fund, 1999a; and CEIC, 1999.

Incentives for Foreign Borrowing

Some governments also provided incentives to encourage foreign borrowing. Banks operating in the Bangkok International Banking Facility, which only borrowed and lent foreign currencies, received special tax incentives. Philippine banks also paid less tax on their foreign currency deposit units (Radelet and Sachs, 1998; and East Asia Analytical Unit, 1998).[5] Also, in the past, foreign borrowing by Korean banks had carried explicit government guarantees.

Market Sentiment

Credit ratings, stock market returns and secondary market sovereign debt prices all influenced capital inflows. Before the crisis, most of these indicators for the region were rising and credit ratings were stable or positive (Table 2.1).[6]

---

[5] Foreign currency deposit units were originally introduced in 1971 to encourage Filipinos to keep their money in the country. They allow Filipinos to deposit and borrow in foreign currencies (largely US dollars).

[6] For example, in the second quarter of 1997, stock markets rose 11 per cent in Taiwan, over 12 per cent in Korea and Indonesia, 15 per cent in Japan, and 25 per cent in Hong Kong. In late June 1997, Indonesian, Thai, Korean, Malaysian and Philippine credit ratings were either stable or positive.

Table 2.1

Ratings Stable or Positive before the Crisis
Standard and Poor's Long Term Foreign Currency Debt Ratings, 1996-97

	15 January 1996		2 December 1996		24 June 1997	
	Rating	Outlook	Rating	Outlook	Rating	Outlook
Indonesia	BBB	Stable	BBB	Stable	BBB	Stable
Malaysia	A+	Stable	A+	Stable	A+	Positive
Philippines	BB	Positive	BB	Positive	BB+	Positive
Korea	AA-	Stable	AA-	Stable	AA-	Stable
Thailand	A	Stable	A	Stable	A	Stable

Source: Radelet and Sachs, 1998.

Corporate Governance and Supervisory Problems

Lax corporate governance, prudential standards and supervision also were critical in allowing capital inflows to escalate to unsustainable levels. In Indonesia and Malaysia, regulations limited banks from taking open positions in foreign currencies and offshore borrowing. However, domestic corporates borrowed directly in foreign currencies from offshore banks and many local banks on-lent foreign currency in domestic and foreign currencies (Fane, 1998).[7]

Banking supervisors in industrial economies also may bear some responsibility for excessive foreign lending by banks in their jurisdictions, as may the 1988 Basle Committee capital adequacy standards. Prudential regulations in creditor countries typically did not factor riskiness of their banks' foreign lending into capital adequacy ratio requirements. Basle standards also did not factor debt maturity and currency mismatches into credit risk assessments.[8] These failings will be addressed by the new Basle standards.

CAPITAL INFLOW COMPOSITION AND THE CRISIS

The scale and composition of capital inflows from the mid 1990s and sudden, equally large outflows in mid 1997 contributed significantly to the financial crisis. Average annual private capital flows to developing Asian economies rose from around US$13 billion in the late 1980s to US$100 billion by 1996, then dropped to an outflow of over US$50 billion in 1998 (Figure 2.6).[9] In particular, capital inflows to

---

[7] To undertake foreign currency lending to domestic firms, some banks accepted foreign currency deposits.

[8] Many regional banks borrowed foreign currency short term and lent it in local or foreign currency for longer terms, exposing them when creditors refused to roll over loans.

[9] Using the definition of Asian developing economies in International Monetary Fund (1998b), data on Asian developing economies, in this chapter includes Afghanistan, Bangladesh, Bhutan, Brunei, Burma, Cambodia, China, Fiji, India, Indonesia, Kiribati, Laos, Maldives, Malaysia, Marshall Islands, Micronesia, Nepal, Pakistan, Papua New Guinea, Philippines, Samoa, Solomon Islands, Sri Lanka, Thailand, Tonga, Vanuatu and Vietnam. China received around half of these flows, mostly as less volatile foreign direct investment.

Capital and the Crisis

Asia-5 economies jumped rapidly after 1994 but plummeted in 1998, so these economies were most severely hit (Figure 2.6). The US$150 billion contraction in Asia-5 liquidity after 1996 explains much of the financial crisis' severity.

To better understand the nature of these capital inflows, they can be grouped into three categories:

- foreign direct investment, FDI
- portfolio investment in bonds and equities
- 'other' flows, mainly bank lending.

FDI forms the largest and most stable Asian capital inflow; it increased steadily before the financial crisis (Figure 2.7). However, China received around two thirds of this FDI flow. Most bank lending was short term; it rose dramatically in the lead up to the crisis and also was the main element of the capital exodus (Figure 2.7). Portfolio flows did fall significantly from 1996, but were much less volatile than bank lending flows.

Figure 2.6

Private Capital Flows Built Up Rapidly before the Crisis
Net Private Capital Flows to Developing Economies and Asia-5, 1990-2000

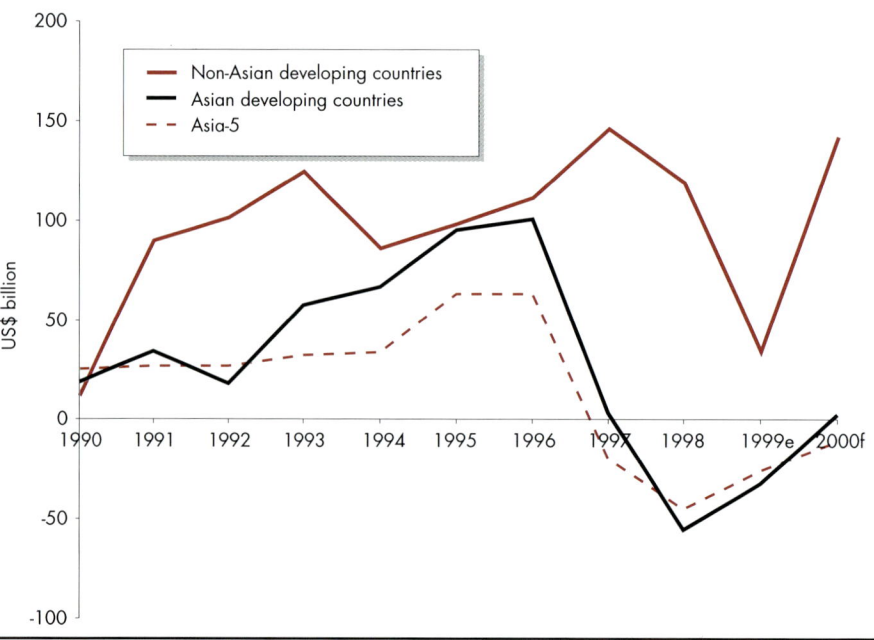

Note: Asia-5 economies are Indonesia, Malaysia, the Philippines, Thailand and Korea.
 e is estimate.
 f is forecast.
Source: International Monetary Fund, 1999b.

Figure 2.7

Bank Lending Most Volatile
Net Private Capital Flows to Asian Developing Economies

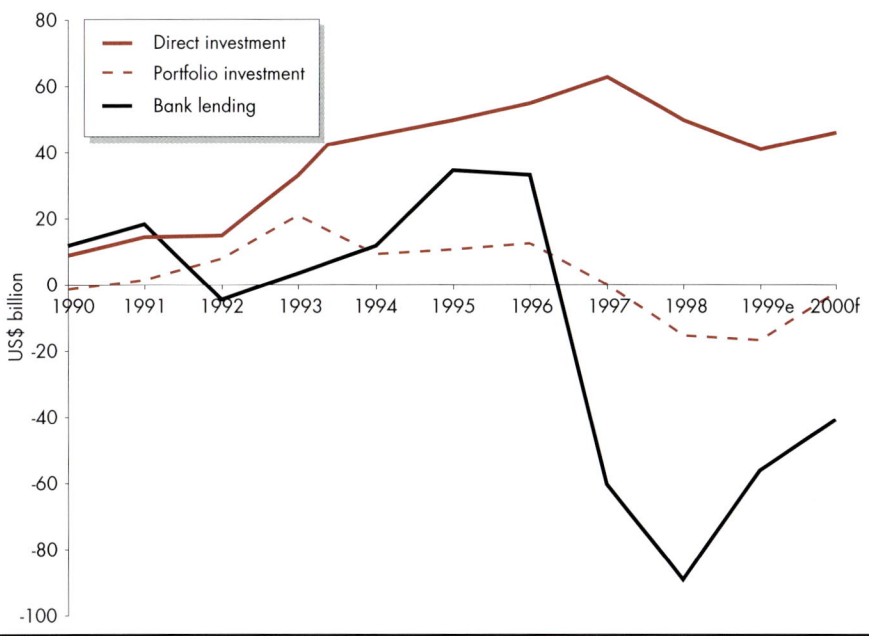

Note: Asian developing economies are those defined by the IMF in footnote 9.
e is estimate.
f is forecast.
Source: International Monetary Fund, 1999b.

Capital Flows to the Asia-5 Crisis Economies

Capital flows to the Asia-5 economies were quite different from those to the rest of developing Asia (Figures 2.7 and 2.8). FDI in Asia-5 economies was relatively small and increased only slowly in the 1990s, unlike other Asian economies, particularly China. In 1996, over 80 per cent of Asia-5 capital inflows were bank loans and portfolio flows (Figure 2.8).[10]

Hence in 1997, the Asia-5 were heavily exposed to bank lending, the most volatile element of capital flows; this switched from an inflow of US$33 billion in 1996 to an outflow of US$45 billion in 1997, and a further outflow of US$44 billion in 1998. Portfolio investment also dropped 42 per cent to US$13 billion in 1997, then became an outflow of US$6.5 billion in 1998, but still was less volatile than bank lending (Figure 2.8). In contrast, Asia-5's modest FDI flows were relatively stable.

---

[10] Bank lending multiplied 6.5 times from 1993 to 1995, while portfolio investment doubled between 1994 and 1996.

Capital and the Crisis

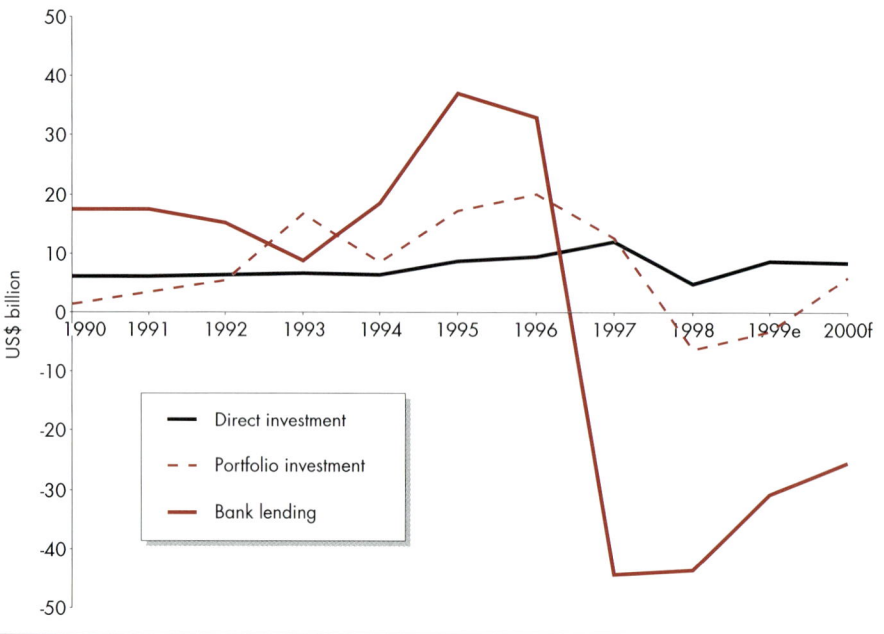

Figure 2.8

Asia-5 Capital Flows Volatile
Private Foreign Capital Flows to Asia-5 Economies, 1990-2000

Note: Asia-5 economies are Indonesia, Korea, Malaysia, the Philippines and Thailand.
e is estimate.
f is forecast.
Source: International Monetary Fund, 1999b.

While all Asia-5 economies had a significant ratio of net private capital inflows to GDP, the composition of these inflows varied markedly (Figure 2.9). Thailand and the Philippines depended most on bank foreign currency lending, while Indonesia and Malaysia had stronger FDI inflows.[11] Korea had a net FDI outflow and a high combined inflow of portfolio investment and bank loans. By contrast, almost all China's net private capital inflows were FDI and it was a net international lender (Figure 2.9).

[11] However, in the Philippines residents held around 63 per cent of Philippine banks' foreign liabilities compared to Thailand where residents held around 1 per cent (East Asia Analytical Unit, 1998). This made Philippine banks less vulnerable to capital flight, and reduced the macroeconomic impact of currency depreciation, as domestic holders of these foreign currency deposits benefited from peso depreciation.

Figure 2.9

Bank Lending Most Important in the Philippines and Thailand
Private Capital Inflows as Percentage of GDP, 1996

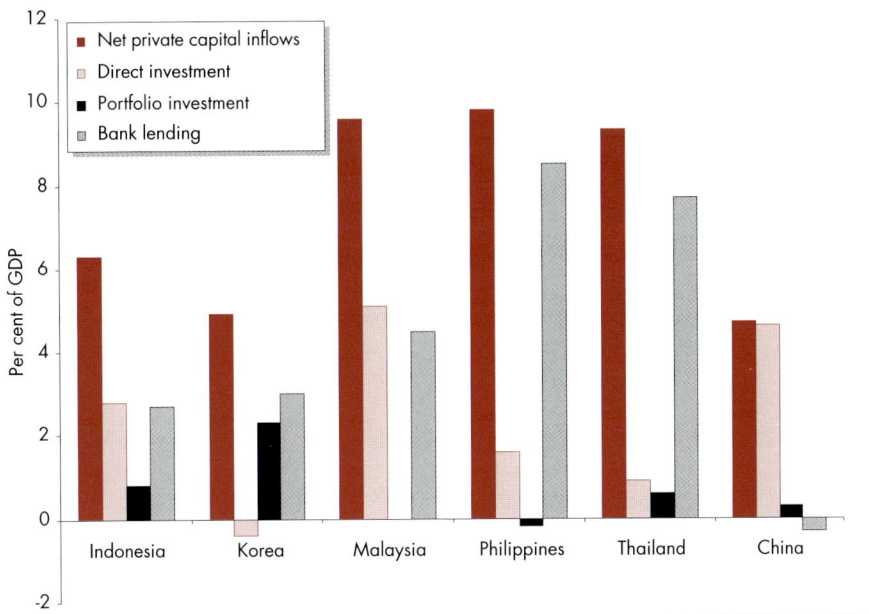

Note: Portfolio investment data for Malaysia is unavailable.
Source: International Monetary Fund, 1997.

Short term foreign borrowing

In the 1990s, short term (less than one year maturity) bank lending increased sharply as a percentage of total international bank lending to Asia-5 economies, particularly to Korea and Thailand (Appendix Table 2.1). By mid 1997, short term external debt exceeded official foreign exchange reserves in Thailand, Indonesia and Korea (Figure 2.10). In Malaysia and the Philippines, official reserves exceeded short term foreign debt; however, these economies had insufficient foreign exchange to roll over all short term debt and still service long term debt (Corsetti et al, 1998).[12]

Asia-5 Vulnerability to Capital Flow Shocks

During 1997, Thai, Indonesian and Korean authorities depleted reserves by unsuccessfully defending pegged exchange rates, thereby compounding vulnerability from exposure to short term foreign borrowing. In late 1997, when creditors realised these economies' short term foreign debt exceeded their foreign exchange reserves, they rushed to call in loans and shed portfolio investments. This amplified exchange rate and stock market falls.

---

[12] Not all official foreign exchange reserves can be used. For example, after the crisis began, Korean authorities admitted some Korean foreign exchange reserves were precommitted and therefore unavailable to service debt. Similarly, forward contracts entered into by the Bank of Thailand constituted a claim on Thai reserves (International Monetary Fund, 1998c).

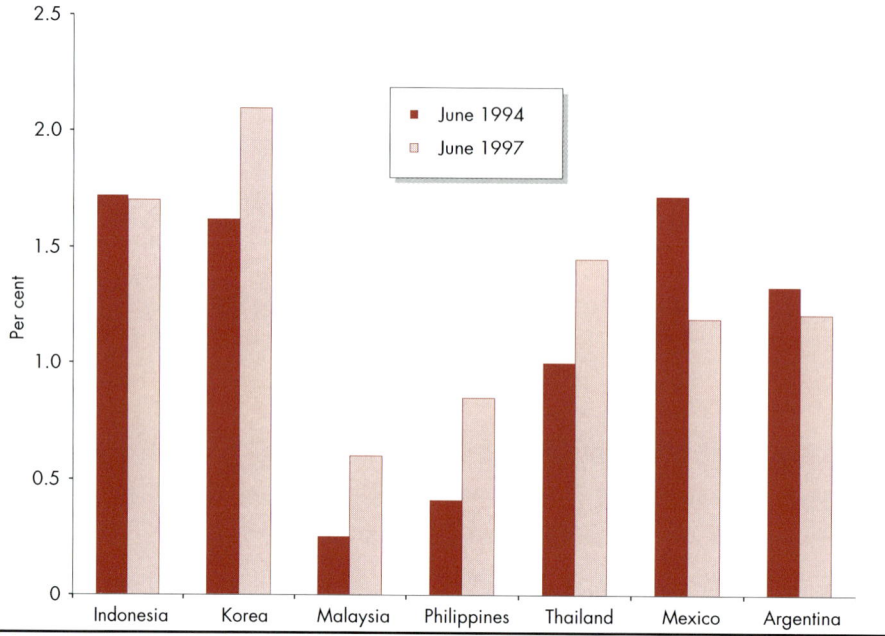

Figure 2.10

Indonesia and Korea Least Able to Service Short Term Debt
Ratio of Short Term Debt to Reserves in Financial Crisis Economies

Source: Radelet and Sachs, 1998.

Failure to hedge most foreign debt increased the Asia-5's vulnerability to capital flow reversal. The foreign currency obligations of banks and corporations became crippling once capital withdrew and exchange rates depreciated sharply. The lack of hedging was partly due to complacency about exchange rate risk. Throughout the 1990s, the Asia-5 had enjoyed prolonged currency stability, supported by occasional central bank intervention. However, lack of liquid instruments for hedging domestic currency and interest rate risk also contributed to low corporate hedging. (See Chapter 5 - *Capital Markets*.)

INTERNATIONAL BANK LENDING IN EAST ASIA

In Korea, the Philippines and China, domestic banks were important intermediators of foreign bank lending; whereas, in Indonesia, Malaysia and Thailand, corporates tended to borrow directly from foreign banks (Appendix Table 2.1). In Korea and China, foreign banks may well have been more willing to lend to domestic banks because creditors believed these banks carried implicit government guarantees.

Shifts in International Bank Lending Sources

Japanese and European Union banks remain East Asia's major creditors; Japanese banks reduced their market share during the 1990s, while European banks increased their Asian exposure (Figure 2.11).[13] Once the crisis began, the decline in volumes of Japanese lending accelerated, and Japanese bank claims on Asian developing economies dropped by US$29 billion to US$86 billion over the year to December 1998 (Bank for International Settlements, 1999a).[14] This exacerbated the regional credit crunch in Indonesia, Korea, Thailand, Hong Kong and elsewhere.

The withdrawal of Japanese capital from Asia is unlikely to be reversed rapidly. Tougher capital adequacy requirements for Japan's international banks caused many weaker institutions to withdraw totally from international operations.[15] (See Chapter 11 - *Japan*.) However, their withdrawal should create opportunities for other foreign financial institutions and result in a more realistic pricing of risk.

Figure 2.11

European Union Banks Are Big Lenders to East Asia
Sources of International Lending to East Asia, 1994-98

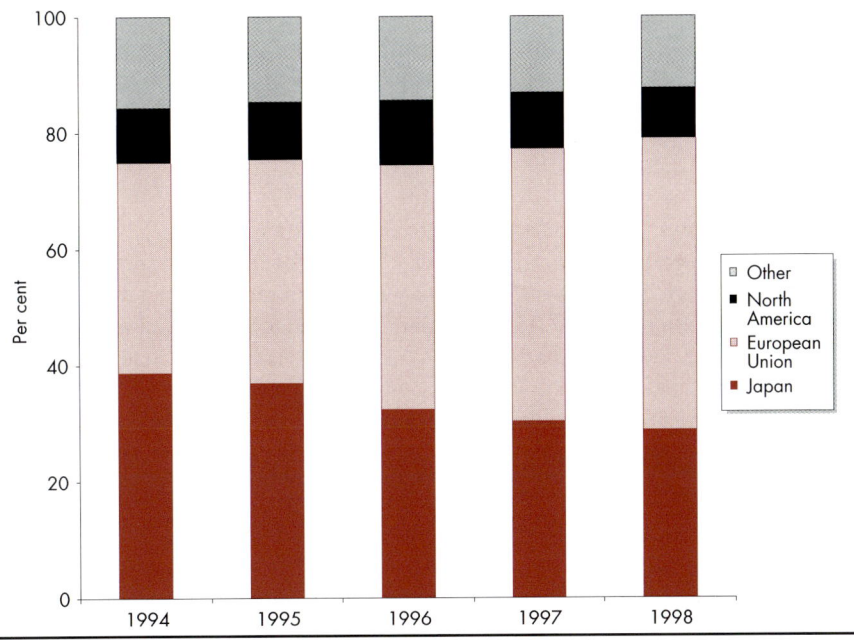

Note: Other includes lending to other countries and official lending.
Source: Bank for International Settlements, 1999a.

---

[13] US banks badly hurt by their exposure to the Latin American debt crisis in the 1980s took on relatively little exposure in Asia.

[14] In the year to December 1997, Japanese exposure to Asian developing economies declined by US$4 billion.

[15] Japanese banks with international operations must have a capital adequacy ratio of 8 per cent while domestic banks only require a 4 per cent ratio. Japanese banks to withdraw from international operations include Mitsui Trust and Banking and Daiwa Bank.

REFORMING INTERNATIONAL FINANCIAL ARCHITECTURE

While domestic policy failures were the main cause of the Asian financial crisis, the crisis highlighted the increasing interdependence of the world financial system and the benefits of strong international financial infrastructure. Apart from supporting IMF led reform programs in Thailand, Indonesia and Korea, the international community has focused its response to the crisis on developing recommendations to improve international financial architecture (Taskforce on International Financial Reform, 1998). Australia, as one of only four non-G7 economies in the Financial Stability Forum, the main institution currently progressing these issues, is closely involved in these efforts.[16] Australia also is a member of the newly formed G20, established by the G7 to address international financial architecture issues. To expedite reform progress, it broadens the dialogue on these issues to include other significant economies as well as the international financial institutions.

Key issues in reforming international financial architecture include:

- improving transparency, by increasing compliance with domestic disclosure rules and cross-border information exchange agreements
- reducing the potential of highly leveraged institutions like hedge funds to destabilise domestic and international markets
- tightening and enforcing prudential standards in offshore financial centres
- reducing capital flow volatility by encouraging more stable capital flows
- facilitating greater private sector involvement in crisis prevention and resolution.

Transparency

The Asian financial crisis highlighted major transparency problems in domestic and international financial systems. Consequently, the Financial Stability Forum compiled a draft *Compendium of Standards*, encompassing internationally accepted principles and codes of good practice followed by sound, well functioning financial systems.[17] This compendium will be updated regularly and covers issues such as transparency of fiscal, monetary and financial policies; dissemination of economic and financial data; regulation and supervision of banking, securities and insurance sectors; disclosure, transparency and risk management practices of financial institutions; corporate governance; accounting standards; bankruptcy procedures; auditing; and payment and settlement systems (Bank for International Settlements, 1999c).

In another significant development, to enhance its traditional surveillance role, the IMF is assessing countries' progress towards these internationally recognised standards (Nellor, 1999). However, ultimately policy makers and private sector analysts must utilise the information disclosed to improve market functioning.

---

[16] The G7 Ministers and Governors initiated the Financial Stability Forum in February 1999 (Bank for International Settlements, 1999b). The G7 members each have three representatives on the forum; Australia, Hong Kong, Singapore and the Netherlands each have one. Australia also has actively promoted international financial reform through the IMF, the Manila Framework and APEC.

[17] The compendium is a joint product of various standard setting bodies, such as the International Organisation of Securities Commissions, the International Association of Insurance Supervisors and the International Accounting Standards Committee.

Highly Leveraged Institutions

Several regional governments feel strongly that highly leveraged institutions like hedge funds destabilised domestic and international markets, exacerbating or even causing, the crisis. Consequently, a working group within the Financial Stability Forum is assessing the advantages and disadvantages of direct and indirect supervisory approaches, and evaluating the adequacy of measures to improve these institutions' disclosure and transparency arrangements (Bank for International Settlements, 1999c).[18] The most effective approaches to regulating highly leveraged institutions are likely to include improving their disclosure standards and improving risk monitoring among institutions that ultimately allow highly leveraged institutions to generate large positions (Reserve Bank of Australia, 1999).

Offshore Financial Centres

Offshore financial centres with weak financial supervision, poor cross-border cooperation and poor transparency can undermine efforts to strengthen the global financial system. They also can destabilise international financial markets by becoming the focus for illegal activities. Consequently, the Financial Stability Forum is identifying appropriate international prudential and disclosure standards for these centres and designing incentives to enhance compliance (Bank for International Settlements, 1999c).

Reducing Capital Flow Volatility

While domestic distortions in Korea, Indonesia and Thailand encouraged a dangerous build up of short term capital inflows, both borrower and creditor economies may be able to reduce capital flow volatility and better assess and manage risks flowing from excessive short term external debt. Key issues being considered include: risk management requirements for realising potential capital flow benefits; the costs and benefits of using capital inflow controls as a preventive risk management tool; and distortions and prudential failures that might bias capital flows and increase volatility. As mentioned previously, the Basle Committee's 1988 capital adequacy standards did not factor debt maturity into credit risk assessments; however, the proposed new framework raises the capital requirements for banks advancing short term interbank credit lines to emerging markets (Nellor, 1999).

Private Sector Role in Crisis Prevention and Management

Early private sector involvement in crisis management could have reduced the severity of the Asian crisis, limiting currency depreciations and maintaining trade and other finance. The key to involving the private sector more in crisis management is to find mechanisms to bind them in to crisis resolution. For example, introducing 'majority voting' or 'collective action' clauses into private and sovereign debt would motivate creditors to register with suitable debt restructuring forums to protect their interests. Such initiatives could facilitate more timely agreement on

---

[18] The Financial Stability Forum should complete its work on this and other architecture issues by April 2000 (Bank for International Settlements, 1999c). Australia, through the Reserve Bank of Australia, is represented on this working group.

rescheduling or suspending debt payments (Taskforce on International Financial Reform, 1998). Experience with the Asian financial crisis suggests bank to bank debt should be an important focus of cooperative efforts; the successful rescheduling of Korean bank debt in December 1997 and January 1998 demonstrates the benefits of collective action in this area (Grenville, 1999).

However, such initiatives depend on developing arrangements acceptable to private sector lenders. The report by the G7 Finance Ministers at the Cologne Economic Summit on 18-20 June 1999 provides a framework for the international community to address individual cases that might arise, with further work planned on implementation (International Monetary Fund, 1999c).

FINANCIAL RESTRUCTURING, CAPITAL INFLOWS AND RECOVERY

To reduce vulnerability to future crises and underpin future investment generated growth, Asia-5 and other Asian economies are undertaking financial restructuring and reform. In Thailand, Indonesia and Korea, IMF packages drive this restructuring and liberalisation (Appendix Table 2.2) but all regional governments now recognise the importance of healthy market oriented financial systems.[19] For example, in addition to domestic reform programs Hong Kong, Indonesia, Japan, Korea, Malaysia, Singapore and Thailand have all ratified the fifth protocol to the General Agreement on Trade in Services since its conclusion in December 1997. This involves new or improved offers to liberalise financial sectors and begins to set the framework for liberalising trade in financial services.

By late 1999, East Asia was recovering rapidly from the financial crisis of 1997 and 1998; all regional economies should achieve positive GDP growth in 1999 (Figure 2.12). East Asian growth was boosted in 1999 because:

- capital flight was exhausted by the end of 1998
- large trade surpluses are being achieved and rebuilding of reserves is underway
- trade financing has resumed in most economies
- monetary conditions have loosened and real interest rates have fallen
- as interest rates fell, the excessive inventory contraction of 1998 halted
- rising budget deficits are providing fiscal stimulus
- consumer confidence and spending is returning in some economies
- substantial excess industrial capacity is allowing production and exports to expand without new investment.

---

[19] Examples of increased intervention include Malaysia's imposition of capital controls and Hong Kong's stock market support. However, these are isolated, and address specific problems.

Figure 2.12

Asia Recovers Rapidly
Real GDP Growth in Asia, 1997-99

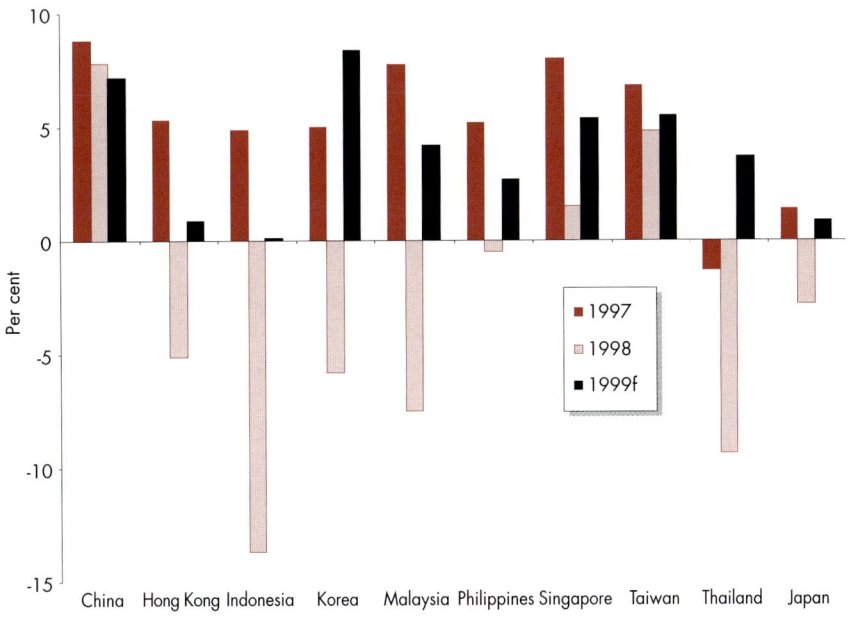

Note: 1999 growth rates are consensus forecasts.
Source: CEIC, 1999; and Consensus Economics, 1999.

However, most factors fuelling recovery are cyclical. As their growth impact diminishes, it will be critical that banking sectors have been recapitalised and restructured so they can finance new private investment, to sustain long term growth. Restructured financial sectors (and other microeconomic reforms) also are essential to improve the efficiency of new investments, and by boosting investor confidence, attract new capital inflows. Renewed inflows are particularly important for Malaysia, Thailand and the Philippines, which relied most heavily on such flows before the crisis (Figure 2.9), and for Indonesia which is incurring huge liabilities to recapitalise its banking system. Well invested foreign capital inflows will allow outstanding foreign debt to be repaid and overall investment to grow more rapidly.

POST-CRISIS EXCHANGE RATE AND MONETARY POLICY TRENDS

The financial crisis broke informal US dollar pegs in Indonesia, Thailand, the Philippines, Korea and Taiwan. Post-crisis, exchange rates should continue to float more freely, better protecting economies from external trade shocks and helping to more effectively transmit monetary policy.[20]

---

[20] Malaysia's fixed exchange rate and capital controls is the main exception to this trend.

During the 1980s and 1990s, the Japanese economy became increasingly integrated with the rest of East Asia, causing the yen's sharp depreciation from mid 1995 to drive significant real exchange rate appreciation in regional currencies. In future, movements of East Asian currencies are likely to become more closely correlated with yen fluctuations, relative to US dollar movements (Hale, 1999). Also, correlation of Indonesian, Philippine and possibly Thai currencies with the Chinese renminbi also should increase, as Chinese exports become more important.

Monetary Policy Evolution

In the post-crisis period, most monetary authorities recognise they can target either prices, such as interest rates and exchange rates, or quantities such as the money supply or total volume of credit created, but not both. Financial market liberalisation usually changes the relationship between monetary aggregates, so monetary policy is harder to formulate. As Australia experienced in the 1980s, this may change monetary policy objectives.

However, as East Asian capital markets liberalise and develop, monetary authorities more frequently can employ open market operations (central bank sales and purchases of government securities) to influence liquidity and interest rates. This should reduce reliance on blunter monetary policy instruments like reserve ratios. Changes in reserve ratios can require large and potentially disruptive restructuring of commercial bank assets, destabilising the financial system and unfairly benefiting non-bank financial institutions (which usually are exempt from such controls).

EVOLUTION OF AUSTRALIA'S MONETARY POLICY OBJECTIVES

After the Australian Government lifted capital controls and deregulated financial markets in the 1980s, the Reserve Bank of Australia's monetary policy objectives changed several times. In 1985, with the relationship between monetary aggregates changing frequently and concern increasing about the current account deficit and foreign exchange market instability, the Reserve Bank abandoned monetary targeting. It replaced this with a checklist approach, which targeted the inflation rate, exchange rate, interest rates, balance of payments and monetary aggregates.

The present system of inflation targeting was developed in the late 1980s, driven by the view that economic agents require some guiding principle on which to base their actions and expectations. Pre-announced rules also provide the market and government with a clear benchmark against which to judge central bank performance.

Source: Smith, 1998.

CONCLUSIONS

Capital flows were a major driving force behind the 'East Asian miracle' but also were central to the Asian financial crisis. Excessive short term lending and portfolio flows to Indonesia, Korea, Malaysia, the Philippines and Thailand precipitated currency volatility and asset price bubbles, making the region vulnerable to capital flight. To reduce their exposure to future crises, East Asian economies recognise they must increase less volatile FDI inflows and develop domestic capital markets. Since the crisis, many regional economies have restructured their foreign debt, lengthening its maturity and liberalising foreign investment regimes to encourage more stable capital inflows. They also are strengthening prudential controls and supervision. (See Chapter 3 - *Prudential Reform*.)

Ongoing efforts to strengthen international financial architecture should complement regional domestic financial sector reform. However, success in reforming and refinancing regional financial systems is crucial to sustain the next stage of investment led growth after the current cyclical recovery. Such reforms also are essential to lift investment efficiency and encourage new capital inflows.

Appendix Table 2.1

Short Term Debt Exposure Increases before the Crisis
Maturity and Sector Distribution of International Bank Lending to Asia-5 and China

		Distribution by maturity (per cent)[a]			Distribution by sector (per cent)[a]		
	Total (US$ billion)	Up to and including one year	Over one year and up to two years	Over two years	Banks	Public sector	Non-bank private sector
Indonesia							
1985-89[b]	16.9	41	9	48	10	46	43
1990-95[b]	31.7	60	9	28	22	21	57
1996	55.5	62	6	28	21	13	66
1997	58.4	61	6	30	20	12	68
1998	44.8	53	7	37	11	15	74
Korea							
1985-89[b]	24.9	54	8	35	40	24	35
1990-95[b]	46.2	71	5	17	63	9	28
1996	100.0	68	4	16	66	6	28
1997	94.2	63	6	17	59	4	36
1998	65.3	45	13	25	57	8	35
Malaysia							
1985-89[b]	9.4	21	6	62	12	57	29
1990-95[b]	11.2	46	6	37	29	28	42
1996	22.2	50	3	33	29	9	62
1997	27.5	53	3	34	36	6	58
1998	20.8	45	5	40	28	9	63
Philippines							
1985-89[b]	12.2	35	9	54	21	58	20
1990-95[b]	7.7	42	4	49	23	48	28
1996	13.3	58	4	31	39	20	40
1997	19.7	60	2	32	45	12	42
1998	16.2	54	6	35	37	13	50
Thailand							
1985-89[b]	8.0	42	7	46	27	39	31
1990-95[b]	32.1	69	6	22	34	8	58
1996	70.1	65	7	23	37	3	60
1997	58.9	66	7	23	30	3	67
1998	40.7	58	8	29	22	5	73

	Total (US$ billion)	Distribution by maturity (per cent)[a]			Distribution by sector (per cent)[a]		
		Up to and including one year	Over one year and up to two years	Over two years	Banks	Public sector	Non-bank private sector
China							
1985-89[b]	12.0	42	4	50	29	47	23
1990-95[b]	33.8	45	7	40	35	33	32
1996	55.0	49	8	36	41	15	43
1997	63.2	53	6	33	43	11	46
1998	58.2	54	6	32	37	12	51

Note: a Percentages do not add up to 100 because of unallocated funds.
       b Annual averages.
Source: Bank for International Settlements, 1999a.

Appendix Table 2.2

IMF Packages Promoted Financial Market and Prudential Reform
Financial Restructuring Measures Agreed with IMF

Thailand		Korea		Indonesia	
Measures	Dates	Measures	Dates	Measures	Dates
Suspension of 58 insolvent finance companies	8/97	New legislation governing supervision, deposit insurance, closure of financial institutions and allocation of losses and equity write-downs	12/97	Closure of 16 insolvent banks; provision of conditional liquidity support to others	11/97
Tightening of loan classification and bank licensing rules	11/97	Closure of 10 (of 14 suspended) merchant banks	1/98	Placement of weak regional development banks under Bank Indonesia supervision	12/97
Guidelines for assessing owners, board members and managers of financial institutions	12/97	Submission of rehabilitation plans by remaining merchant banks; recapitalisation plans required for commercial banks whose 1997 capital adequacy ratios fell below 8 per cent (based on full provisioning)	2/98	Establishment of Indonesia Bank Restructuring Agency; external guarantees to all creditors and depositors of all locally incorporated banks; compensation to small depositors from closed banks	1/98
Amendment of bankruptcy laws; strengthening of loan classification and provisioning rules to meet international standards by 2000	3/98	Establishment of units at Ministry of Finance and Economy under Financial Supervisory Board to coordinate and monitor bank restructuring, and provide public funds	3-4/98	Transfer of 54 weak banks to Indonesia Bank Restructuring Agency; introduction of new loan classification and provisioning rules based on international standards	2/98
Preparation for restructuring and privatisation plan for intervened banks; review of banking supervision laws	6/98	Initiation of consultations with banking community and outside experts on strengthening prudential regulations (regulations issued 11/98)	4/98	Merger of two state owned banks; legislation enabling state bank privatisation and removing limits on private ownership of banks; establishment of new asset resolution entity	6/98

Thailand		Korea		Indonesia	
Measures	Dates	Measures	Dates	Measures	Dates
Memorandums of understanding with financial institutions on implementing stricter loan classification and provisioning rules	8-9/98	Legislation to allow full write-downs of existing shareholders' equity	6/98	Portfolio, systems and financial review of Indonesia Bank Restructuring Agency and major non-Indonesia Bank Restructuring Agency banks by internationally recognised audit firms	8/98
Revision of Bank of Thailand laws; completion of amendments to foreclosure laws	10/98			Preparation of restructuring plan for Indonesia Bank Restructuring Agency banks	10/98
Completion of disposal of assets of 56 (of 58 suspended) finance companies; new prudential regulations; strengthening of rules governing disclosure, auditing and accounting practices; and introduction of new deposit insurance scheme	12/98			Preparation of state banks for privatisation; introduction of deposit insurance scheme	2001
Development of plans for privatising institutions undergoing state intervention					

Note: Dates in this table are the original dates agreed with the IMF; some measures have taken longer to get through parliaments and to implement.
Source: Goldstein, 1998.

REFERENCES

Bank of America, 1999, 'Asian Financial Outlook Issue No. 22', Global Markets Group, Hong Kong, April.

Bank for International Settlements, 1999a, 'Consolidated International Banking Statistics for the End of 1998', www.bis.org/publ/index.htm, accessed on 15 July.

___ 1999b, Press release, 'Financial Stability Forum Establishes Working Groups', Financial Stability Forum, May, Basle.

___ 1999c, Press release, 'Background Brief Made Available to the Press at the Second Meeting of the Financial Stability Forum on 15 September 1999', Financial Stability Forum, September, Basle.

CEIC, 1999, CEIC Database, Hong Kong, supplied by EconData, Canberra.

Consensus Economics, 1999, 'Asia Pacific Consensus Forecasts: September 1999', Consensus Economics, London, October.

Corsetti, G., Pesenti, P. and Roubini, N., 1998, 'What Caused the Asian Currency and Financial Crisis?', www.stern.nyu.edu/~nroubini/asia, accessed on 10 September 1999.

Department of Foreign Affairs and Trade, 1998, 'APEC Region Trade and Investment', Canberra, November.

East Asia Analytical Unit, 1998, *The Philippines: beyond the Crisis*, Department of Foreign Affairs and Trade, Canberra.

Fane, G., 1998, 'The Role of Prudential Regulation', in McLeod, R., and Garnaut, R. (eds), *East Asia in Crisis: from Being a Miracle to Needing One*, Routledge, London.

Goldstein, M., 1998, *The Asian Financial Crisis: Causes, Cures and Systemic Implications*, Institute for International Economics, Washington DC.

Grenville, S., 1999, 'The International Reform Agenda: Unfinished Business', Paper presented at the World Economic Forum 1999 – East Asian Economic Summit, 20 October, Singapore.

Hale, D, 1999, 'Can the US Equity Market Continue Supporting the US Dollar?', *Global Economic Observer*, vol. 20, 27 July.

International Monetary Fund, 1999a, *International Financial Statistics*, IMF, Washington DC, August.

___ 1999b, *World Economic Outlook*, IMF, Washington DC, October.

___ 1999c, 'Communique of the Interim Committee of the Board of Governors of the International Monetary Fund', September, Washington DC, www.imf.org/external/np/sec/pr/1999/PR9946.htm accessed on 22 October.

___ 1998a, *Direction of Trade Statistics*, IMF, Washington DC, September.

___ 1998b, *World Economic Outlook*, IMF, Washington DC, May.

___ 1998c, *International Capital Markets: Developments, Prospects and Key Issues*, IMF, Washington DC, October.

___ 1997, *World Economic Outlook*, Interim Assessment (December), IMF, Washington DC.

Morgan, J.P., 1999, 'Monthly Average for OECD and Emerging Market Currencies', www.jpmorgan.com/MarketDataInd/Forex/currIndex.html, accessed on 15 September.

Nellor, D., 1999, 'A Constitution for the International Financial System', Paper presented at the conference Reform and Recovery in East Asia: the Role of the State and Economic Enterprise, 21-22 September, Canberra.

Radelet, S. and Sachs, J., 1998, 'The Onset of the East Asian Financial Crisis', www.hiid.harvard.edu/projects/caer/index.html, accessed on 7 September 1999.

Reserve Bank of Australia, 1999, 'The Impact of Hedge Funds on Financial Markets', Paper submitted to the Financial Stability Forum Working Group on Highly Leveraged Institutions, 4 June, Sydney.

Smith, H., 1998, 'Macroeconomic Policy and Structural Adjustment in Korea', Paper presented at the conference Financial Sector Reform and Macroeconomic Policy Management in Korea, Australian National University, 3 December, Canberra.

Sutherland, P., 1998, 'Managing the International Economy in an Age of Globalisation,' The 1998 Per Jacobsson Lecture, the annual meeting of the IMF and the World Bank, October, Washington DC.

Taskforce on International Financial Reform, 1998, *Report of the Taskforce on International Financial Reform*, AGPS, Canberra.

Chapter 3

PRUDENTIAL AND FINANCIAL INFRASTRUCTURE REFORM

Most Asian governments now are addressing serious prudential control and structural weaknesses in their financial markets. All the economies severely affected by the Asian crisis suffered from weak or inappropriate financial sector regulations and prudential supervision, low financial institution capital adequacy ratios, poor credit allocation and weak corporate governance. These factors produced fragile and undercapitalised financial systems that misallocated large volumes of foreign capital, and from early 1997, undermined foreign investor confidence. These prudential failings also exaggerated the credit crunch that followed currency depreciations. Consequently, regional governments and international financial institutions are prioritising the reform of regional prudential regulations and supervision.

This chapter briefly discusses the contribution of weak financial system regulation and supervision to the crisis, details post-crisis initiatives to overcome these problems, and finally anticipates future regulation and supervision developments. In particular, it assesses whether new, more robust financial systems will emerge from the crisis, or whether a rapid return to growth will disguise remaining prudential problems, leaving the region vulnerable to future crises and contagion.

The chapter analyses major weaknesses, ongoing reforms and prospects in relation to four major areas of financial market control:

- **prudential regulation** including capital adequacy and liquidity standards, and controls on inappropriate lending practices
- **prudential supervision** including the independence and organisation of financial supervisors
- **disclosure and market discipline** including capital market regulation corporate governance
- **financial market infrastructure** including bankruptcy laws, the payments system and deposit insurance.

PRUDENTIAL FAILURES AND THE CRISIS

A decade of high growth, excessive domestic and foreign investor optimism, poor prudential supervision, weak bankruptcy laws and weak corporate governance encouraged many private firms to imprudently manage financial risk. Many undertook excessive, and often short term foreign currency borrowing to invest in long term, low return or speculative activities. Many regional governments failed to enforce appropriate prudential regulation in rapidly growing and increasingly open financial systems, thus sanctioning these poor decisions on credit allocation. Implicit government guarantees for banks and large corporates created moral hazard for undercapitalised banks and excessively leveraged firms.[1] In this environment, the large exchange rate depreciations and foreign capital outflow in mid and late 1997 caused a vicious cycle of non-performing loans, NPLs, corporate failures, shrinking bank liquidity and ultimately, systemic threats to financial stability.

Financial Liberalisation in the 1980s and 1990s

Most Asian economies partly liberalised their financial sectors in the 1980s and 1990s, reducing government controls on credit allocation and interest rates and liberalising international capital flows, but maintaining some government ownership and direction of credit (Table 3.1). The changes were made to reduce intermediation costs, encourage more efficient capital allocation and assist capital deepening.[2] By opening their economies to international capital flows, governments hoped to attract foreign savings, improve capital allocation by strengthening competition and reduce capital costs for local business.

However, in several cases the reforms were poorly sequenced; liberalisation occurred before adequate supervisory capacity was developed. The more liberal environment enabled many local financial institutions to take on excessive risk, while open capital accounts permitted excessive foreign borrowing that inflated domestic asset prices and exposed economies to unsustainable foreign exchange risk. In such an environment, prudential regulation should have been tightened as domestic and external financial controls were liberalised. While the Philippines, Malaysia and Singapore did tighten prudential regulations as financial sector liberalisation occurred, Thailand and Korea did not vigorously implement new regulations. Indonesia deregulated its financial sector in the 1980s but only tightened controls in the 1990s, and even then implementation was poor.

Rapid Credit Growth

Strong economic growth, interest rate deregulation and large foreign capital inflows drove Asia's rapid credit growth. In the 1990s, inflation adjusted bank credit grew by over 10 per cent per year in most Asian economies, and by almost 20 per cent in some. After their financial markets and foreign borrowing were liberalised in the 1990s, a large proportion of Thai, Indonesian and Malaysian lending was directed to speculative activities like property development and equity markets; this fuelled asset price booms. As asset prices increased, the value of collateral rose and borrowers could borrow more. Often long term projects were financed with short term or variable rate borrowing; risks were not properly assessed. Some banks were highly exposed to one borrower, who often was connected to the lending bank. Many governments also encouraged banks to lend to favoured projects, industries or companies, undermining prudent credit assessment.

---

[1] Moral hazard exists when firms or individuals believe they will not be forced to bear the consequences of their decisions.

[2] Capital deepening is the development of more sophisticated financial markets that offer a wide range of financial products with long maturities.

Table 3.1

Major Financial Liberalisation in 1980s and 1990s
Financial Sector Reforms in East Asia 1973-96

		Credit controls	Interest rates	Entry barriers	Government regulation of operations	Privatisation	International capital flows
Japan	1973	*	**	*	*	***	*
	1996	***	****	***	***	***	****
Australia	1973	*	*	*	na	*	*
	1996	****	****	****	na	***	****
Hong Kong	1973	****	***	**	****	****	****
	1996	****	****	***	****	****	****
Indonesia	1973	*	*	*	*	*	***
	1996	***	****	***	*	*	***
Korea	1973	*	*	*	*	*	*
	1996	***	***	***	**	***	**
Malaysia	1973	*	*	*	***	***	***
	1996	***	****	***	***	***	***
Philippines	1973	*	*	*	**	**	**
	1996	**	***	***	**	***	***
Singapore	1973	****	****	**	****	****	***
	1996	****	****	**	****	****	****
Taiwan	1973	*	*	*	*	*	*
	1996	**	***	***	**	*	**
Thailand	1973	*	*	*	na	**	*
	1996	**	***	**	na	**	*

Note: * is repressed; ** is partially repressed; *** is largely liberalised; **** is fully liberalised; na is not available.
A repressed system is one where the government sets interest rates and makes virtually all credit allocation decisions; a liberalised system is one where the government's role is minimal. Assessments are by Williamson and Maher.
Source: Williamson and Maher, 1998.

PRUDENTIAL REGULATION

As a result of the crisis, many regional governments want to restore market confidence by improving their prudential regulation, strengthening supervision and developing more efficient financial market infrastructure. Most governments regulate and supervise financial systems because:

- the consequences of a financial system break down often severely affect the whole economy (externalities)

- supervision ensures customers/depositors are not exploited because they have less information than financial institutions have (asymmetric information)

- regulation ensures financial institutions expect to bear the full consequences of their actions (moral hazard).

Most East Asian regulatory systems entail:

- minimum capital adequacy ratios; the ratio of unimpaired equity capital to outstanding loans

- minimum reserve ratios; the ratio of liquid and reserve assets to total assets

- limits on lending to 'related' individual borrowers or firms with the same owners or managers as the lending institution

- limits on exposure to currency and interest rate risk, possibly requiring matching of asset and liability maturity

- compulsory disclosure of performance on these criteria and other data like NPL ratios (Fane, 1998).

However, legislated and enforced standards can diverge considerably, and standards also vary between economies. Most governments have tightened controls and enforcement since the onset of the crisis, although implementation still lags in some economies.

Capital Adequacy Standards

Requiring financial institutions to maintain minimum capital adequacy ratios protects depositors and creditors from institutions' risky lending practices and minimises the risk of systemic failure. Enforcing capital adequacy ratios also is the best way to overcome moral hazard, as owners then stand to lose significant amounts of their own capital if their institution fails. Institutions operating in a risky environment need higher capital adequacy ratios, although this increases the cost of borrowing.

Many East Asian economies implemented the 1988 Basle Capital Accord's 8 per cent minimum capital adequacy ratio standard before 1997, but often their enforcement was poor.[3] In particular, lax rules for provisioning for NPLs allowed bank capital to be eroded. Before the crisis, capital adequacy ratios were high only in Hong Kong (18 per cent), the Philippines (17 per cent) and Singapore (19 per cent). In 1994, Indonesian banks reported capital adequacy ratios averaging 11 per cent for private banks, 10 per cent for state banks, and 16 per cent for foreign and joint-venture banks. However, Bank Indonesia did not publish the capital adequacy ratios of individual banks and some had much lower levels (Fane, 1998). For example, in April 1996, Bank Indonesia found 15 banks did not meet the minimum 8 per cent, but it did not force them to take prompt corrective action (Montgomery, 1997).

Furthermore, reported capital adequacy ratios often were overstated because NPL classification standards were below international standards. Consequently, many financial institutions failed to provide adequately for loans which industrialised economies would classify as non-performing. In 1997, banks in Korea, Japan, Thailand, China and Indonesia all faced this problem.

---

[3] The 1988 Basle Capital Accord recommends minimum levels of capital as a proportion of risk weighted assets, and defines the types of capital that can be counted and the weightings that need to be applied. The accord was designed for internationally active banks, but throughout the world, it is widely applied to domestic banks. The 8 per cent level is considered a minimum, and should be raised for banks with riskier asset profiles.

Since the crisis, many governments have tightened their loan classification systems and foreshadowed increases to capital adequacy ratios. In July 1998, Thailand tightened standards for loan classification and loan loss provisioning.[4] Indonesia and Malaysia also tightened their rules in 1998, although Malaysia has since relaxed classification requirements, classifying loans overdue by six months as non-performing (Table 3.2). After lowering its minimum capital adequacy ratio from 8 per cent to 4 per cent during the crisis, Indonesia will raise it to 10 per cent by 2001. In early 1998, Korea also raised banks' minimum capital adequacy ratios to 8 per cent and tightened their loan classifications to international standards; loans overdue by three months now are classified as non-performing.

In China, the crisis also focused policy makers' attention on financial system health. In early 1998, the Government adopted the international five category loan classification system and raised capital adequacy ratios to 8 per cent.[5] (See Chapter 12 - *China*.)

A New Capital Accord

Since the introduction of the 1988 Basle Capital Accord, measuring risk for capital adequacy has been contentious. Critics of the accord argue the quality of assets in the same risk category can vary widely, and the accord does not consider the concentration of banks' loan portfolios (Crockett, 1998).

Between 1999 and 2000, a taskforce of the Basle Committee on Banking Supervision will develop a new capital accord. Proposals include increasing the use of risk assessments from credit rating agencies and, for more sophisticated banks, increasing the use of internal risk management models. The committee is considering new risk weightings for asset classes such as securitisation. The new accord will stress the importance of bank managers in developing internal capital assessment processes and setting targets for capital appropriate to their bank's risk profile and control environment. It also is likely to emphasise market discipline to encourage higher disclosure standards (Basle Committee on Banking Supervision, 1999).

If these proposals are adopted as currently constituted, they will change the global financial services industry by:

- encouraging global banking; the proposed new accord will reduce costs for banks that have well developed credit risk management systems and large, high quality asset portfolios which are amenable to securitisation

- stimulating securitisation and other credit risk hedging instruments; the new framework will have lower capital charges for these assets, creating strong incentives for banks to securitise certain kinds of corporate debt

- emphasising more the judgements of bank managers and credit rating agencies rather than Basle regulators, thereby boosting the credit rating industry (Citibank, 1999).

---

[4] Thai banks will have two years to fully provision under the new rules that include classifying loans as non-performing when they are three months overdue.

[5] However, banks still can make provisions against NPLs for only 1 per cent of total loans. Banks have until 2000 to reach 8 per cent capital adequacy ratios.

Prudential Reform

Table 3.2

Philippines Has More Advanced Prudential Regulations
Selected Prudential Regulations of ASEAN-4

	Philippines	Indonesia	Malaysia	Thailand
Minimum capital adequacy ratio	10 per cent	4 per cent 10 per cent in 2001	8 per cent	8.5 per cent
Limit on real estate lending	20 per cent of loan portfolio, excluding loans for small residential units	Limits on lending to property developers	20 per cent, excluding properties worth less than Ringgit 250 000 and infrastructure lending	none
Single borrower limit	25 per cent	Up to 30 per cent of capital can be lent to any single non-affiliated firm group until December 2001	25 per cent	25 per cent
Past due loan definition	3 months (reduced from 6 months in October 1997)	3 months	6 months (reduced to 3 months in 1997, restored to 6 months in 1998)	3 months
Allowance for loan losses	General provision 2 per cent Special mention 5 per cent Sub-standard 25 per cent Doubtful 50 per cent Loss 100 per cent	Normal 1 per cent Special mention 5 per cent Sub-standard 15 per cent Doubtful 50 per cent Loss 100 per cent Banks can amortise the losses over 4 years from 1998	General provision 1.5 per cent Sub-standard 20 per cent Doubtful 50 per cent Loss 100 per cent	General provision 1 per cent Special mention 2 per cent Sub-standard 20 per cent Doubtful 50 per cent Loss 100 per cent
Liquidity requirements	Reserve requirements between 2 and 8 per cent Liquidity reserves 13 per cent	Reserve requirements 2 per cent (reduced from 15 per cent in the mid 1980s)	Statutory reserve requirement 4 per cent (reduced from 13.5 per cent in 1998) Liquid asset ratio 15 per cent (reduced from 17 per cent in 1998)	na

Source: Banko Sentral ng Philippines, 1999; Fitch ICBA, 1999; Bank Negara Malaysia, 1999; and country chapters of this report.

Reserve Ratios

While most industrialised economies no longer set reserve and liquidity ratios, central banks in many regional economies still require commercial banks to meet minimum reserve requirements. Consequently, they must hold a proportion of deposits in short term and government securities or cash deposits at the central bank. While bank reserves are mainly a monetary policy tool, they also serve prudential purposes because they ensure banks maintain adequate liquidity. However, no internationally agreed bank liquidity standards exist and many economies like the Philippines and China gradually are reducing required reserve ratios to reduce bank intermediation costs. As they do this, they may need to augment compensating prudential requirements.

Bank Negara Malaysia's new framework for liquidity management may provide a model for other regional economies. It relies on banks' internal models for projecting liquidity needs, rather than setting arbitrary minimum requirements. This should encourage a more efficient and proactive approach, but still is subject to supervisory oversight (Bank Negara Malaysia, 1999).

As with other forms of regulation, reserve requirements should be applied comprehensively wherever possible. Typically, non-bank financial institutions are not subject to these reserve requirements, so the requirements can discriminate against the banking sector. As a result, deposits may shift to higher yielding non-bank institutions and banks may take greater risks to compete.

Exposure Limits

To reduce risky lending practices, many regional economies' prudential regulations place limits on:

- loans to single and connected entities
- loans for risky assets like real estate and shares
- borrowing or lending which exposes institutions to currency and interest rate risk.

However, some economies enforce these regulations more successfully than others. For example, strong rules on exposure to real estate helped the Philippines avoid the worst effects of the crisis (East Asia Analytical Unit, 1998).[6] However, while in the 1990s Indonesia attempted to strengthen its prudential rules, including limiting lending to firms in the same group, these regulations were poorly enforced. Before the crisis, banks consistently breached lending limits to related firms, and after the crisis began, authorities found the true situation to be even worse than previously revealed.[7] For example, in mid 1998, the Indonesian Bank Restructuring Agency

---

[6] In June 1997, the central bank lowered banks' ceiling on real estate loans from 30 per cent to 20 per cent of total loans and restricted the use of real estate as collateral for loans, reducing it from 70 per cent to 60 per cent.

[7] For example, in 1993, Bank Indonesia found six of the seven state banks had violated lending limits (Fane, 1994). In 1995, six private banks extended loans to connected firms equal to over 200 per cent of the banks' capital. In April 1996, Bank Indonesia found 41 banks breached legal lending limits and 12 foreign exchange banks exceeded foreign exchange exposure limits (Montgomery, 1997).

found Bank Danamon had loaned 85 per cent of its money to its owner's businesses; Bank Umum Nasionale had loaned 70 per cent of its total loans to its owners Bambang Suharto's and Kaharudin Ongko's companies; and Modern Bank had loaned its entire loan portfolio to its owner, property tycoon Samadikun Hartono (*Asiamoney*, November 1998, pp. 15-21).

Since 1998, Indonesia has actually loosened its limits on lending to related and single entities. Authorities believe viable borrowers are so few and lending is so thin, restrictions would constrain economic activity. However, these rules must be tightened once the economy recovers.

Similarly, Thailand failed to enforce its lending limits, as the collapse of Bangkok Bank of Commerce in 1996 showed. Two senior managers of the bank loaned themselves about two thirds of the bank's loan portfolio, and made loans to politicians, fabricated accounts and embezzled funds (Backman, 1999). Since the crisis began, more cases of illegal connected lending have been uncovered.

As diversified family-owned conglomerates own many Asian banks, several other economies experienced similar problems. For example, Taiwan's Pan Asia Bank was heavily exposed to related companies. (See Chapter 10 - *Taiwan*.) To prevent such conflicts of interest, most industrialised economies, including Australia, do not allow bank ownership to concentrate in a single company or family. The serious impact of related lending abuses in East Asia highlights the crucial role of effective prudential supervision.

PRUDENTIAL SUPERVISION

A major consequence of the crisis is a push for stronger, more independent, efficient and accountable supervisors. In the lead up to and early stages of the crisis, weak prudential supervision in Indonesia, Thailand and Korea generated fear of systemic breakdown, spurred capital flight and contributed to the crisis. Political interference, lack of human and financial resources, and inadequate independence undermined supervisors' authority.

Excessive Forbearance

In several crisis-affected economies, weak and insufficiently independent supervisors contributed to the crisis by allowing insolvent financial institutions to continue operating, sometimes for years. Supervisors were forced to bow to political interference and prevent institutional failures, or in some cases, took illicit payments to show excessive forbearance. For example, many analysts knew from mid 1995 that the Sutowo family's First Pacific Bank was insolvent, but Indonesian authorities allowed it to operate until late 1997, when it became one of 16 banks closed under the IMF's rescue package (Backman, 1999). Similarly, the Japanese Ministry of Finance scandal revealed some supervisors took inducements to cover up the financial problems of institutions they supervised.

In some of the most severely affected economies, supervisory forbearance persisted after 1997, greatly increasing the risk of asset stripping by insiders and the cost of recapitalisation. While forbearance sometimes is necessary to stem systemic risk, it must be implemented according to clear criteria and over a set time frame.

Supervisors' Powers

Supervisory failures have caused crisis-affected countries to upgrade supervisors' powers, giving them greater authority to take action against financial institutions, and less freedom to waive regulations. For example, authorities now can demand additional loan loss provisions from banks when they detect problems. Moreover, most procedures no longer permit earlier supervisory discretion that allowed supervisors to waive regulations, for example by treating loan concentrations on a case-by-case basis (International Monetary Fund, 1999).

Supervisors have more power over the entry and exit of banks. For example, the Philippines and Korea recently passed legislation supporting regulators' power to demand information and withdraw licences from banks; previously it was not clear they had this power. In Indonesia, the central bank rather than the Ministry of Finance now has authority to grant bank licences, and directors must pass a new 'fit and proper' test. (See Chapter 7 - *Indonesia*.)

Many regional authorities are introducing new, tighter exit procedures for problem institutions, including mandatory 'prompt corrective action'.[8] When financial institutions' capital adequacy falls below certain trigger points, authorities must initiate immediate pre-determined actions, culminating in withdrawing bank licences (International Monetary Fund, 1999).

Supervisory techniques also are changing. Supervisors in crisis-affected economies now rely more on on-site examination and less on data submitted by institutions. They also make greater use of examinations by external auditors.

Independence of Supervisory Authorities

Effective supervisors must be able to implement regulations in a consistent, impartial and efficient manner, and resist pressure from banks, debtors, creditors and government. As financial institution owners often are politically influential or may even be governments, supervisors must be independent of government. Independent central banks are more likely to achieve lower inflation rates, less cyclical volatility and better supervision.

---

[8] A prompt corrective action system imposes step by step, obligatory corrective measures on unsound financial institutions that fall below a certain level of capital adequacy. Prompt corrective action measures include improving personnel management and organisation, including changing senior management, reducing capital, restricting profit dividends, merging or purchasing and assuming enterprises, closing institutions and selling risky assets and subsidiaries.

> ## AUGMENTING SUPERVISORS' SKILLS
>
> Many regional prudential supervisors lack the necessary skills to perform their roles effectively. Inadequate resources and poor pay exacerbate this problem. International donors are addressing these problems. Two new centres established since the crisis augment existing training provided by the South East Asian Central Banks Research and Training Centre in Kuala Lumpur:
>
> - the Institute for Financial Stability in Basle trains bank supervisors, holds high-level seminars and coordinates bilateral technical assistance provided by central banks and supervisory bodies. It was established in 1998 by the Bank for International Settlements and the Basle Committee on Banking Supervision
>
> - the Toronto International Leadership Centre for Financial Sector Supervision offers leadership and crisis management training. The World Bank, the Canadian Government, Canadian banks and York University established it in 1997.
>
> The IMF also regularly provides prudential supervision training in Washington DC and at its new training centre in Singapore. Since the crisis began, the World Bank, Asian Development Bank and many bilateral donors including Australia have undertaken extensive training for supervisors.[9]
>
> Source: *Economist*, 17 April 1999; and Bank for International Settlements, 1998.

Lack of central bank and supervisory independence contributed to the crisis.[10] Hence, since the onset of the crisis, several regional governments have enhanced central bank and supervisory independence. The Korean and Indonesian Governments no longer have the authority to replace central bank governors within their term of office and are reducing government representation on central bank boards. Thailand has a new central bank law awaiting legislative approval. Before the crisis Japan, China and the Philippines also increased the independence of their central banks and financial regulators.[11]

---

[9] In March 1999, for example, the Australian aid agency, AusAID, funded a ten day workshop for central bank and ministry of finance officials from East Asia on recent developments in prudential controls run by the National Centre for Development Studies at the Australian National University and the East Asia Analytical Unit of the Australian Department of Foreign Affairs and Trade.

[10] Many regional supervisors failed to close insolvent financial institutions and enforce connected lending and other lending limits because of inadequate independence from governments. Furthermore, several central banks intervened heavily in currency markets, possibly at the urging of governments and other vested interests.

[11] See country chapters for details.

Although many consolidated supervisory agencies still are notionally under the auspices of central banks or ministries of finance, these agencies function more efficiently if financially independent from such bodies.[12] Otherwise, financial institutions and vested interests may exploit conflicts of interest and bureaucratic jealousies, jeopardising supervision.

Supervisors' Accountability and Transparency

To gain the confidence of market participants, government and depositors, more independent supervisors must also be more accountable and transparent. Pioneered by New Zealand and Canada, the impetus for greater supervisory transparency is increasing worldwide, with more supervisors reporting regularly on the conditions shaping their policies.[13] Market participants highly regard Hong Kong, Australia and Singapore for their supervisors' openness in publishing timely data but rate Korea, Indonesia and China poorly (Figure 3.1).

Figure 3.1

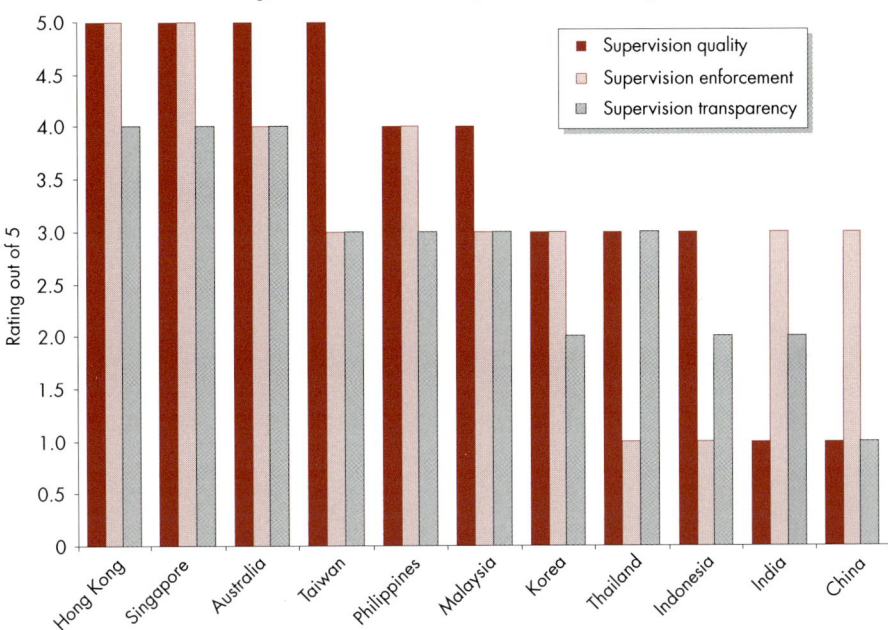

Note: Based on market research on banking regulatory norms, and interviews and assessments from 12 bank economists in the region.

Source: *Asiamoney*, November 1998.

---

[12] Supervisor and central bank independence is enhanced by financial autonomy, so ministries of finance should not fund the activities of supervisors. Hence many economies allow supervisory agencies to collect fees from financial institutions to cover the costs of supervision and to attract, train and hold staff, giving them autonomy over budgetary and personnel matters. For example, in recent years, the Philippines' central bank has gained financial independence from the Ministry of Finance. However, the Korean Financial Supervisory Commission is not yet fully independent from the Ministry of Finance and Economy.

[13] Increasingly, the rationale behind central bank monetary policy decisions is published to demonstrate transparency. Japan and the United Kingdom, for example, both publish minutes of monetary policy committee meetings, while analysts criticise the new European Central Bank for not doing so.

Institutional Arrangements and Consolidated Supervision

Historically, supervisors were organised along institutional lines, with one supervisor for banks, another for securities firms and a third for insurance companies. However, many economies now are removing regulatory barriers between different financial sector industries and allowing single large institutions to enter many markets. Australia, Japan, the United Kingdom, Indonesia, the Philippines, Hong Kong, Korea, and with approval, Singapore now allow financial institutions to operate in bank and non-bank financial institution sectors, allowing a move to universal banking (Institute of International Bankers, 1999). Even in the United States, the repeal of the 1930s Glass-Steagall Act in October 1999 has meant banks, insurers and securities firms now can combine.[14] These developments make it difficult for segmented supervisors to monitor total risk exposure, and are driving the emergence of consolidated supervisors.

Increasing globalisation of the financial industry creates similar dilemmas for supervisors who must attempt to monitor institutions' combined international and domestic exposure. These trends encourage increased cooperation in cross-border information exchanges.

THE GLOBAL TREND TOWARDS CONSOLIDATED SUPERVISION

Since 1997, governments in the United Kingdom, Australia, Japan and Korea have consolidated responsibility for financial institution supervision in new supervisory agencies, allowing central banks to focus on overall financial system stability and monetary policy (Table 3.3).[15]

- In 1997, the United Kingdom's new Financial Services Authority was the first consolidated supervisor, taking over the functions of nine regulatory bodies supervising banks, securities dealers and insurance companies.

- In mid 1998, Australia established the Australian Prudential Regulation Authority, consolidating supervision for all deposit taking institutions, insurance companies and superannuation funds.[16]

- In early 1998, the Korean Government established the Financial Supervisory Commission to take over bank and non-bank financial institution supervisory responsibility from the Bank of Korea, Ministry of Finance and Economy, and securities and insurance supervisory agencies.[17]

- Also in 1998, Japan's new Financial Supervisory Agency took over bank and non-bank financial institution supervisory responsibilities from the Ministry of Finance and Bank of Japan; the new agency is responsible to the Prime Minister rather than the Minister of Finance.

---

[14] Initially, US supervision will remain segmented among several regulators.

[15] Central banks usually have two core functions: to operate monetary policy and maintain financial system stability. Most play a key role in foreign exchange transactions, managing the payments system between financial institutions, acting as a lender of last resort to the banking system, and issuing currency. In addition, central banks traditionally have supervised financial institutions.

[16] In parallel with these changes, oversight of all conduct and disclosure regulation was consolidated in the Australian Securities Investment Commission.

[17] The Financial Supervisory Commission also is in charge of bank and non-bank financial institution restructuring and refinancing. The Ministry of Finance and Economy still has some residual responsibilities for issuing bank licences.

Prudential Reform

Table 3.3

Consolidated Supervision Increasing
Responsibilities for Financial System Stability and Supervision

Country	Prudential Supervision	Responsibilities	Recent developments and comments
Australia	Reserve Bank of Australia	Overall financial system stability and the payments system	Formed in 1998, APRA has taken over prudential regulation and supervision of banks, insurance companies, superannuation funds, credit unions, building societies and friendly societies from the Reserve Bank of Australia, various state agencies and the Insurance and Superannuation Commission
	Australian Prudential Regulation Authority, APRA	All deposit taking institutions, insurance companies and superannuation funds	
	Australian Securities and Investment Commission	Securities companies, capital market regulation and disclosure	
China	People's Bank of China	Banks, trust and investment companies, and credit cooperatives	To reduce provincial interference, nine regional branches recently replaced 31 provincial level branches of the People's Bank of China
	China Securities Regulatory Commission	Securities companies	
	China Insurance Regulatory Commission	Insurance companies	
Hong Kong	Hong Kong Monetary Authority	Banks	Supervision is fragmented with responsibilities shared between these three bodies. No current plans exist to consolidate
	Securities and Futures Commission	Securities companies	
	Insurance Board	Insurance companies	
Japan	Financial Supervisory Agency	Bank and non-bank financial institutions	The Financial Supervisory Agency became the integrated financial supervisor in June 1998. Supervisory responsibility still is shared for some non-bank financial institutions
Indonesia	Bank Indonesia	Banks	A new agency will be created as an integrated financial supervisor in 2003. Powers are yet to be determined
	Capital Markets Supervisory Agency, BAPEPAM	Securities firms	
	Ministry of Finance	Insurance companies	

Prudential Reform

Country	Prudential Supervision	Responsibilities	Recent developments and comments
Korea	Financial Supervisory Commission	Banks, insurance companies, securities and futures, and non-bank financial institutions	Established in 1998, the Financial Supervisory Commission is an integrated financial supervisor, taking over supervisory responsibilities from the Bank of Korea, Securities and Exchange Commission and the Insurance Supervisory Commission. The commission includes the Financial Supervisory Service, and the Securities and Futures Commission
Philippines	Banko Sentral ng Pilipinas	Banks and other deposit taking institutions	Banko Sentral ng Pilipinas is moving towards consolidated supervision
	Insurance Commission	Insurance companies	
	Securities Exchange Commission	Securities companies	
Singapore	Monetary Authority of Singapore	Regulation and supervision of banking, insurance and securities	The Monetary Authority of Singapore is an integrated financial supervisor, and responsible for monetary policy
Taiwan	Ministry of Finance and Central Bank of China	Bank supervision is split between the finance ministry and central bank	The Deposit Insurance Corporation can inspect the records of all institutions. Taiwan is considering a move to a system of consolidated supervision
	The Securities and Futures Commission	Securities companies	
	Department of Insurance	Insurance companies	
Thailand	Bank of Thailand	Banks, finance companies, and finance and securities companies	The creation of a new body to supervise financial institutions is being considered
	Securities and Exchange Commission	Securities companies	
	Ministry of Commerce	Insurance companies	
Malaysia	Bank Negara Malaysia	Banks and non-bank financial institutions	Malaysia is moving to consolidate supervision

Source: Country chapters in this report; and central bank websites.

Developing economies, particularly smaller ones, have been slower to consolidate supervision under integrated financial supervisors. Many still use the central bank as the main supervisor because of difficulty in staffing separate agencies. However, while the central bank knows the banking sector well, its exclusive experience with bank supervision may not necessarily suit it to the consolidated supervision of banks, securities firms and insurance companies. Furthermore, as raising interest rates can adversely affect financial institutions, potential exists for conflict between central banks' supervisory and monetary policy responsibilities. Since the crisis, this conflict has become obvious in some regional economies, leading to plans to separate prudential supervision and monetary policy in Indonesia, and possibly Thailand.

Risk Based Supervision

Following the United Kingdom, Australia and the United States, both Hong Kong and Singapore are moving towards a more risk based approach to supervision. Rather than relying on inspections of banks' current positions, the approach looks ahead, anticipating changes and attempting to detect signs of future weakness. Financial institutions are expected to bear more responsibility and install adequate risk management systems. The approach requires higher calibre supervisors, able to assess the quality of systems rather than merely examine loan books.

MARKET REGULATION THROUGH DISCLOSURE

In recent decades, the expanded scope of financial institutions, transnational financial transactions and technological innovations in financial products all have increased the difficulty of supervision and regulation. This has forced regulation and supervision to evolve from traditional, prescriptive, rules based systems, to newer market based approaches relying almost completely on disclosure.[18]

As a result of the crisis, most East Asian governments recognise their supervisors and their whole financial system require greater transparency and disclosure. For example, Korean and Filipino financial supervisors now require domestic banks to publish data on their capital adequacy ratios and NPL levels. Indonesian banks must publish detailed information more frequently. In this process, credible self-regulatory organisations like accountancy and other professional associations, and institutional investor involvement, are critical.

Capital Market Regulation and Disclosure

To protect investors and preserve market integrity, efficiently functioning capital markets rely on well developed and enforced securities laws and disclosure requirements. Financial results and other information relevant to investor decisions must be disclosed fully and promptly. To enforce this disclosure, independent regulators need to be well resourced and have clear mandates and powers. In East Asia, regulators need adequate enforcement and supervisory powers to effectively implement regulations, and both civil and criminal sanctions; civil actions have a lower burden of proof and have a higher success rate (International Organisation of Securities Commissions, 1998).

---

[18] New Zealand uses a largely disclosure or market based approach.

Bank Regulation through Disclosure

Since the crisis, governments also recognise transparency plays a key role in bank supervision. Since a major review of its supervisory regime in January 1996, New Zealand has relied heavily on a public disclosure regime with limited supervision and few quantitative regulations.[19] To improve transparency in the banking system, the Philippine central bank now requires all listed banks to publish quarterly 'statements of condition', including their returns on equity, NPL levels and prime rates.[20] Since the crisis began, Malaysia, Korea, Thailand and Indonesia also have increased bank disclosure requirements.[21]

THE NEW ZEALAND APPROACH TO BANK SUPERVISION: FOCUS ON DISCLOSURE

In 1996, New Zealand introduced a new bank regulation and supervision regime, relying heavily on disclosure and market discipline, and removing all but a few core prudential regulations.

Financial institutions must release quarterly public 'disclosure statements' publicising information on their financial performance and risk positions. The Reserve Bank of New Zealand's monitoring is based principally on these disclosure statements; it also consults annually with senior bank management on banks' strategic directions and banking industry developments.

New Zealand's prudential regime also relies heavily on external auditors' opinions and attestations by directors. Banks must provide an external audit opinion on whether their year-end disclosure statements comply with generally accepted accounting practices, and provide a true and fair account of their situation. Bank directors must verify the accuracy of quarterly disclosure statements, and affirm their bank employs satisfactory risk management policies.

The Reserve Bank of New Zealand retains only a few prudential requirements. Banks must meet minimum capital requirements in line with the Basle Capital Accord and are subject to limits on lending to related parties.

Source: Reserve Bank of New Zealand, 1997.

---

[19] However, as New Zealand's banking system is almost completely foreign owned, some analysts claim foreign supervisors do most of the supervision for New Zealand. As this system was initiated before full foreign bank ownership, regulators claim this was not a major factor in their decision to adopt a disclosure based system.

[20] The statement must contain information on the level and ratio of NPLs to the total loan portfolio, the level of classified loans and other risk assets, and the value of general and specific loan loss reserves.

[21] See country chapters for details.

CORPORATE GOVERNANCE REFORMS

Weak corporate governance, or a failure to run companies in an open and honest manner, significantly impedes regional capital market development and has undermined regional banking systems. Lack of corporate transparency, investor protection and effective board oversight were severe in Korea, Thailand, Malaysia and Indonesia. Weak corporate governance enabled banks to accumulate risky and concentrated assets via illegal connected lending.[22] This failure also inhibited mechanisms for minority shareholders to ensure assets were managed in their interests and exercise control over corporate insiders, majority shareholders and management. This problem reduced small shareholders' willingness to buy shares and corporate bonds, increasing corporates' reliance on riskier domestic and foreign bank borrowing.

Once a few key events undermined confidence in mid 1997, lack of effective governance systems and poor transparency meant domestic and foreign creditors and lenders could not properly evaluate the riskiness of their loans and portfolio investments; this accelerated capital flight from the region. Since 1997, concern about poor accounting standards and corporate ethics in Thailand, Indonesia, Malaysia and Korea has reduced foreign investor willingness to inject new capital into, or purchase assets from, distressed financial institutions and corporates.

Regional Progress in Corporate Governance

Among the East Asian economies making the greatest efforts to improve corporate governance are Malaysia, Singapore and Korea. Malaysia's National Economic Recovery Plan gives high priority to improving transparency and the regulatory environment, and urges the Kuala Lumpur Stock Exchange and Securities Commission to enforce regulations vigorously and consistently. In 1999, Malaysia tightened its listing rules to require the issue of quarterly financial statements and prevent individuals from sitting on too many boards.

The current corporate governance situation in Malaysia is rather mixed. A recent report listed ten major Malaysian companies with good corporate governance records, including fair treatment of minority shareholders (Dresdner Kleinwort Benson, 1999). However, audit and corporate restructuring reports also point to insider dealings and manoeuvring at the expense of minority shareholders.[23]

---

[22] In most regional economies, accounting and auditing practices are weak and regulators do not demand timely and accurate financial reports. In the lead up to the crisis, this allowed banks to keep NPLs on their books for long periods and use historical rather than market prices to value assets.

[23] For example, Arthur Anderson's 30 June 1998 audited accounts of the Malaysian company Ekran were qualified because of large sums paid to parties related to one of its directors without the relevant approval from the Securities Commission, and possibly in breach of the companies law.

MALAYSIA: CORPORATE GOVERNANCE INITIATIVES

In February 1999, Malaysia produced a corporate governance report containing a 70 point program to improve transparency and board accountability to shareholders, and protect minority shareholders. Malaysia will use the study to lead corporate governance reform discussions in APEC.

The recommendations fall into three categories:

- developing a Malaysian Code of Corporate Governance
- reforming laws, regulations and rules to strengthen the regulatory framework for publicly listed companies
- providing training and education to expand the pool of qualified directors and managers.

These reforms are significant and should help improve Malaysia's corporate governance record. The best practice code recommends independent or outside directors constitute at least one third of corporate boards, directors' attendance records and remuneration details be released and each board establishes committees of non-executive directors and names a lead non-executive director. Other proposed changes include anti-cronyism rules restricting controlling shareholders from voting when they have a conflict of interest and requiring companies to offer mailed proxy votes. The report also argues for greater policing of breaches of minority investor rights.

Changes suggested by the committee to the laws and regulations should be fully implemented by December 2000. Although the code of practice will be voluntary, under proposed new stock exchange listing rules, companies would have to disclose compliance with the code or reasons for non-compliance.

Source: Finance Committee on Corporate Governance 1999.

Before and particularly since the crisis, Singapore has sought to strengthen the banking system by improving bank corporate governance.[24] (See Chapter 9 - *Hong Kong and Singapore*.) Since 1996, Singapore has developed and refined corporate governance rules and principles for listed companies.[25]

Korea has passed significant legislation to improve minority shareholder rights, increase independent membership of boards and introduce international accountancy standards. Korean conglomerates now must release consolidated company accounts for

---

[24] The Monetary Authority of Singapore will require all local banks to appoint nominating committees to handle appointments and reappointments to the board and key management positions. Members of the nominating committees must be chosen from the board and approved by the Monetary Authority of Singapore. The authority also extended its veto over board appointments to cover reappointments (Monetary Authority of Singapore, 1999).

[25] Originally imposed as part of the exchange listing rules, highly prescriptive provisions relating to audit committees have been moved to a best practice guide. The listing rules still require companies to establish audit committees and their annual reports must state whether and how companies have complied with the best practice guide. This focuses more on the substance of compliance than on the form, and is consistent with Australian approaches to corporate governance.

the activities of all subsidiaries (East Asia Analytical Unit, 1999).[26] The Stock Exchange of Thailand requires all listed companies' boards of directors to establish an independent auditing capacity. Furthermore, improved listing rules encourage better disclosure practices, recognition of shareholder rights and development of internal controls (APEC Study Centre, 1998).

However, improving corporate governance requires a significant shift in corporate culture and ethics; this cannot be achieved just by passing legislation. Strict enforcement and some highly publicised convictions can assist in this process.

FINANCIAL MARKET INFRASTRUCTURE

In all seriously affected economies, the crisis revealed structural weaknesses in core financial infrastructure and legal systems; corporate, securities and bankruptcy laws and judicial practice were inadequate. As with corporate governance, regional governments now are prioritising the reform of core financial and legal infrastructure.

Bankruptcy Law Reform

The economic crisis gave urgency to previously muted calls to reform insolvency laws. Until 1997, many Asian corporate and personal bankruptcy laws remained almost unchanged and rarely used since colonial times. For example, until 1998, Indonesia's bankruptcy legislation was based on a 1906 Dutch colonial law, and between 1993 and 1998, only 120 cases were brought to the courts (Linnan, 1999).[27] In Thailand, the old bankruptcy law did not even contain many basic workout provisions.

With the onset of the financial crisis, weak laws prevented creditors from liquidating insolvent companies and securing assets; markets were impotent to resolve corporate debt problems. Consequently, NPLs escalated to extreme levels in economies like Indonesia and Thailand. The absence of efficiently functioning bankruptcy laws constrained the restructuring and recapitalisation of financial institutions, contributing to the liquidity crunch and further deepening the crisis in much of East Asia in 1998.

Throughout 1998, regional governments realised they must strengthen bankruptcy laws and enforcement. Despite opposition from entrenched vested interests, Thailand, Indonesia and Korea passed new laws for bankruptcy and debt workouts, and introduced mechanisms binding dissenting minority creditors to restructuring plans. In March 1999, Thailand's legislature passed four new laws, significantly upgrading the bankruptcy framework. (See Chapter 8 - *Thailand, Malaysia and the Philippines*.) However, the new Commercial Court established in June 1999 is slow in enforcing these laws; time is needed to increase judges' experience, and some landmark cases would help build creditors' confidence in the new procedures. In August 1999, Indonesia submitted a further revision to its bankruptcy law to its legislature and, with World Bank assistance, established a new Commercial Court to

---

[26] Consolidated accounting rules also applied in Japan from 1 April 1999.

[27] Although the old Indonesian law contained most provisions for a workable bankruptcy framework, it rarely was used due to Indonesia's long economic boom, a cultural preference for informal mechanisms for securing debt repayment and the courts' low credibility in dealing with bankruptcy and debt.

implement this law. However, as in Thailand, early court decisions have been slow and often disappointing for creditors; more time is needed to build the court's expertise and credibility. (See Chapter 7 - *Indonesia.*) Korea's bankruptcy laws were significantly amended in February 1998; the new law includes a reasonably successful bank led, out-of-court debt workout mechanism for all distressed corporates except the top five *chaebol* (East Asia Analytical Unit, 1999).[28] However, creditors still are dissatisfied with long enforcement delays.

Singapore and Hong Kong have sound bankruptcy regimes, but during the boom years, these were neglected and now lag well behind those of western jurisdictions. Singapore recently introduced a system to deal with business debt through judicial management. Hong Kong has a considerable body of expertise in its local and expatriate legal community; a court system which efficiently handles insolvency cases; and judges with sound commercial knowledge (Tomasic and Little, 1997). However, Hong Kong's low level of insolvency generated little pressure for further reform.[29]

Malaysia's insolvency laws are quite well developed and favour creditors. However, under Section 176 of Malaysia's companies law, bond issues may be overly protected by court approved schemes of arrangement. Such an interpretation appears contrary to the original intention.[30]

In 1999, Japanese bankruptcy laws were thoroughly reviewed and the Government aims to enact a new corporate rehabilitation law by the end of the year. As bankruptcy and debt workout proceedings can drag on in the courts for many years, facilitating more rapid workouts of corporate debt is a high priority. By 2001, the Government plans to amend the law on bankruptcy and corporate reorganisation, and introduce a new law recognising foreign insolvency proceedings (Matsushita, 1999).

While China began modernising its business laws in the 1980s, bankruptcy law reform stalled. An advanced draft of a new law has been before National Congress for several years, but has not been passed because it could force many unviable state owned enterprises into liquidation. In practice, only Chinese banks and government departments have forced state owned enterprises into bankruptcy; no foreign creditor has attempted to do so.

Prospects for Asian Bankruptcy Laws

Despite considerable progress in the past two years, East Asia's insolvency law reform has only just begun, and much of the new legislation implemented is only partly effective. This is not surprising as new legislation introduces foreign business concepts to environments where powerful stakeholders actively resist their enactment and intervene to prevent their enforcement.

---

[28] Reforms shortened the time of legal proceedings, established standards for managing bankrupt companies to facilitate effective restructuring, and strengthened the rights and status of creditors.

[29] While the Hong Kong Law Reform Commission recommended a system of judicial supervision in 1996, by late 1999, the Government had not updated legislation (Law Reform Commission of Hong Kong, 1996).

[30] A court ruling enables banks that guaranteed bond issues to claim they too are protected by the court when the issuer of the bonds is placed in bankruptcy. This has reduced investors' appetite for low rated corporate bonds.

Prudential Reform

Even in Hong Kong and Singapore, where insolvency laws are well developed and embedded, disputes between small businesses most often are resolved without reference to the courts; foreign businesses are the main users of insolvency laws. Similarly, despite comprehensive bankruptcy legislation, business in Taiwan continues to favour informal workouts outside the formal legal system.

However, with internationalisation and growing western influences, the stigma associated with bankruptcy may be declining, particularly in Hong Kong and Singapore where legal professions are more developed (Tomasic and Little, 1997). Recent upgrading of bankruptcy legislation in Korea, Thailand and Indonesia also should promote its more frequent use, eventually reducing the moral hazard associated with dysfunctional insolvency regimes.

However, for this to happen, upgraded legal infrastructure must complement law reform; increasing the professionalism and remuneration of judges is a top priority. Revisions to the Indonesian bankruptcy laws demonstrate how difficult and time consuming such change can be.

THE PAYMENTS SYSTEM

As the volume and speed of capital movements within and across borders increases, so does the potential for settlement risks and systemic dangers; this makes sound payment and settlement systems a crucial element of financial infrastructure. By settling monetary transactions in a timely and cost effective way, sound payment systems minimise systemic risk. One participant's failure to meet its obligations will not cause other participants to fail.

During the 1980s and 1990s, the huge growth in intra-national and international financial transactions through the world's wholesale payments systems required significant reform of these systems. Most major economies apply a real time gross settlement, RTGS, system for high value interbank transactions.[31] RTGS systems reduce settlement and systemic risks in the interbank settlement process and strengthen securities markets' settlement arrangements by requiring interbank settlement to be finalised when ownership of securities change.

As the RTGS system requires banks to have sufficient balances in their central bank accounts to cover transactions throughout the processing day, it may increase bank costs. However, the benefits from reduced supervision costs, improved system stability and greater market discipline far outweigh the cost to banks (Folkerts-Landau, 1997).

---

[31] RTGS systems settle individual fund transfers continually during the processing day. This helps reduce two major sources of risk in the payment system: the time lag between the execution of the transaction and its final completion, and the lag between the payment and delivery of a transaction.

Prudential Reform

RTGS Progress in Asia

Many of the more advanced East Asian economies have introduced RTGS (Table 3.4). Korea introduced a RTGS system called BOK-Wire in 1994 to undertake most interbank fund transfers previously executed by Bank of Korea telex or cheques.[32] Thailand introduced a real time gross settlement system, BAHTNET, in 1995. However, by 1997, cheques still were used for most large value payments, and in 1999, BAHTNET still accounted for only one tenth of large value payments.[33] In mid 1998, Australia introduced a RTGS system for all large value interbank payments, including the cash settlement of debt securities transactions. With World Bank assistance, China is developing a new payments system to assist with monetary control and reduce systemic risk.

Table 3.4

Many Advanced Regional Economies Adopt RTGS
Real Time Gross Settlement Systems in Asia

Economy	RTGS?	Name of system	Year implemented
Australia	✓	RITS, Austclear	1998
China	x	CNAPS	Planned
Hong Kong	✓	RTGS	1996
Indonesia	x		
Japan	✓	BOJ-NET	1988
Korea	✓	BOK-Wire	1994
New Zealand	✓	KITZ	1997
Malaysia	✓	RENTAS	1999
Philippines	x		
Singapore	✓	MAS Electronic Payment System	1998
Thailand	✓	BAHTNET	1995
United Kingdom	✓	CHAPS	1984

Source: Central bank websites, 1999.

---

[32] With the growing use of electronic payment systems and launch of BOK-Wire, banks can monitor and manage their liquidity position more quickly and accurately, making interbank settlement reserves management more efficient (Bank of Korea, 1999). Through the Monetary and Financial Information System, the BOK-Wire also allows the central bank to monitor the flow of funds among financial institutions and acquire information on banks' positions in markets.

[33] This is mainly because of the lack of legal support for electronic payments, as electronic evidence is not admissible in Thai courts, and the significant amount of liquidity required compared to the parallel netting system for cheques (Bank of Thailand, 1997). The Government plans to amend the evidence law to overcome the first problem.

CHINA'S PAYMENTS SYSTEM

To overcome shortcomings in the Chinese payment settlement system, the World Bank and the People's Bank of China are finalising a new initiative, China National Automated Payments System, CNAPS. The Chinese Government recognises its payments system must be improved to reduce systemic risk and increase the efficiency of monetary policy tools. As the current payment system is not centralised, clearance occurs at separate People's Bank of China branch offices; banks therefore must carry huge cash floats to settle transactions.

The new automated payment system will include a:

- high value payments system on a RTGS basis
- bulk electronic payment system, BEPS, on a net end-of-day settlement basis
- government securities book-entry system
- bank card authorisation system
- financial management information system
- local cheque clearing house.

The system was piloted in 1998 and is being rolled out nationally in 1999, costing around US$600 million. Apart from dramatically lowering systemic risk in China's financial system, the project should facilitate rapid growth in credit card use across China and help develop capital markets.

Source: Morgan Stanley Dean Witter, 1998.

Hong Kong's RTGS system is perhaps the region's most advanced. It currently has a real time delivery-versus-payment capability for debt securities and eventually will have payment-versus-payment capability for foreign exchange transactions via links between the payment systems of Hong Kong and other economies. The Hong Kong Monetary Authority leads the way in building links with other national electronic settlement systems, including Australia's.[34]

DEPOSIT INSURANCE SCHEMES

Most regional governments provide either explicit or implicit guarantees of bank deposits.[35] However, the Asian crisis highlighted the need to approach depositor protection schemes more coherently, possibly including them as part of financial market infrastructure.

---

[34] In December 1997, Hong Kong became linked to Australia's Reserve Bank Information and Transfer System, RITS, for Australian government securities and Austraclear, for Australian private sector debt securities. A similar link was built with Austraclear New Zealand, the clearing system for both government and private sector debt issues operated by the Reserve Bank of New Zealand. Hong Kong is preparing to link to the Chinese government securities book-entry system when it is operational. Hong Kong also is discussing a similar link with Korea's securities depository system (Hong Kong Monetary Authority, 1999).

[35] Explicit guarantees may take the form of a formal deposit insurance scheme, which reimburses depositors for their losses, possibly up to a threshold limit. Implicit guarantees exist when depositors assume the government will either prevent bank failures or bail out depositors if banks fail.

Prudential Reform

The Arguments For and Against Formal Deposit Insurance Schemes

Deposit insurance schemes are controversial. Supporters of these schemes point out few governments would allow local banks to fail and depositors to lose funds, and in any case, most depositors assume their deposits are guaranteed. Consequently, they argue it is better to formalise and limit guarantees, and make bank depositors bear their cost.

Critics of deposit insurance schemes claim they do little to protect depositors in a systemic crisis and can undermine market discipline. While deposit insurance schemes usually only cover smaller borrowers in selected financial institutions, they could impose considerable costs if insured depositors merely seek high interest rates and deposit in risky institutions. Banks also may take more risks if they believe their insured depositors would be protected if the bank failed. This moral hazard danger was well demonstrated during the United States' savings and loan debacle in the 1980s.

However, forcing larger depositors, other creditors, shareholders and managers to face the real consequences of their investment decisions can minimise these moral hazard dangers. For example, some analysts believe insured institutions should be required to raise a specified portion of their funding through uninsured, subordinate debt issues.[36]

East Asian Deposit Insurance

Most East Asian economies already have or are considering deposit insurance schemes. Before the crisis, Japan, Korea, Taiwan and the Philippines all had some form of deposit insurance, directed mainly at small depositors (Table 3.5). During the financial crisis, the Korean, Indonesian and Thai Governments were forced to provide blanket guarantees of bank depositors to restore confidence in their banking systems; these governments now are introducing or expanding formal deposit insurance schemes.

In late 1997, the Indonesian Government made explicit its previously implicit deposit guarantees, initially guaranteeing deposits of up to US$6 000 in closed banks, and finally, all depositors and creditors of all Indonesian banks. Thailand also had to issue blanket guarantees to stem bank runs. Both economies now plan to introduce formal deposit insurance schemes to replace these blanket guarantees. (See Chapter 7 - *Indonesia* and Chapter 8 - *Thailand, Malaysia and the Philippines*.) To prevent bank runs, early in the crisis Korea extended the reach of its deposit insurance scheme to provide blanket cover.

While China has announced it wishes to introduce a deposit insurance scheme, this would expose the budget to huge contingent liabilities, so details still are under discussion. (See Chapter 12 - *China*.) The Chinese Government already implicitly guarantees most domestic depositors, and explicitly guarantees other liabilities of the main state owned commercial and policy banks. In the past, Hong Kong provided *ad hoc* guarantees for domestic depositors of failing banks, but now is considering a formal deposit insurance scheme (Carse, 1999).

---

[36] Subordinated debt holders are least likely to be bailed out when a bank fails, and therefore should monitor a bank's financial condition. Subordinated debt provides no benefit from risky lending so holders will discourage excessive risk taking. Consequently, spreads on subordinated debt should be particularly sensitive to bank performance risk. While some conceptual difficulties still are associated with developing a mandatory subordinated debt policy, the issue is being developed (Meyer, 1999).

Other regional governments usually guarantee the deposits and often other liabilities of government-owned financial institutions. For example, the Singapore Government explicitly guarantees state owned POS Bank deposits and liabilities. In contrast, Australia is not discussing the introduction of any form of explicit deposit insurance. However, as in Hong Kong, Australia provides preference to depositors when banks are liquidated, offering increased, but not total, safety for deposits.

Table 3.5

Most Regional Economies Have Some Deposit Insurance
Explicit Deposit Insurance in East Asia

	Formal deposit insurance scheme?	Details and plans
Australia	x	No explicit guarantee. Depositors are granted preference over other creditors in the winding up of financial institutions. The Wallis Review expanded depositor preference from banks to all regulated deposit taking institutions. This applies to all deposits regardless of size.
China	x	Announced intention to introduce deposit insurance.
Hong Kong	x	Under consideration, but no explicit plans to introduce it as yet. Deposits of up to HK$100 000 are given preference in bank liquidation.
Indonesia	x	In 1998, the Government guaranteed all bank deposits until further notice. The Government is developing a scheme to insure small individual depositors, up to approximately US$5 000, for possible introduction in 2000.
Japan	✓	The Deposit Insurance Corporation has provided coverage since 1971. Scaled back coverage to individual deposits up to ¥10 million from March 2001 is proposed.
Korea	✓	Korea Deposit Insurance Corporation offers compulsory contributory insurance for deposits up to Won 20 million (US$38 000); this was extended during the crisis but is being wound back.
Malaysia	x	Blanket guarantee of deposits issued during the crisis.
Philippines	✓	Philippines Deposit Insurance Corporation provides coverage for all bank deposits up to P 100 000 per depositor.
Singapore	x	Deposits and liabilities of POS Bank are guaranteed until the merger with Development Bank of Singapore is finalised.
Taiwan	✓	Central Deposit Insurance Corporation offers voluntary deposit insurance. Most financial institutions are insured. New legislation requires all financial institutions to be covered.
Thailand	x	In 1997, the Government announced it guaranteed all deposits. This will be replaced with a formal scheme.
United States	✓	Most banks and savings and loans associations are insured by the Federal Deposit Insurance Corporation which covers deposits of up to US$100 000. Credit Unions are insured through the National Credit Union Administration, up to US$100 000 per member.

Source: Financial System Inquiry 1997; country chapters in this report; and central bank websites.

Prudential Reform

Limiting Public Liabilities

However, as a result of the crisis, most East Asian governments are moving to limit their exposure through deposit insurance. Japan's Deposit Insurance Corporation has provided full protection to depositors regardless of amount, but in April 2001, the Government will introduce a ¥10 million (US$84 000) upper limit per depositor. Similarly, in 1998, Korea reduced its deposit insurance protection on new deposits from Won 20 million without accrued interest, to Won 20 million including accrued interest. Indonesia's new scheme will be more limited than the blanket cover provided during the crisis.

While deposit insurance is not a panacea, making depositor protection explicit but limited, and funding it through the banking system, should limit government exposure. Benefits will increase if schemes lead to improved supervision, and market discipline is maintained by leaving large depositors uninsured, by increasing capital adequacy ratios and possibly by requiring the issue of subordinated debt.

FUTURE PROSPECTS

The key issue for regional economies and the international community is whether post-crisis reforms will enhance the vigour and resilience of regional financial systems, or whether a rapid resumption of growth in 2000 will reduce prudential reform commitment, making the region vulnerable to future crises.

Since the crisis began, East Asian governments have progressed significantly in reforming prudential regulation and supervision, and upgrading financial infrastructure. Australia, New Zealand, Hong Kong, Taiwan, Singapore and the Philippines are refining generally well functioning prudential systems. In Korea and Japan, authorities have undergone major shifts in their supervisory culture and significantly upgraded financial and regulatory infrastructure; these changes should permanently and continuously improve their financial systems' prudential control. China, Thailand, Malaysia and Indonesia are embarking on major structural reforms and institutional culture changes.

If successfully completed, in the long term, these reforms should strengthen prudential control and the resilience of these economies' financial systems. However, in the short to medium term, governments still require significant commitment and skill to complete reforms and more importantly, effectively implement them.

REFERENCES

APEC Study Centre, 1998, *Corporate Governance in APEC: Rebuilding Asian Growth*, Symposium report, www.apec.org.au, accessed on 1 November.

Backman, M., 1999, *Asian Eclipse: Exposing the Dark Side of Business in Asia*, John Wiley and Sons, New York.

Bank for International Settlements, 1998, Press release, 'BIS Appoints Leadership of the Financial Stability Institute', 1 December, www.bis.org, accessed on 12 July.

Bank of Korea, 1999, 'The Payment System in Korea', www.bok.or.kr, accessed on 15 July.

Bank Negara Malaysia, *Annual Report 1998*, Kuala Lumpur.

Bank of Thailand, 1997, 'Risk Reduction in Large Value Transfer Systems: the Case of Bangkok, Thailand', www.bot.go.th, accessed on 15 July 1999.

Banko Sentral ng Pilipinas, 1999, 'The Philippines: Staying on Course', Manila.

Basle Committee on Banking Supervision, 1999, Consultative paper on a new capital adequacy framework, www.bis.org, accessed on 12 June.

Carse, D., 1999, East Asia Analytical Unit interview with Deputy Chief Executive, Hong Kong Monetary Authority, Hong Kong, May.

Citibank, 1999, 'The New Regulatory Capital Framework', Global Banking Brief, gcbweb.citibank.com, accessed on 27 October.

Crockett, A., 1998, *Banking Supervision and Financial Stability*, Group of Thirty, Washington DC.

Dresdner Kleinwort Benson, 1999, 'Malaysian Corporate Governance: Better than You Thought', Malaysian Research Team, Singapore.

East Asia Analytical Unit, 1999, *Korea Rebuilds: from Crisis to Opportunity*, Department of Foreign Affairs and Trade, Canberra.

___ 1998, *The Philippines: beyond the Crisis*, Department of Foreign Affairs and Trade, Canberra.

Fane, G., 1998, 'The Role of Prudential Regulation', in McLeod, R., and Garnaut, R. (eds), *East Asia in Crisis: from Being a Miracle to Needing One*, Routledge, London.

___ 1994, 'Survey of Recent Developments', *Bulletin of Indonesian Studies*, vol. 30, no. 1, pp. 3-38.

Finance Committee on Corporate Governance 1999, *Report on Corporate Governance*, Ministry of Finance, Kuala Lumpur.

Financial System Inquiry, 1997, 'Financial System Inquiry Final Report', Canberra, www.treasury.gov.au, accessed on 14 July 1999.

Fitch IBCA, 1999, 'Asia Bank Restructuring', April.

Folkerts-Landau, D., 1997, 'Wholesale Payments and Financial Discipline, Efficiency and Liquidity', IMF Working Paper WP/97/154, www.imf.org, accessed on 14 June 1999.

Hong Kong Monetary Authority, 1999, 'Settlement and Payments Systems', www.info.gov.hk, accessed on 15 June.

Institute of International Bankers, 1999, 'Global Survey 1999: Regulatory and Market Developments', September, www.iib.org, accessed on 28 October.

International Monetary Fund, 1999, *Financial Sector Crisis and Restructuring: Lessons from Asia*, advance copy, September, www.imf.org, accessed on 18 October.

International Organisation of Securities Commissions, 1998, *Objectives and Principles of Securities Regulation*, www.iosco.org, accessed on 14 June 1999.

Linnan, D., 1999, 'Bankruptcy Policy and Reform: Reconciling Efficiency and Economic Nationalism', Paper presented at the International Conference on Current Issues and Future Directions for Bankruptcy Reform in Indonesia: International and Comparative Perspectives, 29-30 April, Jakarta.

Law Reform Commission of Hong Kong, 1996, 'Report on Corporate Rescue and Insolvent Trading', October, www.info.gov.hk/justice/department/6/index.htm, accessed on 14 July 1999.

Matsushita, J., 1999, 'Current Japanese Insolvency Law and the Comprehensive Reform Project', Paper presented at the International Conference on Current Issues and Future Directions for Bankruptcy Reform in Indonesia: International and Comparative Perspectives, 29-30 April, Jakarta.

Meyer, L., 1999, 'Remarks on Market Discipline as a Component of Banking Supervision and Regulation', Speech to the conference on Reforming Bank Capital Standards, 14 June, New York, www.bis.org, accessed on 15 July.

Monetary Authority of Singapore, 1999, 'Liberalising Commercial Banking and Upgrading Local Banks', www.mas.gov.au, accessed on 23 May.

Montgomery, J., 1997, 'The Indonesian Financial System: Its Contribution to Economic Performance and Key Policy Issues', IMF Working Paper 97/45, www.imf.org, accessed on 14 September 1999.

Morgan Stanley Dean Witter, 1998, 'China: Financial Services', Asia Pacific Investment Research, 2 February, Hong Kong.

Reserve Bank of New Zealand, 1997, 'The Role of the Reserve Bank of New Zealand in Supervising the Financial System', www.rbnz.govt.nz/fin/role.htm, accessed on 19 September 1999.

Tomasic, R., and Little, P., 1997, 'Insolvency Law and Practice in Asia', FT Law and Tax Asia Pacific, Hong Kong.

Williamson, J. and Maher, M., 1998, 'A Survey of Financial Liberalization', Essays in International Finance, no. 211, International Finance Section, Princetown University, New Jersey.

Chapter 4

BANKING IN POST-CRISIS ASIA

The scale of East Asian banks' non-performing loans, NPLs compares with that of the Chilean and Argentine crises of the early 1980s. However, in most regional economies efforts to resolve NPL problems are now well advanced, and with ongoing global changes in financial service industries, will dramatically change Asia's banking markets. Since the crisis, many economies have raised foreign equity limits, providing increased opportunities for foreign investors to participate in Asian banking markets. These opportunities include making acquisitions, purchasing specific activities, setting up joint ventures, assisting local banks to reform and outsourcing business.

This chapter analyses the extent of current NPL problems in regional banks, and the expected cost of resolving them and refinancing banks. It then evaluates alternative approaches regional governments are using to reform and restructure banks. It examines global trends in financial service industries and their impact on Asian financial markets, and finally, it highlights emerging opportunities for Australian financial service exporters and investors in regional banking.

BANKS' IMPORTANCE IN EAST ASIA

As in most developing economies, in developing East Asia banks dominate financial intermediation. Banks in non-Japan Asia account for around 70 per cent of total financial sector assets (Figure 4.1). However, while non-Japan Asia depends on banks considerably more than the United States and Japan do, it depends on them less than many Latin American economies do (Figure 4.1).

Banking

Figure 4.1

Banks Dominate East Asian Financial Markets
Bank Assets as a Share of Total Financial Institution Assets in East Asia,ᵃ Latin America, Japan and United States, 1994

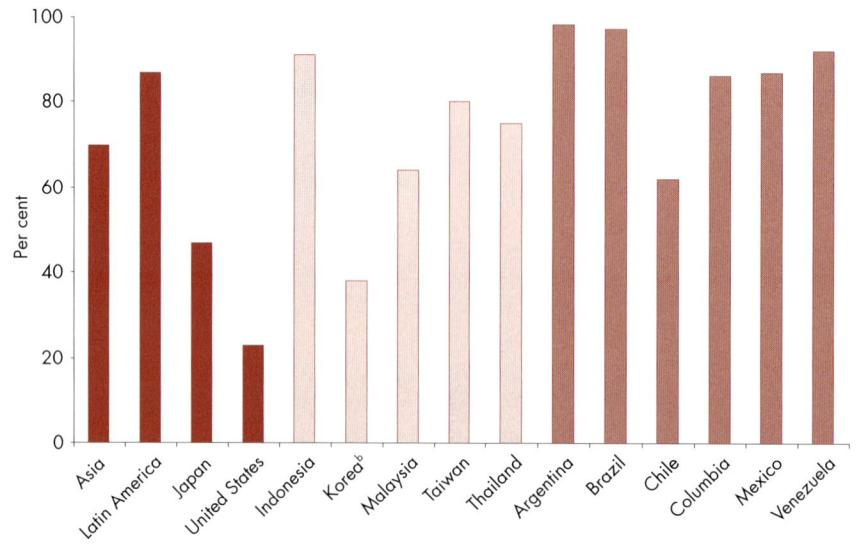

Note: a The figures for Asia and Latin America are averages of the individual Asian and Latin American economies presented in this chart. The average for Asia excludes Japan.

b The estimate for Korea may be an underestimate. In October 1999, the Financial Supervisory Commission indicated commercial banks' share of total financial assets was 54 per cent. (See Chapter 13 - *Korea*, Table 13.1.)

Source: World Bank, 1997.

Even in Japan, Hong Kong and Singapore, East Asia's most developed financial centres, banks retain a prominent role compared to stock and particularly bond markets (Figure 4.2). This contrasts with the United States where bank assets relative to GDP are less important than both stock and bond markets (Figure 4.2).

Figure 4.2

Banking Still Important in Hong Kong, Singapore and Japan
Relative Position of Banking Assets, Equity, and Bonds, 1994 (Per cent of GDP)

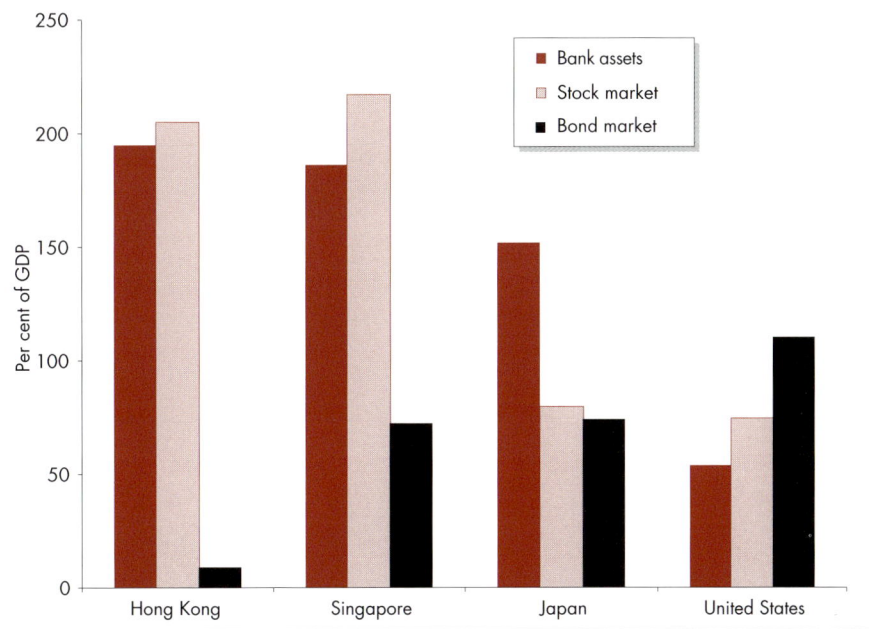

Note: Hong Kong figures only include Hong Kong dollar denominated assets.
Source: World Bank, 1997.

NPL PROBLEMS IN EAST ASIAN BANKS

The financial crisis dramatically raised NPLs in East Asia. NPLs are most serious in Indonesia and Thailand, although in mid 1999, all economies except Hong Kong, Singapore and Taiwan had NPL ratios above 10 per cent (Figure 4.3).

Banking

Figure 4.3

NPL Problems Worst in Indonesia and Thailand
Official Estimates of NPLs in Mid 1999 (Per cent of Outstanding Loans)

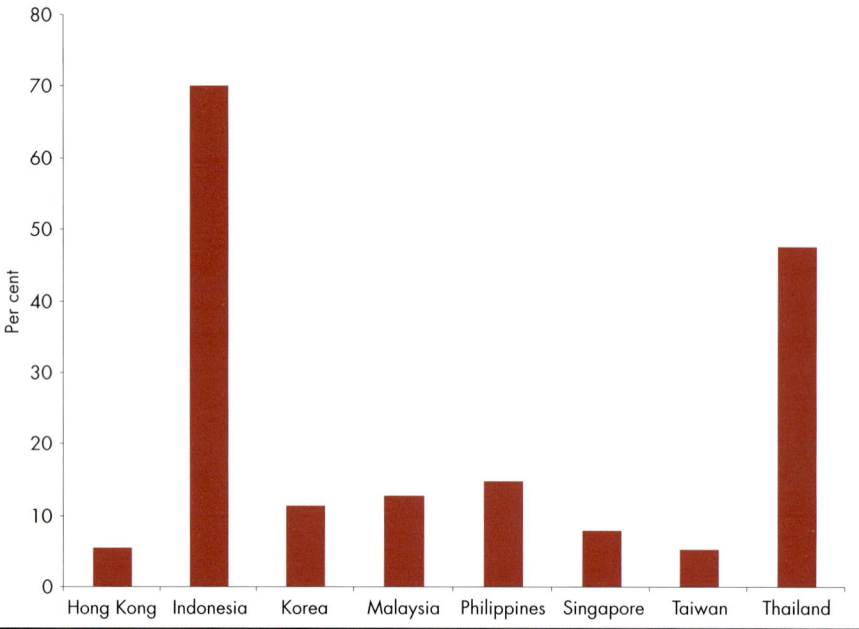

Note: NPLs are loans three or more months in arrears on interest payments.

Figures for Hong Kong, Korea and Singapore are for March 1999; figures for the Philippines and Indonesia are for May 1999; figures for Taiwan are for June 1999, for Malaysia July 1999 and for Thailand August 1999. The Indonesian figure is a Morgan Stanley Dean Witter estimate; the latest official estimate was 25 per cent in December 1997.

For Malaysia gross NPLs, including loans managed by Danaharta were 25.9 per cent in July 1999. (See Chapter 8 - *Thailand, Malaysia and the Philippines*.) Korea's NPLs peaked at 23 per cent in 1998, before Korea Asset Management Company purchased a large share from banks.

Source: Morgan Stanley Dean Witter, 1999.

Provisioning and write-offs associated with these NPLs reduce bank capital adequacy and therefore their lending ability[1]. In the most severely affected regional economies, the resulting credit crunch reduced economic growth by depriving healthy businesses of credit and caused further NPL problems. Credit growth has been weak across all economies most seriously affected by the financial crisis, although this weakness reflects lack of demand as well as banks' unwillingness to lend (Figure 4.4). Only in Korea did credit growth recover substantially in the first half of 1999 (Figure 4.4).

---

[1] Capital adequacy is the ratio of unimpaired capital to outstanding loans. Most economies require banks to maintain the Bank for International Settlements' minimum of 8 per cent.

Figure 4.4

Indonesian and Thai Credit Growth Weakest
Growth of Commercial Bank Credit, 1998 and First Half of 1999

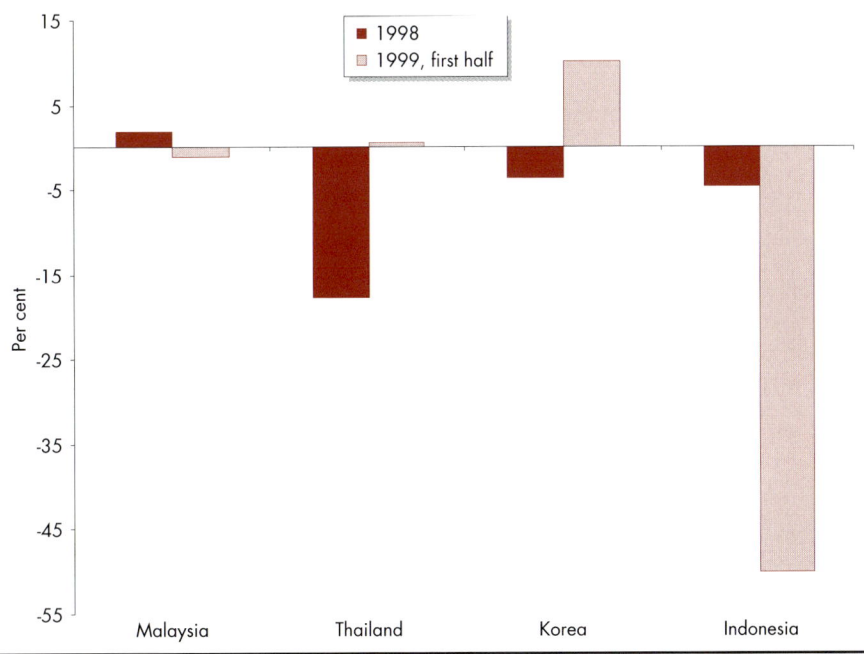

Source: CEIC, 1999.

When the Asian financial crisis peaked in late 1997 and early 1998, banks' weak capital adequacy ratios and large losses associated with NPLs caused depositor concern and even panic. To prevent systemwide bank runs, governments in Indonesia, Thailand, Korea and Malaysia had to introduce comprehensive depositor guarantees. However, these guarantees exposed governments to enormous contingent and actual liabilities. Hence governments now are winding back their exposure, and many are establishing formal deposit insurance schemes. (See Chapter 3 - *Prudential Reform*.)

Concerned depositors also sought out better quality and safer East Asian banks. For example, between October 1997 and June 1998, the deposit share of Indonesian private banks fell from around 60 per cent to around 40 per cent while the share of state owned and foreign/joint-venture banks rose commensurately. (See Chapter 7 - *Indonesia*.) A similar, although less pronounced flight to quality occurred in Japan, Thailand and Malaysia.[2] (See Chapter 8 - *Thailand, Malaysia and the Philippines*, and Chapter 11 - *Japan*.)

---

[2] In Japan, domestic banking sector weakness helped drive up the deposit share of foreign banks from below 1 per cent in mid 1995 to above 2 per cent by mid 1998. (See Chapter 11 - *Japan*.)

Costs of the Banking Crisis

Asian banking sector problems are imposing significant costs on regional economies, reducing economic growth and demanding costly public bailouts. Lower consumer and investor confidence, high interest rates and restricted bank lending reduce economic growth. Over time, costs in terms of foregone growth can be substantial.[3]

The costs imposed by banking crises are distributed according to government policy responses; consequently, these decisions often are highly controversial. For example, forcing corporates to repay all NPLs or enter bankruptcy imposes costs on those who made poor borrowing decisions, but this can slow recovery. On the other hand, excessive public bailouts penalise taxpayers and, by creating moral hazard, can lead to future crises.[4] However, bailouts can accelerate financial and corporate restructuring, and a return to normal economic activity.

Governments can reduce moral hazard problems by requiring bank shareholders to write down their capital to zero, by sacking negligent bank managers, and by requiring unsecured creditors and possibly large depositors to accept losses before injecting government funds, in return for equity.

The Korean Government pursued probably the cleanest, most transparent and efficient approach to bank restructuring and refinancing. Banks below the required 8 per cent capital adequacy ratio had to sell their NPLs to a government-owned asset management company at a significant discount and accept government equity, after writing down their shareholders' equity to nearly zero. By contrast, the Indonesian Government is allowing existing bank owners to become strategic partners with it, on preferential terms; many analysts fear this approach may benefit bank owners at taxpayers' expense. The Thai Government is allowing banks to apply for government equity on a voluntary basis but under strict conditionality; however, this voluntary approach is slowing down bank refinancing.

While the cost of injecting public funds to recapitalise a banking system is frequently used as a proxy to estimate the cost of a banking crisis, this cost depends on policy choices about recapitalisation methods and does not factor in the cost of foregone growth. The estimated cost of recapitalising the Indonesian banking sector is at least 58 per cent of 1998 GDP; this is higher than recapitalisation costs in either Chile or Argentina in the early 1980s (Figure 4.5).[5] Recapitalisation costs will be over 40 per cent of GDP in Thailand and also very substantial in Korea, Malaysia and Japan (Figure 4.5). These costs will impose substantial taxpayer burdens; most of these economies will be forced to carry high government debt burdens for some years.

---

[3] IMF surveys of previous currency and banking crises indicate GDP growth takes over three years to return to pre-crisis trends. Cumulative losses of economic activity over this period average around 14.5 per cent of GDP (International Monetary Fund, 1998).

[4] Moral hazard occurs when creditors, debtors, managers or others do not have to accept the consequences of their poor commercial decisions.

[5] Some estimates of the cost of recapitalising Indonesia's banking sector are as high as 82 per cent of GDP. (See Chapter 7 - Indonesia.)

Figure 4.5

Asia's Bank Recapitalisation Costs Match Latin America's
Bank Recapitalisation Costs as a Per cent of 1998 GDP

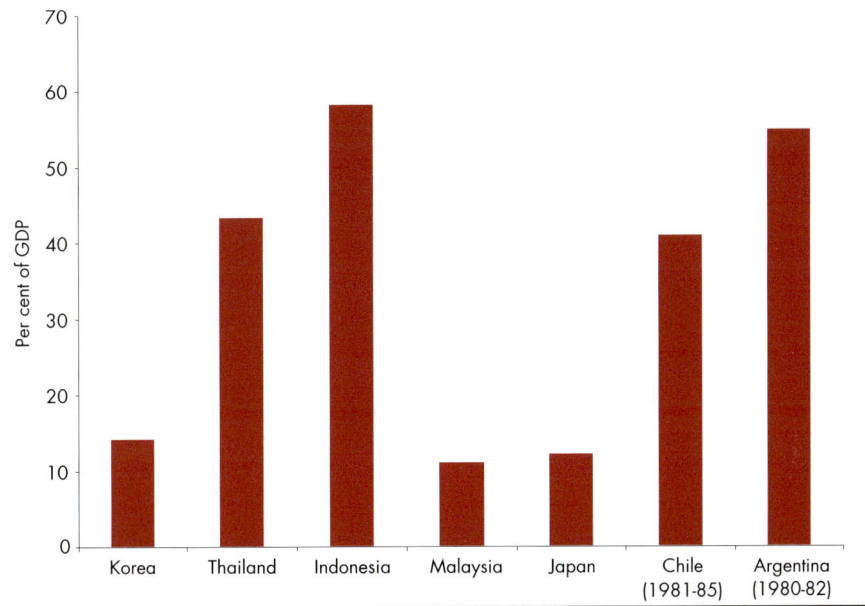

Source: Bank of America, 1999a; and Eslake, 1998.

APPROACHES TO BANKING REFORM

Asian governments are using different approaches to refinance and restructure their banking systems depending on the seriousness of banking sector problems, political constraints and their fiscal capacity. Their intervention aims to protect bank depositors and prevent systemic collapse of banking systems, with its serious consequences for economic activity.

Many regional governments are resolving serious NPL problems by requiring banks to sell NPLs, at a significant discount on face value, to government-owned and financed asset management companies. Many also are injecting government capital into weak but viable banks in return for equity. In the process, these governments are closing, merging and nationalising banks, and requiring them to attract external capital.

Asset Management Companies

As their basic strategy to resuscitate virtually paralysed banking systems, most of the severely affected economies established asset management companies to buy banks' NPLs. Korea and Malaysia lead this approach. Japan also now has a strong asset management company; the Resolution and Collection Corporation, authorised to purchase NPLs from both failed and healthy banks.[6] In 1999, China established an

---

[6] Before April 1999, the Resolution and Collection Corporation's predecessors could not purchase NPLs from healthy institutions. This hindered these institutions' ability to move debt off their balance sheets. (See Chapter 11 - *Japan*.)

Banking

asset management company at each of the four major banks. (See Chapter 12 - *China*.) In Thailand, a public asset management company purchased low quality finance company loans and by late 1999 this asset management company had sold off all core assets (Bank of America, 1999b). Private banks are encouraged to set up their own asset management companies; Thai Farmers Bank was the first to do so.[7] (See Chapter 8 - *Thailand, Malaysia and the Philippines*.) However, without a public asset management company for surviving banks, Thailand's NPL disposal is slow compared to Korea's and Malaysia's (Figure 4.6).

Government asset management companies require significant injections of public funds to purchase and hold NPLs. Their loan disposal strategies vary: Korea's asset management company started disposing of some NPLs quite quickly, while Malaysia's asset management company puts more emphasis on managing and restructuring assets and only started disposal in the second half of 1999. This approach can improve prices through restructuring loans and underlying assets and waiting for market recovery. However, holding NPLs involves paying considerable interest costs on bonds issued to banks in return for these assets.[8]

Figure 4.6

Korea and Malaysia Making Most Progress in NPL Disposal
NPLs Restructured as a Share of Total NPLs, September 1998 to June 1999

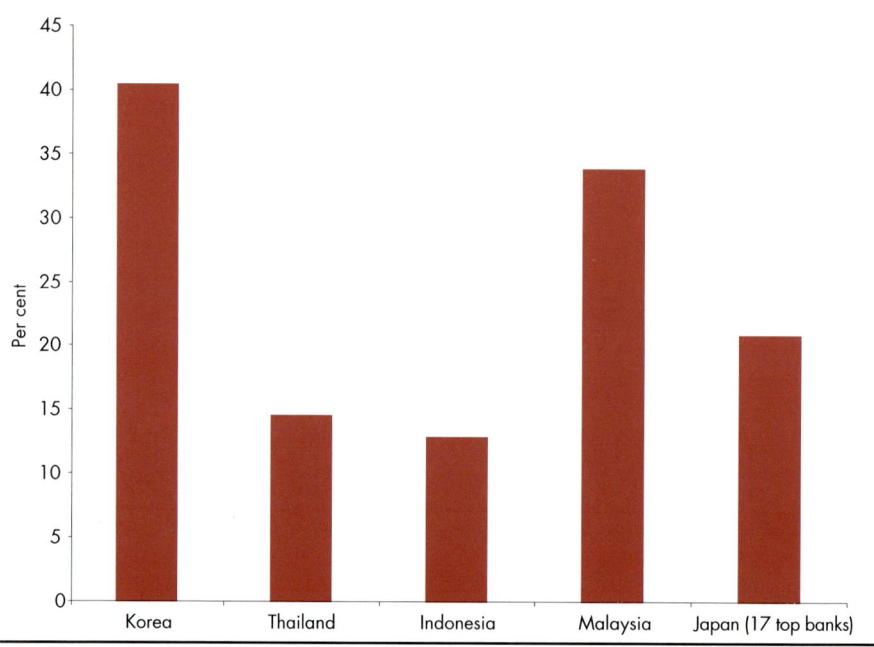

Source: Bank of America, 1999b.

---

[7] Despite majority ownership of these asset management companies by third parties and some government incentives, lack of funding is the main constraint.

[8] For example, interest costs associated with Thailand's financial system rescue may reach 4 per cent of GDP (Flatters, 1999).

The political difficulty of admitting the full cost of bank rescues to the public means governments often understate required funding. Consequently, banks may continue to hold excessive NPLs and be unable to resume normal lending. For example, Daewoo's recent problems may lead to a further rise in Korean NPLs. The Chinese Government still has not announced whether it will pay to purchase state bank NPLs through their asset management companies, or how much this will cost. Given the strong powers of asset management companies, accusations of bias in NPL purchases also can arise.

KOREAN AND MALAYSIAN ASSET MANAGEMENT COMPANIES

Korea and Malaysia both successfully used asset management companies.

KAMCO - The Korean Asset Management Company

Korea is well advanced in purchasing NPLs. By March 1999, the Korea Asset Management Company, KAMCO had bought NPLs worth US$37 billion, 63 per cent of the Government's target, at an average discount of 56 per cent on face value. KAMCO is expected to buy all targeted NPLs in 1999 (Bank of America, 1999b; and East Asia Analytical Unit, 1999).[9] By March 1999, these massive purchases and the improving macroeconomic situation reduced Korean banks' NPLs from their peak of 23 per cent to 8.5 per cent.

KAMCO also is disposing of assets quite rapidly. During the first half of 1999, it disposed of over US$4.2 billion of NPLs, 32 per cent of its planned 1999 NPL disposal (Bank of America, 1999b). Goldman Sachs and the Lone Star Fund bought the bulk of auctioned NPLs (Slater, 1999). By 2003, KAMCO aims to have disposed of 98 per cent of acquired NPLs, mostly as asset-backed securities, and to have recovered 91 per cent of its outlays (Bank of America, 1999b).

Danaharta - Malaysia's Asset Management Company

By June 1999, Malaysia's asset management company, Danaharta, had completed its NPL acquisition plan six months ahead of its deadline (Bank of America, 1999b). It acquired 36 per cent of the NPLs in the financial system, at an average discount of 57 per cent. Danaharta has significant powers to facilitate loan recovery, including restructuring debtors' businesses after only 30 days' notice of foreclosure.[10] (See Chapter 8 -*Thailand, Malaysia and the Philippines*.)

Danaharta started disposing of NPLs in mid 1999, with options including liquidation and asset sales, securitisation, joint ventures and stock exchange listing. It has a relatively small number of large NPLs to deal with and plans to maximise returns from their disposal. This implies a slower disposal process than in Korea.[11] Danaharta aims to reduce NPLs to around 10 per cent, believing commercial banks then can write off the remainder (Slater, 1999).

---

[9] Expected NPLs are around double the level of targeted NPLs, but the Government expects banks to write off the remainder from their capital.

[10] In addition, once Danaharta buys a NPL, other parties lose their claims on the loan and any collateral. This gives buyers from Danaharta a clear picture of what they are purchasing.

[11] According to Danaharta's Managing Director, Danaharta only has around 2 000 accounts (Slater, 1999).

Public Capital Injections

Public capital injections often complement the activities of asset management companies. By June 1999, Malaysia's Danamodal, which recapitalises banks, had injected US$1.6 billion into ten banking institutions.[12] Similarly, the Korean Deposit Insurance Corporation had issued government bonds worth Won 16 trillion (US$13.3 billion). In mid 1998, the Thai Government allocated Baht 300 billion (US$8 billion) to recapitalise private banks which adopt new loan classification and provisioning requirements. However, many banks initially viewed these conditions as too onerous and were reluctant to apply for funds. By early 1999, only two of the remaining seven private banks and the two state banks had sought capital injections.[13]

After many years, the Japanese Government has accepted the use of significant public funds to recapitalise weak but viable banks. (See Chapter 11 - *Japan*.) In March 1999, 15 of Japan's 17 major banks received injections totalling around US$62 billion, around 32 per cent of the public funds allocated to recapitalise banks.[14] To access these funds, banks must write off high levels of NPLs and comply with other stringent conditions.[15]

As part of the Indonesian Government's September 1998 recapitalisation program, 61 banks with capital adequacy ratios between -25 per cent and 4 per cent will receive government funds for up to 80 per cent of their recapitalisation needs.

Nationalisation

Most regional governments also nationalised banks, either outright or *de facto* via large capital injections to boost their capital adequacy. In January 1998, the Korean Government nationalised the two major commercial banks in greatest difficulty, Korea First Bank and Seoul Bank.[16] The Thai Government nationalised seven of Thailand's 15 commercial banks, while the Japanese Government nationalised the Long Term Credit Bank and Nippon Credit Bank. In April 1998, Indonesia nationalised seven banks, adding to the existing seven state banks.[17] Indonesia's public capital injections into private banks will produce further *de facto* large scale nationalisations.

When banking system distress is extreme, nationalising banks allows governments to force reluctant shareholders to write down their shareholdings or share the burden of writing off NPLs. Before the Korean Government nationalised Korea First and Seoul Banks, it wrote down each bank's existing capital from Won 820 billion to

---

[12] This capital was injected via 'exchangeable subordinated capital loans'. Danaharta signed agreements with nine of these banks to convert these funds into permanent tier-1 or tier-2 capital. Danamodal also is involved in facilitating mergers.

[13] In January 1999, after discussions with all commercial banks, the Bank of Thailand decided six banks, accounting for 56 per cent of deposits, had adequate capital. Two banks, accounting for 15 per cent of deposits, raised private capital and also received public funds, while the Government remained committed to fully recapitalising the two state banks (Bank of America, 1999b).

[14] Of these 17 banks, only Bank of Tokyo-Mitsubishi and Nippon Trust and Banking did not apply for funds; Yasuda Trust and Banking will receive funds through Fuji Bank.

[15] During Japanese fiscal year 1998-99, Japan's top 17 banks wrote off US$86.8 billion in NPLs and other banks seeking public funds wrote off a further US$80.4 billion (Bank of America, 1999b).

[16] In September 1999, after lengthy negotiations, Newbridge Capital purchased a 51 per cent share in Korea First Bank. Negotiations for the sale of Seoul Bank to Hong Kong Shanghai Bank failed.

[17] These banks were taken over by the Indonesian Bank Restructuring Agency.

Won 100 billion. Then it raised each bank's capital to Won 1.6 trillion through injecting public capital, raising the Government's share in each bank to 94 per cent (East Asia Analytical Unit, 1999). Nationalisation also increases the capacity to negotiate debt forgiveness and restructuring deals with foreign creditors and local borrowers, and to change management.

However, after so many bank nationalisations, when and how governments return banks to private ownership will be a vital issue.[18] Increasing globalisation of financial services and continuing development of new financial products mean banking will continue to be fraught with risk. Banking therefore remains an inappropriate industry for long term government investment, particularly given the pressing need to improve education, infrastructure and social welfare in most East Asian economies. To limit public exposure to contingent liabilities from privatised banks, governments also must refrain from making excessive performance and risk related guarantees.

Bank and Other Financial Institution Closures

In the most severely affected economies, authorities have closed many non-viable financial institutions. Since the crisis began, the Thai Government has closed 53 finance companies and one bank, while the Indonesian Government has closed 67 banks.[19] By August 1999, the Korean Government had closed five commercial banks and 17 merchant banks.[20] The Japanese Government also closed one major bank, Hokkaido Takushoku Bank in 1997. The Chinese Government closed the Hainan Development Bank in 1997, the Guangdong International Trust and Investment Corporation in 1998 and numerous smaller trust and investment corporations and credit cooperatives over recent years. In all cases, government capital injections protected depositors.

Mergers

Another tool frequently used to resolve failed banks' problems is government supported mergers, often involving the purchase of NPLs and capital injections. The Korean Government used Korea Asset Management Company NPL purchases and government capital injections to facilitate the 1998 mergers of Hanil Bank with the Commercial Bank of Korea and Hana Bank with Boram Bank.[21] Similarly in October 1998, Sumitomo Bank took a 49 per cent stake in the ailing Bank of Kansai before applying for US$3.8 billion in public funds to strengthen its capital base (*Nikkei Weekly*, 31 October 1998, p. 22). In Malaysia, Danamodal is injecting public funds so four commercial bank mergers can be completed by the end of 1999 (Bank of

---

18   Korea already is discussing disposal of its nationalised banks with the IMF. Indonesia is aiming to fully privatise all state banks in 2001.

19   The Indonesian Government closed 16 banks in November 1997, 13 in 1998 and 38 more in March 1999 (Bank of America, 1999b).

20   The assets and liabilities of the five closed commercial banks were transferred to five healthy banks, after the Government paid US$7.2 billion to acquire NPLs and inject capital (Goldstein, 1998; and Bank of America, 1999b).

21   The Government purchased US$1.8 billion in NPLs and provided capital injections of US$2.8 billion to bring the newly merged banks' capital adequacy ratio to 10 per cent (Bank of America, 1999b).

Banking

America, 1999b).[22] In addition, the Malaysian Government is pushing for a new round of mergers; local commercial and merchant banks, and finance companies must submit proposals for broad groupings to the central bank by the end of January 2000 and complete the merger process by January 2001. (See Chapter 8 - *Thailand, Malaysia and the Philippines*.)

In Indonesia, the merger of four state banks into the newly established Bank Mandiri will give it 30 per cent of banking system deposits. (See Chapter 7 - *Indonesia*.) With the Government seeking to further reduce private bank numbers, mergers also are likely among the private banks.[23] The Philippine Government also encourages mergers by raising banks' minimum capital requirements.

However, on their own mergers cannot resolve NPLs and to be beneficial, they must produce longer term saving benefits. For example, Krung Thai Bank, Thailand's second largest, faces huge write-offs and few benefits from its forced merger with First Bangkok City Bank and takeover of Bangkok Bank of Commerce. Korea has a much better record for extracting efficiency increases from mergers. For example, by January 1999, the merged Kookmin-Korea Long Term Credit Bank had shed 18 per cent of staff and had only 6 per cent more branches than the original Kookmin Bank (East Asia Analytical Unit, 1999; and *Far Eastern Economic Review*, 11 February 1999, p. 53).

Raising External Capital

Regional governments also are requiring local banks to recapitalise by raising external capital through seeking foreign partners or issuing bonds and shares. However, this approach only is useful for banks with fundamentally sound prospects, not entire banking systems. Thailand relies most on this approach to refinancing. Thai banks have issued bonds and specialised debt and equity instruments, and received several direct equity injections.[24] For example, ABN Amro purchased a 75 per cent share in Bank of Asia, Standard Chartered purchased a similar share in Nakornthon Bank and the Development Bank of Singapore purchased a share in Thai Danu Bank.

Japanese and Korean banks also are raising external capital. Japanese banks have focused largely on bond issues, raising ¥2 trillion in the year to 31 March 2000. In contrast, Korean banks mainly seek foreign equity, with four major equity injections completed by late 1999 (Appendix Table 4.1).

....

[22] These are the mergers of Sime-RHB Bank, Perwira Affin-BSN Commerce Bank, Bank Bumiputra-Bank of Commerce and Southern Bank Berhad- Ban Hin Lee Bank Berhad.

[23] In July 1997, there were 160 private banks. The Government reportedly seeks a two thirds reduction in this pre-crisis number (Bank of America, 1999b). Thus far, it has closed 67 private banks, so another 38 closures or mergers are possible.

[24] In the first half of 1998, Thai Farmers Bank raised US$875 million and Bangkok Bank raised US$1.1 billion via bond issues. In early 1999, Thai Farmers Bank raised a further US$1.1 billion by issuing securities that combined preferred shares and subordinated debt (*Far Eastern Economic Review*, 4 February 1999, p. 54).

GLOBAL TRENDS IN FINANCIAL SERVICES INDUSTRIES

Over the last two decades, regulatory reforms and new financial technologies and products have revolutionised financial service industries in most industrialised economies. These forces should become increasingly important in post-crisis Asia.

Unbundling Bank Business

Unbundling banking business is an important trend in global financial service industries. Increasingly, new entrants can bid separately for components of banks' traditional business without needing to offer a comprehensive range of services. This lowers entry barriers. To foster this development, capital market and non-bank financial institution growth are essential, because they allow different institutions to provide deposit and lending services. On the deposit side, cash management trusts and insurance companies offer services akin to deposit taking without making loans. On the lending side, merchant banks, finance companies and mortgage managers make loans without taking deposits. This unbundling process pressures banks to price each service competitively and remove cross subsidies. Consequently, interest margins tighten while transaction charges and account keeping fees proliferate.

Outsourcing administrative services also is increasingly common. In the United States, banks have long outsourced mortgage processing and administration to specialist non-financial institutions. Outsourcing now occurs across borders. For example, Westpac and National Australia Bank process New Zealand mortgages in Australia.

These trends could transform East Asian banking, particularly as many regional economies now allow increased access to their markets by foreign financial institutions. Large incumbent banks with extensive retail networks are naturally protected from new retail banking entrants, but efficient, internationally reputable cash management trusts and funds managers can quite readily enter poorly serviced markets.

Securitisation

Another major trend is the growth of securitisation. This financial technique repackages assets or receivables with a regular cashflow, such as mortgage repayments, export payments or toll-road revenues, into tradable securities. In the right regulatory environment, securitisation has tremendous growth potential. The Australian securitisation market grew from zero in 1983 to A$16 billion in 1998 (*Asiamoney*, May 1999, p. 17). In Australia, the National Australia Bank no longer keeps home loans on its balance sheet, but passes them straight through to mortgage originators, who package them for loan securitisation portfolios. Mortgage originators, such as Aussie Home Loans, also compete directly with banks. Similarly, in the United States, many small banks are largely originators of home and consumer lending; they analyse lending risks and advance loans, but immediately on-sell the loans for packaging into loan securitisation portfolios. By creating new business and consumer funding sources, securitisation increases the competitive pressure banks face. It also allows banks to create new products and earn fee income.

Removing Barriers between Financial Markets

In many markets, such as Australia, Japan, the United States and the United Kingdom, regulatory barriers between banks, insurance and securities companies are disappearing.[25] Australian banks already offer insurance services, and insurance companies increasingly offer banking services.[26] Japanese insurance companies now can establish banking subsidiaries and from 2001, banks will be able to enter the insurance sector. Because of the substantial sums required to set up many new financial sector businesses, such regulatory changes favour large, well capitalised financial institutions. Many of these financial institutions have relevant expertise and existing retailing networks, and are recognised company names; therefore, they are much better placed than unknown new entrants to provide serious competition for incumbent firms. This development also is spurring consolidation, as takeovers can facilitate market entry.

Electronic Banking and Banking Technologies

Electronic banking also is important in many industrialised economies. Telephone banking, Internet banking and EFTPOS are convenient for consumers, and banks actively promote them, as they cost less to deliver than traditional services.[27] The United States leads Internet banking, with around 7.5 million households, or 8 per cent of all American households, banking online (*Economist*, 10 April 1999, p. 75). Internet banking also is growing very rapidly in Australia.

A related trend is the increasing importance of bank expenditure on new technologies to upgrade banking systems, marketing and distribution. Large multinational banks, such as Citibank, spend over US$1 billion per year on new technology (Casserly and Gibb, 1999). Major multinational financial institutions often are better placed to adopt new technologies because they can spread such costs over a large network. This advantage encourages financial institution consolidation.

EAST ASIAN FINANCIAL MARKET TRENDS

These global trends already are evident in East Asia, especially in the relatively sophisticated financial markets of Tokyo, Hong Kong and Singapore. In future, pressures induced by the Asian financial crisis and ongoing deregulation should accentuate these forces, dramatically influencing East Asian banking.

---

[25] Most recently, in October 1999, the US Congress repealed the Glass-Steagall Act which prevented mergers of US banks, insurers and securities houses (*Australian Financial Review*, 25 October 1999, p. 1).

[26] Major recent developments by Australian companies include the Colonial Mutual Group's takeover of the State Bank of New South Wales and the decision by AMP to establish a bank.

[27] Internet banking is an exception. At this stage, Internet banking services generally cost banks money, although Citibank claims to have broken even (*Economist*, 10 April 1999, p. 75).

Unbundling of Pricing

Nationwide banks that dominate economies such as China, Indonesia, Malaysia, Thailand, the Philippines and Taiwan rely on branch networks to attract enough deposit and loan business to justify their presence. Such banks considerably cross-subsidise small, low value accounts in rural areas and small business from high value urban and corporate accounts. The substantial difference between borrowing and lending rates covers bank costs.

In the post-crisis environment, this system is likely to come under increasing pressure, as large lenders and borrowers pursue more profitable and lower cost options. Interest rate deregulation now is largely complete, so banks can differentiate between prime and riskier borrowers.[28] Capital market development is receiving higher priority; over time, this should expand investment options for large savers and borrowers. (See Chapter 5 - *Capital Markets*.)

Moreover, removal of entry barriers and sales of NPLs and other assets help new domestic and foreign players enter East Asian financial markets. This will increase competition between existing banks and new banking market entrants which, unburdened by large branch networks, will be able to offer more attractive rates for certain financial products.

These forces create pressure to reduce interest margins and increase fee income. In Singapore, the trend towards fee-for-service banking is underway; annual membership fees and spending based fee waivers are the norm for credit cards (*Business Times*, 27 May 1999, p. 38). In August 1999, Deputy Prime Minister and Monetary Authority Chairman Lee Hsien Loong indicated in Parliament, the Monetary Authority of Singapore would not interfere with banks' commercial decisions to impose fees (Lee, 1999).

Electronic Banking

EFTPOS, ATMs, GIRO, telephone and Internet banking are well established in the region's more advanced financial sectors. Singapore's ATM network is one of the most sophisticated in the world.[29] The Government actively encourages cashless payments by requiring GIRO payment for services like school and university fees and power bills.

In future, electronic banking will not be limited to high income East Asian markets like Singapore, Hong Kong, Japan, Taiwan and Korea. In China, the national roll out of the China National Automated Payments System, CNAPS, in late 1999 and 2000 should facilitate rapid growth of credit card business and electronic banking (Morgan Stanley Dean Witter, 1998). China Construction Bank already offers Internet banking services in Beijing and Guangzhou (Asian Banker Interactive, 1999a).

---

28 China is the major exception, although even there, banks can vary rates by 20 to 25 per cent around the benchmark rate. Hong Kong's remaining interest rate restrictions should be removed by July 2001. (See Chapter 9 - *Hong Kong and Singapore*.)

29 From some machines, customers can purchase sporting and concert tickets, and even stocks.

Eroding Business Boundaries

Consistent with worldwide trends, traditional barriers between banks, insurers and securities companies are disappearing in East Asia. This process is most advanced in Japan. (See Chapter 11 - *Japan*.) However, similar reforms are underway in Korea where the top four banks are likely to evolve into universal banks (East Asia Analytical Unit, 1999). The merger of Bank of the Philippine Islands and Ayala Insurance represents the first full integration of a bank and insurance group in South East Asia (Asian Banker Interactive, 1999b).

Government led financial sector consolidation also helps blur financial sector boundaries. For example, the Thai Government offers banking licences to encourage non-bank financial institution mergers.[30] The major Malaysian mergers planned for 2000 will encompass banks and non-bank financial institutions, except insurance companies; and some Korean merchant banks have merged with commercial banks.

This erosion of barriers between different financial markets favours large, well capitalised institutions, including foreign financial institutions, with resources to invest in profitable new business areas. The Commonwealth Bank of Australia is one Australian financial institution taking advantage of this situation in Japan; it is establishing a niche securities presence to complement its banking business. This trend to cease segregation of financial markets will further strain bundled pricing and stimulate merger activity. These developments already are driving considerable merger activity in Japan. (See Chapter 11 - *Japan*.)

THE COMMONWEALTH BANK: ESTABLISHING A JAPANSE SECURITIES OPERATION

Japanese financial market deregulation has enabled the Commonwealth Bank to extend its services to a broader range of customers and products. In July 1999, the Ministry of Finance granted Commonwealth Securities (Japan) a Japanese securities registration. As a niche market player in Japan's increasingly competitive financial marketplace, the Commonwealth Bank considers a dual banking and securities presence necessary to facilitate the development of its financial markets business.

Commonwealth Securities (Japan) offers Australian and New Zealand dollar securities; securities issued by Australian, New Zealand and other borrowers; foreign currency denominated securities; structured debt products; investment fund agency services; and solutions to securities related businesses. Operating in the same time zone as Sydney it leverages off Australian based expertise and connected infrastructure.

Source: Commonwealth Securities, 1999.

---

[30] Since December 1998, the Bank of Thailand has granted restricted banking licences to merging non-bank financial institutions with capital of at least Baht 10 billion. At least five finance and securities companies have applied.

Mergers

Between 1987 and 1997, while many banks merged in the United States, Europe and Australia, only 22 out of 1 700 banks merged in Asia (Casserly and Gibb, 1999). However, as was discussed previously, the financial crisis and higher capital requirements now drive a major consolidation of East Asian banking. As government driven mergers are completed, an increasing number of market driven mergers are likely. In future, increased competition, reduced barriers between financial markets, and larger technology expenditures will drive consolidation. These mergers will occur both among domestic financial institutions and also between domestic and foreign financial institutions.

Securitisation Growth in East Asia

Hong Kong and Japan have the most advanced East Asian securitisation markets, with the Korean market growing rapidly. Hong Kong's strong securitisation industry reflects the presence of many issuers affiliated with international banks, the well developed legal framework and the availability of suitable securitisation assets. Mortgage backed securitisation by institutions like Sanwa Finance and Dah Sing Bank dominates the market.[31] For example, in June 1997, of their Hong Kong residential mortgage portfolios, Sanwa Finance securitised HK$1.1 billion and Dah Sing Bank securitised HK$2.3 billion (*Asiamoney*, January 1998, p. 29). However, the government-owned Hong Kong Mortgage Corporation soon will become the major driver of business as it securitises its large portfolio of property loans.[32]

Since 1996, Japanese institutions have used securitisation in a range of areas including car loans, lease receivables and credit card receivables. Japanese banks also use securitisation to strengthen capital adequacy. For example in late 1997, the Bank of Tokyo-Mitsubishi completed securitisation transactions worth US$3 billion to bolster its capital base (*Asiamoney*, special supplement, January 1998, p. 34). Many Japanese banks securitise loan portfolios from overseas branches (*Asiamoney*, May 1999, p. 25).

Securitisation is a rapidly growing source of finance in Korea. In December 1998, the Export Import Bank of Korea sold US$265 million worth of bonds backed by trade related promissory notes. In February 1999, the Industrial Bank of Korea securitised US$106 million in bonds and syndicated loans to investors in the United States, Europe and Asia (Marriott, 1999). Moreover, Korea Asset Management Company intends to dispose of 63 per cent of its NPL portfolio by securitisation (Bank of America, 1999b).

By late 1999, in most other regional economies, embryonic pre-crisis securitisation markets had not recovered. However, legal frameworks gradually are improving. Tight credit situations in Indonesia, Thailand and Malaysia are likely to increase pressure to find innovative new funding sources, giving a new impetus to the region's securitisation industry.

---

[31] The commercial mortgage backed securitisation market also shows strong signs of growth. For example, Wharf Holdings raised HK$575 million by securitising retail and office space in its Harbour City Development in Hong Kong (Marriott, 1999).

[32] The Hong Kong Mortgage Corporation began business in October 1997; it buys real estate loans from banks to reduce their on-balance sheet property exposure. By 31 December 1998, it had acquired a mortgage portfolio of HK$11.4 billion. Ultimately, it will securitise its mortgage portfolio. The first pilot scheme was announced on 21 July 1999 (Hong Kong Monetary Authority, 1999).

Implications of Securitisation

For banks strong enough to participate in the market, securitisation is attractive. As in the United States and Australia, securitisation allows banks to act largely as lending originators, particularly in home lending and credit finance. The post-crisis emphasis on capital adequacy ratios will make loan origination increasingly attractive, as originating banks do not have to keep loans on their books. It also allows small banks to offer clients a wider range of loan products.

The spread of securitisation may open up opportunities for partnerships between large, well rated foreign financial institutions and local banks which may have the branch networks to originate loans, but lack the strong balance sheets to hold them. This also will allow local banks to retain clients by more quickly offering new products. For some foreign financial institutions, these partnerships may present attractive new business, allowing them to use their skills in risk management and loan packaging. Macquarie Bank, an Australian leader in securitisation, currently promotes mortgage securitisation in a joint business initiative with the China Construction Bank.

MACQUARIE BANK EXPLORES SECURITISATION IN CHINA

State enterprise housing sales, rapid income and savings growth, and government reforms to the banking, mortgage and private housing markets drive China's demand for private housing.[33] Only 5 per cent of urban housing is privately owned, so the growth potential is huge. To tap this market, Macquarie Bank and AMP have formed joint ventures with municipally-owned construction companies in Beijing, Shanghai and Tianjin to construct 100 000 m^2 of apartments for middle to higher income earners.

To finance these housing projects, Macquarie is promoting a new concept in China, mortgage securitisation, through a joint business initiative with the China Construction Bank. Macquarie wants to be an early participant in this market, which eventually should be big enough to handle many participants.

To promote mortgage securitisation, Macquarie officials discussed this proposal with Premier Zhu Rongji who promised support; now they are consulting with Ministry of Finance and People's Bank of China officials. As a result, Chinese officials have begun to formulate guidelines for a domestic securitisation market. A mortgage insurance industry also is slowly taking shape. Initially, the mortgage backed bonds will be sold to the China Construction Bank, with the aim of refining the product and later marketing it to international institutions.

Source: Macquarie Bank, 1999.

---

[33] To encourage this process, the Government has cut taxes and administrative fees on property development and sales, increased the average rental on state owned housing from 3 to 15 per cent of monthly household income, allowed commercial banks to provide 15 year mortgages, lifted the loan-to-valuation ceiling from 70 to 80 per cent and urged the major commercial banks to enter the mortgage business.

FOREIGN BANKS IN EAST ASIA

Improved foreign bank market access in the post-crisis environment, combined with new product and technological developments create many exciting new business opportunities for foreign financial institutions. These institutions in turn bring host economies many benefits.

Benefits of Foreign Banks

The presence of foreign banks improves product choice and increases competition. For example, in Japan, Citibank pioneered 24-hour ATMs, retail foreign currency bank accounts and telephone banking (*Australian Financial Review*, 28 August 1996, p. 15). Similarly, in Hong Kong, ABN Amro introduced fixed rate mortgages (*Asian Banker*, 1999a). In Vietnam, ANZ Bank introduced ATMs.

Foreign banks also train local employees, many of whom move back to domestic institutions. In 1997, the Philippines' three largest domestic banks were run by ex-Citibank staff (*The Economist*, 12 April 1997, p. 37). These well trained staff may have helped major Philippine banks avoid the critical problems many other regional banks experienced. In Indonesia, the President of Bank Mandiri and many other senior bank officials also are ex-Citibank staff (*Far Eastern Economic Review*, 30 September 1999, p. 50).

Foreign banks also provide liquidity options for domestic financial sectors during difficult times. In January 1999, all ten foreign banks in Indonesia had capital adequacy ratios above 4 per cent and did not need capital injections, while all 32 foreign joint-venture banks could recapitalise from their own sources, typically their foreign partners (Bank of America 1999c).

Foreign banks also are an important source of new financial market technology. Typically, major investments serve the global networks of foreign banks; consequently, they rapidly introduce technological advances to local banking systems. For example, ABN Amro's current roll out of global information technology infrastructure should benefit its East Asian acquisitions, Bank of Asia in Thailand and Great Pacific Savings Bank in the Philippines (*Asian Banker*, 1999a).

Major international banks also can provide in-country examples of best practice restructuring. For example, like local Thai banks, Hong Kong Shanghai Bank accumulated large amounts of NPLs in Thailand. However, Hong Kong Shanghai Bank in Bangkok moved quickly to introduce an independent line of credit officers, answering directly to Hong Kong, with veto power over local lending officers (*Far Eastern Economic Review*, 30 September 1999, p. 44). Citibank in the Philippines was organising creditors' debt workout committees for large borrowers with liquidity problems as early as June 1997 (Montes, 1997).

Increasing Access for Foreign Banks

Since the crisis began, regional governments have liberalised considerably rules governing foreign equity limits, including in banking (Table 4.1). Liberalisation was most dramatic in Indonesia, Korea and Thailand, where foreign investors now can own 100 per cent of existing local banks.[34] In Korea, foreigners also can own

---

[34] However, in Thailand, after ten years foreign banks will not be able to take up additional equity unless their equity share is below 49 per cent.

100 per cent of new banks which confers greater flexibility in the type of operation that can be established. Japanese and Korean sentiment towards foreign financial sector investment has improved considerably, contributing to greatly increased foreign direct investment inflows to these sectors.

Table 4.1

Foreign Equity Limits Easing
Foreign Equity Limits in Existing Local Banks, Pre and Post-crisis

Economy	Foreign ownership limit (per cent)		Comment
	Pre-crisis	Post-crisis	
Indonesia	49	100	Branching restrictions on foreign joint-venture banks lifted. However, foreign banks cannot establish new, fully foreign-owned banks
Korea	49	100	Foreign investors have acquired a majority share in Housing and Commercial Bank and in Korea First Bank
Thailand	25	100	After ten years, foreign investors will not be forced to sell their shares, but they cannot purchase any additional shares unless they hold less than 49 per cent of total shares
Malaysia	30	30	The 30 per cent figure does not apply to existing fully foreign-owned banks, and can be relaxed on a case-by-case basis
Philippines	60	60	Full foreign ownership of distressed banks is allowed by the central bank although this ruling is yet to be given legislative approval. New foreign owners must reduce their share to 85 per cent within five years, and to 70 per cent within ten years
Singapore	40	100	Full foreign takeovers of local banks are unlikely to be approved, but a new extended class of foreign bank licence was created for six banks
Hong Kong	100	100	Under proposed reforms, branching restrictions on foreign banks will be eased somewhat and most foreign bank licences will be upgraded
Taiwan	15	50	At this stage this is only a Ministry of Finance proposal, and yet to be ratified by Parliament
Japan	100	100	No formal ownership restrictions exist, but as yet no takeovers have occurred; a US investment company has first negotiating rights to purchase the Long Term Credit Bank of Japan from the Government
China	100	100	Tight branching, location and business scope restrictions apply to fully foreign-owned banks, but these are less restrictive for joint-venture banks. Restrictions will gradually ease upon entry to the World Trade Organisation

Source: Country chapters of this report.

Banking

OPPORTUNITIES FOR FOREIGN BANKS

The post-crisis environment is generating opportunities for large and small foreign banks, ranging from full acquisitions and targeted purchases of specific activities to assistance with local bank reforms and outsourcing.

Acquisitions

Since the crisis began, many foreign financial institutions have acquired full or part equity stakes in Asian banks (Appendix Table 4.1). Standard Chartered, ABN Amro and the Development Bank of Singapore are among the most active foreign banks. Australian financial institutions, such as the ANZ Bank, National Australia Bank and CMG Asia, also are actively assessing acquisition opportunities in East Asia and have undertaken some investments. ANZ has taken a share in Panin Bank and increased its share in its joint venture-bank with Panin, while CMG Asia has acquired Guardian Assurance in Hong Kong. Thailand is the most active acquisition market, followed by Korea, the Philippines and Hong Kong.

A major issue for post-crisis acquisitions is the allocation of responsibility for new and existing NPLs. When the Development Bank of Singapore acquired Thai Danu Bank in December 1997, it also acquired all outstanding NPLs; by mid 1998, Thai Danu accounted for 44 per cent of the Development Bank of Singapore's NPLs (*Far Eastern Economic Review*, 4 February 1999, p. 45). Since then, most purchases have included explicit agreement on NPL responsibility. In ABN Amro's March 1998 purchase of a 75 per cent share in the Thai Bank of Asia, the final price will depend on the state of the bank's books in mid 2000. The Development Bank of Singapore's purchase of Kwong On Bank in Hong Kong included a similar provision. In Newbridge Capital's purchase of a 51 per cent share in Korea First Bank, the Government agreed to take full responsibility for any NPLs arising during the first year after the takeover, and a portion of NPLs arising in the second year (East Asia Analytical Unit, 1999).

Another factor complicating many Asian bank acquisitions is the prevalence of family ownership. Up to 60 per cent of Malaysian and Philippine banks are family owned, and even in Singapore, three of the big four banks are family owned (*Asian Banker*, 1999b). Family ownership tends to inflate prices and increase resistance to surrendering management control.

A further danger with acquisitions is that institutions wanting to sell shares may be the most troubled. However, other factors may provide a motive for sale. In the Philippines, increased minimum capitalisation requirements means many small banks need to merge or find partners. Some of these banks have quite strong management and balance sheets.

Looking forward, acquisition opportunities are likely to increase. As large scale, across-the-board consolidations are completed, banks are likely to increase their focus on mergers that offer scope for franchise enhancement through acquisition of synergistic businesses.

Targeted Purchases of Specific Activities

Foreign financial institutions also can take over a particular activity of local banks or form partnerships. Many US financial institutions in Japan have adopted this approach; rather than purchase the troubled Toho Mutual Life Insurance Company, GE Capital established a joint venture that assumed much of Toho's former business. (See Chapter 11 - *Japan*.) GE Capital also is buying the entire US loan portfolio of the Long Term Credit Bank of Japan (Bank of America, 1999b).

Foreign financial institutions also have purchased distressed bank assets at auctions to enter credit card and finance company markets. By aggressively bidding for good assets under the government led finance company restructuring process, GE Capital and AIG Consumer Finance bought small Thai finance company platforms (Morgan Stanley Dean Witter, 1998). Similarly, PT ANZ Panin Bank bought the credit card business of a defunct bank in an Indonesian Bank Restructuring Agency sale (Bank of America, 1999b).

Assisting Local Bank Reform Efforts

Foreign banks and other financial institutions also can advise governments and individual banks on reform strategies. For example, Goldman Sachs and GE Capital are helping Thai Farmers Bank restructure its loans (*Far Eastern Economic Review*, 30 September 1999, p. 44). As part of acquiring a stake in Panin Bank in Indonesia, ANZ signed a technical service agreement and will appoint a senior executive to transfer experience from Australia's banking industry. (See Chapter 7 - *Indonesia*.) Technical assistance agreements also are commonly used as a first step to gain access to China and Vietnam. For example, foreign insurance companies, including CMG Asia, are assisting the Chinese Government with pension policy.

In these activities, banks need to avoid perceptions of conflict of interest, which can arise if different branches of a business advise governments and buy assets. For example, American investment banks, Lehman Brothers and Goldman Sachs, were subject to conflict of interest allegations in both Thailand and Indonesia (*Far Eastern Economic Review*, 19 November 1998, p. 19).

Outsourcing

Another area of opportunity is the outsourcing of administrative and financial services, as regional banks strive to become more competitive. Cheque clearing, funds transfers, credit card processing, call centres and data base processing are services that banks increasingly will outsource. American Express in Asia seeks to capitalise on these trends, transforming itself from purely a card provider to a processor and service provider. It is working on over 20 deals with banks and non-bank financial institutions. GE Capital also is reputedly looking for third party processing deals (*Asian Banker*, 1999c). First Data Resources, an Australian based business, is seeking to break into this market.

> **FIRST DATA: INVESTING FOR ASIAN OUTSOURCING BUSINESS**
>
> First Data Resources Australia was formed when US based First Data Corporation became established in Australia in 1992. First Data is Australia's largest independent provider of electronic funds transfer and credit card transaction processing services. Its clients include major banks and credit unions, charge card organisations, government utilities and telecommunications providers. In June 1999, First Data announced a A$20 million investment to establish an Asia-Pacific regional processing centre; from the centre, it plans to expand its electronic funds transfer and credit card business from Asian financial institutions and credit card issuers.
>
> Source: First Data Resources Australia Limited, 1999.

CONCLUSIONS

Governments in the most severely affected East Asian economies are making considerable progress resolving bank NPL problems and refinancing banks; Korea and Malaysia lead this process. The bank restructuring involved will have a major impact on the future structure of East Asian banking. Global banking trends like the unbundling of banking business, erosion of business boundaries, electronic banking and outsourcing also increasingly will shape regional banking. This rapid process of change is likely to create significant new opportunities for Australian and other foreign financial institutions.

Appendix Table 4.1

Philippines and Thailand Most Active Acquisition Markets

Bank Mergers and Acquisitions in East Asia Involving Foreign Financial Institutions, January 1998 to September 1999

Target organisation	Acquirer	Type of deal	Date	Size of investment
Korea				
Kookmin Bank	Goldman Sachs	Investment	April 1999	US$500 million
Korea First Bank	Newbridge Capital	Acquisition	Announced December 1998	US$584 million, 51 per cent share
Korea Exchange Bank	CommerzBank	Investment	1998	29 per cent share
Housing and Commercial Bank	ING Netherlands	Investment	July 1999	US$275 million
Philippines				
Bank of Southeast Asia	DBS	Acquisition	August 1998	US$34 million
Great Pacific Savings Bank	ABN Amro	Acquisition	June 1999	Unavailable
Westmont Bank of Philippines	United Overseas Bank	Acquisition	July 1999	US$74 million; 60 per cent share
Thailand				
Bank of Asia	ABN Amro	Acquisition	September 1998 to April 2000	US$185 million September 1998; next payment based on book value in December 1999; 75 per cent share
Thai Danu Bank	Development Bank of Singapore	Acquisition	Completed March 1998	US$130 million
Bangkok Metropolitan Bank	HSBC Holdings	Acquisition	April 1998	Unavailable
Bangkok Bank of Commerce	Sakura Bank	Acquisition	April 1998	US$71.2 million
Thai Farmers Bank	Government of Singapore Investment Corporation	Investment	April 1998	US$265.6 million
Nakornthon Bank	Standard Chartered Bank	Acquisition	September 1999	US$126 million; 75 per cent share

Target organisation	Acquirer	Type of deal	Date	Size of investment
Hong Kong				
International Bank of Asia	Credit Suisse	Acquisition	Completed May 1999	Unavailable
Dah Sing Financial Holdings	Mitsui Trust and Banking	Acquisition	Completed May 1999	US$17.9 million
Kwong On Bank	Development Bank of Singapore	Acquisition	Completed July 1999	87.3 per cent share
Indonesia				
Panin Bank	ANZ	Investment	February 1999	ANZ to acquire an additional 19.5 per cent
Bank Bali	Standard Chartered	Acquisition	July 1999	US$123 million

Note: US dollar values are based on prevailing exchange rate in the month of the deal.
Source: *Asian Banker*, 1999d.

REFERENCES

Asian Banker, 1999a, 'Is Universal Banking a Sum of Its Disparate Parts?', *Asian Banker Journal*, issue 18, April/May, pp. 44-47.

___ 1999b, '13 Truths about the Future of Mergers and Acquisitions in Asia', *Asian Banker Journal*, issue 19, special issue, pp. 18-27.

___ 1999c, 'Shifting Dynamics in Asia's Cards Business', *Asian Banker Journal*, issue 18, April/May, pp. 20-24.

___ 1999d, 'Bank Mergers and Acquisitions in Asia: January 1998-July 1999', *Asian Banker Journal*, issue 19, special issue, pp. 51-53.

Asian Banker Interactive, 1999a, 'Account Update', subscriber service for *Asian Banker*, 15 July, www.asianbanker.com.sg, accessed on 21 September.

___ 1999b, 'Account Update', subscriber service for *Asian Banker*, 2 September, www.asianbanker.com.sg, accessed on 29 September.

___ 1999c, 'Account Update', subscriber service for *Asian Banker*, 15 August, www.asianbanker.com.sg, accessed on 10 September.

Bank of America, 1999a, 'Banking Reform in Asia: Comparative Rankings of Progress Made', *Asian Financial Outlook*, pp. 18-23.

___ 1999b, 'A Survey of Banking Reform in Asia', *Asian Financial Outlook*, July, pp. 1-57.

___ 1999c, 'Restructuring and Recapitalising Banks in Asia', *Asian Financial Outlook*, February, pp. 92-23.

Casserly, D. and Gibb, G., 1999, *Banking in Asia: the End of Entitlement*, John Wiley and Sons, Singapore.

CEIC, 1999, CEIC Database, Hong Kong, supplied by EconData, Canberra.

Commonwealth Securities, 1999, Information supplied to East Asia Analytical Unit, September.

East Asia Analytical Unit, 1999, *Korea Rebuilds: from Crisis to Opportunity*, Department of Foreign Affairs and Trade, Canberra.

Eslake, S., 1998, 'The Asian Financial Crisis: Origins, Dimensions and Implications,' ANZ Banking Corporation, Melbourne.

First Data Resources Australia Limited, 1999, Information supplied to East Asia Analytical Unit, October.

Flatters, F., 1999, 'Thailand, the IMF and the Economic Crisis: First in, Fast Out?', Paper presented at the Brookings/CIER conference on the Asian Financial Crisis and Taiwan's Role in the Region, 5 April, Washington DC.

Goldstein, M., 1998, *The Asian Financial Crisis: Causes, Cures, and Systemic Implications*, Institute for International Economics, Washington, DC.

Hong Kong Monetary Authority, 1999, 'Mortgage Corporation', www.info.gov.hk/hkma/eng/mortgage accessed on 1 October.

International Monetary Fund, 1998, *World Economic Outlook*, Washington DC, May.

Lee, Hsien Loong, 1999, 'Service Charges Imposed by Banks', Response to Parliamentary Question, 17 August, Singapore, www.mas.gov.sg/newspeeches/parliamentary, accessed on 2 November.

Macquarie Bank, 1999, Information supplied to East Asia Analytical Unit, September.

Marriott, C., 1999, 'Securitisation Comes of Age', *Finance Asia*, vol. 3, issue 5, March, pp. 41-49.

Montes, V., 1998, East Asia Analytical Unit interview with Vice President, Citibank, Manila, May.

Morgan Stanley Dean Witter, 1999, Information provided to East Asia Analytical Unit, August.

___ 1998, 'Financial System Reform: the Journey Has Just Begun', *China: Financial Services*, 2 February, p. 11.

Slater, D, 1999, 'White Knights in Tarnished Armour', *Finance Asia*, vol. 3, issue 9, pp. 24-27.

World Bank, 1997, *Private Capital Flows to Developing Countries: the Road to Financial Integration*, World Bank Policy Research, Oxford University Press, New York.

Banking

Chapter 5

CAPITAL MARKETS

The relative immaturity of many East Asian capital markets contributed significantly to the financial crisis. Many enterprises relied on foreign borrowing, volatile foreign portfolio flows and highly leveraged short term bank loans. Therefore, strengthening Asia's capital markets is important to prevent further financial crises and mobilise funds to assist sustainable recovery. Deeper capital markets also will improve investment efficiency and expand funds for long term investment.

This chapter analyses the scope and growth of major regional equity, bond and futures markets, assessing main barriers to their development and the effectiveness of post-crisis capital market reforms.

THE IMPORTANCE OF CAPITAL MARKETS

Bank loans dominate financing in East Asia. (See Chapter 4 - *Banking*.) However, healthy capital markets are critical to sustain recovery. They reduce reliance on predominantly short term local and foreign bank borrowing, as primary equities and bonds markets allow issuers to raise long term funding. Long term local currency bond and equity financing also is needed to fund around US$1 trillion in East Asian infrastructure spending between 1995 and 2005 (East Asia Analytical Unit, 1998) and to continuously upgrade industrial capacity to retain competitiveness as incomes rise.

Secondary markets in equities and bonds also are important in allowing investors to restructure the maturity and level of their share and bond holdings. Lack of secondary markets inhibits East Asian bond market development; where secondary markets are thin, primary markets also struggle, as investors are reluctant to buy bonds if they cannot sell them quickly. Healthy secondary markets also will help keep East Asian capital in the region rather than encouraging its flow to highly liquid markets like the United States. At the end of 1997, Asian investors, excluding Japan, held almost US$165 billion in US treasury securities alone (Sobol, 1998). This is close to the combined GDPs of Malaysia and the Philippines.[1]

Well developed capital markets also put competitive pressure on banks to cut their lending margins, as larger corporates can directly access share and bond finance for funds. Furthermore, over time, well supervised capital markets can improve corporate governance and disclosure standards.

Improved access to futures markets helps mitigate corporate risk exposures. Asian currency values recovered significantly in the first three months of 1998, suggesting corporates could have used short term currency hedging to reduce the flow-through effects of currency volatility on profitability and real economic activity. Futures markets also stimulate secondary markets in bonds and equities by providing traders with a means to cover their positions.

---

[1] Malaysia's 1997 GDP was US$98 billion; the Philippines' 1997 GDP was US$82 billion (Department of Foreign Affairs and Trade, 1998).

Capital Markets

Deepening local primary and secondary share, bond and futures markets will significantly contribute to alleviating financing problems faced by East Asian corporates and foreign investors who want to finance investments in local currency.

EAST ASIAN EQUITY MARKETS

Before the crisis, rapid economic growth, shallow share markets, large foreign portfolio capital inflows and poor disclosure produced rapidly growing market capitalisation and liquidity in non-Japan East Asian equity markets. However, these markets remained relatively unsophisticated and inadequately regulated, except in Hong Kong and Singapore. In the post-crisis period, markets around East Asia have surged. The challenge now is to maintain reform momentum, improve supervision enforcement to ensure sustainable recovery and prepare exchanges to operate in a world dominated by electronic trading.

Market Capitalisation

Between 1990 and 1996, the market capitalisation of some East Asian exchanges grew enormously; only in Korea and Japan did capitalisation less than double (Figure 5.1).[2]

Figure 5.1

Market Capitalisation Increased Most in Indonesia and the Philippines
Market Capitalisation Growth of East Asian Exchanges, 1990-98

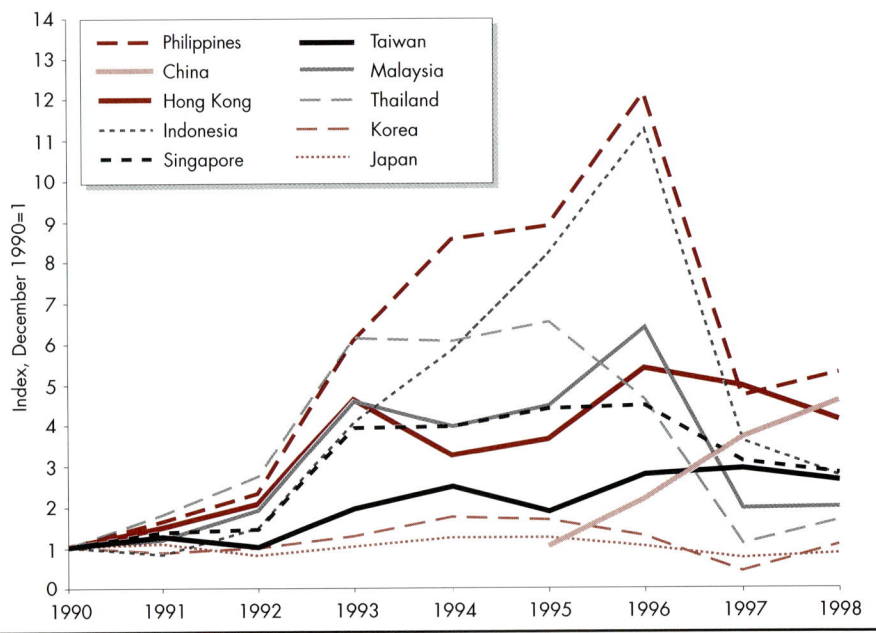

Note: Chinese data come from CEIC database and is only available from December 1995.
Source: Federation of International Stock Exchanges, 1999; and CEIC, 1999.

[2] For example, market capitalisation of the Philippine and Indonesian exchanges increased more than ten fold, while capitalisation of China's exchanges doubled in 1996 and increased a further two thirds in 1997.

Japan has by far the largest market capitalisation in East Asia; other East Asian exchanges are very small compared to major world equity markets (Figure 5.2). In September 1999, the market capitalisation of East Asian exchanges, excluding Japan, but including Australia and New Zealand, was only 17 per cent of that of the New York Stock Exchange.[3] The small size of East Asian exchanges and the worldwide trend to consolidate and trade across borders represents a major challenge for these exchanges.

Relative to their GDP, Hong Kong, Singaporean and Malaysian equity markets are the most important, while the Chinese market is least important (Figure 5.3).[4]

Figure 5.2

Non-Japan Asian Exchanges Are World Minnows
Market Capitalisation of East Asian and Major World Exchanges, September 1999

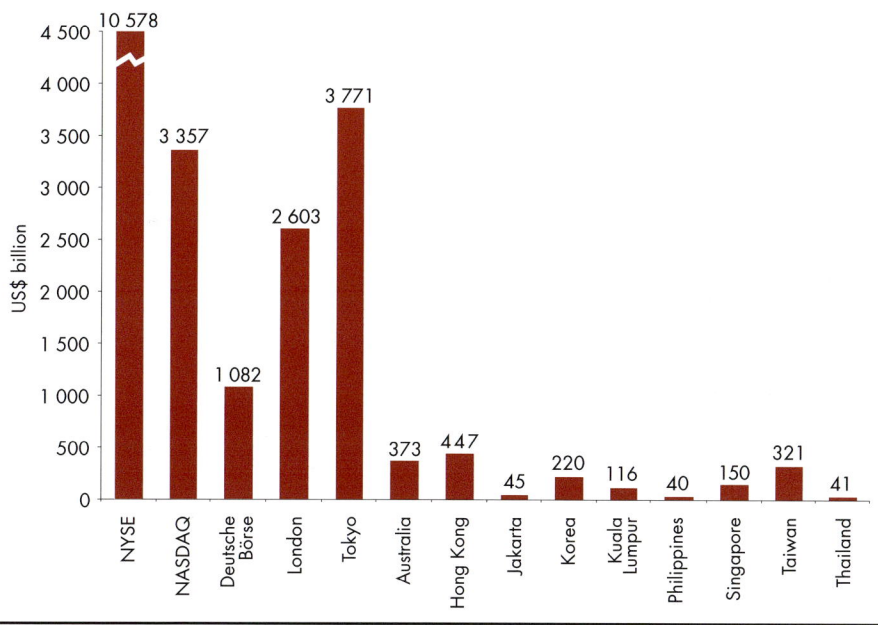

Note: Data on market capitalisation include common and preferred shares and shares without voting rights, but exclude investment funds, rights, warrants, convertibles and foreign companies.
Source: Federation of International Stock Exchanges, 1999.

---

[3] These comparisons are based on US dollar capitalisation. Economies included in this calculation for East Asia are Australia, Hong Kong, Malaysia, Korea, New Zealand, the Philippines, Indonesia, Singapore, Taiwan and Thailand.

[4] Malaysia's market capitalisation was around three times its GDP in 1996, but fell to below 150 per cent of GDP in 1997 and 1998; however, with 21 per cent growth in market capitalisation in the nine months to September 1999, its market capitalisation relative to GDP again is increasing.

Capital Markets

Figure 5.3

Equity Markets Most Important in Hong Kong, Malaysia and Singapore Pre-crisis

Market Capitalisation as a Percentage of GDP, 1996-98

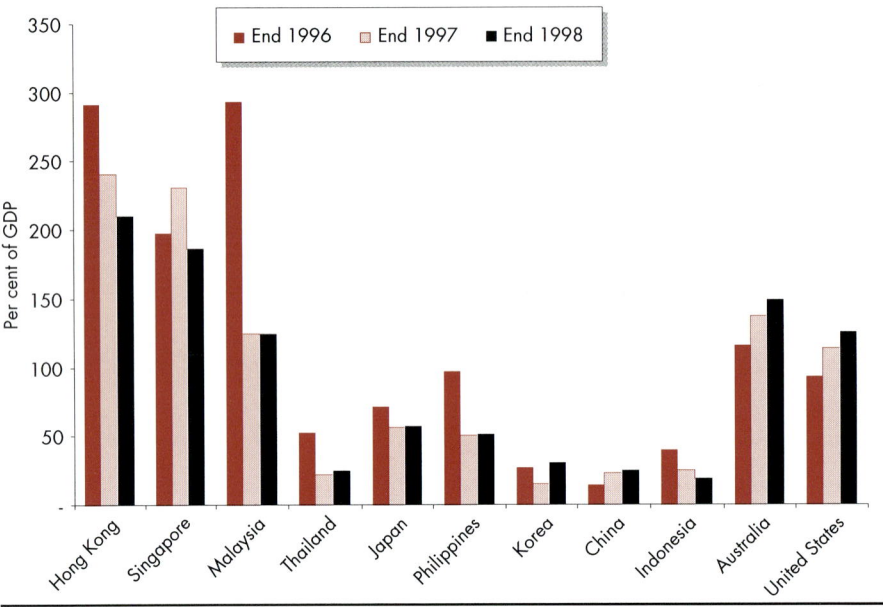

Note: Data on market capitalisation include common and preferred shares and shares without voting rights, but exclude investment funds, rights, warrants, convertibles and foreign companies.
Source: Federation of International Stock Exchanges, 1999; and CEIC, 1999.

Between June and December 1997, all East Asian markets except China lost significant market capitalisation, even in local currency terms (Figure 5.4).[5] Many declined further until August 1998 when they began to rebound sharply. High levels of domestic liquidity and returning foreign capital drove this rebound.

New Trading Technology

During the late 1980s and early 1990s, East Asian exchanges quickly adopted new trading and settlement technologies. In 1986, the Stock Exchange of Hong Kong introduced automated trading followed by the Australian Stock Exchange in 1987. All regional exchanges now use fully automated trading systems, except Japan, which combines screen and floor based trading. Automated trading reduces costs and bottlenecks, and facilitates volume increases. However, settlement and surveillance improvements often were less rapid, creating significant problems.

---

[5] US dollar losses were even more extreme due to exchange rate deprecations.

Stock Market Participants

Compared to industrialised economies, family controlled, listed companies are more prevalent in East Asia, and to maintain majority owner control, many companies only partially list. For example, in June 1997, more than 90 per cent of companies listed on the Jakarta Stock Exchange publicly traded less than half their equity (Backman, 1999). Many listed companies also have unlisted subsidiaries; majority owners of listed companies can transfer profits to these, thereby creating a corporate governance minefield. These practices reduce disclosure and minority shareholder influence, decrease liquidity and facilitate stock price manipulation. Ultimately, such activities undermine the credibility of many Asian share markets with domestic and foreign investors.

Figure 5.4

Korean Rebound Strongest
Total Market Capitalisation in Local Currencies

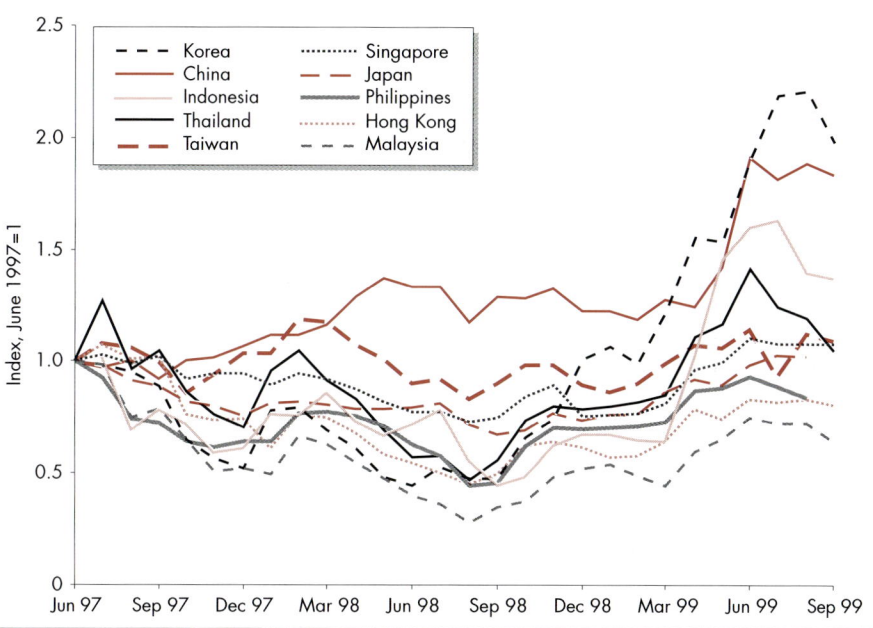

Note: Data are converted to index form with June 1997 equal to 1.
Source: CEIC, 1999.

Institutional investors are much less important in East Asian equity markets than in the United States, Europe or Australia. This is partly due to weak minority shareholder rights in Asian family controlled companies, increasing the riskiness of shareholdings and reducing their suitability for institutional investors, but also due to lower penetration levels of life insurance and pension funds. The dominance of government-owned and managed pension funds in Singapore, Malaysia and Taiwan further constrains local institutional participation in those equity markets. (See Chapter 6 - *Non-bank Financial Institutions*.) More formal barriers also deter institutional investors; for example, the Chinese Government does not allow institutional investors to purchase shares because it considers them too risky. Before the crisis, Indonesia's regulations favoured small share market investors (Linnan, 1994).

In the post-crisis period, many East Asian exchanges are keen to increase the role of institutional investors. Management of public pension funds in Singapore, Malaysia and Japan is being reformed to varying degrees. (See Chapter 6 - *Non-bank Financial Institutions*.) Moreover, Korea, Thailand, Indonesia and Taiwan have dramatically liberalised limits on foreign equity holdings, increasing opportunities for foreign institutional investors to participate in their equity markets. However, in many regional economies, corporate governance must improve considerably for equity investments to attract greater interest from international institutional investors. (See Chapter 3 - *Prudential Reform*.)

POST-CRISIS STOCK EXCHANGE REFORMS

Many East Asian stock exchanges initiated reforms well before the Asian financial crisis. However, regulatory changes often were *ad hoc* and enforcement weak (Radelet and Sachs, 1998). For example, enterprises widely used nominees to avoid restrictions on related party transactions and flaunted listing rules (Backman, 1999).

Since the crisis, many regional governments have strengthened stock exchange regulation, including through improved:

- information disclosure procedures
- accounting standards
- corporate governance
- foreign ownership liberalisation
- settlement procedures
- market surveillance
- enforcement.

However, regulatory reform is lengthy and difficult. New securities regulation must be compatible with the overall legal framework, and enforcement requires stronger institutional and human resources.

Information Disclosure

Inadequate disclosure is a major problem due to weak laws, poor enforcement and lack of appropriate technology. While most regional exchanges require the continuous disclosure of all price sensitive information, outside Singapore, Hong Kong and Australia, disclosure often is poor.

> **DISCLOSURE RULES ON THE AUSTRALIAN STOCK EXCHANGE**
>
> Australian Stock Exchange listing rules require firms to continuously disclose relevant market information. All company information is promulgated to the market through the exchange's Companies Announcements Platform. When a firm determines information is material or price sensitive, trading in the stock is halted for ten minutes to allow all market participants time to assimilate the information.
>
> Source: Australian Stock Exchange, 1999.

Many exchanges now are improving disclosure mechanisms, often assisted by the Internet. For example:

- in August 1997, the Korea Stock Exchange introduced a new disclosure system and raised penalties for non-disclosure; all listed companies electronically submit disclosure documents for dissemination on the Internet

- in mid 1999, the Kuala Lumpur Stock Exchange introduced an electronic disclosure system; companies electronically send market sensitive announcements to the exchange, which it publishes at its website. The exchange also is increasing traders' disclosure requirements[6]

- the Taiwan Stock Exchange introduced an electronic investor information system to disseminate market sensitive information; listed companies enter data into the system, which investors access in real time.

Accounting Standards

Since the crisis, most East Asian equity markets, including Thailand, China, Indonesia and Taiwan have required listed companies to adopt international accounting standards; however, compliance varies. Equity markets in Hong Kong, Singapore, Malaysia and the Philippines required international accounting standards before the crisis, and generally effectively enforced them.[7] While Chinese authorities require local companies issuing shares to foreign investors to meet international accounting standards, these standards are not enforced after listing. Standards also are weak for locally listed companies.

---

[6] In September 1997, the exchange expanded the 'know your client' rule requiring stockbroker clients dealing on behalf of third parties to disclose these parties' identity. These reforms also restricted off-market trading, increasing market transparency.

[7] Some economies exempted banks from these laws before the crisis. For example, Singapore only made disclosure standards for banks consistent with international accounting standards from 1998.

Standards covering the treatment of foreign exchange losses have declined in some economies since the crisis. Before the crisis, Indonesian and Thai companies had to deduct foreign exchange losses immediately from profits. However, now these governments allow firms to spread these losses over five or more years. Hence insolvent firms can appear profitable and can remain listed (*Economist*, 20 December 1997, p. 111).

Japan still has considerable problems with accounting standards, including valuing assets at book, rather than market value, and disclosure problems with loan guarantees.[8] However, since 1 April 1999, a major advance has been to adopt consolidated accounting rules, making it harder to hide losses in subsidiaries. From April 2001, securities holdings will be valued at book rather than market value (*Nikkei Weekly*, 12 April 1999, p. 1).

The treatment of affiliates remains problematical in many regional economies. In a major advance in 1998, Korea forced the 30 largest *chaebol* conglomerates to prepare consolidated certified financial statements for all affiliates by 1999. The Korean Government also prohibited cross lending guarantees within *chaebol* (East Asia Analytical Unit, 1999).

Improved Corporate Governance

Several regional exchanges have attempted to improve corporate governance since the crisis. In April 1997, the Kuala Lumpur Stock Exchange required companies to appoint outside directors and auditors. In October 1997, it improved the rights of minority shareholders by lowering the class action requirement and strengthening the disclosure requirement on listed companies. Korea introduced similar reforms in 1998. In 1998, the Korea Stock Exchange also required listed companies to appoint two independent directors to their boards and established a committee to ensure these directors were appropriately qualified (East Asia Analytical Unit, 1999).[9] The Stock Exchange of Thailand also required all companies to establish audit committees before January 1999.[10]

The Australian Stock Exchange encourages good corporate governance by emphasising disclosure of practice. In 1993 and 1995, the exchange required companies to disclose whether they had an audit committee and the nature of their corporate governance policies. This disclosure based approach recognises companies of different sizes and types have different governance needs, and imposing corporate governance models on listed firms may not be effective; it therefore may be appropriate for East Asian exchanges. The Australian Stock Exchange has had enquiries from the Jakarta Stock Exchange, the Kuala Lumpur Stock Exchange and the Stock Exchange of Thailand on its corporate governance model, with Thailand already applying aspects of this approach (Australian Stock Exchange, 1999).

---

[8] Regulations allowing land and securities to be valued at book rather than market value were introduced just before the end of March 1997. Furthermore, companies often fail to show loan guarantees on their balance sheets. In June 1997, Tokai Kogyo, a construction company listed on the Tokyo Stock Exchange, released a balance sheet showing assets of ¥352 billion and liabilities of ¥344 billion. A month later, it declared bankruptcy, having failed to disclose ¥161 billion in loan guarantees, some of which were called in (*Far Eastern Economic Review*, 9 April 1998, p. 65).

[9] The Hong Kong and Thai exchanges required this before the crisis (Harrison, 1997).

[10] Other corporate governance initiatives in the region will affect equity markets and other areas of the economy. (See Chapter 3 - *Prudential Reform*.)

Foreign Ownership Restrictions

Since the crisis, the IMF-3, Korea, Thailand and Indonesia, have reduced significantly foreign ownership restrictions.[11] In mid 1998, except on a few selected stocks, like Pohang Iron and Steel Corporation, the Korean Government removed all foreign investment ceilings on shares, ahead of the agreed IMF timetable (Korea Stock Exchange, 1998). In January 1998, it also legalised hostile cross-border takeovers of local firms, including securities firms and other financial institutions. In late 1997, Indonesia removed its 49 per cent foreign ownership restriction for all firms, except new banks. In Thailand, foreigners now can have 100 per cent ownership of financial institutions, although after ten years, they cannot purchase any new shares until their equity is less than 49 per cent.

The Philippines, Japan, Hong Kong and Singapore already were fairly open to foreign participation before the crisis. Taiwan removed some major restrictions in a series of steps in 1996, 1997 and 1999. However, with foreign ownership of a company's shares limited to 50 per cent until 2001, and participation restricted to qualified investors, it is less open than Korea.

Malaysia's new capital controls constrain foreign participation in its equity market. Initially, funds withdrawn after less than one year faced a prohibitive tax penalty, but progressively, the Government has reduced tax restrictions to a 10 per cent tax on repatriated profits. Critical service industries also face foreign equity limits such as 61 per cent for telecommunications, 30 per cent for banking and 51 per cent for insurance.

Foreign participation in China's equity markets is the most restricted in the region. Foreign investors can only buy one class of share, B-shares, although other shares are listed on the Hong Kong and New York exchanges. These B-shares can be purchased only in US dollars by other foreign investors; this can create severe liquidity problems when the market is weak. (See Chapter 12 - *China*.)

Settlement and Market Surveillance

Automated trading systems increase the need for better settlement systems. For example, Indonesia's lack of a central share registry often caused investors lengthy delays, particularly when they sold only part of their holding and had to send certificates for splitting and registering (Rosser, 1999).

Since the crisis, some regional markets have introduced new settlement systems. For example, in December 1998, Malaysia created a central depository for all share script, thus facilitating more rapid settlement. Australia established its computerised, scriptless settlement system in September 1994.

Automated trading increases the need for sophisticated electronic surveillance. Australia has a strong internally developed system. If any trade moves outside set price or volume parameters, an alert is raised; if sufficient evidence of insider trading or market manipulation is uncovered, the investigation is referred to the Australian

---

[11] As foreign institutional investors provide considerable expertise in security pricing and risk assessment, and can influence companies to adopt better disclosure practices, they significantly assist equity market development.

Securities Commission.[12] In mid 1999, the Kuala Lumpur Stock Exchange enhanced its market surveillance with an online system allowing it to check compliance of member organisations with capital adequacy requirements.[13] The Hong Kong and Indonesian exchanges all use an advanced Australian-made, real time surveillance system, Securities Markets Automated Research, Training and Surveillance, SMARTS. Taiwan also made a major effort on surveillance in 1998; 70 stocks faced disciplinary action (Taiwan Stock Exchange Corporation, 1999). However, several other regional exchanges need to raise their market surveillance capacity to match improved trading and settlement procedures.

SMARTS: AUSTRALIAN-MADE SURVEILLANCE TECHNOLOGY

SMARTS is the world's leading off-the-shelf stock exchange surveillance technology. Six international regulators and exchanges use it, including the Stock Exchange of Hong Kong, the Securities and Futures Commission of Hong Kong and the Jakarta Stock Exchange. SMARTS is supplied by the publicly listed company, Australian Computershare Limited, the world's largest independent supplier of automated securities market systems. The technology was first released in 1996.

SMARTS assists in research, training and market surveillance. The program's surveillance element examines trading activity in the context of historical activity to identify 'unusual' variations from the norm. After identification, SMARTS provides detailed analysis using sophisticated visualisation tools.

Source: Computershare Limited, 1999.

Enforcement

The crisis showed that weak enforcement of stock exchange regulations often undermined regulatory effectiveness. Governments can lack the political will to enforce regulations, fearing stringent regulations could inhibit market growth or upset vested interests. For example, in 1997, the Korean Stock Exchange sanctioned companies failing to file earnings statements and other price-sensitive information by merely suspending offenders from share trading for one day. Similarly, in the Philippines, late filing of earnings statements incurred a token penalty of around US$13 per day (*Economist*, 20 December 1997, p. 112). Although the Jakarta Stock Exchange requires information be disclosed to it before it is revealed to the market, regulations are not enforced, and rumour rather than regular corporate disclosure often drives stock prices.

In the post-crisis environment, listing rules continue to be inadequately enforced. Despite escalating insolvency, including among listed firms, the number of companies listed on many East Asian exchanges continued to grow in 1997 and 1998 (Figure 5.5). The only East Asian exchanges to record fewer listings in 1997 and 1998 were Thailand and Korea. Efforts to enforce Thai listing rules continue, with

---

12 The Australian Stock Exchange's real time surveillance system is called Surveillance of Market Activity.
13 Brokers' liquidity requirements now are assessed on the basis of risks to which they are exposed.

Capital Markets

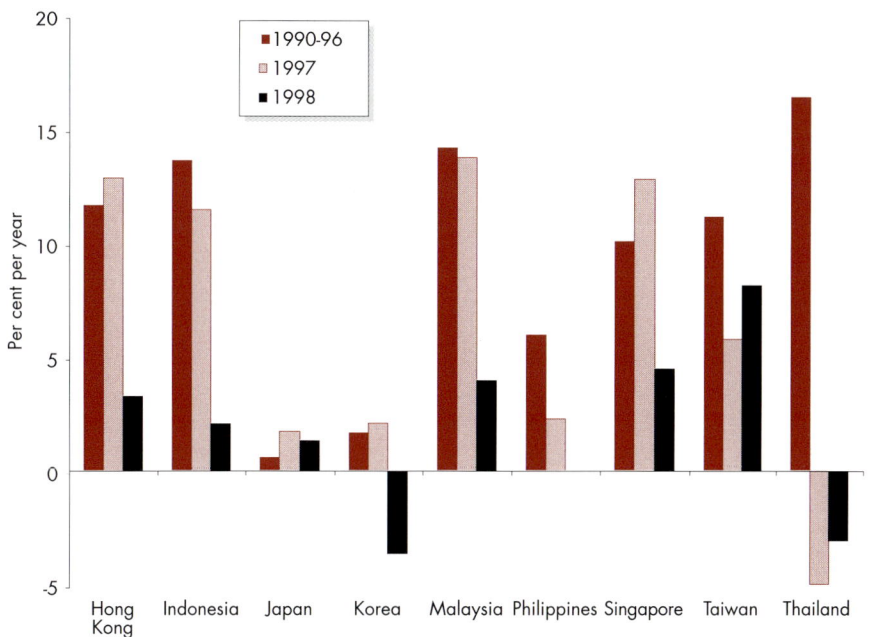

Figure 5.5
Listings Did Not Fall during the Crisis
Change in Number of Listed Companies on East Asian Exchanges, Per cent per Year

Note: There were no new listings in the Philippines in 1998.
Source: Federation of International Stock Exchanges, 1999.

15 companies identified for possible delisting in March 1999 (Stock Exchange of Thailand, 1999). Indonesia's listing rule enforcement reportedly is the most problematic; although around 80 per cent of listed companies are reportedly technically insolvent, the number of listed companies grew by 2 per cent in 1998.

In lower income economies in East Asia, a key to improving securities and other law enforcement is to raise regulators' salaries. Low salaries make regulators more vulnerable to corruption and reduce the calibre of staff attracted to a regulatory career.

Demutualisation

Demutualisation, or separating exchange ownership from access to brokering rights, is an important new trend reinforcing regional stock market reform. Demutualisation removes important barriers to stock exchange growth and efficiency. For example, some smaller Hong Kong stock exchange members opposed technological changes like computer trading which conflicted with their financial interests. Electronic trading demands a broad distribution network, so removing growth restrictions is increasingly important. In October 1998, the Australian Stock Exchange was the first exchange in the world to demutualise and become a public company which lists on itself. The Singapore and Hong Kong Stock Exchanges are following this lead. (See Chapter 9 - *Hong Kong and Singapore*.) As exchanges move from non-profit to profit oriented organisations, they should seek to reduce costs and find new business opportunities. Mergers and cooperation with other regional and international exchanges will be viewed in commercial rather than nationalistic terms. For example, since the Australian Stock Exchange demutualised, it has become allied with the United States' second largest exchange, the North American Securities Dealing and Automated Quotation System, NASDAQ. Ultimately, shares listed on each market will be traded on the other (*Australian Financial Review*, 15 July 1999, p. 23). Demutualised exchanges also are likely to aggressively seek new listings and increase transaction volumes to boost liquidity and reduce transaction costs. Greater outsourcing of technology requirements also should minimise costs.[14]

STOCK MARKET CONSOLIDATION

The worldwide trend is for equity markets to consolidate. Consolidated markets benefit from reduced trading costs, harmonised regulations and standardised admission procedures. They also are better able to attract remote access by a worldwide network of regulated participants. In November 1998, NASDAQ Stock Market bought out the United States' fourth largest exchange, the American Stock Exchange. The London Stock Exchange and Deutsche Börse, the German stock exchange, are leading moves to establish a single European market, initially for the most liquid securities.

The global trend towards consolidation significantly threatens East Asian exchanges, which, except for Japan, are small compared to major US and European markets. Their small size and consequent lower liquidity make them more costly for traders. For example, in the mid 1990s, average bid-ask spreads, the difference between the best buy price and the best sell price, for the top ten stocks by turnover on NASDAQ were one third of those of Australia which in turn were one third of those of Indonesia (Aitken and Swan, 1995).[15]

East Asian exchanges' small size makes them vulnerable should NASDAQ or the New York or London Stock Exchanges extend their electronic network to the region and attract top stocks. This vulnerability is very evident in the Philippines where in 1998, only ten companies accounted for 63 per cent of market capitalisation. Even in Singapore, 16 companies account for 67 per cent of market capitalisation (Federation of International Stock Exchanges, 1999).

Thus far, East Asian exchanges have made limited progress in consolidating even within one economy. China continues to have equity markets in Shenzhen and Shanghai; Indonesia has exchanges in Jakarta and Surabaya; Japan has exchanges in Tokyo and Osaka; and Indonesia and Thailand both plan to open new futures exchanges. Malaysia is introducing its third stock exchange, the Malaysian Exchange of Securities Dealing and Automated Quotations, MESDAQ, despite the existence of a technology exchange, the Stock Exchange of Singapore Dealing and Automated Quotation System, SESDAQ, in Singapore (*Far Eastern Economic Review*, 27 May 1999, p. 54).[16]

---

[14] To date, exchanges have been cautious of outsourcing because they do not want to depend on other businesses.

[15] In fiscal year 1997-98, expenses were 81 per cent of the revenue of the Australian Stock Exchange, one of the region's largest markets, compared to 65 per cent for the London Stock Exchange and 76 per cent for the New York Stock Exchange (Reuters, 1998).

[16] The MESDAQ has no minimum requirement for profit or period of operations; instead, it focuses on transparency.

On the positive side, in March 1994, the Manila and Makati stock exchanges were unified. In December 1998, the Kuala Lumpur Stock Exchange and the Kuala Lumpur Futures and Options Exchange merged; by December 1999, the stock and futures exchanges in Singapore will merge; and in 2000, the Hong Kong stock and futures exchanges will merge.[17]

Exchanges around the world also are moving into closer alliances. The Australian Stock Exchange and Singapore International Monetary Exchange already are well placed in these alliances.[18] For other regional exchanges, becoming part of a close alliance will become increasingly important; however, for many exchanges, further regulatory strengthening and consolidation may be needed first.

TRENDS IN STOCK MARKET CONSOLIDATION

One model for stock market consolidation is for a pan-national exchange, with trading facilitated through the Internet or other means. Such an exchange would require very tight listing and compliance requirements, with national exchanges serving as 'preparatory boards'. This type of exchange would eliminate the need for multiple listing fees and improve liquidity by allowing investors from within the whole region covered by the exchange to actively trade listed stocks. This is broadly the model proposed by eight European exchanges led by the London Stock Exchange and Deutsche Börse. As an interim step, from November 2000, the eight bourses will create a web of connections through a single electronic interface.

An alternative model to a pan-national exchange is to link liquidity pools. Under this model, exchanges remain the 'listing sites', but these sites become accessible to multiple pools of investors. This model forms the basis of the alliance between the Australian Stock Exchange and NASDAQ to co-list and co-trade stocks. This alliance currently is going through regulatory approval in Australia and the United States. It is likely to become operational in 2000 and will allow parallel listing of stocks on the two exchanges. It also will allow Australian investors to invest directly in NASDAQ listed stocks (through their Australian brokers) and US investors to invest directly on the Australian Stock Exchange (through their US brokers), providing Australian companies access to a vast new pool of potential investors. The Australian Stock Exchange is investigating more alliances of this type; ultimately, alliances similar to airline groups could emerge with a group of linked exchanges.

Source: Australian Stock Exchange, 1999; *Financial Times*, 1999; and London Stock Exchange, 1999.

[17] The Australian Stock Exchange planned to merge with the Sydney Futures Exchange. However, these plans have been abandoned due the Australian Consumer and Competition Commission's ruling that the merger would be anti-competitive.

[18] The Singapore International Monetary Exchange is part of the GLOBEX alliance of futures exchanges. The Australian Stock Exchange is finalising an alliance with NASDAQ in North America.

Capital Markets

ASIAN BOND MARKETS

Deeper and more liquid corporate bond markets are critical for providing longer term domestic currency funding for business investment. Government bond markets provide benchmark yield curves, important in pricing corporate bonds, and also assist in macroeconomic management. However, they can crowd out private sector bond issues if they are too large for too long. This section analyses the scope and growth of East Asia's corporate and government bond markets, barriers to their development and recent reforms removing such barriers.

TRENDS IN THE SIZE AND ROLE OF BOND MARKETS

As in industrialised economies, East Asian bonds predominantly are sold over the counter, although many also are listed on stock exchanges.[19] For example, in the mid 1990s, all bonds in Korea were traded over the counter, even though more than 80 per cent of bonds outstanding were listed on the Korean Stock Exchange (Dalla, 1995). Unlike exchange-traded markets, which have a central repository of transaction information, over-the-counter markets are dispersed geographically with no central market. Thus aggregate data, particularly on corporate bonds, are scarce. The best available data on government and corporate bonds are presented below.

Government Bonds

Deep and liquid government bond markets act as fundamental building blocks for corporate bond markets, as they provide a low risk pricing benchmark. Before the crisis, conservative fiscal policies meant outstanding government bonds were below 10 per cent of GDP in Thailand, Singapore, Korea and Hong Kong.[20] In 1997 and 1998, driven by fiscal stimulus packages and financial sector restructuring and refinancing, outstanding government bonds rose as a proportion of GDP in most East Asian economies (Figure 5.6). The largest rises occurred in Japan, Thailand, China and Korea.

---

[19] Over-the-counter bond trading offers less restrictive trading times, no minimum trading amounts and prompt settlement. For example, the turnover of bonds on the Australian Stock Exchange in 1997-98 was around A$182 million, compared with the over-the-counter market turnover of A$1 183 billion.

[20] In Hong Kong, most of these bonds were exchange fund notes rather than more conventional government bonds.

Figure 5.6
Government Bond Markets Growing in East Asia
Government Bonds Outstanding as a Proportion of GDP, 1996-98

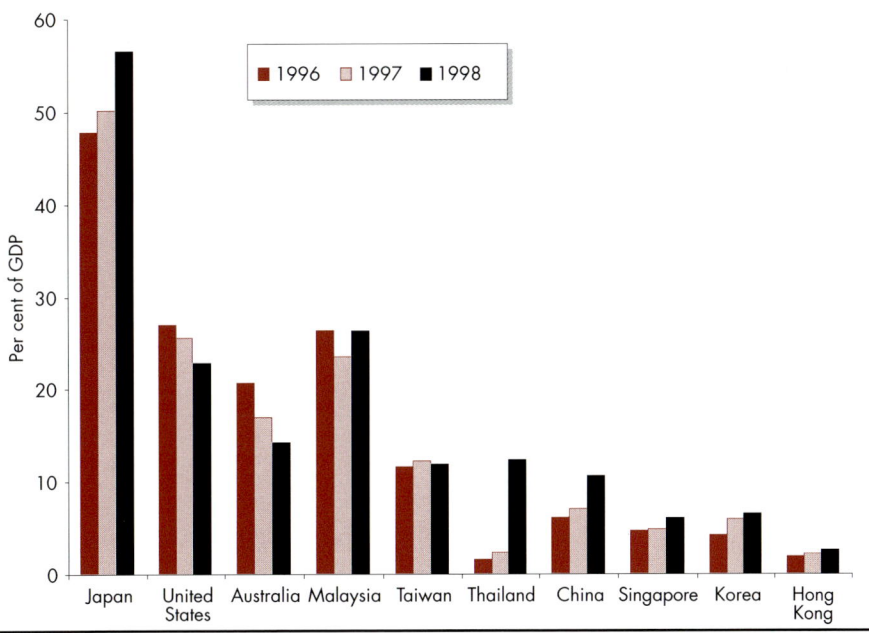

Note: Bonds outstanding for Hong Kong include exchange fund notes.
Source: Central bank annual reports, quarterly and monthly bulletins and websites.

Corporate Bonds

The importance of corporate bond markets was well recognised in East Asia before the crisis and Japan, Korea and Malaysia all had established significant markets (Table 5.1). From the mid 1980s, Japan gradually relaxed restrictions on corporate bond issues, enabling its numerous large corporations to issue bonds. In the mid and late 1990s, Japanese corporations' credit ratings often were better than banks, enabling them to directly access credit more cheaply; this drove bond issues. However, relative to GDP, Korea's and Malaysia's corporate bond markets were larger than Japan's (Table 5.1).[21] Growth in the Malaysian corporate bond market was stimulated by Cagamas, the National Mortgage Corporation. Established in 1986, it supplies liquidity to financial institutions providing housing loans by purchasing their mortgage portfolios (Dalla, 1995).[22] Before the crisis, Hong Kong also had a sizeable corporate bond market (Table 5.1). A sound government security market and the associated Hong Kong dollar benchmark yield curve supported liquidity and enhanced the acceptance of Hong Kong dollar debt instruments.

---

[21] However, Korea's secondary corporate bond market trading was small before the crisis. Most issues had administratively determined yields and were bank guaranteed, making them more like loan packages (Dalla, 1995).

[22] Between 1990 and 1994, Cagamas issued Ringgit 9 billion of bonds, around 45 per cent of corporate bond issues over that period. These bonds had an active secondary market due to their high credit ratings and the quality of their collateral (Dalla, 1995).

Table 5.1

Japan's Corporate Bond Market Dominates the Region
Selected Asia-Pacific Corporate Bond Markets

	Year	Amount outstanding	
		US$ billion	Per cent of GDP
Japan	1996	282.4	6.2
Korea	1996	90.0	26.9
Malaysia[a]	1994	12.5	17.0
Hong Kong	1995	7.0	4.9
Indonesia	1996	4.8	2.2
Taiwan	1996	4.0	1.5
Singapore	1996	3.6	4.2
Thailand			
- Corporate	1996	1.9	1.2
- State owned enterprise	1996	3.3	2.0

Note: a Data for Malaysia are from Dalla, 1995.
Source: Webster, 1997; and Dalla, 1995.

While the crisis has stimulated some Asian corporate bond markets, most have suffered. Growth in new issues has been strongest in Japan; Japan's large corporations responded to continued low interest rates and banking sector problems by increasing bond issuance (Figure 5.7). Since the crisis, Korea's corporate bond market also has remained large in terms of the value of new issues; bond issues grew strongly in 1998, driven by a significant increase in bond issues by the top five *chaebol* as banks restricted their lending (Figure 5.7). However, the market currently is very unstable due to potential mass redemptions of Daewoo bonds, concerns about the solvency of Korean bond funds, concerns about the lack of a requirement for the value of bond holdings to be marked down to current market values, and the lack of a framework for sharing losses from the bankruptcy of a major *chaebol*. (See Chapter 13 - *Korea*.) Corporate bond issues also increased in Taiwan. (See Chapter 10 - *Taiwan*.) Hong Kong bond issues remained stable in 1997 and 1998, while in Singapore new issues fell by 37 per cent (Figure 5.7). However, in both these markets issuance has picked up in 1999 (*Asiamoney*, April 1999, p. 24 and September 1999, p. 123). The corporate bond market hardest hit by the financial crisis was Indonesia; the severe economic contraction caused Indonesia's corporate bond market to dry up completely in 1998.

Figure 5.7

Varying Patterns In Corporate Bond Markets
Corporate Bond New Issues, US$ billion

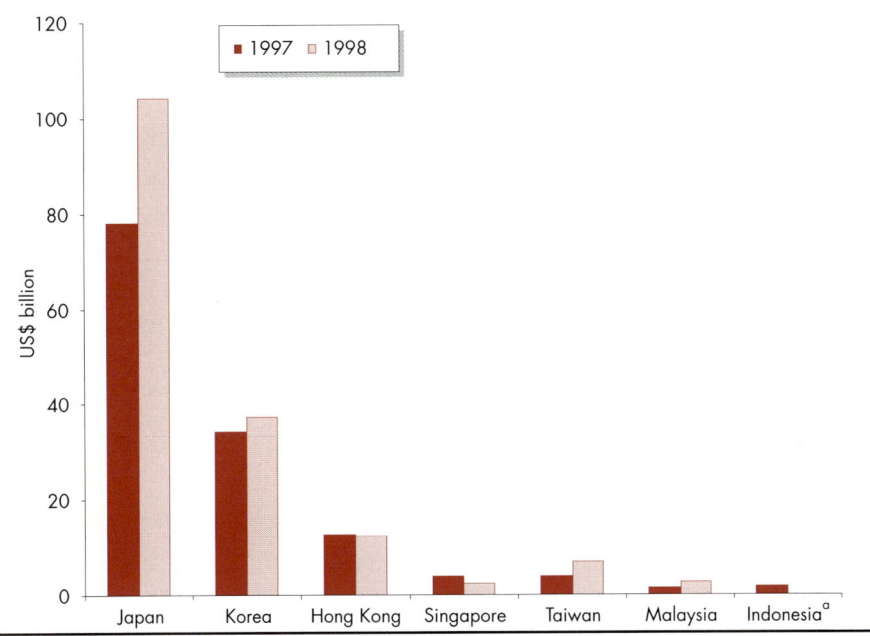

Note: a Indonesia had no corporate bond issues in 1998.
Source: Central bank annual reports, quarterly and monthly bulletins and websites.

MAJOR CONSTRAINTS ON EAST ASIAN BOND MARKETS

Before the crisis, major barriers to East Asian bond market development included inadequate prudential frameworks, unfavourable tax regimes, supply and demand problems, lack of benchmark yield curves, lack of credible domestic rating agencies, and settlement system and liquidity support problems. Governments were tackling these issues, but have intensified their efforts since the financial crisis.

Inadequate Prudential Framework

In many regional economies, more than one body has prudential control of bond markets; this reduces supervisory effectiveness and can cause delays in approval for bond issues. For example, the Indonesian national securities regulator, BAPEPAM, regulates financial instruments with maturities exceeding one year, while the central bank, Bank Indonesia, regulates money market instruments with maturities less than one year. In Malaysia, the Securities Commission officially regulates bond markets, but Bank Negara Malaysia and rating agencies also are involved, so approving bond issues can take up to six months; this causes particular problems when market conditions change.

By comparison, the Monetary Authority of Singapore regulates all financial instruments. Australia and China also now have unified capital market supervision.[23] In China, regulatory consolidation should assist enforcement.

Taxation Regimes

Asian tax regimes often discourage bond trading. For example, private debt security trades in the Philippines are subject to a 0.75 per cent documentary stamp tax; this strongly discourages secondary trading of private debt securities. In addition, private Philippine investors in corporate and government debt securities are subject to a 20 per cent withholding tax. Similarly, Taiwan's tax authorities impose a 0.1 per cent transaction tax on corporate paper and a 20 per cent withholding tax on interest income earned from it (*Asiamoney*, April 1999, p. 28). Furthermore, in many East Asian economies, interest on bonds is taxed while dividends are tax exempt (Quila, 1997).

Many regional economies also differentiate between local and foreign investors, and institutions and individuals in their tax arrangements. In Indonesia, rates of withholding tax differ for domestic corporations, pension funds, banks and offshore investors depending on where they are domiciled. To avoid these tax liabilities, participants allegedly undertake 'coupon-washing' transactions; bonds are sold to a tax-exempt institution when coupons are due, then bought back afterwards avoiding tax, but adding to the cost of bond investments (*Euromoney*, 1997).

Supply Side Problems

Before the crisis, because they ran fiscal surpluses, few East Asian governments issued large quantities of government bonds, making it difficult to establish liquid benchmark yield curves. However, since the crisis, most East Asian governments are running fiscal deficits to stimulate economic activity.

Traditionally, major corporations relied on equity and bank financing, restricting corporate bond supply. The bias against bond financing was partly due to the ease of access to bank finance and to some East Asian firms' dislike of the discipline imposed by bond prospectuses and credit ratings (Tsang, 1998).[24] In the post-crisis environment, many banks are tightening lending conditions; listing rules are tighter; and creditors and regulators require greater transparency. Consequently, the bias against bond markets could decline.

Demand Side Problems

Bond market demand also is weak, particularly in Indonesia, Thailand and the Philippines. Weak demand for government and corporate bonds often reflects investor concerns about future trends in economic growth and inflation. Inadequate transparency, corporate accountancy standards and regulatory controls also can constrain corporate bond demand. Restrictions on local institutional investors such

---

[23] The relevant institution in Australia is the Australian Securities and Investment Commission; in China, it is the newly established China Securities Regulatory Commission.

[24] Disclosure rules for bond issues usually are more stringent than accounting standards imposed on published accounts.

as insurance companies and pension funds participating in bond markets, significantly reduce demand for corporate bonds. In China, institutional investors cannot hold corporate bonds, and even Japan still restricts the asset allocation of pension funds. (See Chapter 12 - *China* and Chapter 11 - *Japan*.) Moreover, in many economies where institutional investors do buy bonds, they hold them to maturity, stifling secondary market trading. This problem is particularly acute in Malaysia, Singapore, Taiwan and China where state run pension schemes dominate the pension market. (See Chapter 6 - *Non-bank Financial Institutions*.)

Nevertheless, investor demand should further develop as savings rates in most East Asian economies are high, and reforms in insurance, pension and fund management industries are ongoing. (See Chapter 6 - *Non-bank Financial Institutions*.) Yields are now market determined in all East Asian bond markets; China was the last to introduce auctions of newly issued government bonds.[25] Furthermore, China's new securities law, introduced in mid 1999, strengthened and formalised regulations governing corporate bond issues; this should boost future demand for these securities. (See Chapter 12 - *China*.)

Lack of Benchmark Yield Curves

A government bond yield curve is a vital pricing benchmark for corporate bonds, but this curve often is poorly developed.[26] Hong Kong probably has the best established yield curve in East Asia. Singapore and Taiwan successfully established benchmark yield curves, although Taiwanese market participants claim liquidity would increase if authorities issued more bonds at each maturity (*Asiamoney*, April 1999, p. 28). The Philippines has a long benchmark yield curve, but issues are infrequent and secondary trading limited (*Asiamoney*, April 1999, p. 26). Japan has issued vast amounts of government bonds in recent years, but is trying to improve its yield curve by reducing reliance on ten year bonds and introducing five year bonds (*Nikkei Weekly*, 26 April 1999, p. 15).[27] Korea has established a benchmark yield rate for three year bonds and gradually will extend this to a full yield curve. (See Chapter 13 - *Korea*.)

Indonesia, Malaysia and Thailand all use substitutes for government benchmarks. For example, Malaysia uses debt issued by the national oil company, Petronas, to proxy a risk free domestic yield curve.[28] However, this strategy may inhibit restructuring of state owned enterprises.

As regional governments move back into fiscal balance, it will be important to foster and maintain these yield curves. Hong Kong and Australia have achieved this. In 1994, while running fiscal surpluses, the Hong Kong Government established the successful exchange fund note program, which issued bonds and reinvested funds raised

---

[25] For bonds issued at par, the interest rate is market determined; for bonds where the Finance Ministry sets the interest rate, the issuing price is market determined.

[26] The yield curve represents the relationship between yield and time, and embodies expectations concerning future fundamental economic indicators such as growth and inflation.

[27] The distressed long term credit banks used to issue at this maturity (*Nikkei Weekly*, 26 April 1999, p. 15).

[28] In Indonesia, the swap curve is a surrogate for the yield curve in the absence of long term government bond issues. The swap curve provides an inappropriate measure of spreads on local credits because it is an offshore curve rather than an onshore curve. In Thailand, state enterprise debt and issues by the Industrial Finance Corporation of Thailand are used to construct a domestic yield curve.

Lack of Credit Rating Agencies

Lack of credible East Asian rating agencies inhibits the development of regional bond markets, as ratings often are a prerequisite for successful bond issues. As conglomerates and cross-shareholdings are common in many regional economies, one corporate downgrade can affect a rating agency's relationship with many companies. This acts as a disincentive for accurate and credible ratings. Agencies themselves also see accounting, compatibility and disclosure standards as further constraints (Mariano, 1999).

Nonetheless, most East Asian economies now have domestic rating agencies; these provide a base to build on. In Indonesia, Korea, Malaysia, Taiwan, the Philippines and Thailand, ratings are compulsory for some or all debt issues, stimulating demand for ratings agencies.[29] A Taiwanese rating agency recently established a joint venture with Standard and Poor's, significantly increasing its credibility. Korea has gone even further, opening the credit rating market to foreign competition, and promoting joint ventures between foreign and local rating agencies. Already Moody's and Korea Investors Services have formed a joint venture.[30]

Harmonising agency rating scales in developing East Asian bond markets would increase comparability across countries, industries and economies; consequently, member agencies of the ASEAN Forum of Credit Rating Agencies are taking steps to harmonise rating standards, processes and classifications (Mariano, 1999).

In the medium to long term, addressing the ownership structure of East Asian rating agencies would improve credibility. Large international rating agencies avoid conflict of interest perceptions by having owners which are not financial institutions.[31] However, in economies such as Korea, Malaysia and Thailand, groups of financial institutions own rating agencies.[32]

---

[29] Such regulations probably are justified given the critical role of rating agencies in reducing information asymmetries between providers and users of capital.

[30] This joint venture was formed in 1998. Korea Investor Services is owned by 70 non-bank financial institutions.

[31] For example, Standard and Poor's is part of McGraw Hill while Fitch IBCA is wholly owned by Finilac and listed on the Paris Stock Exchange.

[32] For example, the Rating Agency of Malaysia is owned by Malaysian commercial banks, finance companies and merchant banks, while Malaysian Rating Corporation is owned by Malaysian insurance companies, stockbrokers and discount houses. Malaysia, Thailand and Korea all have limits on the share any one financial institution can own in a rating agency.

Lack of Efficient Settlement Facilities

Several regional bond markets suffer from a lack of up-to-date trading infrastructure; this reduces bond trading and settlement efficiency, and exposes investors to settlement and systemic risk.[33] Linking antiquated local settlement systems with international settlement institutions' automated systems also is difficult, reducing the attractiveness of regional bond markets to foreign investors and depriving these markets of much needed liquidity.

However, most regional economies are moving towards simultaneous delivery and payment for securities. Malaysia is quite close to establishing such a system while in the Philippines, rivalry over which settlement system to employ has caused major problems (*Asiamoney*, April 1999, p. 26). Singapore and Hong Kong have the most sophisticated settlement systems, already providing simultaneous delivery and payment. In December 1998, the Stock Exchange of Singapore implemented a new scriptless bond trading system connected to the Monetary Authority of Singapore's electronic payments system. In Hong Kong, the Central Moneymarkets Unit debt market clearing and settlement system is linked with Euroclear and Cedel, the principal settlement and clearing mechanisms for European and eurodollar transactions, as well as Australian and New Zealand systems. Hong Kong has offered to share technical experience in software, hardware and market making arrangements with any Asian economy willing to work to develop an *Asiaclear* network to link regional bond settlement systems. This could provide a major boost to Asian bond markets.

Despite its size and income levels, Japan continues to have surprising settlement problems. In secondary markets for government and corporate bonds, settlement takes up to three days compared to electronic real time settlement for all US treasuries, Australian Commonwealth Government bonds and Hong Kong exchange fund paper.

Lack of Liquidity Support

Another factor hampering regional bond market development is the lack of liquidity support available to market makers.[34] This support is critical for market makers' highly leveraged operations and generally is provided through repurchase markets or central bank re-discount windows.[35] Such support is best developed in Hong Kong, Singapore and Japan.

---

[33] Settlement risk is that faced by individual participants in the domestic payments system. For example, one participant may write a 'bad' cheque. Systemic risk refers to risk inherent in the financial system. It arises when one or more participants are unable to meet their obligations, and this causes other participants to be unable to meet theirs. (See Chapter 3 - *Prudential Reform*.)

[34] A market maker is a dealer prepared to buy or sell at the quoted bid and offer prices.

[35] Repurchase facilities and re-discount windows enable price makers to quote two way market prices. Repurchase facilities enable them to borrow and lend stock to meet settlement commitments, whilst re-discount windows provide additional liquidity to bond markets in the form of a committed purchase arrangement from the government.

Foreign Participation

Further opening East Asian bond markets to foreign investors would boost liquidity, strengthen links between domestic and global markets, broaden the investor base and increase risk diversification potential for investors. Smaller local companies then could secure bond financing. With greater foreign participation, pressure would increase to standardise bond market regulation and practices, and increase domestic market sophistication via the transfer of intermediation technology (Dalla, 1995).

However, in the post-crisis environment, to increase foreign participation, governments must consider broad strategies to develop bond markets, not just remove restrictions. For example, Korea removed all restrictions on foreign investment in the local bond market in 1998, but the foreign investor base has barely grown. Not only are investors concerned about the health of Korea's corporate sector, but the market lacks a proper benchmark yield curve and as yet, does not employ standard international bond trading practices.

Both Hong Kong and Singapore with their more advanced bond market infrastructure have successfully increased foreign participation. Hong Kong's tax free, locally issued, long term Hong Kong dollar and foreign currency bonds have attracted considerable foreign interest. Foreign issues of Singapore dollar bonds for offshore use have increased since the Monetary Authority of Singapore first permitted these in August 1998.[36]

OUTLOOK FOR ASIA'S BOND MARKETS

The financial crisis reinforced the importance of developing bond markets as an alternative to short term domestic and foreign borrowing. Some economies are undertaking significant reforms to boost domestic bond markets; however, a more proactive approach is needed. Required tax reforms are reasonably straightforward. Other important areas requiring action include:

- reducing barriers to foreign investors
- establishing efficient trading and settlement mechanisms
- providing stable and unambiguous regulatory environments
- establishing risk free yield curve benchmarks
- broadening the range of permitted issuers and investors
- increasing the credibility of domestic rating agencies.

The interrelated nature of these issues implies large gains from comprehensive reform efforts.

---

[36] Together, Ford, the European Bank for Reconstruction and Development, and General Electric Capital Corporation issued bonds worth almost S$1 billion in early 1999 (*Asiamoney*, April 1999, p. 27).

These reform efforts are at different stages in different economies, with Hong Kong and Singapore the most advanced. In the short term, by developing these economies as regional bond issuing centres, quality companies around the region should be able to access long term capital. However, if growth is sustained and reform ongoing, bond issues also should increase steadily in other regional economies, led by Korea, Taiwan and Malaysia.

RISK MANAGEMENT INSTRUMENTS

If risk management markets were more developed, they could have protected regional corporates better during the financial crisis. This section outlines the different types of risk management tools available in East Asian financial markets, assesses the size and growth potential of various risk management markets and examines recent regulatory reforms and developments.

DERIVATIVES AND FINANCIAL RISK REDUCTION

Derivative products are contracts whose payoffs depend on changes in the value of an underlying asset.[37] Derivatives are available on a wide range of assets but the most actively traded financial derivatives are on currencies, equities and government bonds, a proxy for interest rates.[38] In well regulated markets, derivatives can enhance risk management. They enable investors to insure against price falls while they are holding a security, or price rises when they cannot hold a security (Aitken et al, 1996; Harris, 1989; and Hodgson and Nichols, 1990). The risk hedging provided is paid for by a premium or by a large deposit or margin, as well as by commissions charged by derivative brokers.

The Role of Derivatives in the Financial Crisis

Some analysts and regional governments believe the large and concentrated derivative positions taken by highly leveraged institutions like hedge funds contributed to Asian financial market instability. As part of international efforts to strengthen global financial architecture, a working group within the Financial Stability Forum currently is assessing means to improve the supervision of highly leveraged institutions and strengthen their disclosure requirements. (See Chapter 2 - *Capital and the Crisis.*) Certainly, such institutions took large positions during the financial crisis by using derivatives; as they were heavily leveraged they may have contributed to financial market volatility.[39] On the other hand, during the financial crisis, East Asian corporates could have reduced the adverse effects of currency and interest rate volatility on their solvency if they had used derivatives, particularly as from early 1998, many exchange rates partially rebounded and interest rates fell.[40]

---

[37] The most common financial derivatives are options, futures and forwards. Options are contracts conferring a right to buy or sell an underlying asset at a fixed price. Futures and forwards are transactions in underlying assets taking place at a future date whose terms, such as price and quantity, are determined today.

[38] Derivatives also are available on commodities including energy, agricultural products and precious metals.

[39] For further details see International Monetary Fund (1999).

[40] In the first half of 1998, Korean, Malaysian, Philippine and Thai currencies significantly recovered and interest rates also started to fall.

Capital Markets

DERIVATIVES USE IN EAST ASIAN MARKETS

Before the crisis, East Asian corporates did not extensively use derivatives because they believed exchange rates would remain stable, and as hedging possibilities for local currency and interest rate risk were limited. Since the crisis, with the benefits of risk management tools clearly illustrated, demand for derivatives is likely to increase. Like bonds, derivatives can either be traded on exchanges or sold in the over-the-counter markets.

Exchange Traded Markets

The Korea Stock Exchange has the largest number of futures contracts traded in Asia (Figure 5.8). However, these contracts are exclusively equities based. (See Chapter 13 - *Korea*.) After Korea, the Sydney Futures Exchange is the region's largest financial futures and options exchange by contract volume, with 30 million contracts in 1998.

Figure 5.8

Sydney a Large Regional Futures Exchange
Trading Volume on the Six Largest Asia-Pacific Financial Futures and Options Exchanges, 1998

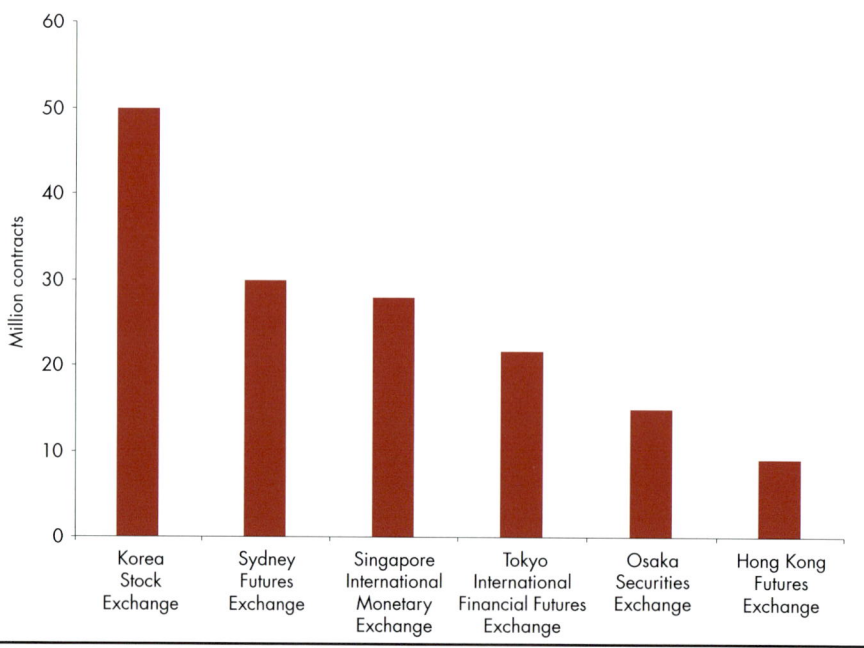

Source: Sydney Futures Exchange, 1999; and Korea Stock Exchange, 1999.

Theoretically, most Asian economies offer exchange traded interest rate or currency derivatives, but many lack adequate depth or liquidity (Tables 5.2 and 5.3). Only Australia and Japan provide sufficiently deep and liquid futures markets for local or offshore corporates to hedge Australian and Japanese interest rate and currency risk (Table 5.3). In the past, the Singapore International Monetary Exchange did not offer futures on domestic assets and securities because the Government discouraged internationalisation of the Singapore dollar (Monetary Authority of Singapore, 1998). However, this is changing rapidly. In 1998, the Singapore International Monetary Exchange launched a Singapore stock index future and in 1999, introduced a three month Singapore dollar interest rate future. In another encouraging development in October 1999, the Korean Futures Exchange launched its three year government bond future, with initial volumes reported to be around 6 000 contracts per day.

Lack of opportunities to hedge domestic interest rate or currency risk offshore exacerbates the lack of liquid hedging products in domestic markets. Except for euroyen and eurodollar products which hedge yen and US dollar currency and interest rate risk, East Asian futures exchanges do not list offshore interest rate or exchange rate contracts.[41]

Over-the-counter Markets

Theoretically, East Asia has many over-the-counter markets for currency and interest rate derivatives. However, active exchange traded markets are an important prerequisite for successful over-the-counter markets. They provide transparent price signals for valuing derivatives, and cheap mechanisms for over-the-counter market traders to reduce their risk.[42] Consequently, Australia, Singapore, Japan and Hong Kong, which have the most active exchange traded derivative markets also have the most active and successful over-the-counter derivatives markets.

---

[41] Euroyen and eurodollar products are yen and US dollar products offered in markets other than Japan and the United States. Singapore's futures exchange is the region's most active in euroyen and eurodollar products.

[42] Other reasons for the poor state of regional over-the-counter interest rate derivative markets are in Banks (1996).

Capital Markets

Table 5.2
Seemingly Wide Range of Hedging Options ...
East Asian Currency and Interest Rate Derivative Markets

	Exchange-traded markets			Over-the-counter markets		
	Currency derivatives[a]	Interest rate derivatives	Other derivatives[b]	Currency derivatives[a]	Interest rate derivatives	Other derivatives[b]
Australia		✓	✓	✓	✓	✓
China		✓	✓	✓		
Hong Kong	✓	✓	✓	✓	✓	✓
Indonesia			✓	✓	✓	
Japan	✓	✓	✓	✓	✓	✓
Malaysia		✓	✓	✓	✓	
Philippines	✓	✓	✓	✓	✓	✓
Singapore	✓	✓	✓	✓	✓	✓
Korea		✓	✓	✓	✓	
Taiwan			✓	✓	✓	✓
Thailand			✓			

Note: a Only derivatives on home currencies and interest rates are indicated in these columns.
       b 'Other' refers to derivatives on stocks and commodities.
       Blank entries indicate product is not offered.

Source: *Handbook of World Stock, Derivative and Commodity Exchanges*, 1998; Futures Communication, 1998; Banks, 1996; and country chapters of this report.

Capital Markets

Table 5.3

But Liquid Markets Are Rare
Exchange Traded Futures and Options on East Asian Currencies and Interest Rates

Market/exchange	Futures contract	Daily volume (contract numbers)[a,b]
Australia		
Sydney Futures Exchange	3 year bonds[c]	37 910
	10 year bonds[c]	24 162
	90 day bank accepted bills[c]	23 094
China		
Beijing Commodity Exchange, China Commodity Futures Exchange of Hainan, China Zhengzhou Commodity Exchange, Guangdong United Futures Exchange, Shanghai Stock Exchange, Shenyang Commodity Exchange, Shenzen Metal and United Futures Exchange, Shenzhen Stock Exchange and Wuhan Securities Exchange Centre	2 year treasury notes 3 year treasury notes 5 year treasury notes 10 year treasury notes	Trading suspended since 1995, following market manipulation incidents
Hong Kong		
Hong Kong Futures Exchange	3 month Hong Kong interbank offer rate	1 802
Japan		
Tokyo International Financial Futures Exchange	3 month euroyen[c]	107 012
	US dollar/Japanese yen	170
	1 year euroyen	0
Tokyo Stock Exchange	5 year Japanese government bond	1 198
	10 year Japanese government bond[c]	58 098
	20 year Japanese government bond	9
Korea		
Korea Futures Exchange	3 month interest rate future	na
	3 year government bond[d]	6 000

Capital Markets

Market/exchange	Futures contract	Daily volume (contract numbers)[a,b]
Malaysia		
Commodity and Monetary Exchange of Malaysia[e]	Kuala Lumpur interbank offer rate	302
Singapore		
Singapore International Monetary Exchange	3 month Singapore dollar Interest rate future[f]	1 517
	Euroyen contract[g]	29 790
	Eurodollar contract	37 879
Philippines		
Manila International Futures Exchange	US dollar/peso currency	na
	Philippine interest rate	na

Note: a The nominal value of positions traded better indicates the value of derivatives trading, but most exchanges do not report this information.
b All statistics are for the year ended 31 October 1998, unless otherwise indicated.
c This indicates options traded as well as futures.
d This was introduced in late 1999. The reported figure is anecdotal from market contracts.
e Malaysian data is for year ended December 1998.
f From 10 September 1999, volume given is for the first day's trading.
g Figures for the euroyen and eurodollar contract are daily averages from January to July 1999.
na means not available.

Source: *Handbook of World Stock, Derivative and Commodity Exchanges*, 1998; *Futures Magazine*, 1998; and country chapters of this report.

DERIVATIVES REGULATION

Due to the highly leveraged nature of derivatives trading and its possible effects on growth prospects in the event of market failure, strong regulation is critical in derivative markets. Regulation should protect market integrity while minimising the impact on liquidity and efficiency. Two key areas of exchange traded derivatives regulation relate to ensuring contract performance and market fairness.

Contract Performance

A major risk associated with derivatives markets is systemic failure. Failure to fulfil obligations under derivative contracts can squeeze counter-parties causing them to default and leading to market collapse. The main regulatory tools used to minimise systemic risk associated with contract performance are margining, guarantee funds, and price limits and trading halts.

Margining

'Initial margins' are cash deposits or liquid securities which traders must deposit with an exchange or clearing house before trading. They are costly, as more profitable uses of these funds must be foregone. Margins are designed to cover possible losses arising from default by one party to a derivative transaction. Exchanges regulate the minimum margin size but it can vary across exchanges for an identical product.[43]

At the end of each day, the gain or loss on outstanding futures trades is calculated for all traders and added to or subtracted from their margin account. This is known as the 'marking-to-market' feature of futures. If the margin account drops below a certain level known as the 'maintenance margin', the exchange will send out a request for funds to keep the balance of the margin account above the maintenance margin level. While initial margins vary across exchanges, maintenance margins are fairly similar and based on a system developed by the Chicago Mercantile Exchange.

Guarantee funds

Financial guarantees are large funds available to settle transactions in the event of a default; they enhance market stability. Their size and composition varies considerably across exchanges.[44] The costs of setting up these guarantees are subsumed into exchange fees and brokers' clearing and settlement commissions.

---

[43] For example, both the Osaka Securities Exchange and Singapore International Monetary Exchange trade a futures contract on the Nikkei. Currently, the margin on a Nikkei futures contract in Osaka is 27 per cent higher than the margin on an equivalent position in Singapore.

[44] For example, the Hong Kong Futures Exchange has A$113 million (HK$553.7 million) available, the Singapore International Monetary Exchange A$37 million (S$42 million) and the Sydney Futures Exchange has a fund size of A$100 million. In terms of composition, the Sydney Futures Exchange largely relies on members' deposits (60 per cent) and insurance (30 per cent) while Singapore relies on retained earnings (69 per cent) and its cash based fidelity fund (31 per cent).

Capital Markets

Price limits and trading halts

Price limits are regulated maximum allowable price movements on a futures contract. All East Asian futures exchanges except the Sydney Futures Exchange set such price limits.[45] Some commentators believe price limits calm markets during volatile trading, but increasingly, evidence indicates price limits can exacerbate price volatility, denying market agents the ability to trade when they are most keen to (Lee et al, 1994).

Effects on the cost of trading

While margins, financial guarantees and price limits safeguard markets from collapse, they increase trading costs. For example, trading costs for a Nikkei contract are implicitly higher in Osaka than Singapore because of higher margins and tighter price limits. While Osaka may well be a 'safer' place to trade, it has lost liquidity to Singapore and reduced the ability of market participants to adjust to new information, such as macroeconomic data.

Market Fairness

Market fairness regulation attempts to ensure all participants face the same trading conditions (Aitken and Berry, 1991). Key regulations creating fair markets include:

- banning dual trading so brokers cannot trade on their own account as well as for clients
- improving trading reporting procedures.

Many East Asian exchanges strongly regulate dual trading and reporting procedures, due in part to lessons learned from the Barings incident in 1995. However, enforcement can be problematic.

With fully computerised trading on most East Asian futures exchanges, new mechanisms to enhance reporting procedures and audit trails should be available. As in equity markets, improvements in market surveillance must keep pace with trading volumes to ensure market credibility.

THE BARINGS INCIDENT

Nick Leeson's unauthorised trading in the Nikkei stock index future on the Singapore International Monetary Exchange resulted in a £1 billion loss to Barings, rendering it insolvent. Leeson was able to conduct this unauthorised trading because he controlled both the trading and reporting function, preventing either Barings or the Singapore exchange becoming aware of the problem until it was too late to intervene.

Source: Hogan, 1997.

---

[45] For example, the Nikkei future traded on the Osaka Stock Exchange has a price limit of about 5 per cent from the previous day's closing price, while the price limit on a Nikkei future in Singapore is about 7.5 per cent.

MOVES TO AUTOMATED EXCHANGES

East Asia is at the forefront of fully computerised derivatives trading. Derivatives trading in Japan and Hong Kong already is fully computerised. The Sydney Futures Exchange closed its remaining three open outcry contracts on 15 November 1999. The Kuala Lumpur Options and Financial Futures Exchange had fully computerised trading at its inception in 1995, a trend repeated on East Asia's other smaller and newer exchanges. The Singapore International Monetary Exchange plans to introduce a new electronic trading system by the end of 1999, then will let the market decide between open outcry and fully computerised trade (SIMEX, 1999a). In contrast, the world's two largest futures exchanges, the Chicago Mercantile Exchange and Chicago Board of Trade, have yet to move to computerised trading.

As in equity markets, computerised trading is likely to increase competition among regional and world futures exchanges, improving investor access to products and stimulating alliances. Eurex, a major European exchange, currently uses a screen based electronic system to trade derivatives; it has won business from London due to the cost advantages of screen based trading and to the installation of trading terminals in foreign countries, including the United States.[46] Similar moves in East Asia by large regional or world exchanges could undermine the competitive position of smaller East Asian derivatives markets.

FOREIGN TRADERS IN DERIVATIVE MARKETS

Foreign traders can help East Asian futures markets to develop, contributing expertise, providing liquidity and raising risk bearing capacity. Foreign exchanges, in East Asia or elsewhere, can contribute significantly to regional economic health by listing derivatives based on assets or securities in other economies. This increases the range of products East Asian corporates can use to hedge risk.

Currently, euroyen and eurodollar products are the only offshore interest or exchange rate contracts listed on Asian futures exchanges. However, the Singapore International Monetary Exchange, SIMEX offers stock index derivatives for Thailand, Taiwan, Japan and Hong Kong; the Japanese and Taiwanese indices are well established. From 2000, the Sydney Futures Exchange jointly with Dow Jones will offer index products based on the Hong Kong and Japanese stock indices.

One barrier to East Asian futures exchanges listing offshore based products is the tendency for governments to see such futures contracts as national property. For example, the Stock Exchange of Hong Kong banned the supply of real time information to support a futures contract based on the Hang Sang Index listed on the Singapore International Monetary Exchange (*Australian Financial Review*, 9 November 1998).

---

[46] Eurex was formed from the alliance of the German Futures Exchange, Deutche Termin Bourse and the Swiss Option and Financial Futures Exchange.

However, this is gradually changing. The Korean Futures Exchange plans to allow listing of its products on foreign exchanges from 2000. (See Chapter 13 - *Korea*.) In future, trends towards demutualisation and mergers of futures and equities exchanges should foster more listing of foreign derivative products as increasingly, such opportunities will be judged commercially.

LIKELY FUTURE TRENDS IN EAST ASIAN DERIVATIVES MARKETS

The financial crisis should help regional derivative markets to develop, as price volatility drives derivatives volumes. The crisis also has alerted many regional companies to the benefits of hedging.

In the emerging era of fully computerised trading, exchanges must find the right balance between the stabilising effects of regulation and its costs. Smaller exchanges will need to form alliances and even merge, as liquidity is likely to congregate in large regional and global exchanges which will intensify efforts to increase access to their products. Pressure to merge and form comprehensive alliances is likely to increase after the alliance announced between the Chicago Board of Trade and Eurex in September 1999 (*Australian Financial Review*, 13 September 1999, p. 38).

THE SYDNEY FUTURES EXCHANGE AND SINGAPORE INTERNATIONAL MONETARY EXCHANGE: STRATEGIES TO IMPROVE PRODUCT DISTRIBUTION

The Sydney Futures Exchange is building trading hubs in London, New York, Chicago, Tokyo and Hong Kong, allowing members of the exchange or registered affiliates to access Sydney markets from these centres. The Sydney Futures Exchange also is moving to offer a wider range of international products; trading on Dow Jones compiled stock indices for Hong Kong and Japan will begin in early 2000. Opportunities for alliances with other exchanges also are being considered, although none has yet been confirmed.

Singapore International Monetary Exchange is a member of the GLOBEX alliance of futures exchanges, along with the Chicago Mercantile Exchange, Paris Bourse, Canada's Montreal Exchange and Brazil's Bolsa de Mercadorias and Futures. All these exchanges use a common electronic trading system, with each alliance member receiving direct access to all products of all markets in the alliance through one technical access. Cross margining of products is allowed to reduce the capital requirements of customers and members. From 2000, Singapore International Monetary Exchange also will begin placing trading terminals outside Singapore.

Source: Sydney Futures Exchange, 1999; and Singapore International Monetary Exchange, 1999a and 1999b.

CONCLUSIONS

Capital market regulation, particularly to ensure disclosure and market transparency, has not kept pace with the growth of markets and new trading technology. Enforcement of regulations, such as listing rules, also is a major constraint on the orderly growth of many regional exchanges. Hong Kong, Singapore and Australia have the most advanced regulatory and trading infrastructure; other economies are attempting to improve regulation and supervision.

Inadequate regulatory and settlement systems, discriminatory taxation, and a lack of credible credit rating agencies and benchmark yield curves constrain regional bond markets. Since these issues are interrelated, large gains should flow from comprehensive reforms.

Even if regulatory progress continues, smaller regional exchanges must face the challenge their lack of critical mass presents. This problem is particularly acute on many newer futures exchanges, where volume is minimal. Except for Japan, most East Asian equity markets are small in world terms and relatively costly to trade. Misplaced energy is spent on competition between exchanges; cooperation rarely extends beyond sharing surveillance information. By contrast, North American and European markets actively seek regional alliances and court cross-listings of companies from outside the region. Regional segmentation and competition run counter to international trends towards demutualisation and mergers of equities and futures exchanges, and ultimately disadvantage regional corporates seeking to raise finance and hedge risks.

REFERENCES

Aitken, M. and Berry, J., 1991, 'Market Surveillance: an Overview', Working Paper, Securities Industry Research Centre of Asia Pacific, University of Sydney, Sydney.

Aitken, M. and Swan, P., 1995, 'The Cost and Responsiveness of Equity Trading in Australia', Working Paper no. 9 5001e, Securities Industry Research Centre of Australia, University of Sydney, Sydney.

Aitken, M., Frino, A. and Jarnecic, E., 1996, 'Are Options Beneficial for Investors of Underlying Stocks?', *ASX Perspective*, third quarter, pp. 72-76.

Australian Stock Exchange, 1999, Information supplied to the East Asia Analytical Unit, October.

Backman, M., 1999, *Asia's Eclipse: Exposing the Dark Side of Business in Asia*, John Wiley and Sons, New York.

Banks, E., 1996, *Asia Pacific Derivatives Markets*, MacMillan, Basingstoke.

CEIC, 1999, CEIC Database, supplied by EconData, Canberra.

Computershare Limited, 1999, Information supplied to East Asia Analytical Unit, October.

Dalla, I., 1995, *The Emerging Asian Bond Market*, World Bank, Washington DC.

Department of Foreign Affairs and Trade, 1998, *The APEC Region Trade and Investment, November 1998*, Market Information and Analysis Unit, Canberra.

East Asia Analytical Unit, 1999, *Korea Rebuilds: from Crisis to Opportunity*, Department of Foreign Affairs and Trade, Canberra.

___ 1998, *Asia's Infrastructure in the Crisis: Harnessing Private Enterprise*, Department of Foreign Affairs and Trade, Canberra.

Euromoney, 1997, 'Building Bonds in a Floating Market', February, Internet publication, www.emwl.com, accessed on 11 September.

Federation of International Stock Exchanges, 1999, Annual and Monthly Reports 1990-1999, at www.fibv.com/ accessed on 23 August.

Financial Times, 1999, 'Companies and Markets: Plan for Single Europe Bourse Shelved. Eight Biggest Exchanges Rein in their Ambitions and Settle for Compromise Solution', Press release, 24 September, www.ft.com, accessed on 30 September.

Futures Communication, 1998, *Futures Magazine*, January, pp. 76-101.

Handbook of World Stock, Derivative and Commodity Exchanges, 1998, International Financial Publications, London.

Harris, L., 1989, 'S&P 500 Cash Stock Price Volatilities', *Journal of Finance*, vol. 46, no. 5, pp. 1155-75.

Harrison, M., 1997, *Asia-Pacific Securities Markets*, Third Edition, Financial Times, Financial Publishing, Asia Pacific.

Hodgson, A., and Nichols, D., 1990, 'The Impact of Index Futures Markets on Australian Sharemarket Volatility', *Journal of Business Finance and Accounting*, vol. 18, no. 2, pp. 267-80.

Hogan, W., 1997, 'Corporate Governance: Lessons from Barings', ABACUS, vol. 33, no. 2, pp. 252-65.

International Monetary Fund, 1999, *International Capital Markets: Development, Prospects, and Key Policy Issues*, Washington DC.

Korea Stock Exchange, 1999a, 'Review of the Korean Securities Market in 1998', www.kse.or.kr, accessed on 20 March.

___ 1998, *Fact Book: 1997*, Seoul.

Lee, C., Ready, M. and Seguin, P., 1994, 'Volume, Volatility and New York Stock Exchange Trading Halts', *Journal of Finance*, pp. 183-14.

Linnan, D., 1994, 'Indonesian Capital Market Development and Privatization', in McLeod, R.H. (ed.), *Indonesia Assessment 1994: Finance as a Key Sector in Indonesia's Development*, Australian National University, Canberra and Institute of South East Asian Studies, Singapore, pp. 223-47.

London Stock Exchange, 1999, 'European Stock Exchanges Agree Market Model - Electronic Market of Markets for European Bluechips by November 2000', Press release, 22 September, www.stockex.co.uk/new/new.asp, accessed on 25 October.

Mariano, R., 1999, 'An Assessment of Credit Rating Services in APEC Economies', Background paper for the APEC Consultative Group Workshop on The Credit Rating Industry in APEC Economies: Critical Issues for Capital Market Development, Asian Development Bank, 8-9 February, Manila.

Monetary Authority of Singapore, 1998, Notice 109, MAS, Singapore.

Quila, J., 1997, 'Developing a Regional Bond Market', Paper presented at the Third Asia Securities Forum, Asian Development Bank, Manila.

Radelet, S. and Sachs, J., 1998, 'The Onset of the East Asian Financial Crisis', Harvard Institute for International Development, Harvard University.

Reserve Bank of Australia, 1999, 'Australian Financial Markets', *Reserve Bank of Australia Bulletin*, March, pp. 1-12.

Reuters, 1998, 'Australia: Business - Stock Exchange's Cost Levels High by Global Standards', Reuters Business Briefing, 7 October.

Rosser, A., 1999, 'Creating Markets: the Politics of Economic Liberalisation in Indonesia since the Mid 1980s', PhD dissertation, Murdoch University.

SIMEX, 1999a, Singapore International Monetary Exchange Limited, 'SIMEX ETS: Electronic Trading System', www.simex.com.sg/ets.html, accessed on 26 October.

___ 1999b, 'Canada's Montreal Exchange Joins Globex Alliance with CME, Parisbourse, Simex, OM&F', Press release, 15 September, www.simex.com.sg/news50.html, accessed on 15 October.

Sobol, D., 1998, 'Foreign Ownership of US Treasury Securities: What the Data Show and Do Not Show', *Current Issues in Economics and Finance*, Federal Reserve Bank of New York, New York, May.

Stock Exchange of Thailand, 1999, '15 Companies Face Possible Delisting', Press release no. 16, www.set.or.th, accessed on 20 July 1999.

Sydney Futures Exchange, 1999a, *SFE Bulletin*, January, p. 1.

___ 1999b, Information supplied to the East Asia Analytical Unit, October.

Taiwan Stock Exchange Corporation, 1999, 'Major Progress in 1998, www.plan.tse.com.tw/plan_depart/publish/Eannual, accessed on 1 October 1999.

Tsang, D., 1998, 'Asian Bond Market', Speech to Asian Debt Conference, 6 July, Hong Kong, www.info.gov.hk/hkma/eng/speeches, accessed on 8 November.

Webster, R., 1997, 'The Emergence of an Invigorated Domestic Bond Market', International Banks and Securities Association of Australia, Paper presented at Issuing and Investing in Corporate Bonds Forum, IBC Conferences.

World Bank, 1997, 'Philippines: Managing Global Integration', vol. 1, Report no. 17 024-PH, East Asia and Regional Office, Manila.

Chapter 6

NON-BANK FINANCIAL INSTITUTIONS

In some regional economies, poorly regulated non-bank financial institutions, NBFIs, contributed significantly to the financial crisis. However, in the medium term, as East Asia resumes normal growth, NBFIs should grow rapidly and help deepen and broaden the region's financial systems. In developed economies, life insurers and pension funds play an important role in lengthening the term structure of savings and investable funds and fostering bond market development. Stronger regulation and more liberal market access should reinforce NBFIs' growing importance in East Asia and generate many opportunities for foreign financial institutions.

This chapter first assesses the role poorly regulated NBFIs played in triggering the financial crisis and reviews the main trends in regulatory reform affecting NBFIs. It then examines market developments in regional life insurance and pension fund industries, and finally assesses prospects and opportunities for foreign financial institutions.

THE NATURE AND ROLE OF NBFIs

The myriad of NBFIs fall into three broad categories:

- deposit taking institutions, such as credit cooperatives, credit unions and finance companies, which do not hold a banking licence but take deposits and lend, often in closely defined areas

- risk hedging institutions, such as life and general insurers, which provide risk cover in return for the payment of regular premiums

- pension and superannuation funds, which provide vehicles to accumulate funds for retirement income.

Generally, NBFIs become more important as populations become wealthier, as people can afford to pay for the services of life and general insurers, accumulate savings for old age, and use consumer credit from finance companies (Drake, 1980; and Fry, 1988). Before the crisis, all these NBFIs were growing rapidly and as regional economies recover, NBFIs' role in financial markets should grow. Improving these institutions' regulatory frameworks therefore is a high priority for regional governments.

Well supervised NBFIs encourage financial sector innovation, expand the range of savings and risk management vehicles, and contribute to economic stability and development. For example, the growth of Latin American pension funds promoted asset-backed securitisation, thus assisting in establishing a major new type of financial product in Latin America (Quessier, 1999).[1] As pension fund and insurance company liabilities generally are long term, they help lengthen the term structure of saving and investment finance, reducing vulnerability to short term bank lending cycles and international capital flows.[2] By demanding and actively trading long term commercial paper, NBFIs also encourage primary and secondary bond markets.[3]

Credit cooperatives often constitute the first form of deposit taking institution in many rural areas. Even in very low income economies, they can play an important role pooling rural savings and making them available for investment. For example, China's rural and urban credit cooperatives still are growing rapidly and hold 10 per cent of financial assets (Figure 12.1). Credit cooperatives also significantly helped mobilise savings in Japan and Taiwan. Lack of rural credit cooperatives has inhibited Philippine savings performance (East Asia Analytical Unit, 1998).

POORLY REGULATED NBFIs AND THE CRISIS

As NBFIs sometimes are established to avoid the tight prudential controls applied to banks, NBFIs were prominent in financial system failure in Thailand, Malaysia and Korea. For example, in Thailand, local finance companies obtained funds from high yielding promissory notes and foreign currency borrowing, then lent in local currency to relatively high risk clients who often could not obtain bank loans. Between January 1990 and December 1996, Thai finance company loans and receivables increased more than five fold (Figure 6.1), but the very risky structure of this lending made them the first financial institutions to fail in 1997.[4] (See Chapter 8 - *Thailand, Malaysia and the Philippines*.) The Thai Government was forced to close 69 insolvent finance companies and auction their assets.

Malaysia's finance companies also experienced major problems. As in Thailand, a key growth area was hire purchase loans; these were affected adversely by rising interest rates and sharply slowing growth flowing from the onset of the crisis.[5] In both Thailand and Malaysia, poor regulatory oversight of finance companies and their rapid lending growth also contributed to the financial crisis indirectly, by increasing pressure on banks to lower lending standards and increase lending volumes to maintain their market share.

---

[1] Institutional investors, such as pension funds and insurance companies, are likely to be particularly interested in asset-backed securities as they often do not have the expertise and information to assess loan risk and directly collect repayments (Quessier, 1999).

[2] Chile's pension funds reduced that economy's vulnerability to volatile international capital flows. After 1981, Chile developed a comprehensive pension system, replacing its public pay-as-you-go scheme with a fully funded, privately managed system. In both the 'Tequila' financial crisis in 1995 and the Asian financial crisis of 1997-98, Chile enjoyed relative calm, partly because it relied more on domestic funds available through its pension funds (Quessier, 1999).

[3] Deeper bond markets also assist macroeconomic management by dampening yield volatility associated with large government bond issues.

[4] In early 1997, high interest rates associated with the baht's defence caused Thai stock and property prices to fall and escalated non-performing loans, NPLs. When the baht sharply depreciated in mid 1997, many finance companies could not service their foreign borrowings.

[5] Between 1990 and 1997, hire purchase loans from Malaysian finance companies grew on average by 22 per cent per year (CEIC, 1999). Like Thailand, the industry also was highly fragmented with 39 companies.

Figure 6.1

Pre-crisis, Thai Finance Companies Expand Rapidly
Loans and Receivables of Thai Finance Companies, January 1990 to December 1996

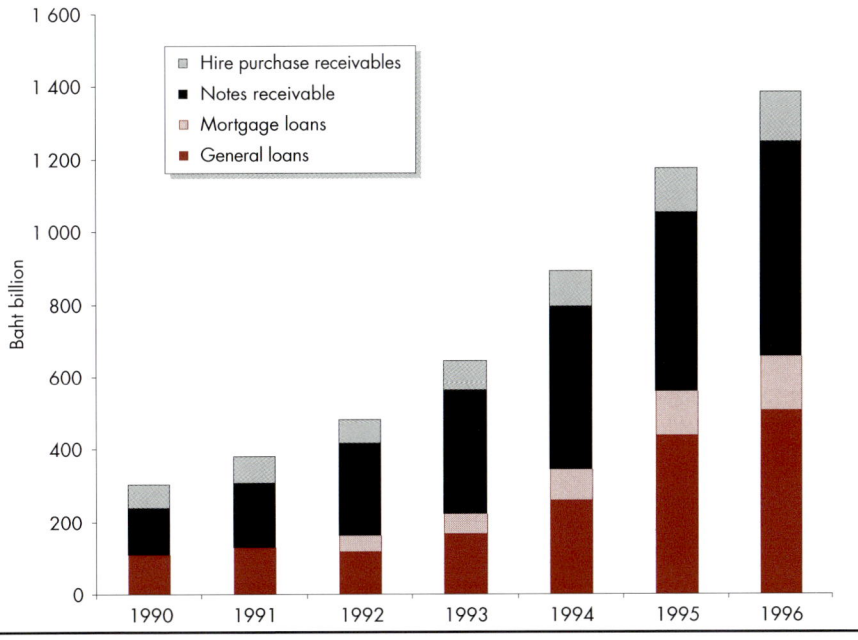

Source: CEIC, 1999.

Korea's merchant banks engaged in similarly risky borrowing and lending practices, borrowing offshore and at high interest rates from local financial markets to lend in local currency to marginal projects. By October 1997, they had borrowed US$20 billion in short term funds from international financial markets to lend to highly leveraged *chaebol* for excessive capacity expansion (East Asia Analytical Unit, 1999). This borrowing contributed significantly to the build up of short term foreign debt; this was central to the rapid reversal of foreign investor sentiment towards Korea in late 1997. As the won rapidly depreciated, many merchant banks became insolvent. Soon after signing the IMF package in December 1997, the Korean Government closed 16 merchant banks and by early 1999, only 14 remained.

China's international trust and investment companies also undertook large scale foreign borrowing and made speculative local investments, causing many to become insolvent. Guangdong International Trust and Investment Corporation went bankrupt in October 1998 with liabilities of around US$4 billion to foreign creditors, and many other trust and investment companies are being closed or restructured. (See Chapter 12 - China.)

Causes of Poor NBFI Performance

The poor supervision and enforcement which contributed to regional economies' NBFI problems were most obvious in Thailand and Korea, where NBFIs' unhedged foreign exchange exposure rose rapidly without regulators intervening to prevent it. Chinese regulators also permitted trust and investment corporations to enter speculative business areas well beyond their original business scope. Similarly, Japan's agricultural cooperatives were permitted to acquire a dangerously high exposure to the real estate sector.

Lack of clear regulatory responsibility for NBFIs often exacerbated supervisory problems. For example, in Japan, the Ministry of Finance shared responsibility for supervising the *jusen* or housing loan companies and farmers' cooperatives with the Ministry of Agriculture, the Ministry of International Trade and Industry, and other agencies; this shared responsibility contributed to the regulatory failure in regard to the *jusen* (East Asia Analytical Unit, 1997).[6] Similarly, the Ministry of the Interior, the Ministry of Finance and the Council of Agriculture jointly supervise Taiwan's credit cooperatives (*Taipei Times*, 26 July 1999, p. 3). In China, the Agricultural Bank of China, which had little supervisory capacity, previously oversaw rural credit cooperatives, many of which have failed.

NBFIs often are exposed to risk because they service a limited sector of the economy or have a narrow product range. For example, once interest rates rose, high exposure to hire purchase lending weakened Malaysian finance companies. East Asian property and housing lending, another important NBFI business area, also was hurt by falling property values and rising interest rates. The specialised nature of NBFIs also implies a narrow skills base, so poor investment decisions become more likely once NBFIs move beyond core business areas. For example, Japan's agricultural cooperatives are supposed to serve the financial needs of farmers, but lent funds to Japan's failed housing loan companies to access Japan's booming property market. Major difficulties followed.

Non-financial companies also owned NBFIs, further contributing to their poor performance. For example, in Korea, *chaebol* owned many merchant banks and other NBFIs which undertook high risk activities to raise funds to finance *chaebol* activities.[7]

Recent Tightening of Regulatory Regimes

The financial crisis' severe effect on banking systems caused most regional governments to initially give priority to tightening banking regulations; as banking problems are resolved, focus should shift to NBFI regulatory regimes. A vital NBFI regulatory reform underway in several regional economies is supervisory consolidation. Consolidation should help clarify regulatory and supervisory responsibility for NBFIs straddling several sectors. (See Chapter 3 - *Prudential Reform*.)

---

[6] During the 'bubble economy' period of 1987 to 1991, Japan's seven housing loan companies, the *jusen*, lent increasing amounts to property development. When the bubble burst, land values collapsed and NPLs soared. In June 1996, the *jusen's* business was assumed by the Housing Loan Administration Corporation with the Government contributing ¥685 billion (approximately US$6 billion) to repay depositors (*Economist*, 23 December 1995, pp. 93-95).

[7] In 1997, the 70 largest *chaebol* owned 109 financial affiliates, concentrated among securities firms, merchant banks and non-life insurance firms (Smith, 1999). The *chaebol* used their affiliated NBFIs, especially their overseas branches, to finance the activities of group subsidiaries (Nam et al, 1999).

> **CONSOLIDATING NBFI SUPERVISION**
>
> Many regional economies, including Australia, Korea, Japan and Indonesia, are consolidating prudential control of NBFIs and banks. In 1998, the Australian Prudential Regulatory Authority was formed to consolidate Australian NBFI and bank supervision, with state based NBFIs transferring to this new regime from July 1999. In January 1999, the Korean Financial Supervisory Service was created to bring together four pre-existing supervisory authorities including those responsible for NBFIs.[8] Japan also has consolidated supervisory power, although the Financial Supervisory Agency continues to share regulatory authority for some NBFIs with other ministries. Indonesia has announced it will undertake a prudential consolidation in 2002. (See Chapter 7 - Indonesia.)
>
> Several other regional economies are consolidating some supervision, although there are also contrary trends. For example, the People's Bank of China now regulates Chinese credit cooperatives, but in November 1998, the China Insurance Regulatory Commission was split off from the People's Bank to become the insurance industry regulator. Similarly, analysts expect the ongoing review of Thailand's banking laws probably will produce some consolidation of NBFI supervision, but the Ministry of Commerce will continue to supervise insurance.

Another important prudential reform is to apply banking capital adequacy and provisioning regulations to NBFIs, making regulation of banks and NBFIs more consistent. For example, in 1998, the Korean Government extended to insurance companies, newly tightened bank regulations on loan classification, capital adequacy, provisioning, large exposures, connected lending and disclosure. Similarly, Japan and Indonesia now impose risk weighted capital requirements on their life insurers.[9]

General regulatory regime tightening also affects many NBFIs. (See Chapter 3 - Prudential Reforms.) For example, governments adopting international accounting standards for stock and property portfolio valuations usually also require insurance and pension funds to value their assets at market value.

INSURANCE COMPANIES

As East Asian incomes rise, life insurers and pension funds should become increasingly important. While the primary purpose of life insurance is to provide individuals with a means of protecting themselves from risks, such as death and injury, a well managed life insurance and pension fund sector plays an important financial role, pooling large volumes of long term savings for productive investment

---

[8] The Financial Supervisory Service brings together the Banking Supervisory Authority, the Securities Supervisory Board and the Non-bank Supervisory Board (East Asia Analytical Unit, 1999).

[9] Japan introduced a 200 per cent solvency margin ratio, or ratio of capital and unrealised profit to risk weighted assets. In July 1999, Indonesia also moved to a risk based capital system and raised minimum capitalisation requirements from Rp 3 billion to Rp 100 billion.

NBFIs

in long term assets. Insurers and pension funds boost demand in bond and security markets, developing alternative corporate financing sources. Regional insurance, pension and capital markets all provide increasingly significant opportunities for foreign financial institutions.

Patterns of Life Insurance Demand

East Asian trends in per capita life insurance uptake mainly reflect economies' per capita GNP. Japan has by far the highest life insurance use, and Indonesia the lowest (Figure 6.2).[10] However, Korea, Taiwan, Malaysia, Singapore and Thailand all have high life insurance demand compared to other economies at their income level (Figure 6.3).[11] In Indonesia, the Philippines and China, life insurance demand is about average for economies at their respective income levels, while in Hong Kong, life insurance demand is below average.

Figure 6.2

Japan Is Asia's Largest Life Insurance Market
Life Insurance Density Premiums Per Capita and GNP Per Capita, 1997

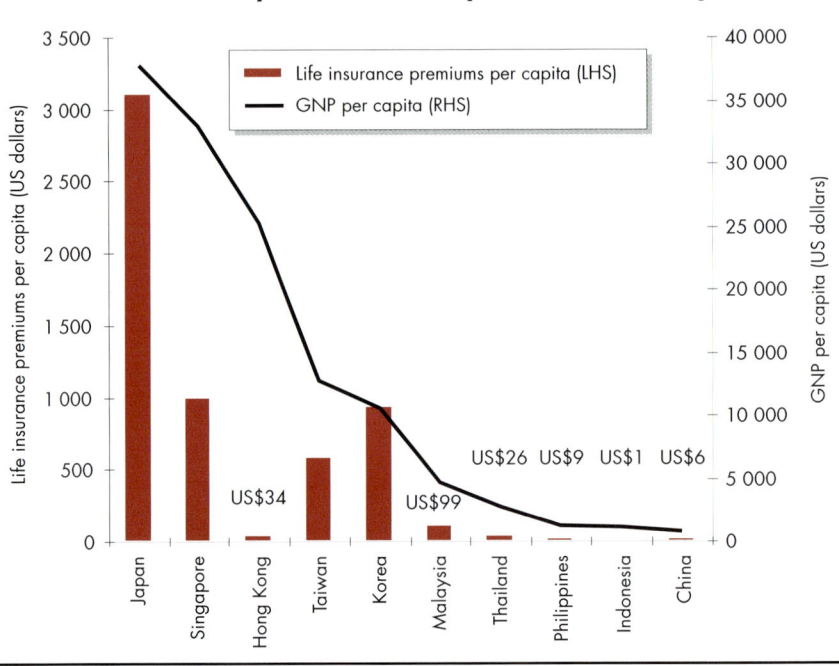

Source: Sigma, 1999; and World Bank, 1998.

[10] Korea is the main exception. Its insurance demand is around the same level as Singapore's despite having only one third the per capita GNP. Korea's high level of life insurance demand is mainly because insurance companies also tend to provide banking services (Sigma, 1998).

[11] The statistically estimated average level of demand for insurance for any particular income level is represented by the S shaped curve in Figure 6.3.

Figure 6.3

Insurance Demand Relatively High in Many East Asian Economies
Life Insurance as a Share of GDP Relative to Per Capita GDP, 1997

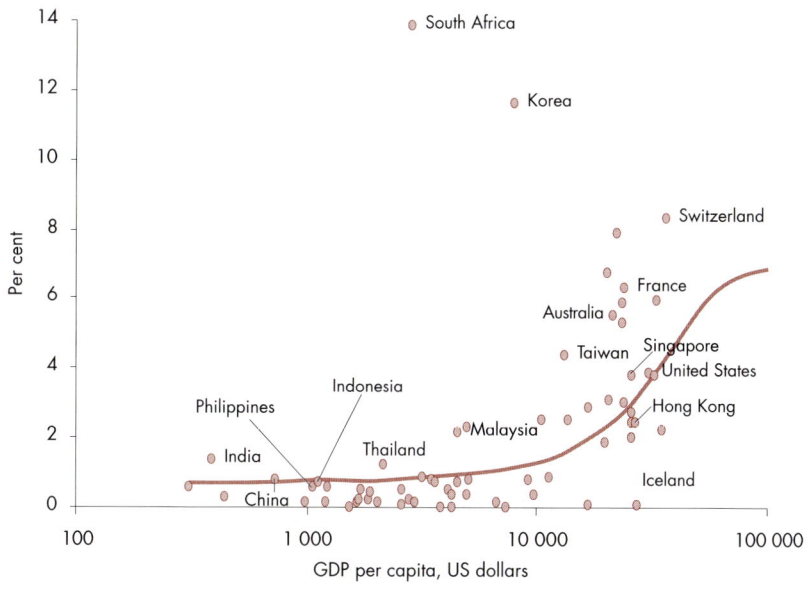

Note: The S shaped curve represents the statistically estimated best fit relationship between per capita GDP and insurance premium share of GDP.
Source: Sigma, 1999.

In 1996 and 1997, gross local currency life insurance premiums expanded by over 10 per cent per year in all East Asian economies except Japan, Korea and Thailand (Figure 6.4).[12] China's market grew the most rapidly.

Impact of the Financial Crisis

In 1998, many distressed households and corporates cashed in policies, so local currency premium growth declined significantly. The crisis most severely affected premium growth in Thailand, Indonesia and Malaysia, while it had the least impact in the Philippines. China's slowing economic growth also reduced new business growth there.

The proliferation of under-performing assets and loans also severely affected many East Asian insurers, diminishing their capital. In 1998 and 1999, authorities closed five insolvent Korean life insurers and a further 16 insurers are being rehabilitated (East Asia Analytical Unit, 1999). Two Japanese life insurers have gone bankrupt

---

[12] The large exchange rate depreciations in 1997 caused premium income, measured in US dollars, to fall in Thailand, Korea and Japan (Figure 6.4).

Figure 6.4

Strong Life Insurance Premium Growth before 1997

Growth of East Asian Local Currency and Insurance Premium Income

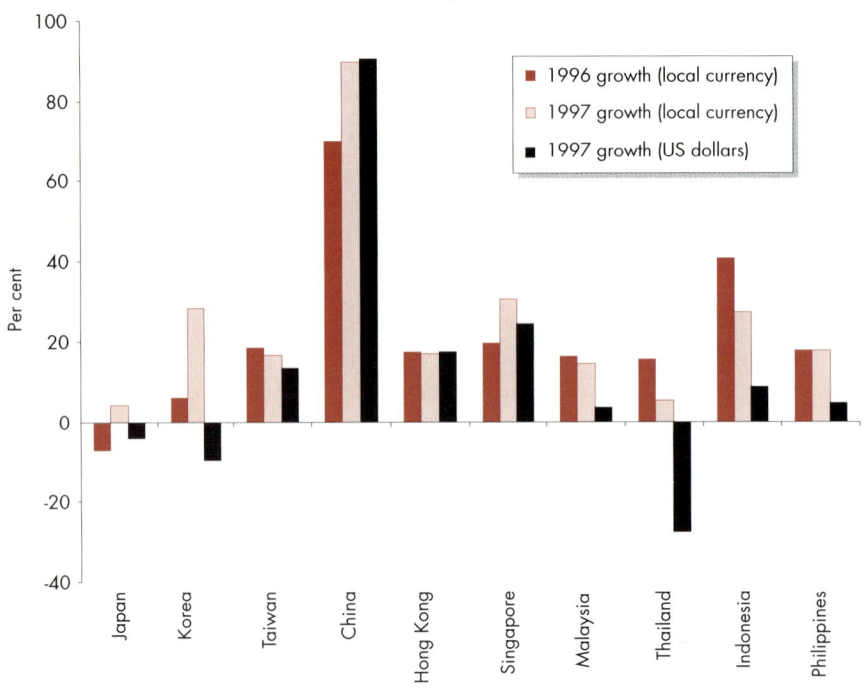

Note: Growth in US dollar premium income is only shown for 1997.
Source: Sigma, 1999.

since 1997.[13] (See Chapter 11 - *Japan*.) No Malaysian insurers closed but the Government delayed implementing new minimum paid up capital and solvency margin requirements.[14] Throughout the region, further closures of poorly capitalised insurers are possible.

Insurance beyond the Crisis

Despite these setbacks, the regional life insurance industry's outlook is good. As demand for life insurance usually exceeds GDP growth, once household income growth recovers, life insurance demand is likely to grow rapidly.[15] Furthermore,

---

[13] Nissan Mutual Life collapsed in April 1997 and Toho Mutual Life collapsed in mid 1999.

[14] Capital and solvency margin requirements were phased in from early 1997, and set to increase again in January 1999, but were postponed in October 1998. In July 1999, the Government introduced a new timetable for these measures, with full implementation by the end of 2000 (Bank Negara Malaysia, 1999a and 1999b).

[15] For example, gross Chinese premiums written grew 32 per cent per year between 1987 and 1997, considerably higher than the annual average growth of nominal GDP, 20.7 per cent. Similarly, in the Philippines, gross premiums of life insurance companies increased by 17.6 per cent in 1996 and 28.6 per cent in 1997 compared to annual nominal GDP growth of 13.9 per cent and 11.5 per cent (CEIC, 1999).

Korea, Taiwan, Thailand, Indonesia and the Philippines have rather rudimentary and poorly enforced public pension schemes; employees and employers contribute less than 10 per cent of wages to these schemes (Sigma, 1998).[16] Consequently, demand for private life insurance and pension schemes will increase to provide supplementary retirement benefits.

Furthermore, the aging of many East Asian populations is likely to boost demand for life insurance. In 1995, 9 per cent of Asia's population was over 60, but by 2025 this proportion will double (World Bank, 1994). By 2025, Japan, Hong Kong, Singapore, Taiwan and Korea will have more than 22 per cent of their populations over 60. The rising ratio of dependants to workers will strain in-family old age care and public pension systems. Consequently, policy makers are likely to encourage retirees to provide more for themselves, including through life insurance.

Additional Challenges in Asian Life Insurance Markets

The immediate challenge for many regional life insurers is lack of capital. Relaxing restrictions on foreign equity participation would help solve this problem. Introducing and strengthening capital and solvency margin requirements also would help raise capital levels over time.

Many economies also need to relax restrictions on insurers' investment strategies to enable them to maximise risk weighted returns for policy holders. In particular, because offshore markets often are less volatile than small domestic markets, increased foreign investment would increase insurance company rates of return and spread risks.[17]

Regulations in many regional economies require life insurers to offer policy holders guaranteed yields rather than market determined returns. As long term interest rates have fallen below returns guaranteed, many Korean, Japanese and Chinese insurers have incurred large unfunded liabilities, so called 'yield gaps'. For example, in fiscal 1998, Japan's seven major life insurers reported a negative yield gap of ¥1.3 trillion (*Nikkei Weekly*, 14 June 1999, p. 8).[18] A lack of actuarial understanding among regulators also can result in insurers being forced to set unrealistic premiums.[19]

Some regional governments also favour incumbent, often state owned insurers. In China, new domestic or foreign life insurance companies can only operate in either life or property and casualty insurance, increasing the cost of marketing infrastructure and reducing cross-selling opportunities. (See Chapter 12 - *China*.) In Indonesia, state owned insurers receive most of the business of state owned enterprises which dominate the overall insurance market. (See Chapter 7 - *Indonesia*.)

---

[16] Thailand does not have a general public pension scheme at all. (See Table 6.1.)

[17] Many regional governments restrict life insurance companies to investing mainly in bank accounts, blue chip stocks and government bonds. However, in Indonesia and China, these restrictions saved life insurance companies from high exposure to risky assets. Hence, liberalising these restrictions will need care and should be accompanied by skills upgrading and close supervision.

[18] Despite lowering the guaranteed minimum return in April 1996, a large proportion of Japan's outstanding stock of insurance policies still carries a guaranteed yield of 5 per cent (International Monetary Fund, 1998).

[19] For example, in Thailand, regulators are unwilling to accept that the rapid spread of AIDS will affect life insurance payouts and therefore, must be reflected in premiums.

A further challenge in regional insurance markets is to reduce the cost of reinsurance and stimulate more active reinsurance markets.[20] The high cost of reinsurance can discourage its use, exposing domestic and foreign insurers to excessive risk. Furthermore, the high cost of reinsurance or lack of reinsurance options can deter international companies from taking on particular risks.

Openness to Foreign Investment

Before the crisis, Singapore, Hong Kong and the Philippines had the region's most open insurance markets (McGuire et al, 1998). In 1994, the Philippine life insurance market was liberalised substantially, allowing foreigners to fully own insurance companies; by 1997, 14 major foreign insurers serviced 58 per cent of the Philippine market (Insurance Commission, 1998).[21] However, other economies also were liberalising their markets. In 1992, Taiwan partially liberalised international entry to its insurance industry, but US life insurers, which gained priority entry from an earlier bilateral agreement dominate the market. (See Chapter 10 - *Taiwan*.) Japan has few formal barriers to international entry; consequently, the grave problems and large portfolios of domestic life insurers are attracting many international life insurers, particularly from the United States. (See Chapter 11 - *Japan*.)

Since the crisis, several East Asian economies have liberalised international access to their insurance industries. Foreign insurers' role in the Korean market should increase; Korea lifted all restrictions on foreign equity in the insurance industry in 1998. Korea's Financial Supervisory Commission is accepting bids from domestic and foreign investors for five ailing insurance companies and holding an international auction for Korea Life Insurance, the third largest life insurer.

Chinese authorities also are cautiously liberalising the insurance sector, issuing nine licences to international insurance companies by the end of 1998. However, foreign insurance companies must operate as joint ventures with Chinese firms and most only can operate in Shanghai.[22] Moreover, like new domestic entrants, they can enter only the life or property and casualty markets. Consequently, foreign insurers' market share remains small; the main benefits for consumers are improved products and services. (See Chapter 12 - *China*.)

In mid 1999, Thailand raised the foreign ownership ceiling for life and non-life insurers from 25 to 49 per cent, while Indonesia lifted its limit to 99 per cent. In both economies, struggling local firms seek foreign partners. In Singapore, international life insurers already supply over 50 per cent of the market, and the Government is likely to allow new entrants following a report due by the end of 1999 (Lee, 1999).[23]

These moves throughout the region will open many new opportunities for foreign insurers, particularly given the Asian insurance market's bright medium term outlook.

....

20   Reinsurance is the spreading of insurance risk between insurers. In return for a premium, an insurer may pass all or part of the insurance risk to another insurer.

21   Up to 40 per cent foreign equity was allowed for 60 years prior to that. Under the new rules, foreign insurers must be in the top ten insurers in their country of origin and in the top 200 insurers in the world.

22   Exceptions include AIA, which already operates in four cities, and in 1999, John Hancock, Prudential and Sunlife which, as part of China's bid for World Trade Organisation membership, received provisional approval to operate in four cities other than Shanghai.

23   After 1986, Singapore's insurance market was closed to most new domestic and foreign entrants; only one direct life insurer was admitted (Lee, 1999).

> ### CMG ASIA – THE ASIAN CRISIS AND BEYOND
>
> The Colonial Group is a diversified, Australian, international financial services group with core businesses in insurance, superannuation, banking and funds management, and a presence in 12 markets. The Colonial Group entered Asia in 1990 through its wholly-owned subsidiary, CMG Asia. It operates wholly-owned businesses in Hong Kong and the Philippines, and has joint-venture partnerships in Thailand, Malaysia and Indonesia. In 1998 it was the eighth foreign life insurer invited to apply for a licence to set up a life insurance business in China, where it recently signed a contract with China Life Insurance Company to form a joint venture. (See Chapter 12 - China.)
>
> While the Asian crisis affected CMG Asia in 1998, given the difficult operating environment, CMG Asia's performance exceeded expectations. CMG Asia's Thai operation gained market share in a depressed market; new Philippine business sales increased 24 per cent; new Malaysian business increased 2 per cent; and even new Indonesian sales rose 4 per cent in local currency terms. An expanding sales force and new products significantly increased new Hong Kong business in 1999.
>
> CMG Asia is continuing to expand its role in the region. By acquiring Guardian Assurance, the group is well placed to participate in Hong Kong's Mandatory Provident Fund. Recently, it also signed a joint-venture agreement to develop a life insurance business in Vietnam. CMG Asia plans to continue expanding its presence in Asia through organic growth, with joint-venture partners and through acquisition, as opportunities arise.
>
> Source: Colonial Mutual Group Asia, 1999.

PENSION FUNDS

While improved pension fund management is critical to finance the retirement of East Asia's aging populations; the maturity of the industry varies significantly across the region.

Public Pension Schemes

East Asia's most comprehensive pension schemes are Singapore's Central Provident Fund and Malaysia's Employees Provident Fund. Both schemes were established in the 1950s, and require compulsory employer and employee contributions. By 1996, pension fund assets equalled 56 per cent of Singapore's GDP and 47 per cent of Malaysia's (Quessier, 1999). However, one concern with these schemes is poor returns. For example, between 1987 and 1996, the estimated real average annual returns in Singapore's Central Provident Fund was -0.3 per cent (*Asia Pensions*, 1998).[24] Reasons for these low returns include a tendency to 'buy and hold' bonds, the limited range of permitted investable assets, favouring government bonds, and a tendency to sometimes invest on non-economic grounds.[25]

---

[24] A World Bank study estimated a real rate of return of 3 per cent per year between 1980 and 1990 (*Asia Pensions*, 1998).

[25] For example, since October 1997, Malaysia's Employees Provident Fund lent Ringitt 1 billion to the new international airport and Ringitt 710 million to a local steel maker that the government had twice before bailed out of bankruptcy (*Asia Pensions*, 1998).

Japan, Taiwan, the Philippines, Indonesia and Korea also have state pension schemes but their coverage and compliance vary greatly (Table 6.1). Taiwan's obligatory public scheme has low compliance as penalties often are less than the required contributions, and only 30 per cent of the population participate in the Philippines' compulsory public pension scheme (*Asia Pensions*, 1998). While Indonesia's Provident Fund was established in the 1950s, less than 10 per cent of the population participate in any pension scheme (*Asia Pensions*, 1998). Korea's pension system still is rudimentary and retirees receive only a few years' salary (Sigma, 1998).

Table 6.1

Singaporean and Malaysian Public Pension Systems Most Comprehensive
Public Pension Plans in East Asia

	Pension system	Coverage	Financing (per cent gross salaries)
Hong Kong	Mandatory Provident Fund (from 2000) - obligatory - fully funded	Old age, disability	Employer: 5 Employee: 5 Maximum contribution HK$1 000 per month
Indonesia	Public social security plan - obligatory - pay as you go	Old age, disability, death	Employer: 3.7 Employee: 2
Korea	Public old age insurance - obligatory - pay as you go	Old age, disability, death	Employer: 2 Employee: 2
Malaysia	Public social security plan (Employees Provident Fund) - obligatory - fully funded	Old age, disability, death, health	Employer: 12 Employee: 11
Philippines	Public old age insurance - obligatory	Old age, disability, death, pregnancy	Employer: 5.1 Employee: 3.3
Singapore	Public social security plan (Central Provident Fund) - obligatory - fully funded	Old age, disability, death, health, accident	Employer: 10 Employee: 20
Taiwan	Public old age insurance - obligatory - pay as you go	Old age, disability, death	Employer: 6.5 Employee: 1.4
Thailand	No obligatory, general pension Government Pension Fund (for government employees only)		

Source: Sigma, 1998.

China and Hong Kong both are introducing major new pension schemes. China's unified pension system reform law provides the framework for the staged introduction of a universal, funded pension scheme, initially for the urban population. This scheme will be managed at provincial and municipal levels with strict investment strategy guidelines, and is based on a three pillar approach:

- universal benefits (the basic state pension) financed by payroll taxes to provide subsistence living for a retiree after 40 years' employment
- a fully funded mandatory employer contribution to top up the basic state pension with contributions maintained in individual accounts
- an optional supplementary pension offered by enterprises or subscribed to by individuals.

Funds accumulated under the third pillar are likely to be managed by life insurance groups outside the formal pension system. These opportunities are a major area of interest of foreign life insurance companies in China. At least on a pilot basis, foreign insurance companies also are keen to assist in efficiently investing and managing funds invested under the first two pillars.

Hong Kong's Mandatory Provident Fund, to be introduced in November 2000, will be Hong Kong's first universal pension scheme. Employers will be free to select their private sector Mandatory Provident Fund provider and employees will be able to invest in a range of unit trusts and mutual funds. Only 30 per cent of fund managers' assets need be in Hong Kong dollars (*Asia Pensions*, 1998). Fierce competition among domestic and foreign fund managers should promote financial product innovation and capital market development. However, strict pricing regulations and the scale economies flowing from a large customer base mean participants will need to win a substantial market share to generate satisfactory rates of return.[26] Australian based AXA National Mutual Holdings and CMG Asia are actively targeting this market.

Important issues affecting the Mandatory Provident Fund's operation include ensuring compliance from smaller, labour cost conscious employers and a highly mobile workforce. The high degree of labour force mobility makes fund portability a major issue and will raise administrative costs (*Asia Pensions*, 1998). The supervisory framework of the Mandatory Provident Fund also is fragmented; fund managers will be supervised by three different supervisory bodies. (See Chapter 9 - Hong Kong and Singapore.)

Private Sector Pension Schemes

All regional economies offer private sector pension cover in at least one sector, or offer proxies that replicate pension provision (Table 6.2). Most private sector retirement provision is occupational. Generally funds are managed internally, so the fund is closely aligned to the company offering the scheme. This is dangerous due to lack of investment expertise, potential for investment in company related projects and risk of losing invested funds if a company becomes insolvent.

---

[26] Scale economies likely to arise include reduced unit costs for providing infrastructure, such as computing facilities, and account maintenance software and cross-marketing opportunities.

> **AXA CHINA REGION AIMS TO DEVELOP HONG KONG OPPORTUNITY**
>
> As the second largest insurer in Hong Kong with one million clients, Australian based financial services group, AXA National Mutual Holdings, through its subsidiary, AXA China Region, expects to be a key provider of services to Hong Kong's Mandatory Provident Fund. AXA China Region will tap the global AXA group's experience in managing retirement and superannuation funds.
>
> AXA National Mutual Holdings currently owns 75 per cent of AXA China Region. In October 1999 it made an offer to acquire outstanding shares from minority shareholders.[27] This offer aims to increase AXA National Mutual Holdings' exposure to the Hong Kong market and to AXA China Region's newly established Shanghai joint-venture operation, consistent with its long term strategy to be a leading financial services group in the Asia-Pacific region.
>
> Source: AXA National Mutual Holdings, 1999.

In principle, except for Indonesia, all regional providers of occupational funds must fund pensions through a separate pension fund rather than the company balance sheet (*Asia Pensions*, 1998). Only Thailand requires all occupational schemes to be managed externally (Table 6.2). In Hong Kong, Japan, Singapore and Taiwan, a mixture of internal and external management exists. Indonesian legislation passed in 1992 gave companies five years to establish independent funding of pension liabilities (*Asia Pensions*, 1998). However, widespread corporate insolvency caused by the financial crisis will disastrously affect the retirement provisions of many Indonesians as many pensions still were funded through company balance sheets.

Another major issue with occupational pensions is that often they cannot be transferred between jobs. In mid 1998, pensions were not portable in Hong Kong, Japan or Korea (*Asia Pensions*, 1998). In Korea and Japan, this is largely due to a tradition of lifetime employment with the large employers. However, with intensifying pressure on large Japanese and Korean companies making lifetime employment guarantees untenable, pension portability is becoming important.

---

[27] At the time of printing this offer had not been finalised.

Table 6.2
Many Private Insurance Funds Managed Internally
Private Pension Provision and Management in East Asia

	Private sector occupational schemes	Private sector non-occupational schemes	Externally managed private schemes
China[a]	✓		
Hong Kong	✓		P
Indonesia	✓	✓	
Japan	✓	✓	P
Malaysia	✓	✓	
Philippines	✓	✓	
Singapore	✓		P
Korea	✓	✓	
Taiwan	✓		P
Thailand	✓	✓	✓

Note: a In China, occupational pension schemes are permitted for joint ventures, for foreign firms and among the self employed.
P means partial external management is permitted.
Source: Adapted from *Asia Pensions*, 1998.

Restrictions on Fund Management

Most regional governments are easing previously tight restrictions on what pension fund investments are permitted and who manages assets. This trend is likely to accelerate, driven by the need to reduce risk, raise returns on funds as populations age and minimise unfunded liabilities.[28] While Hong Kong's Mandatory Provident Fund will have the region's most liberal regulatory regime, other economies also are reforming pension policy. Over the years, the Singapore Government has liberalised the Central Provident Fund's rather restrictive regulatory regime. Participants now can invest in major world markets via unit trusts.[29] In a separate reform, between 1998 and 2000, the Government will put out S$35 billion of Central Provident Fund assets for private fund management. However, two government-owned companies still manage most funds.

Since November 1996, the Malaysian Government also has allowed Employees Provident Fund participants to invest in some approved fund management institutions. To date, the amounts are small compared to total Employees Provident Fund assets, and investments in foreign funds are negligible.[30]

---

[28] In a funded scheme, contributions are invested to 'fund' the eventual benefit payments to members. In an unfunded scheme, benefits are paid from current contributions and a possible subsidy from the sponsor of the scheme.

[29] In 1986, Singapore made its first significant reform, allowing fund participants with balances over a set minimum, currently S$50 000, to invest in unit trusts or prescribed stocks on the Singapore Stock Exchange.

[30] In November 1996, the Government introduced the Members' Savings Investment Scheme allowing individuals to invest in approved fund management institutions. In 1998, the amount of these withdrawals doubled to Ringitt 1.2 billion or 0.7 per cent of assets. Foreign investment accounted for only 0.3 per cent of pension fund assets in 1998; the Employees Provident Fund dominates Malaysia's pension fund industry with 94 per cent of accumulated contributions (Bank Negara Malaysia, 1998).

In response to poor performance, the Japanese Government is substantially liberalising public and private pension fund management regulation, allowing fund management to be outsourced, including to foreign companies. (See Chapter 11 - *Japan*.) While Taiwan has not yet made major changes to its public pension system, with no private management of public pension funds permitted, the issue of pension system reform is on the agenda (*China Post*, 7 May 1999, p. 13). When reform occurs, high per capita incomes could make this a lucrative market.

Among the private funds, Malaysia and the Philippines have the most liberal regimes, with unrestricted investment strategies, provided funds maintain an appropriate balance between fixed interest securities and higher risk, variable return securities and property (*Asia Pensions*, 1998).

Continuing liberalisation of pension fund management should generate significant opportunities for foreign financial institutions, which frequently have superior skills in managing diverse portfolios and risk to obtain higher returns. Japan typifies the opportunities likely to be available, with foreign financial institutions now increasing their share of public and private pension funds management.

CHALLENGES IN THE NBFI SECTOR

To contribute positively to East Asia's future economic development, NBFIs must overcome several important challenges. Many smaller NBFIs need to consolidate, but this must be done in a manner that maintains consumer confidence. In Taiwan, Japan, China and Korea, successful approaches will include liquidations and mergers with banks and other NBFIs.

Another important challenge for NBFIs is to respond creatively to increasing competition from banks; they are entering traditional NBFI business sectors of life insurance, retirement provision and consumer lending. Similarly, NBFIs often can exploit opportunities in areas banks once dominated. They can also adopt technology based selling mechanisms, like the Internet, and reduce reliance on large pools of often poorly skilled agents. For many NBFIs, more adequate capitalisation, better staff skills and the ability to form foreign alliances also are essential for success. Some governments may need to further tighten prudential regulations, and encourage human resource and systems development to assist East Asia's troubled NBFIs in regaining customer confidence. In several economies depoliticising NBFIs also is important.[31]

Finally, while governments have progressed significantly in consolidating supervision, these efforts need to continue as economies recover and NBFI regulatory reform receives priority equal to bank regulatory reform. In economies like Indonesia, Thailand and Korea, where NBFI problems are considerable, governments must tackle NBFI regulation, restructuring and recapitalisation as soon as they have dealt with their major banking sector problems.

---

[31] For example, some analysts believe political interference undermined the performance of Taiwan's cooperatives (*Taipei Times*, 26 July 1999, p. 3). In November 1997, the Indonesian government-owned insurer, PT Jamsostek, was one of a number of state controlled companies required to support the stock market. Its selective purchases targeted the state controlled telecommunications company and the stocks of a range of Suharto affiliated companies (Backman, 1999).

CONCLUSIONS

While poorly regulated NBFIs contributed to the financial crisis, with improved regulation and greater competition, they can contribute significantly to the region's future economic development. Before and particularly since the financial crisis, regional governments increasingly have recognised the need for efficient pension and insurance industries to finance retirement incomes for aging populations, manage risk and finance long term investments. Governments also want to avoid future contingent liabilities from bailing out failed insurers, pension funds and credit cooperatives. Consequently, many regional governments are strengthening NBFI regulation to protect savers and reduce contingent liabilities. They also are liberalising foreign participation to improve efficiency, returns and corporate governance standards. For pension funds, the regional trend is to ease restrictions on investable asset classes and eligibility requirements of pension asset managers; many life insurance markets also are opening further.

As East Asia recovers, rising incomes will drive increasing demand for NBFI services and products. Because this growth will occur concurrently with continuing liberalisation of foreign access to regional NBFI markets, it will generate significant opportunities for foreign financial institutions.

REFERENCES

Asia Pensions, 1998, 'Asia Pensions', summer 1998, Special report by the Global Custodian, Asset International Incorporation, Connecticut.

AXA National Mutual Holdings, 1999, Information supplied to East Asia Analytical Unit, August.

Backman, M., 1999, *Asian Eclipse: Exposing the Dark Side of Business in Asia*, John Wiley and Sons, New York.

Bank Negara Malaysia, 1999a, Press release, 'New Measures for the Insurance Industry at the International Conference for Emerging Markets in a Globalising Economy', www.bnm.gov.my/pa, accessed on 9 September.

___ 1999b, Press release, 'New Licences for Local Incorporation of Five Foreign Insurance Companies', www.bnm.gov.my/pa, accessed on 9 September.

___ 1998, *Annual Report 1998*, BNM, Kuala Lumpur.

CEIC, 1999, CEIC Database, Hong Kong, supplied by EconData, Canberra.

Colonial Mutual Group Asia, 1999, Information provided to the East Asia Analytical Unit, August.

Drake, P., 1980, *Money, Finance and Development*, Martin Robertson, Oxford.

East Asia Analytical Unit, 1999, *Korea Rebuilds: from Crisis to Opportunity*, Department of Foreign Affairs and Trade, Canberra.

___ 1998, *The Philippines: beyond the Crisis*, Department of Foreign Affairs and Trade, Canberra.

___ 1997, *A New Japan? Change in Asia's Megamarket*, Department of Foreign Affairs and Trade, Canberra.

Fry, M., 1988, *Money, Interest, and Banking in Economic Development*, John Hopkins University Press, Baltimore.

Insurance Commission, 1998, *Annual Report 1998*, Department of Finance, Republic of the Philippines, Manila.

International Monetary Fund, 1998, *International Capital Markets: Developments, Prospects and Key Issues*, International Monetary Fund, Washington DC.

Lee, Hsien Loong, 1999, 'Life Insurance in the 21st Century', Speech presented at the 19th Pacific Insurance Conference, 16 August, Singapore.

McGuire, P., Conroy, J. and Thapa, G., 1998, 'Getting the Framework Right: Policy and Regulation for Microfinance in Asia', The Foundation for Development Cooperation, Brisbane.

Nam, Il Chong; Kang, Yeongjae and Kim, Joon-Kyung, 1999, 'Comparative Corporate Governance Trends in Asia', Paper presented at the OECD/KDI conference on Corporate Governance in Asia: a Comparative Perspective, 3-5 March, Seoul.

Queisser, M., 1999, 'The Role of Pension Funds in the Stabilisation of the Domestic Financial Sector' in Queisser, M. and Brooks, D. (eds), *Financial Liberalisation in Asia: Analysis and Prospects*, Asian Development Bank and Development Centre of the Organisation for Economic Cooperation and Development, Paris.

Sigma, 1999, no. 3, Swiss Reinsurance Company, Zurich.

___ 1998, no. 1, Swiss Reinsurance Company, Zurich.

Smith, H, 1999, 'The State, Banking and Corporate Relationships: Korea and Taiwan', Paper presented at the conference on Reform and Recovery in East Asia: The Role of State and Economic Enterprise, Australian National University, 21-22 September, Canberra.

World Bank, 1998, *World Development Report 1988/89*, Oxford University Press, New York.

___ 1994, *Averting the Old Age Crisis: Policies to Protect the Old and Promote Growth*, Oxford University Press, Oxford.

Chapter 7

INDONESIA

Until mid 1997, the Indonesian economy performed very well. Annual real GDP growth averaged 7 per cent between 1980 and 1997, and real per capita income more than doubled from US$500 to US$1 100. Inflation averaged 9 per cent per year and fiscal policy generally was conservative.

Despite seemingly sound macroeconomic fundamentals, in 1997 and 1998, Indonesia suffered the world's worst banking crisis since the 1970s. Estimates put the cost as high as US$87 billion, or 82 per cent of Indonesia's GDP (Standard and Poor's, 1999).[1] With non-performing loans, NPLs, expected to reach 75 to 85 per cent of total loans by the end of 1999, financial sector recovery will be protracted. Much of Indonesia's financial and real sectors remains insolvent, requiring massive public funding injections and debt restructuring before it can begin to function normally again.

This chapter briefly examines the impact of the crisis on Indonesia's financial sector and financial indicators. It then assesses progress in banking and corporate sector restructuring, and analyses capital and insurance market developments. Finally, it outlines recent reforms to strengthen Indonesia's financial infrastructure and assesses future challenges.

IMPACT OF THE CRISIS

At the height of the crisis, the rupiah fell to below Rp 16 000:US$1, losing 85 per cent of its pre-crisis value (Figure 7.1). Consumer price inflation reached 82 per cent in September 1998, while interest rates peaked at 70 per cent in late August 1998, up from pre-crisis levels of 10 to 15 per cent (Figure 7.2). In 1999, the economy stabilised, helped by the exchange rate appreciating to around Rp 7 000:US$1, although political uncertainties continued to undermine confidence until the announcement of the new president in late October 1999. However, exchange rate appreciation and improved food availability reduced inflation to an estimated 2 per cent for 1999, and interest rates fell to 13 per cent by October 1999.

---

[1] This estimate includes the cost of bank recapitalisation and unrecovered loans to banks from the central bank, and is 24 per cent higher than the Indonesian Government's estimate of US$70 billion (Standard and Poor's, 1999).

Indonesia

Figure 7.1
The Rush for US Dollars
Exchange Rate (Rupiah:US Dollars)

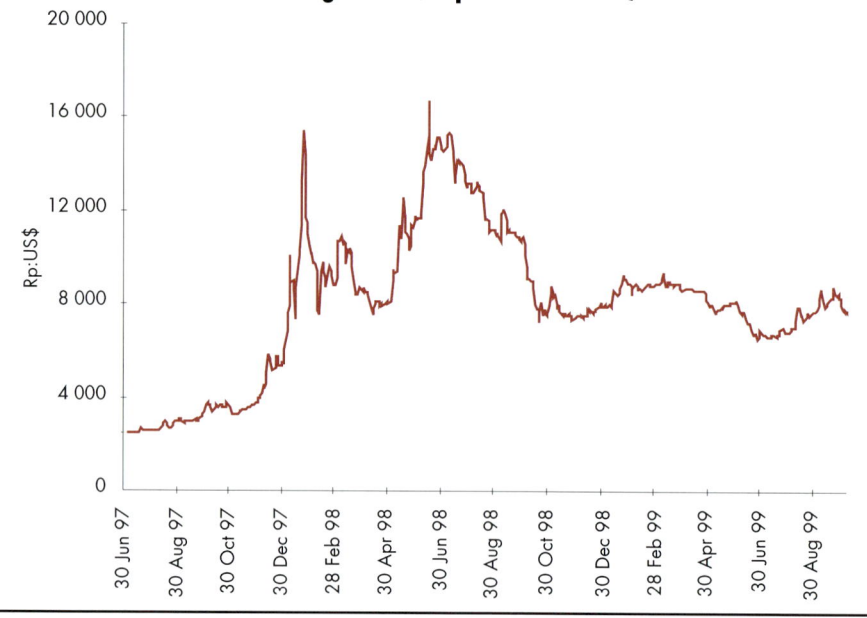

Source: Datastream Research Service, 1999.

Figure 7.2
Interest Rates Climb Sharply
One Month, Bank Indonesia Certificates and Rupiah Deposit Interest Rates

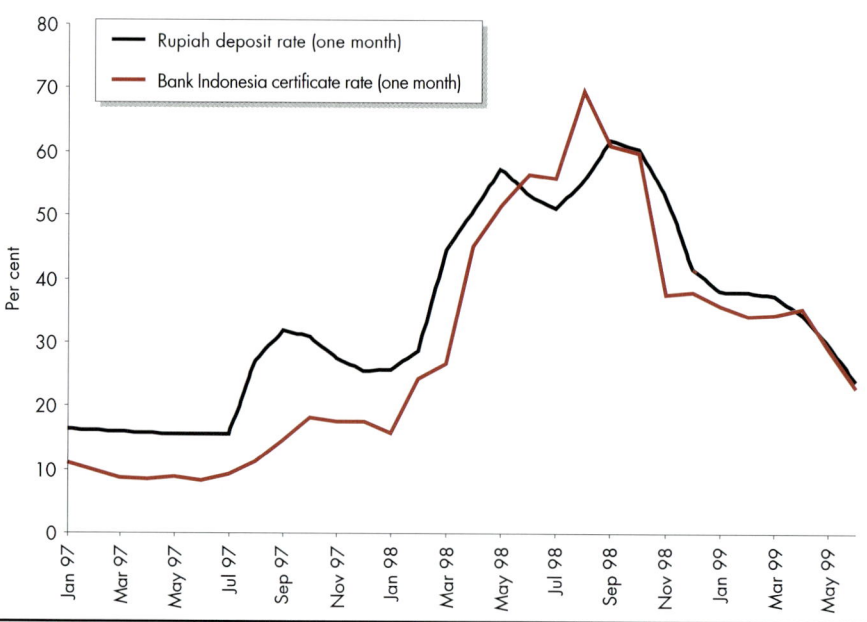

Source: CEIC, 1999.

By late 1999, the banking system was still in crisis. The central bank, Bank Indonesia, estimated pre-crisis NPLs at 10 per cent. By the end of 1999, NPLs should stabilise at 75 to 85 per cent (Bank of America, 1999). The massive banking system losses will be funded by the Government issuing bonds worth US$50 billion, repaid through future government budgets and asset sales. Consequently public debt, which was 24 per cent of GDP in June 1997, could exceed 100 per cent of GDP by the end of 1999. Also over much of 1998, interest margins between loans and deposits were negative, compounding bank problems (Figure 7.3). Banks had to keep deposit rates high to avoid losing funds, but were unable to pass high rates on to borrowers. Moreover, with most borrowers not servicing their loans, banks faced negative net interest income; this dramatically eroded bank capital.

On equity markets, share transactions fell dramatically in line with the share price index. In late 1998, daily share market transactions sank to Rp 200 billion from their pre-crisis levels of around Rp 500 billion. However, in mid 1999, the value of transactions surged again as the Jakarta Stock Exchange Composite Index recovered to pre-crisis levels after more than halving in 1997 and 1998.

Indonesia faces an enormous task to revive its banking system, restructure corporate debt, rebuild its capital markets and reform its financial and legal infrastructure. Reviving the banking system requires massive recapitalisation, NPL resolution, retrieval of central bank loans to private banks, and state bank restructuring. Success is critical to Indonesia's ability to regain strong economic growth and attract foreign investors, including foreign financial institutions.

Figure 7.3

Banks Faced Negative Spreads in 1998

Deposit and Loan Rates (Per cent per year)

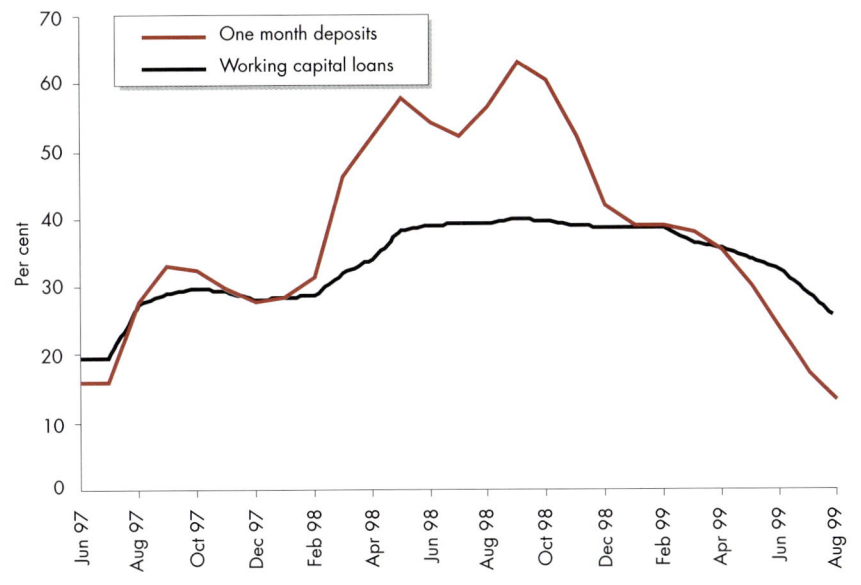

Source: Bank Indonesia, 1999a.

BANKING GROWTH AND CRISIS

The Indonesian banking sector's sharp decline in 1997 and 1998 contrasts with its massive growth following financial deregulation in the late 1980s.

Deregulation in the 1980s

Until the mid 1980s, seven state owned banks dominated the banking sector. Cheap funds from Bank Indonesia were channelled through the state banks, as subsidised loans to selected categories of borrowers. Lending ceilings and branch network limits severely constrained private bank operations.

However, bank deregulation in the mid 1980s:

- removed quantitative lending controls
- removed controls on state bank interest rates
- permitted the entry of new private domestic and foreign joint-venture banks
- provided greater freedom for domestic banks to expand their branch networks
- eased requirements on domestic banks seeking foreign exchange licences.[2]

In the deregulated environment, the private sector rushed to satisfy latent banking demand and to capitalise on the advantages of holding a banking franchise while regulation and supervision were weak. Bank numbers more than doubled from 115 in 1985 to 239 in mid 1997; branch numbers and bank assets grew even more rapidly (Figure 7.4).[3] Despite official disclaimers, the public believed the Government guaranteed bank deposits; this perception fuelled rapid bank deposit expansion.

Pre-crisis Vulnerabilities

Due to lax lending controls, inadequate supervision and enforcement, and the lack of viable bank exit policies, the banking system suffered from substantial asset quality problems well before the crisis. The problems in state banks culminated in the 1995 rescue of Bapindo, the Development Bank of Indonesia. Among the private banks, Bank Summa failed in 1992. In 1997, a significant number of undercapitalised banks remained licensed, and breaches of rules on lending limits, connected lending and net open foreign exchange exposure continued (Montgomery, 1997).[4]

---

[2] Other policy changes included reducing the required reserves ratio from 15 per cent to 2 per cent, allowing banks to introduce customised savings deposit products, and allowing foreigners to purchase shares in listed domestic banks (McLeod, 1999a).

[3] The number of banks owned by the national government ('state banks') and provincial governments ('regional development banks') remained constant at 7 and 27, respectively. The number of private banks grew from 63 to peak at 164 before the crisis. Foreign and foreign joint-venture banks increased from 11 to 44, while the number of 'people's credit banks' grew from 7 711 to peak at 9 037.

[4] According to Bank Indonesia, 15 banks did not meet the required 8 per cent capital adequacy ratio in April 1996; 41 banks did not comply with the legal lending limit; and 12 licensed foreign exchange banks did not meet the rules on net open foreign exchange exposure (Montgomery, 1997).

Indonesia

Figure 7.4

Banking Deregulation Spurred Rapid Expansion
Number of Branches and Total Bank Assets, 1985-97

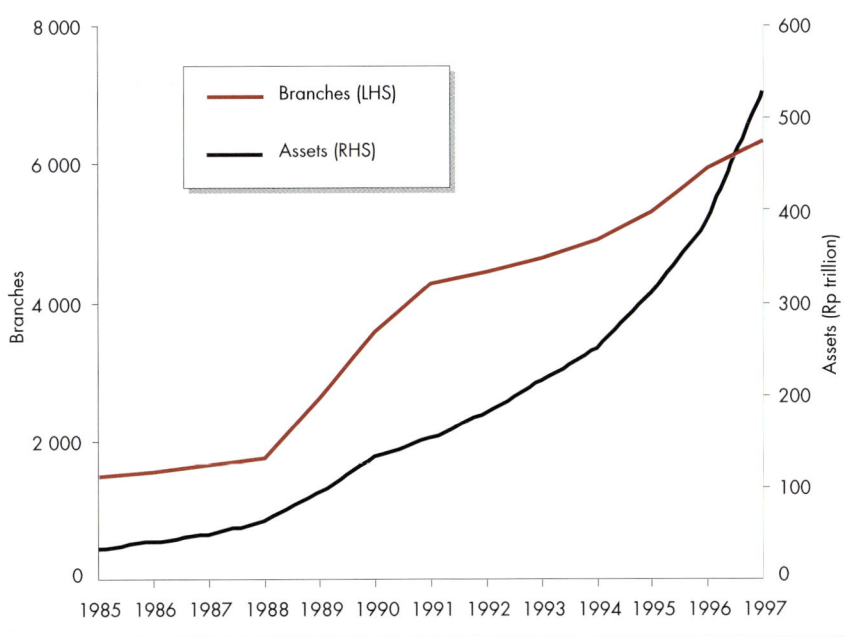

Source: Bank Indonesia, 1999a.

Bank Closures and Depositor Panic

Initial efforts to deal with Indonesia's banking crisis actually deepened it. In November 1997, the Government closed 16 private domestic banks. The IMF and the Government hoped closing these insolvent banks would demonstrate commitment to enforcing prudential regulations, boost confidence in the banking system and end the shift of deposits into state and foreign banks. Instead, the closures hastened the capital flight to state banks, which depositors assumed carried government guarantees, and to foreign banks. In the three months to January 1998, private banks' deposit share fell from 59 per cent to 49 per cent; they have recovered little since then (Figure 7.5). To stem this private bank deposit exodus, on 27 January 1998, the Government guaranteed all depositors and other creditors of domestically incorporated banks.[5] During this period, to prevent systemic collapse, Bank Indonesia provided large scale liquidity support to banks in the form of loans.[6]

---

[5] The guarantee was initially provided until January 2000. Six months' notice is required before adjusting the guarantee, and no notice had been given by November 1999.

[6] Private bank owners owe Bank Indonesia around Rp 140 trillion (US$20 billion) lent to them for liquidity support between July 1997 and February 1998. The Indonesian Banking Restructuring Agency, IBRA, has taken over US$10.5 billion in conglomerates' assets in part payment for bank debts.

Indonesia

Figure 7.5

Depositors Shift Funds to State Banks
Deposit Shares of Major Bank Groups

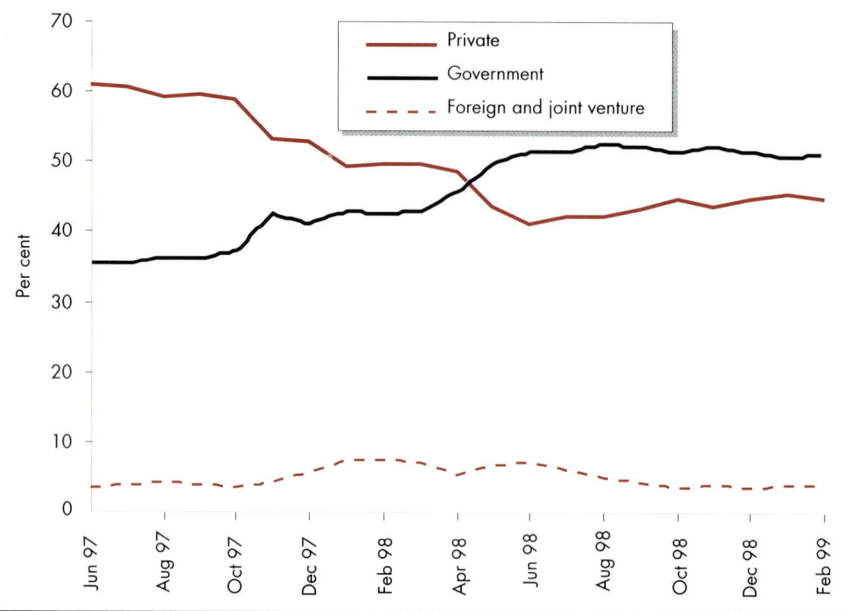

Source: Bank Indonesia, 1999a.

BANK RESTRUCTURING

Government led banking sector consolidation significantly shifted banking assets and liabilities to the Government. Of the 160 private banks operating before the crisis, over 60 were closed; 12 were taken over by the Government; and eight were deemed capable of joint recapitalisation by the Government and owners.[7] Probably around 98 private banks will survive, of which 20 will be wholly or majority government owned (Table 7.1). Most of the closed banks' liabilities were transferred to state banks, while their assets were transferred to the government-owned Indonesian Bank Restructuring Agency, IBRA.

---

[7] Four criteria were used to determine which banks would be given government funds for recapitalisation: the capital adequacy ratio had to be between -25 per cent and 4 per cent; a business plan had to show future viability; management and directors had to pass a 'fit and proper' test; and the bank owners had to contribute 20 per cent of recapitalisation costs (World Bank, 1999).

Table 7.1
Government Drives Consolidation in the Banking Sector
Government Actions and Numbers of Banks, 1997-99

Pre-crisis bank numbers						
		Private	Foreign	Regional	State	Total
		160	43	27	7	237
1997	November	16 small to medium sized banks liquidated				
1998	April	7 banks suspended, assets transferred to IBRA				
		7 banks taken over by IBRA, 6 later declared insolvent				
1999	March	38 banks closed				
		7 banks taken over by IBRA				
		8 banks to be jointly recapitalised				
	July	4 state banks merged to form Bank Mandiri				

Post-crisis bank numbers						
Fully private	Recapitalised	Nationalised	Foreign	Regional	State	Total
74	8	12	41	27	4	166

Source: Bank of America, 1999; Brown, 1999; and Bank Indonesia, 1999a.

THE INDONESIAN BANK RESTRUCTURING AGENCY, IBRA

IBRA was created in January 1998 to take over the assets of nationalised banks and recover state and private bank NPLs. By May 1999, IBRA was responsible for assets worth Rp 243 trillion (US$35 billion). It has taken control of 48 failed banks, and has stakes in about 200 companies. Its assets include:

- Rp 155 trillion in NPLs which it must recover or write off
- Rp 87 trillion in assets received from bank owners repaying Bank Indonesia's liquidity support of early 1998.

The key challenge for IBRA is to balance the need to maximise long term revenue realised from bank asset sales with the short term need to fund the budget deficit and bank recapitalisation. In the year to March 2000, the Government asked IBRA to raise Rp 17 trillion from assets sales. However, by August 1999, it had raised only Rp 800 billion from the sale of five operating companies, including a stake in PT Indofood owned by the Salim group. IBRA is exploring asset sale options including private sale, sale to foreigners or listing on the stock exchange. For example, in late 1999, IBRA hopes to raise Rp 2 trillion (US$286 million) by listing part of Bank Central Asia on the stock exchange (*Asia Pulse*, 15 July 1999).

Another challenge is to adequately conserve assets. For example, a scandal over illegal commissions paid by Bank Bali reinforced questions about IBRA's human and financial resources; only a due diligence study by Standard and Chartered Bank revealed the scandalous transaction.

Privatising State Banks

In the long term, restructuring and privatising the state banks will create a healthier banking system. The state now owns 19 banks,[8] 12 more than before the crisis, accounting for 75 per cent of banking system liabilities and 90 per cent of its negative net worth (World Bank, 1999). Before recapitalisation, all the state banks had less than -25 per cent capital adequacy ratios. On 31 July, as its first step to restructure state banks, the Government merged four of the original state banks to form a new bank, Bank Mandiri, which now accounts for around 30 per cent of total deposits.[9] The merger, originally planned to be completed by March 2000, involves reforming management, shedding 12 000 staff, injecting capital (US$19.5 billion) and transferring NPLs to IBRA. However, planned recapitalisation of Mandiri has suffered ongoing delays in part due to inadequate government funding (*Far Eastern Economic Review*, 26 August 1999, p. 47). The Government intends to recapitalise and restructure the remaining three original state banks in late 1999, in preparation for privatisation. It intends to privatise all state banks, including those taken over during the crisis, in 2000-01.

Bank Recapitalisation

The scale of Indonesia's banking sector crisis and the Government's guarantee of deposits forced the Government to bear the bulk of bank recapitalisation and depositor compensation costs. Based on their capital adequacy ratios, IBRA determined which banks should be closed and which recapitalised. However, the selection process involved controversy and allegations of cronyism.

As a first step towards recapitalisation, in late 1998, the Government employed the five big international accounting firms to do due diligence audits of all private banks. Few banks met the required 4 per cent minimum capital adequacy and many had a negative capital adequacy (Table 7.2).

Owners who wanted to keep managing the eight private banks eligible for recapitalisation injected around 20 per cent of new capital requirements (Rp 5.3 trillion); owners' previous equity in these banks was written down to zero. The Government injected its share of new capital (Rp 24.1 trillion) by issuing government bonds in return for equity.[10] For three years, the former owners will have first right to buy back shares from the Government.

---

[8] Of these, four banks have been merged to form Bank Mandiri.

[9] The four merged banks in Bank Mandiri are Bapindo, Bumi Daya, BDN and EXIM. At the time of merger, they had combined losses of Rp 117 trillion.

[10] The Government will issue three types of bonds: floating rate bonds where the interest rate is linked to the three month, Bank Indonesia certificate; fixed rate bonds at 10 per cent interest for five year maturity and 12 per cent for 12 year maturity; and inflation indexed bonds. Around 60 to 70 per cent of the issue will be floating rate bonds. By issuing long maturity bonds at close to market interest rates, the funding burden will be spread over many years. Most bonds will be inflation indexed to remove uncertainty over their real value and their cash flow effect on the budget.

Table 7.2

Insolvent Banks Hold Bulk of Deposits
Private Bank Recapitalisation Needs and Action Taken, 1999

Category	Number of banks	Status of banks	Comments
A	74	CAR is greater than 4 per cent	These banks represent only 5 per cent of bank deposits and are operating without government capital injections
B	37	CAR is between -25 per cent and 4 per cent	These banks represent 12 per cent of bank deposits
			The fate of one bank is yet to be decided
	of which:	9 will be recapitalised	Eight have injected the required 20 per cent of new capital; the Government will inject 80 per cent. One subsequently was nationalised
		21 will be liquidated	
		7 will be nationalised	
C	17	CAR is less than -25 per cent	Closed on 13 March 1999
Total	128		

Note: CAR is capital adequacy ratio.
Source: Bank of America, 1999.

The Government also issues bonds to banks taking on the liabilities of closed banks. Banks can sell these bonds on the secondary market to make new loans or settle liabilities. Initially, however, low capital adequacy ratios will continue to constrain new lending.

Recapitalisation Costs

The estimated cost of bank recapitalisation rose throughout 1998 and 1999, reflecting final due diligence audit results and the impact of negative interest rate spreads in 1998. In May 1999, IBRA estimated it would need to issue bonds worth Rp 351.6 trillion (US$50 billion); it had issued Rp 103.8 trillion of these by June 1999 (Bank Indonesia, 1999b). The capitalisation costs are split as follows:

- seven state banks, 66 per cent
- banks taken over by the Government in 1998, 23 per cent
- banks taken over by the Government in 1999, 3 per cent
- nine private banks eligible for recapitalisation, 7 per cent
- 21 regional development banks, 0.4 per cent (Bank Indonesia, 1999b).

The Government aims to complete the recapitalisation program by March 2000; it will recapitalise private and nationalised banks by December 1999. After missing several deadlines, on 13 October, the Government issued the first tranche of bonds to recapitalise Bank Mandiri. The second and final tranche is due in December following a due diligence audit to determine the amount required.

FOREIGN PARTICIPATION IN BANK RESTRUCTURING

The new banking law of November 1998 opens significant new opportunities for foreigners to participate in Indonesia's banking sector. Important changes include:

- permitting foreign banks to take over Indonesian banks and invest in unlisted and listed banks, subject to some restrictions[11]
- allowing foreign non-bank institutions to purchase Indonesian banks
- lifting restrictions on the expansion of branch networks of foreign joint-venture banks.[12]

Despite the opening of the banking sector, to date, new foreign investment has been limited as most local banks are considered too risky to invest in. However, in July 1999, UK based Standard Chartered Bank signed a management contract with Bank Bali and agreed to take a 25 per cent share in the bank through a rights issue in October (*Associated Press*, 18 August 1999). ABN AMRO and GE Capital are considering investing in Bank Niaga, and ANZ Bank recently took a 25 per cent stake in Panin Bank, one of Indonesia's strongest private banks (*Associated Press*, 27 July 1999). As in Singapore, foreign management is increasing; Lippo Bank recently hired two foreigners, including an Australian who was appointed its chief executive officer.

ANZ THE FIRST INTO INDONESIA SINCE THE CRISIS

When the ANZ Bank took a 25 per cent stake in Panin Bank in late 1998, it was the first foreign bank to take a share in an Indonesian bank since the crisis. Panin Bank currently is the twelfth largest bank in Indonesia, with a 35 per cent capital adequacy ratio, and 104 branches. At the time of the purchase, ANZ had a direct interest in Panin of 4.9 per cent in shares and an option over a further 19.9 per cent.

ANZ has also signed a technical service agreement with Panin. ANZ will transfer its experience of major restructuring in Australia's banking industry by appointing a senior executive to advise Panin, and provide additional project resources as required. The investment adds to ANZ's existing joint-venture arrangement in ANZ Panin Bank, a foreign joint-venture bank in which ANZ bought an 85 per cent share from Westpac in 1993.

Source: ANZ Bank, 1999.

---

[11] Although the law still does not permit foreign banks to establish new fully foreign-owned banks in Indonesia, foreigners can acquire 99 per cent of existing banks' shares. Takeover suitors must have an 'A' credit rating from a major credit ratings agency and a minimum Rp 3 trillion in capital. One director of every bank must be an Indonesian citizen.

[12] The Government also abolished network restrictions for any fully foreign-owned banks that may emerge from Indonesian bank buyouts. However, foreign banks must incorporate locally and inject considerable capital before expanding branch networks.

Opportunities for Foreign Investment

While investing in Indonesia's banking sector requires careful due diligence, Indonesia's large population and future growth potential will ensure it attracts many foreign investors. Foreign banks' skills and technology should make them highly competitive. The removal of most restrictions on foreign ownership of Indonesian banks and state bank privatisations present major long term opportunities. Indonesian authorities also increasingly recognise the financial sector's need for foreign capital and expertise.

The disposal of assets held by IBRA presents another set of opportunities for foreign financial service firms. For example, in a June 1999 IBRA tender process, ANZ's joint-venture bank, PT ANZ Panin, bought the credit card business of Papan Sejahtera, one of 38 banks the Indonesian Government took over in March 1999.

CORPORATE DEBT RESTRUCTURING

Bank and corporate restructuring are inextricably linked. Without debtor-creditor agreements to reschedule loans, undercapitalised banks cannot re-start lending and corporations cannot access new working capital.

By early 1998, most of the Indonesian corporate sector was insolvent.[13] Until mid 1999, initiatives to restructure private debt attracted little response from debtors or creditors. Since then, the Government with international financial institution assistance, has introduced two restructuring initiatives, the Jakarta Initiative and the Indonesian Debt Restructuring Agency, INDRA.

The Jakarta Initiative

The Government's September 1998 Jakarta Initiative seeks to encourage borrowers and creditors to renegotiate domestic and foreign debt contracts. While the process offers no direct financial assistance to creditors or borrowers, it provides professional advice and assistance to help creditors and debtors negotiate out-of-court debt restructuring agreements. It also seeks to remove bureaucratic hurdles to debt restructuring. For example, it established a 'one-stop shop' to expedite restructuring filings and removed company law limits on debt-equity swaps. However, the initiative lacks budgetary and administrative support (World Bank, 1999).

By September 1999, around 170 companies had sought assistance from the Jakarta Initiative Task Force to restructure a total of US$21 billion of foreign debt. However, only 24 companies had reached agreement with their creditors, covering foreign debts of about $US3 billion and domestic currency debt of Rp 600 billion (US$89 million) (Jakarta Initiative, 1999).[14]

---

[13] In February 1998, corporate foreign debts were around US$72.8 billion (68 per cent of 1998 GDP) consisting of US$14.6 billion in bank loans, US$5.9 billion in state company loans and US$57.7 billion in non-bank private company loans (Bank of America, 1999).

[14] By comparison, total private sector foreign debt is about US$80 billion, while total domestic bank rupiah loans are about Rp 300 trillion (US$43 billion).

Indonesian Debt Restructuring Agency

The Indonesian Government established INDRA in August 1998 to help companies deal with foreign debt problems once they reach restructuring agreements. The INDRA arrangements reschedule short term loans and convert foreign debts to rupiah at a favourable rate; and INDRA bears the exchange rate risk. While INDRA places itself between the debtor and the creditor—receiving payments from the former and passing them on to the latter—it does not incur commercial risk. If the debtor fails to pay, INDRA is not obliged to make payments to the creditor.

By June 1999, only one borrower-creditor agreement was registered with INDRA, and it involved a government-owned securities company whose officials were intimately involved in setting up INDRA. Consequently, the Government extended the deadline for joining INDRA from June to December 1999. Most borrowers and their creditors will attempt to negotiate debt write-offs or debt to equity swaps before joining the INDRA scheme. The Jakarta Initiative is likely to facilitate such restructuring.

STOCK MARKET DEVELOPMENT

When Indonesia revised the capital market law in 1995, it aimed to become the largest capital market in South East Asia by 2020, but the crisis has delayed many planned reforms needed to achieve this goal. Buoyant economic conditions and reforms which enabled foreigners to buy local shares dramatically expanded the stock market between 1990 and mid 1997 (Figure 7.6) (Noerhadi, 1994). However, the crisis more than halved market capitalisation from June 1997 to September 1998,[15] upsetting plans to upgrade market infrastructure and further develop the bond market. In 1998, the Government postponed planned increases in securities firms' capital adequacy requirements because the crisis undermined their viability (BAPEPAM, 1999). While securities market supervision ultimately will be transferred to the new Financial Supervisory Agency, for now, BAPEPAM, the securities market regulation department of the Ministry of Finance, will retain regulatory authority.

Going against the worldwide trend, the Government decided not to combine Indonesia's two stock exchanges, but to segment the market. The Jakarta Stock Exchange will list large companies, while the Surabaya Stock Exchange will list small and medium sized enterprises, and mining exploration companies. However, the share markets' segmentation will reduce liquidity, increase relative trading costs and may well prove unsustainable. (See Chapter 5 - *Capital Markets*.)

---

[15] Almost 60 per cent of listed companies were in the financial sector and many of the largest listed companies were banks. Many banks are among the delisted companies.

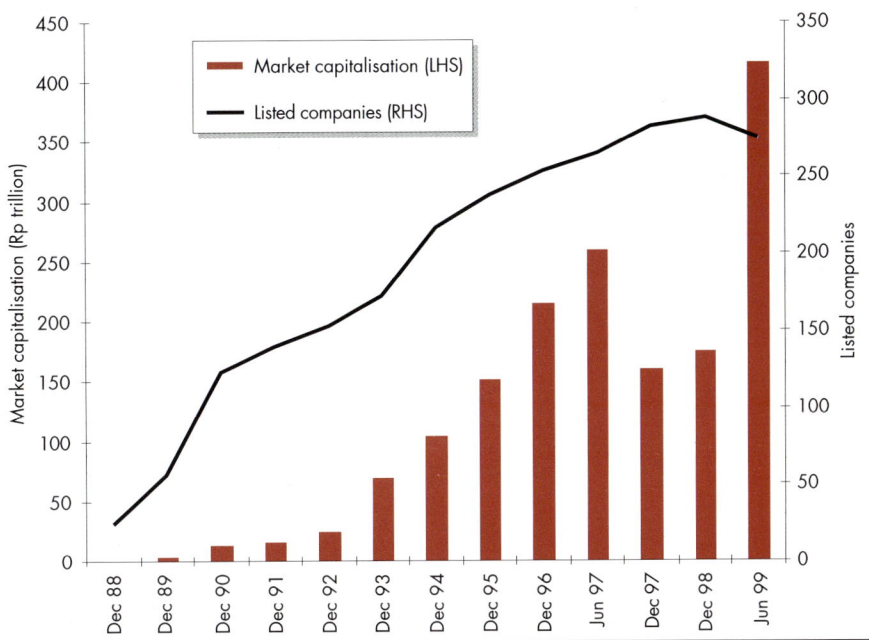

Figure 7.6

Stock Market Recovers Post-crisis

Listed Companies and Market Capitalisation, Jakarta Stock Exchange

Source: Jakarta Stock Exchange, 1999a.

Despite the setbacks, some innovations now are progressing. Falling trading values initially set back plans to introduce scriptless trading and book-entry settlement, and centralise the back office functions of broker-dealers, but now these initiatives are underway (Jakarta Stock Exchange, 1999b). The stock exchanges also are developing new risk management products. In 1999, the Surabaya Stock Exchange will introduce a share market index futures contract and the Jakarta Stock Exchange is considering an options market.

THE BOND MARKET

While bond markets are important in reducing enterprise reliance on bank finance and providing long term capital, in 1994, Indonesia had East Asia's smallest bond market (Dalla, 1995).[16] (See Chapter 5 - *Capital Markets*.) However, its bond markets grew quickly after the 1995 capital markets law liberalised regulations and provided a comprehensive regulatory regime. From 1995 to 1997, the number of corporate bonds on issue more than doubled (BAPEPAM, 1999).

---

[16] The balanced budget law kept the Indonesian Government out of the market while Bank Indonesia mainly issued bonds as money market instruments. High issuing costs also limited the domestic market as interest rates were well above international levels.

Indonesia

Unsurprisingly, the bond market languished in 1998 (Figure 7.7) and new issues only resumed in September 1999 after interest rates fell to manageable levels and confidence improved. The first issue was by Bank NISP, one of the healthier private banks.

Dealers drive the current corporate bond market. The Surabaya exchange provides the computer system for an over-the-counter market; no significant secondary market exists. As of August 1999, of 70 bonds listed on the Surabaya exchange, five also were listed on the Jakarta Stock Exchange. The Jakarta Stock Exchange is exploring the prospect of an order-driven market (Jakarta Stock Exchange, 1999b).

While new corporate bond issuers must compete with over Rp 300 000 billion of government bonds issued to recapitalise banks, government bond sales and trading also assist broader bond market development. They help produce benchmark yield curves and secondary trading markets. BAPEPAM, the capital markets' agency and Bank Indonesia encourage this process.

Figure 7.7

New Bond Issues Dried Up Post-crisis
Public Offerings of Shares, Rights and Bonds

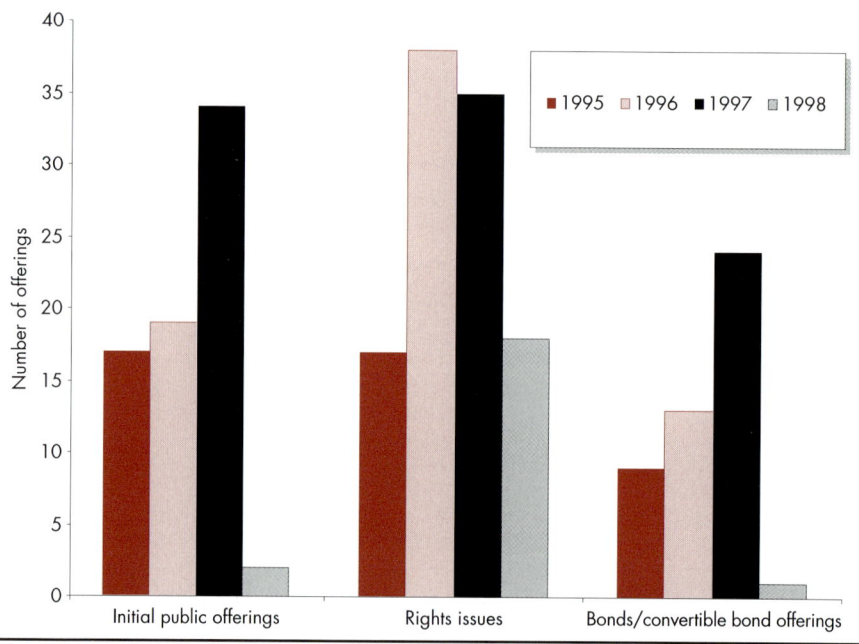

Source: BAPEPAM, 1999.

THE INSURANCE SECTOR

Insurance premiums, particularly life insurance, grew rapidly before the crisis (Figure 7.8). However, the insurance industry suffered heavily from rupiah devaluation, with many people cashing in their policies. Unlike in banking, large scale corporate failures have not occurred among insurers, mainly because regulations required insurers to hold a high proportion of their funds in bank deposits.[17] Non-life insurers suffered heavily from arson and looting in the May 1998 Jakarta riots, with claims reported to be around Rp 8 trillion (US$1.1 billion) (Data Consult, 1999).

State owned enterprises strongly influence the insurance market, particularly non-life insurance by buying around 70 per cent of general insurance, and they favour state owned insurers (Data Consult, 1999). For example, the insurance business of state owned oil and gas company, Pertamina, is monopolised by its subsidiary, PT Tugu Pratama (Data Consult, 1999).

Figure 7.8

Life Insurance Grew Most Rapidly Pre-crisis

Asset Values in the Indonesian Insurance Sector, 1993-97

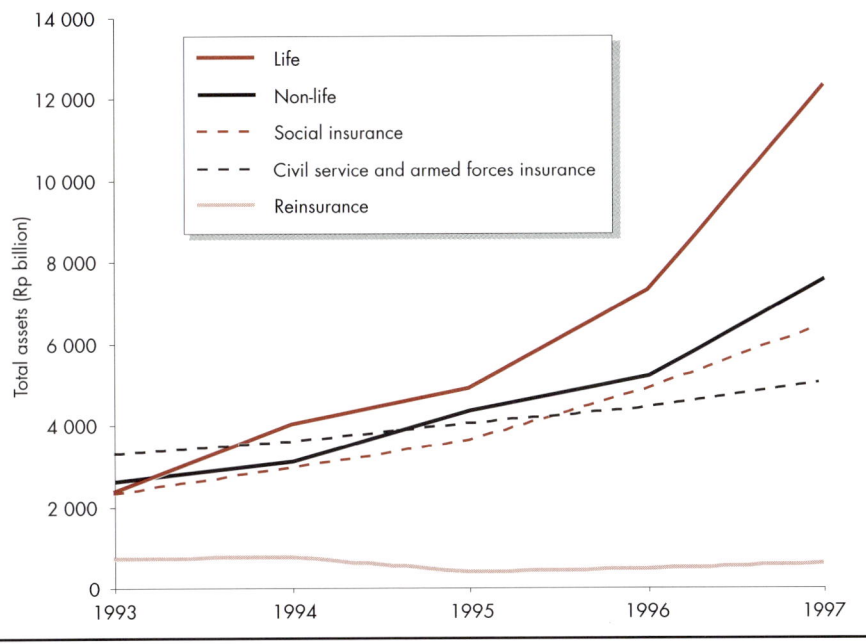

Source: Ministry of Finance, 1998.

---

[17] These deposits were relatively safe and lucrative when interest rates were high. At 31 December 1996, the industry held 70 per cent of its assets in bank deposits and Bank Indonesia certificates (Ministry of Finance, 1999, p. 11, Table 1.7).

The Government has introduced some important regulatory changes for insurers since the crisis, including a new risk weighted capital adequacy regime to encourage mergers and increase capital requirements for new insurance companies. Authorities are allowing a grace period so existing firms can meet these requirements. (See Chapter 6 - *Non-bank Financial Institutions*.)

Furthermore, to enable insurers to meet increased capital requirements, the Government now allows foreigners to own up to 99 per cent of listed insurance companies. Local insurers are actively seeking partners. For example, Lippo Life will increase its capital by allying itself with a leading US insurance company (Data Consult, 1999). Foreign companies are likely to move into life insurance first, then health insurance.

REFORMING THE FINANCIAL AND LEGAL INFRASTRUCTURE

The IMF program prioritised developing Indonesia's financial and legal infrastructure. It focused on drafting new laws and regulations, upgrading prudential regulation and supervision, deposit insurance, corporate governance, bankruptcy and accounting standards. However, even the best designed regulatory framework is ineffective without adequate enforcement; this relies on well trained, honest regulators and a supportive system of penalties and incentives. These take longer to develop than drafting new regulations.

Prudential Regulation

During 1998 and 1999, falling public confidence in the banking system and growing bank insolvency forced the Government to review banks' prudential regulation. Initially, it actually relaxed some regulations, accommodating previous breaches, but regulations will progressively tighten as the financial sector recovers (Table 7.3). Before the crisis, the minimum required capital adequacy ratio was 8 per cent. However, the Government recognised the banks' parlous condition, and temporarily reduced capital adequacy ratios to 4 per cent; they will increase to 8 per cent by December 2000 and 10 per cent by December 2001. Also, as many banks have lost capital during the crisis, to allow them to restructure, the Government temporarily has lowered the minimum capital requirement for existing banks from Rp 175 billion to Rp 105 billion (US$25 million to US$15 million). As minimum capital and capital adequacy requirements increase, conglomerate owners will need to choose between being bankers and concentrating on their real sector activities.

New regulations for loan loss provisioning emphasise valuing assets at market prices rather than historical prices. However, these provisions also will be phased in over several years; in the short term, banks can continue spreading NPL losses over four years. Temporarily banks also will be allowed to meet more lenient loan loss provisions (Table 7.3).

Table 7.3

Regulations Loosened Short Term, Tightened Long Term
Key Changes to Prudential Regulations

	Pre-crisis regulation	**Current regulation**	**Expected future regulation**
Capital adequacy ratio	8 per cent, in line with the Basle Capital Accord	4 per cent	8 per cent by December 2000 10 per cent by December 2001
Loan loss provisions	Four categories of loan classification	• Normal • Special mention (overdue 1 to 90 days) at 5 per cent Substandard (overdue more than 90 days) at 15 per cent • Doubtful (overdue more than 180 days) at 50 per cent • Loss (overdue more than 270 days) at 100 per cent Banks can amortise the losses over four years from 1998	Provisions as in current regulation, but with immediate recognition of full loan losses
Concentrated lending	25 per cent of capital	Up to 30 per cent of capital can be lent to any single non-affiliated firm group until December 2001	25 per cent of capital from 2002 20 per cent of capital from 2003

Source: Bank Indonesia, 1999c.

Similarly, to encourage lending and stimulate economic activity, in 1998, Bank Indonesia softened rules on concentrated lending to non-affiliated firms, raising the limit from 20 per cent to 30 per cent of capital. The new limit only applies until the end of 2001, when it falls back to 25 per cent and to 20 per cent by 2003.

The unprecedented depth of Indonesia's financial crisis dictated this two stage prudential regulation reform process. As regulations strengthen, improved enforcement and supervision will be critical to avoiding future crises.

Financial Supervision

While regulations have been progressively strengthened since 1993, supervision and enforcement remain inadequate. The main reform to the supervisory framework announced post-crisis is a new independent bank supervisor, provisionally named the Financial Supervisory Agency, to take over bank supervision from Bank Indonesia from the end of 2002. In line with the worldwide trend towards consolidated supervision, the new institution also will supervise insurance companies, pension funds, securities firms, venture capital and other non-bank financial institutions.[18] This structure facilitates the regulation of financial institutions whose activities span several financial markets, in line with the worldwide trend to dismantle financial sector firewalls. Moreover, separating responsibility for bank supervision and monetary policy should help avoid future conflicts of interest. However, unlike Korea, where the new Financial Supervisory Commission established in April 1998 quickly improved the efficiency and credibility of Korean supervisors, Indonesia's planned new structures are not available to assist in improving supervision in the current crisis.

November 1998 amendments to the banking law allow Bank Indonesia to use private accountants to undertake bank examinations, further strengthening supervisory arrangements. During the crisis, Bank Indonesia extensively used foreign accounting firms for due diligence assessments on distressed banks, and they may be employed to examine banks in the future.

Recent reforms also clarify confidentiality provisions; whereas, previously banks hid the identity of defaulting borrowers. Now secrecy applies only to depositors. Nevertheless, little information has emerged on defaulting borrowers.

Revisions to supervisory arrangements also include significant increases in penalties. However, previous regulations also contained heavy penalties; the key challenge is to improve enforcement.

POOR PENALTY ENFORCEMENT FOR REGULATION BREACHES

In the 1990s before the crisis, the three most famous cases of bank failure involved Bank Duta, Bank Summa and Bank Pembangunan Indonesia (Bapindo). A director of Bank Duta, tried for corruption outside the banking law, was jailed but permitted to go 'on leave' from prison. Staff from Bank Summa were not prosecuted over the bank's wilful flouting of prudential regulations. Only in the Bapindo case were offenders successfully charged, again, outside the banking law, but the defaulting debtor bribed his way out of jail.

Authorities have not yet laid charges against major shareholders, commissioners or directors of banks that failed during the financial crisis, although some at least have been banned from travelling internationally. Others had to resign their directorships after failing the Bank Indonesia 'fit and proper test'.

Source: McLeod, 1999b.

---

[18] Japan, Korea, the United Kingdom and Australia recently established independent, integrated supervisory agencies. (See Chapter 3 - *Prudential Reform*.)

Central Bank Independence

The new central bank law, enacted in May 1999, significantly increases Bank Indonesia's independence. Previously, the central bank was effectively an arm of government; the Governor was a member of Cabinet. The central bank also experienced politically motivated dismissals of its top management and government interference in monetary policy (Kenward, 1999).

New legislation precludes presidential dismissal of Bank Indonesia board members, except for specified criminal acts.[19] The new law also specifies Bank Indonesia must maintain the rupiah's stability. In addition to providing greater independence for the central bank, the new law introduces two other important initiatives:

- Bank Indonesia no longer can lend to the Government or purchase government bonds except in the secondary market; consequently, the Government will no longer be allowed to print money to finance its deficit
- if Bank Indonesia acts as lender of last resort to the banks, it may only provide credit which is fully secured by sound and liquid collateral for a maximum of 90 days.

Deposit Insurance

Irrespective of the lack of formal protection, the public believes bank deposits are government guaranteed; the Government has decided to formalise this situation through a fully funded insurance scheme. The Government initially announced a new deposit insurance scheme would replace the current guarantee of bank deposits when it expired in January 2000. However, the new scheme will not be operational by then, and the guarantee will continue, subject to six months' notice of any change.

An early proposal was for all banks to pay an annual premium equal to 0.5 per cent of insured deposits into a government operated, deposit insurance institution. As staff skills increase, the Government intends to charge differentiated premiums based on the riskiness of contributing banks.

Bankruptcy Legislation and the New Commercial Courts

In its April 1998 Letter of Intent to the IMF, the Government recognised the importance of an effective bankruptcy regime for financial system recovery, and committed to a two stage overhaul of the bankruptcy law. In the first stage, effective 20 August 1998, the Dutch statute dating back to 1905 was updated. In the second stage, a comprehensive new law was submitted to parliament in August 1999 (Churchill, 1999).

To enforce the new legislation, with World Bank assistance the Government has created a new Commercial Court with 17 specially trained judges and *ad hoc* judges with commercial experience. It has improved procedures and simplified the appeals process. In addition, judges' salaries will be increased to reduce corruption.

---

[19] In addition, the Department of Finance now has virtually no role in financial supervision.

Judges also will be subject to much greater scrutiny. They must provide written, reasoned opinions when handing down decisions. Already, the Centre for Legal Studies has launched a new journal to analyse and publicise court decisions, and the Department of Justice has created a Commercial Court website to publish the full text of Commercial and Supreme Court decisions.[20]

Although observers criticised some early decisions of the new court and are frustrated with the slow pace of reform, legal institutions cannot be developed instantly. Building the Commercial Court's credibility will require sustained improvements in judges' skills, knowledge, salaries and accountability. Government could further contribute to the bankruptcy reform process by initiating proceedings against state bank and IBRA loan defaulters in the new Commercial Court.[21]

Corporate Governance

Protecting bondholder and minority shareholder interests is crucial to develop Indonesia's financial markets. Major corporate governance weaknesses include inadequate transparency, single shareholder dominance and inadequate independence of outside board directors.[22]

The March 1999 IMF Letter of Intent foreshadows recommendations to improve corporate governance, including strengthening securities regulation, stock exchange listing requirements, and company and accounting laws.[23] By September 1999, the main reforms achieved included:

- requiring unlisted companies with assets over Rp 50 billion to publish financial statements audited by public accountants
- requiring banks to promptly publish detailed quarterly and annual financial reports, with annual reports audited by a public accountant.

Accounting Standards

Before the crisis, company accounting standards were extremely weak.[24] Official standards were lax compared with industrialised countries. Foreign accountants were only permitted to operate in joint ventures, weakening their potential to improve standards.

However, some steps have been taken to improve accounting standards. As yet, only banks must regularly publish more comprehensive financial data; the Government has not yet required all corporates to meet this standard. The Government and aid

---

20 The website is at www.pengadilan-niaga.go.id.
21 In September, IBRA announced it would issue bankruptcy proceedings against 17 of Indonesia's top 200 debtors, with a total of US$515 million in bad debts and owing US$770 million. These debtors have not signed a letter of commitment to IBRA to repay loans with assets from other businesses.
22 In Indonesia these directors are known as commissioners.
23 In addition to regulatory strengthening, it also is important to foster a competent and objective financial press, free to report on business affairs, and to develop a stock exchange willing and able to act strongly against listed firms, members and powerful shareholders who abuse their positions.
24 Many enterprise owners routinely had multiple sets of financial statements: one for themselves, one for the tax office, one for the bank, and perhaps one more for minority shareholders.

donors are assisting the finance professionals, including actuaries and insurance appraisers, to meet international professional standards through tougher entrance requirements, continuous learning, higher professional and ethical standards, and member discipline.[25] An effective way to upgrade standards is to allow foreign and domestic accounting and actuarial firms to compete freely, and require international best practice disclosure statements.

FUTURE CHALLENGES FOR FINANCIAL SYSTEM RECOVERY

Recapitalising, restructuring and privatising the banking system represents a massive challenge for Indonesia, as does corporate debt restructuring. Nevertheless, it now has institutions and mechanisms in place to achieve these objectives, even though funding is a possible constraint. Furthermore, regulatory changes made in 1998 and 1999 reflect government commitment to greater financial sector transparency and accountability, and improved financial sector supervision. However, enforcement of new laws and regulations must improve dramatically to enable a return to financial sector stability, a necessary precondition for economic recovery.

As the immediate crisis recedes and relative stability returns to financial markets, the challenge is to rebuild a financial sector better able to avoid future crisis and panic. Challenges for the new Indonesian Government include:

- over time, raising and enforcing capital adequacy requirements and enforcing connected lending limits to ensure bank owners have strong incentives to manage risks effectively
- enhancing prudential regulation and supervision to better monitor financial institutions' asset quality and loss provisioning
- implementing a well designed and implemented deposit insurance scheme to replace implicit government deposit guarantees
- improving the functioning of bankruptcy courts to encourage timely repayment of loans
- substantially progressing corporate governance reform
- further opening the finance sector and professions to international competition.

These challenges are enormous, and it will be several years before Indonesian regulators establish credibility in supervising the financial system. Success in these areas would significantly strengthen Indonesia's financial system, reducing the likelihood of another financial crisis and underpinning a return to robust growth; however, a return to normalcy is still some way off.

---

[25] The project is operating in the Indonesian Department of Finance funded by the Canadian International Development Agency.

REFERENCES

Asia Pulse, 1999, Asia Pulse News Service, www.asiapulse.com, accessed on 9 October.

Associated Press, 1999, AFX-Asia New Service, www.indoexchange.com, accessed on 10 October.

ANZ Bank, 1999, Information supplied to the East Asia Analytical Unit, August.

Bank of America, 1999, 'A Survey of Banking Reform in Asia', Global Markets Group Asia, Hong Kong, July.

Bank Indonesia, 1999a, Indonesian Financial Statistics, www.bi.gov.id, last accessed on 10 October.

___ 1999b, Press statement on government bonds, www.bi.gov.id/intl/press/govbond.html, accessed on 17 June.

___ 1999c, Bank Indonesia website, www.bi.gov.id, accessed on 31 August.

BAPEPAM, 1999, *BAPEPAM (Capital Market Supervisory Agency) Annual Report 1998*, Ministry of Finance, Jakarta.

Brown, M., 1999, The Indonesian Banking Crisis, Unpublished paper by the Senior Financial Adviser, Indonesian Bank Restructuring Agency, Jakarta.

CEIC, 1999, CEIC Database, Hong Kong, supplied by EconData, Canberra.

Churchill, G., 1999, 'Indonesian Bankruptcy Reforms: a Chronological Overview', Paper presented at the Conference on Current Issues and Future Directions for Bankruptcy Reform in Indonesia, 29-30 April, Jakarta.

Dalla, I., 1995, *The Emerging Asian Bond Market*, World Bank, Washington DC.

Data Consult, 1999, 'Life Insurance Industry amidst Crisis', Indonesia Commercial Newsletter, Jakarta, 13 April.

Datastream Research Service, 1999, Datastream International Limited, London.

Jakarta Initiative, 1999, Information supplied to the East Asia Analytical Unit, September.

Jakarta Stock Exchange, 1999a, *JSX Monthly Statistics*, vol. 8, no. 3, March.

___ 1999b, Information supplied to the East Asia Analytical Unit by the Jakarta Stock Exchange, July.

Kenward, L., 1999, 'What Has Been Happening at Bank Indonesia?', *Bulletin of Indonesian Economic Studies*, vol. 35, no. 1, April, pp. 121-27.

McLeod, R., 1999a, 'Control and Competition: Banking Deregulation and Re-regulation in Indonesia', *Journal of the Asian Pacific Economy*, vol. 4, no. 2, pp. 258-96.

___ 1999b, Consultancy prepared for the East Asia Analytical Unit, June.

Ministry of Finance, 1999, *Insurance Annual Report 1998*, Directorate of Insurance, Ministry of Finance, Jakarta.

Montgomery, J., 1997, 'The Indonesian Financial System: Its Contribution to Economic Performance and Key Policy Issues', IMF Working Paper no. 97/45, Washington DC.

Noerhadi, D., 1994, 'The Role of the Indonesian Capital Market', in McLeod, R., (ed.), *Indonesia Assessment 1994: Finance as a Key Sector in Indonesia's Economic Development*, Research School of Pacific and Asian Studies, Canberra, and Institute of Southeast Asian Studies, Singapore, pp. 202-22.

Standard and Poor's, 1999, 'Credit Week', 23 June.

World Bank, 1999, 'Indonesia: from Crisis to Opportunity', Jakarta, July.

Chapter 8

THAILAND, MALAYSIA AND THE PHILIPPINES

Thailand, Malaysia and the Philippines suffered similar exchange rate, interest rate and stock exchange shocks in 1997 and 1998. They are pursuing similar reform agendas and responding to similar financial sector problems, albeit at different scales and over different time frames. While Malaysia and Thailand did not suffer a systemic breakdown like Indonesia's, they face serious non-performing loan, NPL, problems; NPLs also rose in the Philippines. All three economies are consolidating their fragmented banking systems, upgrading prudential controls and developing capital markets. Malaysia and Thailand have larger, more developed financial markets than the Philippines, but the Philippines has implemented reforms driven by earlier financial crises. Policy makers in all three economies are conscious of impending regional and global liberalisation of financial services, potentially by 2003, and the need to upgrade the competitiveness and stability of their financial systems.

This chapter discusses the impact of major financial sector regulatory and legal reforms undertaken before and during the crisis, and assesses the impact of the financial crisis on financial markets in these three South East Asian economies. It also examines the progress in restructuring and recapitalising banks in Thailand and Malaysia, and their financial sectors' medium to long term prospects, including further opening to foreign investment. The chapter then analyses the ongoing opening of the Philippine banking system to foreign competition, and some major challenges it faces including increasing competition and reducing intermediation costs.

THAILAND

While Thailand's financial crisis is not as severe as Indonesia's, the major depreciation, capital flight and corporate insolvencies since 1997 have wrought havoc on the financial sector. The crisis eroded most of the banking system's capital, undermined nascent capital markets and highlighted serious shortcomings in the financial sector's regulatory, supervisory and legal framework. The Government opted not to bail out the banking system with public funds or impose tight recapitalisation and provisioning timetables, but mainly left bank owners to determine their own solution. This policy approach has delayed financial and corporate restructuring, the resumption of lending and a return to self-sustaining economic growth. Political manoeuvring by vested interests and cultural factors have frustrated the Government's reform agenda.

Nevertheless, the Thai Government has undertaken significant reforms in a reasonably short time, and financial and corporate restructuring seems to have accelerated since March 1999.

PRELUDE TO THE CRISIS

After experiencing considerable economic success in the 1980s, Thailand's economy became increasingly vulnerable from 1993 due to a build up in short term foreign debt, strong credit expansion and asset booms. In 1996 and 1997, conditions deteriorated rapidly after the Thai baht appreciated in real terms, export and GDP growth slowed sharply, and the current account deficit widened to 8 per cent of GDP. Heavy foreign borrowing pushed external debt to 50 per cent of GDP. Growing difficulties in the property sector, a sharp stock market correction and a weaker government fiscal position compounded problems. The financial system, particularly finance companies, showed serious weaknesses. Corruption scandals in government also restricted economic and political reforms, undermining investor confidence.

In the 1990s, while Thailand's public debt fell, private sector foreign debt expanded rapidly. For nine years, government budget surpluses reduced public sector debt from over 50 per cent of GDP in 1987 to under 16 per cent of GDP by 1996. However, over the same period, private sector foreign debt rose from US$6 billion to over US$70 billion; 40 per cent of this was short term foreign borrowing (Figure 8.1) (World Bank, 1999b). Thailand experienced external pressure from foreign creditors refusing to roll over short term bank loans and currency speculation. A lending boom, mainly to real estate, and a history of poor risk management and credit assessment by domestic and foreign financial institutions, accentuated this vulnerability.

Figure 8.1

Short Term Private Sector Debt Outstrips Public Debt
External Private and Public Debt, 1985-97

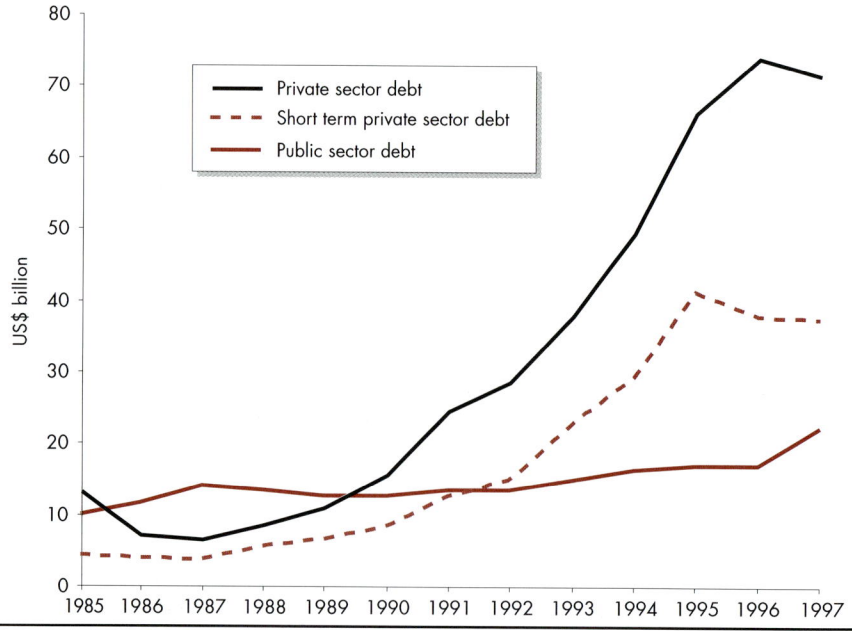

Source: World Bank, 1999a.

In early 1997, as the economy slowed and asset prices fell, concerns deepened about the health of banks and finance companies, resulting in a series of speculative attacks on the baht. In early 1997, the Thai central bank sold a large proportion of Thailand's foreign exchange reserves to defend the pegged exchange rate. On 2 July 1997, the Thai Government abandoned the peg and introduced a managed float, allowing a 20 per cent depreciation. Net usable reserves had fallen to only US$1 billion, a few weeks of imports, when the Thai Government negotiated an emergency support package with the IMF (Nomura Securities, 1999). However, weak political leadership, reports borrowers were having difficulty rolling over short term debt and indecisive treatment of 58 suspended finance companies precipitated a widespread loss of confidence in the Thai economy. Over the second half of 1997, the baht's value halved. In November 1997, the new, reformist Chuan Government embraced a stronger IMF program, calmed markets and eventually enabled currency and financial stability to return.

IMPACT OF THE CRISIS ON FINANCIAL MARKETS

By the third quarter of 1997, the currency crisis had quickly become a major financial crisis. Bank assets, already poor due to excessive credit growth and weak credit analysis, weakened dramatically after devaluation, and Thailand faced systemwide financial sector problems. High corporate and financial sector exposure to unhedged, short term foreign borrowing undermined corporate and financial institution viability. This and the high interest rates needed to defend the baht caused the economy to contract sharply, in turn raising banks' NPLs, eroding bank capital and constraining new lending. The Government incurred huge liabilities supporting insolvent financial institutions through the Financial Institutions Development Fund. New bank lending almost ceased; interest rates rose dramatically; consequently investment collapsed, causing the real economy to contract 9.4 per cent in 1998.

MAJOR POST-CRISIS REFORMS

In July 1997, Thai authorities abandoned their unsuccessful defence of the baht, and announced they would replace its peg to a basket of currencies with a managed float system. The pegged exchange rate system had encouraged unhedged foreign borrowing, which, with yen depreciation from mid 1995 contributed significantly to Thailand's declining export competitiveness, weaker GDP growth and diminishing creditor confidence.

In October 1997, to prevent major bank runs, the Government extended depositor guarantees to all domestic bank and non-bank customers via its Financial Institutions Development Fund. Once the banking system stabilises, the Government will replace this blanket guarantee of financial system liabilities with a limited, self-financing deposit insurance system (World Bank, 1999c).

Prudential Reforms

As part of the IMF program, the Thai Government has introduced many new reforms to tighten prudential regulations and supervision, ensure systemic stability and increase financial sector transparency and competition. In October 1997, it amended the commercial banking law; now the Bank of Thailand can take prompt corrective action including changing management, recapitalising distressed financial institutions and ultimately suspending their operating licences.[1] In March 1998, the Government determined banks needed to classify all their loans according the standard international five tier system by the end of 1998; stop accruing interest income on NPLs in January 1999; and meet tighter capital provisioning for classified loans by the end of 2000.[2] The Government also tightened eligibility guidelines for owners and managers of financial institutions (Bank of Thailand, 1998). These reforms increased confidence in the banking system, but were introduced gradually to reduce the negative effects on bank liquidity and lending capacity.[3]

In July 1998, to increase transparency, the Government announced all financial institutions must review their on and off-balance sheet loan portfolios; at the end of each quarter, they must submit results, including data on loan classifications and provisioning to the Bank of Thailand.

International Competition

The most important reform to promote financial institution competition and efficiency was to allow 100 per cent foreign ownership of Thai financial institutions for a ten year period.[4] When international banks buy a major share in distressed or nationalised Thai banks, the Bank of Thailand typically agrees to pay around 85 per cent of the losses incurred by banks' asset management companies in disposing of NPLs.

Before the crisis, 15 domestic banks and 91 finance companies held 85 per cent of household savings and extended 90 per cent of loans (Bank of Thailand, 1998; and Nidhirabha and Warr, 1999). Some analysts believe as few as six of the original 15 banks will survive in Thai ownership in the medium term (Noruma Securities, 1999). Of the 15 banks, Thai Danu and Bank of Asia already are foreign owned; deals have been agreed for foreign takeovers of Nakornthon and Radhanasin banks; and two more banks are for sale by the end of 1999. Most other banks are seeking strategic foreign partners, although some may remain Thai controlled.

---

[1] This initiative required the authorities to develop standard exit procedures for failing banks and introduce new legislation to close and liquidate financial institutions.

[2] The new classifications and provisioning requirements are pass (1 per cent), special mention (2 per cent), sub-standard (20 per cent), doubtful (50 per cent) and loss (100 per cent or write-off). Previously only loans overdue by more than 12 months were classified as NPLs; now ones overdue by three months are classified as sub-standard.

[3] Other regulatory changes are designed to make finance companies subject to the same regulatory standards as banks and encourage financial sector consolidation. For example, larger finance companies now can amalgamate and apply for banking licences. The Government's new financial institutions law will upgrade the regulatory framework to cover both banks and finance companies, and replace existing commercial bank and finance company laws. The new law will cover licensing, supervision, ownership, governance and other aspects of financial institutions' activities. Restructuring of government-owned, specialised financial institutions like the Thai Savings Bank also is underway.

[4] After ten years, new capital injections must come from Thai entities unless the foreign holding has fallen to below 49 per cent. However, international financial liberalisation agreements between 1997 and 2007 may well make these sell-down provisions redundant.

Debt Restructuring

In June 1998, the Government issued regulations covering debt restructuring procedures, and defining debtor and creditor responsibilities and accountability (Bank of Thailand, 1998). The Government's 'Bangkok approach' involved establishing a more informal, out-of-court mechanism to restructure debt, based on the London approach, widely used in out-of-court debt workouts. The Government established a Corporate Debt Restructuring Advisory Committee and legislated tax and other incentives to encourage debtors and creditors to reach market based debt workouts under Bank of Thailand supervision. Most foreign and local banks have signed debtor-creditor agreements and inter-creditor agreements to speed up the process of restructuring syndicated loans.[5] The Government has targeted around 690 major corporate debtors with debts of nearly Baht 1.5 trillion for this process, 56 per cent of total NPLs (World Bank, 1999d).

Despite these initiatives, corporate debt restructuring initially was slow, inhibiting NPL write-offs and recovery. By August 1999, banks had restructured only 26 per cent of reported NPLs (World Bank, 1999d). Corporate restructuring completions and loans under negotiation started to accelerate in the second half of 1999. However, many analysts are concerned that many debt rescheduling deals may be inappropriate; many completed deals just could reschedule loans which will become non-performing when payments become due.

IMPROVING FINANCIAL AND LEGAL INFRASTRUCTURE

Reforming the legal framework to stipulate creditors' foreclosure rights and provide debtors with bankruptcy protection is a key component of the IMF support package and the Government's reform agenda. Serious failings in legal and financial infrastructure contributed to foreign creditors losing confidence in Thailand's financial system, and constrain the recovery of collateral from NPLs and the resumption of credit flows.

Bankruptcy and Asset Recovery

In March 1999, after much prevarication, the Thai Senate passed four new bankruptcy reform bills, significantly reforming the bankruptcy framework.[6] They also provide a stronger framework for voluntary debt restructuring and eventually should reduce transaction costs during debt workouts. The pre-crisis framework for enforcing security and bankruptcy strongly favoured debtors (Thomasic and Little,

---

[5] Signatories to debtor-creditor agreements and inter-creditor agreements agree to defined procedures for case entry, information sharing, negotiations and 75 per cent majority voting approval. The agreements provide options for mediation and arbitration (World Bank, 1999a).

[6] Changes include improved security for new lending to financially distressed companies, voting by creditor class, rescission of related party transfers, limits to discretion for court action, and conversion of currency denominated claims (World Bank, 1999b). Further reforms are planned to improve creditors' access to collateral, including a law to establish a centralised registry of mortgage collateral.

1998).[7] Under the pre-crisis bankruptcy system, debtors could prolong proceedings almost indefinitely, so debtors could stall restructuring negotiations and make their loans strategically non-performing, even if they were able to pay (Flatters, 1999).[8]

In June 1999, the Government created a special commercial court to handle bankruptcy cases. However, this court will need time to establish its record as creditor-friendly. While the pace of reorganisation and bankruptcy filings has increased since the March amendments, new filings still stand at only two to three per month, suggesting creditors remain reluctant to use the court process (World Bank, 1999b).

Implementing the new law in the courts has been slow and some analysts argue, largely unsatisfactory. The new foreclosure law would only reduce the time required to resolve a claim from ten to five years, still too long to apply real leverage on uncooperative debtors.[9] However, the improved legal framework probably increases incentives for debtors to reach out-of-court settlements.

Other Legal Reforms

In October 1999, the Thai Parliament passed a new alien business law, the last of 11 key economic laws the Government undertook to revise in its agreement with the IMF.[10] The new law reduces the sectors restricted to majority Thai-owned companies and requires an annual review of remaining restrictions, making future liberalisation easier. The land law also has been amended to allow foreigners to own and mortgage land.

RECAPITALISING THE BANKING SYSTEM

In late 1999, Thai banks still were struggling to raise sufficient new capital to meet required capital adequacy ratios while providing for and writing off NPLs. As existing bank losses have depleted the banking system's capital, banks must attract new capital to write off debts without breaching capital adequacy rules.[11] This encourages banks to enter debt workouts, including extending debt maturity and reducing interest rates, rather than writing off loans and recognising losses. Bank liquidity is no longer a problem as the Government's deposit guarantee ensures a surplus of deposits. However, while bank capital remains low, banks cannot undertake new lending.

---

[7] The courts have not yet successfully prosecuted former executives of failed financial institutions. Even executives implicated in the infamous Bangkok Bank of Commerce loan scandal of several years ago have not been convicted.

[8] One analysis estimates one third of bank NPLs are strategic bad debts; debtors could repay but refuse to do so because of the weak insolvency laws and lack of progress in debt restructuring negotiations (Nidhiprabha and Warr, 1999).

[9] Furthermore, the courts currently interpret insolvency as liabilities exceeding assets, rather than a company's inability to meet its debts as and when they fall due, as is common in western jurisdictions. This allows debtors to avoid insolvency by over-valuing assets and under-valuing liabilities. However, the Government plans follow-up legislation, which would streamline summons procedures for taking debtors to court (*Far Eastern Economic Review*, 4 November 1999, p. 11).

[10] The economic laws proposed and enacted by the Chuan Government included the bankruptcy, foreclosure and commercial court laws; a state enterprise corporatisation law; amendments to the civil and commercial code; amendments to the laws on property leasing and condominiums; and an amendment to the application of the land law to foreigners.

[11] In 1998, the ten main commercial banks recorded a combined loss of Baht 262.3 billion (US$7.1 billion) by writing off loan losses.

Under its August 1998 recapitalisation program, the Thai Government announced it would provide matching public funding to recapitalise private banks, subject to certain conditions.[12] However, this program has not been successful. So far only one commercial bank and one finance company have applied for government assistance.[13] Most large bank owners are reluctant to ask for government support, fearing loss of control. This delays recapitalisation and NPL write-offs, increasing the overall cost of bank recapitalisation, as most banks operate at or close to negative margins (World Bank, 1999b).

Up to late 1999, banks have recapitalised mainly by raising new capital through innovative hybrid capital instruments called 'SLIPs' and 'CAPs', which target depositors.[14] While they can be counted as bank capital for prudential control purposes, they are short term and costly with interest rates of between 12 and 22 per cent per year. Hence most banks cannot become profitable until they retire these instruments (Nomura Securities, 1999). Furthermore, such hybrid capital cannot absorb losses as well as equity capital can, and therefore is of lower quality (Standard and Poor's, 1999).

Some Thai banks have begun attracting foreign partners to assist them recapitalise. ABN Amro took a majority share of Bank of Asia; Development Bank of Singapore took a 58 per cent share in Thai Danu; in September 1999, Standard Chartered finalised the purchase of 75 per cent of Nakornthon Bank; United Overseas Bank of Singapore won the tender for the government-owned Radhanasin Bank; and several other bank takeovers and joint ventures are being negotiated. With insufficient capital available in the domestic market to meet recapitalisation needs, recapitalisation cannot occur without further major foreign capital injections or participation in the government-sponsored recapitalisation scheme (Standard and Poor's, 1999).

Cost of Recapitalisation and Depositor Guarantees

The cost of financial restructuring and recapitalisation is high. Estimates of the capital required for full loan loss provisioning of surviving financial institutions range from Baht 300 billion to Baht 400 billion (US$8.1 billion to US$10.8 billion) (Ministry of Finance, 1999) to Baht 700 billion to Baht 1 trillion (US$18.9 billion to US$ 27 billion) (Flatters, 1999). The total cost of supporting banks and finance

---

12 The package provides for up to Baht 300 billion (US$8.1 billion) in capital injections to viable private financial institutions. The Ministry of Finance matches funds raised by new or old shareholders by providing ten year government bonds in return for equity in the bank. Bank owners can buy back these shares at some future date, if they can recapitalise from other sources. For tier-1 capital injections, banks must adopt up-front year 2000 loan loss provisioning requirements; financial institutions unable to recapitalise will be nationalised (Ministry of Finance, 1999).

13 Siam Commercial Bank raised Baht 32 billion of new investor capital which the Government will match (Nomura Securities, 1999). Tisco Finance also has received approval for a government capital injection. Thai Military Bank had sought approval, but has delayed its recapitalisation plans until 2000.

14 Stapled Limited Interest Preferred Structures, SLIPS, are non-cumulative preferred shares, which qualify as tier-1 capital when calculating bank capital adequacy, while Capital Augmented Preferred Securities, CAPS, are subordinated debentures. The securities usually are non-voting and do not dilute banks' existing ownership structures, and have a maturity of up to seven years, although issuers can repay them after three years. Holders receive fixed payments for the life of the security. Banks cannot hold more than one third of tier-1 capital in this form (World Bank, 1999b). Thai Farmers Bank, Bank of Ayudhya, Bangkok Bank and Thai Military Bank issued such securities in 1998 and 1999.

companies and repaying depositors could reach Baht 2 trillion (US$54 billion) or 35 to 40 per cent of projected 1999 GDP (Fitch IBCA, 1999). Privatising nationalised banks and liquidating closed financial institutions' assets will provide part of this cost; however, Thai taxpayers will bear most of it. To date, the Government has issued bonds to finance:

- the Financial Sector Restructuring Agency which manages the affairs of the failed finance companies
- the Asset Management Corporation, which purchased the lowest quality assets of the failed finance companies
- capital injections to Nakornthon Bank
- the Financial Institutions Development Fund, which supplied huge amounts of liquidity support to weak financial institutions.[15]

The state enterprise privatisation program will not be large enough to repay the capital costs of bonds issued. The IMF/Thai Government's latest estimate of the annual interest cost of financial restructuring bonds is 4 per cent of GDP (Flatters, 1999).

RESOLVING NPLS

NPLs appeared to peak in May 1999 at around Baht 2.7 trillion (US$73 billion), 48 per cent of outstanding loans and 54 per cent of 1998 GDP (World Bank, 1999b). In the second half of 1999, NPLs started to fall due to lower interest rates and some debt restructuring; in August NPLs were 46.7 per cent. A return to growth, the Government's fiscal stimulus and corporate restructuring should help reduce NPLs further towards the end of 1999 (Figure 8.2).

The Government established the Asset Management Company to dispose of the NPLs of closed finance companies; however, existing privately-owned banks are encouraged to set up their own asset management companies to dispose of their NPLs. The Government offers exemptions from taxes and transfer fees to encourage this process. However, unlike the Korean Government, the Thai Government does not purchase surviving banks' NPLs through a central, government-owned asset management company (Fitch IBCA, 1999; and East Asia Analytical Unit, 1999). To remove NPLs from bank balance sheets, these special purpose companies must be majority-owned by third parties. However, banks have no guaranteed source of funds for this process; consequently progress is slow. Banks had disposed of less than 15 per cent of their NPLs by April 1999, mainly by write-offs (Fitch IBCA, 1999).

---

[15] The Financial Institutions Development Fund also guaranteed ailing financial institutions' deposits and other liabilities. Financial institutions with excess liquidity had to deposit it with the Financial Institutions Development Fund. In the eight weeks before mid July 1997, the fund lent financial institutions Baht 160 billion (US$5.2 billion). By November 1998, the fund had accumulated liabilities of over Baht 1 trillion (over US$30 billion) on behalf of the Government (Ministry of Finance, 1999). Analysts expect the Government will recover no more than half of these funds (Flatters, 1999).

Figure 8.2

Thai NPLs Decline Only Gradually
Non-performing Loan Ratios of Thai Financial Institutions (Per cent)

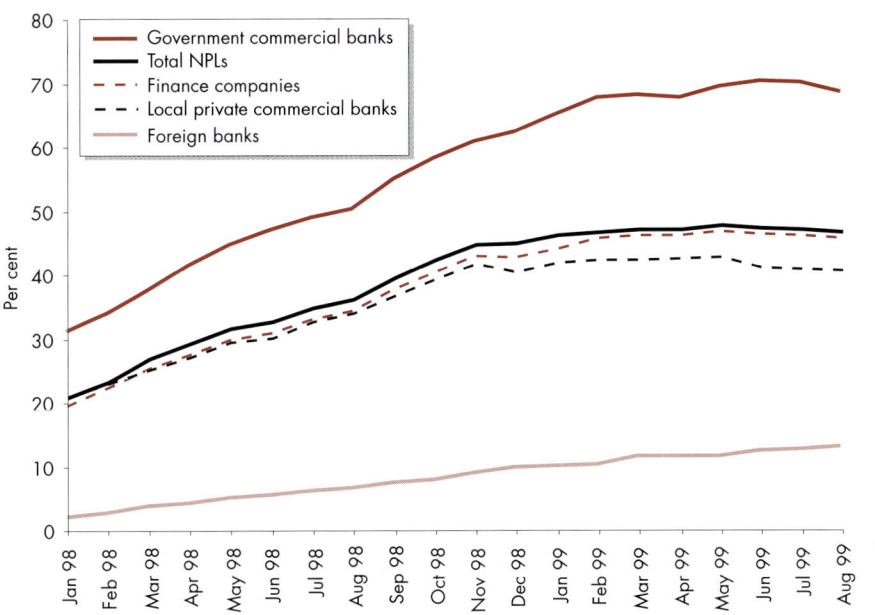

Source: CEIC, 1999.

In early 1999, Thai Farmers Bank announced it would set up the first asset management company and transfer its NPLs at 55 per cent of book value.[16] Joint-venture partners, Goldman Sachs and GE Capital, will help the bank maximise the value realised from these NPLs. In late 1999, more banks were establishing their own asset management companies; others will have to follow soon (Collins, 1999).[17] Consequently, a significant increase is expected in late 1999 (World Bank, 1999b).

DISPOSING OF NATIONALISED BANKS AND FINANCE COMPANIES

Since the crisis began, the Government has closed 69 finance companies and nationalised seven mostly small or medium sized banks pending recapitalisation and sale (Table 8.1).[18]

---

[16] However, some analysts believe 15 per cent of book value may be more realistic, given the extent of asset price depreciation and the difficulty of securing assets under Thailand's bankruptcy laws. This divergence probably explains why asset management companies are slow to take on NPLs.

[17] In September, Bangkok Bank and Bank Ayudhya announced plans to establish asset management companies (AFX-Asia, 24 September 1999).

[18] The nationalised banks are Siam City Bank, Bangkok Metropolitan Bank, Bangkok Bank of Commerce (absorbed into the 95 per cent state owned Krung Thai Bank), First Bangkok City Bank, Laem Thong Bank (absorbed into the newly created Radhanasin Bank), Bank Thai and Nakornthon Bank.

Table 8.1

Many Banks Are Nationalised and Finance Companies Closed
Government Intervention in Financial Institutions 1997 to October 1999

Pre-crisis number of banks and finance companies			
		Commercial banks	Finance companies
		15	91
1997	56 finance companies closed	Taken over by the Financial Restructuring Authority. Assets auctioned during 1998 and 1999	
1998	12 finance companies closed	Taken over by the Financial Restructuring Authority. Assets auctioned during 1998 and 1999	
	6 banks nationalised	Small and medium sized banks (20 per cent of banking system assets)	
1999	1 bank nationalised	Nakornthon Bank	
	1 finance company closed	Bank of Thailand appointed a liquidator for the small and insolvent Ocean Finance	

Post-crisis number of banks and finance companies			
Commercial banks		Finance companies	
Original owners	Merged or new ownership	Surviving	Taken over or closed
6	9	22	69

Source: Ministry of Finance, 1999a; World Bank, 1999b; and Fitch IBCA, 1999.

The nationalised banks still face major problems. The seven nationalised banks are severely undercapitalised and have high NPLs. Thailand's largest bank, the 70 per cent government-owned Krung Thai Bank, has NPLs exceeding 60 per cent of outstanding loans; another report estimates NPLs exceed 80 per cent of outstanding loans.[19] A rule holding state bank directors liable for losses caused by their business decisions constrains progress in restructuring state bank NPLs, transferring them to special purpose vehicles and realising losses. This rule also encourages illegal accounting practices.

The Government plans to sell the nationalised banks as soon as possible, realising some of the funds it has injected into them since 1997, and using these to recapitalise surviving banks. In doing so, it hopes to encourage banking sector consolidation and new foreign investment. However, so far privatisation has been slow.[20] Deals have been agreed for Nakornthon and Radhanasin Banks; and under Thailand's eighth Letter of Intent to the IMF, Siam City and Bangkok Metropolitan Banks should be sold by the end of 1999. The Government also hopes to privatise Krung Thai Bank within two or three years; this will present a major challenge, requiring significant modernisation and inroads into the bank's NPLs.

---

[19] A report by PricewaterhouseCoopers, commissioned by Krung Thai Bank and leaked to the press in August 1999, estimated the bank's NPLs at 84 per cent of total loans, raising questions over the NPL estimates the bank itself made, and the resultant recapitalisation cost.

[20] The original deadline of December 1998 to privatise Siam City and Bangkok Metropolitan Banks was not met due to delays in recapitalising banks and gaining government approval of loss-sharing arrangements with new buyers.

THAILAND'S FINANCE COMPANIES

The Thai Government's decision to close 69 finance companies was particularly courageous as powerful political interests and former bureaucrats partly owned or controlled these companies (Nomura Securities, 1999).

Before the crisis, the Bank of Thailand poorly supervised these finance companies; many were used as a means to avoid regulations imposed on banks (Pakorn, 1999). They could not legally take deposits, but issued promissory notes returning investors 12 to 15 per cent per year. They also often borrowed unhedged foreign funds and on-lent them to Thai customers in baht, exposing themselves to considerable foreign exchange risk. To cover their high capital costs, they lent to very risky projects, often ones that could not obtain bank loans. Most banks had their own finance companies; riskier borrowers were referred to these.

Since the crisis, most surviving finance companies have faced rising NPLs, falling earnings and increasing competition, with only a few strong companies showing good prospects. The remaining 22 finance companies now hold less than 10 per cent of financial system assets.

Disposing of failed finance company assets also presented a challenge. The Ministry of Finance's Financial Restructuring Agency ran five large auctions between July 1998 and August 1999 to liquidate finance company assets such as cars, construction loans and mortgages worth Baht 584 billion. In a protracted and at times controversial process, most assets eventually were sold, netting around 25 per cent of their book value.[21]

PRUDENTIAL CONTROL PROSPECTS

Inadequate financial system regulation and supervision reinforced Thailand's financial crisis. The Thai Government liberalised financial markets in the late 1980s and early 1990s, lifting interest rate ceilings and allowing financial institutions greater flexibility in their domestic and international activities (Bank of Thailand, 1998). However, it failed to substitute prudential regulation when it removed controls on asset allocation and foreign borrowing. With weak supervision, malpractice was frequent; risky connected lending and unhedged foreign borrowing were excessive (Pakorn, 1999). Supervisory skills were low and political intervention often compromised enforcement.

Improving Bank of Thailand Supervision

While the Government has introduced many prudential regulation reforms, it recognises it must strengthen the Bank of Thailand's capacity to enforce these regulations in supervising financial institutions. This requires training, reorganisation and outside expertise. The Bank of Thailand already has been reorganised and

---

[21] Local and foreign finance companies and banks bought assets; Goldman Sachs and GE Capital (Thailand) were the biggest single purchasers in the fifth and final auction on 11 August, 1999.

improved its recruitment; staff exchanges between it and local financial institutions, and multilateral and bilateral assistance training programs should build supervisory skills; the new central bank law should clarify its role and responsibilities.

The Bank of Thailand and World Bank recognise prudential aspects requiring strengthening include:

- methods and procedures for off-site monitoring and on-site examination
- requirements for consolidating supervision
- revision and streamlining of commercial bank reports
- design of bank and finance companies' public disclosure data
- improved enforcement (Ministry of Finance, 1999).

FINANCIAL SYSTEM PROSPECTS AND OPPORTUNITIES

The post-crisis banking system will have fewer banks, be more competitive and have a much greater foreign presence. As family controlled banks decline, competition and foreign presence is increasing, bringing greater pressure for higher standards. Top bankers realise the basis of lending must change from connections and collateral to balance sheet and cash flow analysis. Competition already is raising credit requirements and accounting standards. Credit approval is more closely scrutinised and more arms-length than before; several banks now approve credit through committee rather than individual decisions (Nomura Securities, 1999).

International banks will be the single most important force increasing competition and improving efficiency, risk management, transparency and technological development. New prudential controls and improved bankruptcy proceedings also will be crucial in improving the sector's performance and reducing exposure to future crises. Together these factors should help the Thai banking system gradually achieve international standards in transparency and efficiency. These developments also should expand opportunities for Australian suppliers of banking system technologies, as local banks seek to compete with new foreign entrants and foreign owners attempt to upgrade local systems.

Capital Markets

The Thai equity and bond markets are relatively underdeveloped. The equity market had recovered by late 1999, but remains small and vulnerable to volatility and competition from Internet based stockbrokers. The floating of Baht 500 billion in government bonds to refinance the Financial Institutions Development Fund's short term debt is forcing the development of a government bond market, including what promises to be a large secondary market. Capital market prudential controls require strengthening to develop these markets. Many opportunities should arise for foreign fund managers and suppliers of financial system technologies, as local institutions seek to compete with new foreign entrants.

Insurance

Thailand's insurance industry is progressively opening and liberalising; 12 new licences were issued in 1997 including several with minority foreign participation. Licences have a maximum of 25 per cent foreign participation, but this will be lifted to 49 per cent in 2000.

Insurance penetration in Thailand remains low; premiums are 1.2 per cent of GDP, compared to Malaysia's 2.2 per cent. While the sector grew by 15 per cent per year over 1992-97, it fell by 25 per cent during the crisis. After the crisis began, some insurers developed solvency problems from losses on property and equity investments. However, these were limited to some extent by restrictive government investment regulations; furthermore Thai policies are payable in baht, not in US dollars as in Indonesia.[22]

Future Prospects

Since the crisis began, the Thai Government has adhered to its IMF program and made significant structural reforms in a relatively short period. In doing so it has overcome significant domestic political resistance. It has overhauled financial sector prudential requirements, enacted basic economic laws, including strengthening the bankruptcy law, and opened the financial sector to foreign investment. By mid 1998, the Government had started to relax fiscal and monetary policy, expanding the budget deficit and allowing interest rates to fall. Consequently, by the third quarter of 1999, GDP growth was starting to recover.[23] In late 1999, it announced it would not require the last tranche of disbursements agreed under its IMF program.

However, concerns remain about the pace and extent of bank NPL write-offs and refinancing, and the effectiveness of new bankruptcy laws. Unless addressed rapidly, these problems could undermine sustainable growth once the effects of the Government's fiscal stimulus package are exhausted. Successful bank recapitalisation and corporate debt restructuring and effective implementation of new laws and prudential controls are essential to foster a more robust financial sector and underpin sounder, more sustainable long term growth.

MALAYSIA

Malaysia's comparatively small foreign debt and modest exposure to short term borrowing helped it avoid the most severe problems of the 'three IMF economies', Indonesia, Thailand and Korea. Nevertheless, the Malaysian Government had to intervene to restore health in the banking system and stimulate financial sector restructuring. It also raised interest rates and eventually introduced capital controls to defend the ringgit. To resolve banks' high NPLs, the Government followed the Korean and Japanese approach, establishing an asset management company to buy NPLs from the banking system and injecting government funds to boost banks' capital adequacy ratios.

---

[22] Insurance is regulated by the Ministry of Commerce, which currently is segregating life and non-life businesses. The life insurance sector is inhibited by regulations guaranteeing policy benefit levels to policyholders, negatively affecting industry viability.

[23] In November 1999, the Bank of Thailand expected 1999 GDP growth to reach 3.5 per cent, well up on its earlier estimate of 1 per cent (*Far Eastern Economic Review*, 4 November 1999, p. 11).

IMPACT OF THE CRISIS

Before the Asian financial crisis, Malaysia had one of the region's most diversified financial sectors. While bank finance still dominated funding, domestic debt markets raised around 33 per cent of net financing (Figure 8.3). Malaysia's economy also had many other strengths including high national savings, large fiscal surpluses, low external debt and low inflation (World Bank, 1999b).

After Singapore, pre-crisis Malaysia had the strongest banks in South East Asia. Balance sheets were sound; NPLs were low; and banking supervision exceeded average regional standards (*Fortune*, 24 November 1997). Pre-crisis NPLs officially were only 3.6 per cent of total bank loans, while the banks' average risk weighted capital adequacy ratio was 11.8 per cent, well above the Bank for International Settlements' 8 per cent minimum (Ministry of Finance, 1998). While Malaysia's current account deficit was high at 5.8 per cent of GDP, it had a relatively good match of foreign liabilities and assets, and foreign reserves exceeded short term debt.

However, like Indonesia, Thailand and Korea, Malaysia had high pre-crisis rates of private sector credit growth, a rapidly growing economy with increasing real estate and equity price inflation, real exchange rate appreciation and slowing exports (World Bank, 1999b). New credit expanded over 25 per cent per year between 1995 and 1997; property and business services were the biggest destinations (Delhaise, 1999). Consequently, Malaysia's corporate sector became highly leveraged; by 1997, bank loans were around 170 per cent of GDP, similar to levels in Korea and Thailand.[24]

Figure 8.3

Pre-crisis Domestic Debt Markets Important
Share of Net Funds Raised in Malaysian Financial Markets, 1996

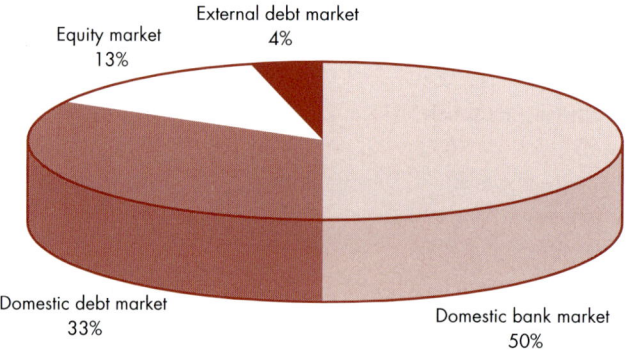

Source: Thillainathan, 1998.

---

[24] Leverage, measured by the average corporate debt to equity ratio, rose from around 90 per cent in 1991 to close to 200 per cent by 1996.

In late 1997, liquidity concerns in smaller banks caused a flight to quality as depositors switched to foreign banks and major local banks. The situation began to stabilise in January 1998 when Bank Negara issued a statement guaranteeing it would pay principal and accrued interest on deposits at financial institutions it supervised.[25] Although Malaysia did not seek an IMF program, the Government voluntarily adopted many elements of programs in the three IMF economies, initially including a tight monetary policy.

Throughout 1998 and 1999, NPLs grew to levels where, without external assistance, some banks' capital adequacy ratios would have fallen below the mandated 8 per cent. By the end of 1998, the banking system's gross NPLs reached 20 per cent of outstanding loans (Fitch IBCA, 1999).[26]

PRUDENTIAL REGULATION AND SUPERVISION REFORMS

Bank Negara is considered one of the best regulators in Asia, renown for its strict interpretation of rules and transparency (Delhaise, 1999). *The Banking and Financial Institutions Act 1989* vested Bank Negara with wide ranging responsibilities and powers to oversee banks, finance companies and insurance companies. In April 1997, the Government introduced measures to restrain excessive bank lending to real estate, shares and units in unit trusts (Delhaise, 1999).

After the crisis began, the Government further tightened many prudential regulations, although some subsequently were relaxed temporarily to ease the severity of the ensuing credit crunch (Bank Negara Malaysia, 1999a).

Loan Classification and Provisioning

From late 1997, the Government strengthened many prudential regulations. In September 1997, it tightened loan classifications so NPLs became loans overdue by three months instead of six months. It required provisioning of at least 1.5 per cent of total loans and 20 per cent of the uncollateralised portion of sub-standard loans; it strengthened bank disclosure requirements and introduced a monthly stress test of bank credit positions (Malaysian Ministry of Finance, 1998). Bank Negara instructed all banking institutions to establish loan rehabilitation units to separate the management of NPLs from daily credit management and administration (Bank of America, 1999).

However, in September 1998, as a result of the unexpectedly severe recession and credit crunch, the Government temporarily relaxed the NPL classification system to six months and allowed restructured and rescheduled loans to be re-classified as performing loans (Malaysian Ministry of Finance, 1998). The Government judged tighter provisioning rules were deterring banks from lending and undermining viable businesses and projects. The new provisions also gave borrowers more time to restructure loans before they were classified as non-performing. As in Indonesia, the Malaysian Government plans to tighten prudential controls as the economy recovers.

---

[25] Malaysia did not have a formal deposit insurance scheme. Now a scheme is being considered.

[26] Malaysia defines NPLs as those that have not repaid interest or capital for over three months and include NPLs sold to Danaharta, the government asset management company.

Finance Company Capital Requirements

Many finance companies experienced severe difficulties during the crisis. To stimulate consolidation and raise public confidence in finance companies, the Government significantly raised their minimum capital requirements.[27] In addition, it increased the risk weighted capital adequacy ratio for finance companies from 8 per cent to 9 per cent by December 1998 and to 10 per cent by December 1999. These new policies are forcing mergers and acquisitions among finance companies and with commercial banks.

Rather than adjusting banks' capital requirements, the Government is using official directives and Danamodal, the agency it established to recapitalise and strengthen the banking industry, to force banking sector restructuring and consolidation.

Supervisory Reforms

Since the crisis, Malaysia also has upgraded significantly its financial supervisory practices. Bank Negara's new liquidity requirement policy replaces previous high liquidity ratios with liquidity requirements; these are based on a bank's ability to meet short term liquidity needs arising from its liabilities' maturity profile. Over time, this new approach should improve liquidity management practices. Bank Negara also is introducing consolidated supervision of all financial institutions in accordance with international best practice. (See Chapter 3 - *Prudential Reform*.)

Bankruptcy Reform

As in other crisis affected economies, the Government is upgrading the bankruptcy framework. The Government closed legislative loopholes to stop companies applying for restraining orders against creditors without their knowledge. Companies can seek protection against creditors while restructuring schemes are worked out (Fitch IBCA, 1999). New rules require borrowers to submit a statement of financial condition, so they cannot acquire additional debts or dispose of assets during the period of the restraining order. In addition, to protect creditors' rights, restructuring companies must appoint independent directors to their boards, nominated by a majority of creditors, to oversee the restructuring process. However, unlike in some other regional economies, the bankruptcy regime does not require independent judicial oversight of corporate workout schemes (Fitch IBCA, 1999).

CAPITAL MARKET REFORMS

The Government also recognises the need to reduce reliance on bank lending and upgrade capital market regulation. In 1999, new risk based capital adequacy rules will force brokers who take on risks to have adequate capital protection. The Government also is improving disclosure standards and moving stock market regulation from a merit based to a disclosure based system. Other recent reforms include tightening regulations on related-party transactions, introducing new

---

[27] The minimum capital requirement increased from Ringgit 5 million to Ringgit 300 million by the end of 1999, and to Ringgit 600 million by the end of 2000.

disclosure requirements for nominee accounts, tightening definitions and penalties for insider trading and increasing Securities Commission inspection and enforcement powers.

Other initiatives will address impediments to capital market development. In 1999, the Securities Commission established a Capital Market Strategic Committee to develop a capital market master plan by early 2000 (AFX-Asia, 23 September 1999).[28] In addition, in February 1999, a high level government finance committee proposed a code of corporate governance and recommended reforms to laws, regulations and rules to improve corporate governance (Finance Committee on Corporate Governance, 1999). Such reforms should improve confidence and market discipline in the share market and corporate bond market. To eventually expand the corporate bond market and enable institutional investors to impose market discipline on corporates, the Government is relaxing restrictions on insurance companies holding corporate bonds.

Bank Negara is revising its guidelines on issuing private debt securities to streamline the corporate bond market and introducing guidelines on securitisation. This development will diversify risks away from the banking system, increase the variety of fundraising instruments in the market and widen the spectrum of papers available for investment.

Malaysian capital markets should start to grow in 1999-2000, stimulated partly by the large bond issues by Danamodal, to recapitalise the banks, and Danaharta, the government agency which purchases NPLs from the banking system. The Government's capital market regulation and supervision reforms, stamp duty exemption on corporate bonds and relaxation of insurance company bond purchases also should assist capital market growth. (See Chapter 5 - *Capital Markets*.)

CAPITAL CONTROLS

On 1 September 1998, the Government introduced controls on international capital inflows and outflows, reversing its relatively open pre-crisis capital market regime. The Government aimed to eliminate the offshore ringgit market, which authorities believed fuelled speculative attacks on the local currency and constrained authorities' ability to reduce interest rates (World Bank, 1999b; and Bank Negara Malaysia, 1998). The Government's capital controls:

- introduced a fixed exchange rate at Ringgit 3.8:US$1

- required all ringgit held abroad to be brought onshore within one month

- imposed a one year holding period on all foreign accounts in Malaysia and the foreigners' proceeds of Malaysian securities' sales

- terminated offshore trading in ringgit instruments and domestic credit facilities for overseas banks and stockbrokers

---

[28] Impediments include lack of an over-the-counter market, a poor clearing system and lack of foreign participation. Another constraint is the approval process for corporate bonds; sometimes it takes six months and involves Bank Negara, the Ratings Agency of Malaysia and the Securities Commission.

- required all importers and exporters to pay and receive foreign currency for imports and exports[29]
- required those needing foreign currency to seek central bank approval.

The Government believes its controls allowed it to stabilise the currency, eliminate speculative attacks and regain control of interest rates. Between August 1998 and August 1999, lending rates declined from 13 per cent to 8 per cent. Lower interest rates encouraged investment and consumption, and gave relief to corporate borrowers. However, Malaysia possibly could have achieved lower interest rates and a stable currency without capital controls (World Bank, 1999b). From late 1998, most other regional economies' interest rates also fell significantly and currencies appreciated as speculative attacks subsided; capital inflows to the region also resumed in 1999, as investor confidence returned (World Bank, 1999b).

The main risk Malaysia faces from capital controls is negative foreign investor reaction and lower future foreign direct investment, FDI. However, *bona fide* current account and FDI related transactions were exempt from the controls. While FDI did fall significantly, as of November 1999, it is too early to judge whether capital controls contributed to this. The Government also has indicated controls are temporary, and it will remove them when the global financial environment normalises (Bank Negara Malaysia, 1998).

While the controls initially locked foreigners into the market for one year, exit provisions were relaxed progressively, lessening the effect on foreign portfolio investors. In February 1999, the Government introduced a graduated exit levy, or tax on repatriated principal, with tax rates of between 30 per cent and 10 per cent. In September 1999, the exit levy was fixed at 10 per cent, simplifying administration for foreign fund managers (Bank Negara Malaysia, 1999b). This one tier exit levy will help Malaysia achieve a higher weighting when it returns to the Morgan Stanley international share index in May 2000. Malaysia did not experience a massive exodus of foreign funds in September 1999 when, after the first 12 months of controls, funds could be withdrawn without the need to pay the exit tax.

RESOLVING NPLS AND RECAPITALISING THE BANKING SYSTEM

In mid 1998, the Government established three institutions to resolve serious banking sector NPL problems and implement refinancing and restructuring:

- Danaharta purchases NPLs from the banking system and maximises the recovery value of acquired assets
- Danamodal injects capital to strengthen banking institutions
- the Corporate Debt Restructuring Committee facilitates voluntary out-of-court restructuring of corporate debt through voluntary agreements between creditors and debtors (Kawai, 1999).

---

[29] This provision was considered necessary to curb the offshore market in ringgit, and hence currency speculation.

Danaharta: Managing and Resolving NPLs

In May 1998, to strengthen domestically-owned financial institutions' balance sheets and enhance their lending ability, the Government established an asset management company, Danaharta, to acquire these institutions' NPLs. Using government guaranteed bonds, Danaharta purchases NPLs from financial institutions whose NPL ratio exceeds 10 per cent.[30] If Danaharta recovers more than it pays for a NPL, the financial institution gets 80 per cent of the surplus back.

Danaharta only buys loans above Ringgit 5 million, bidding for NPLs at a discount to book value. While sales to Danaharta technically are voluntary, banks that reject a Danaharta NPL bid must write down the NPL's value to 80 per cent of Danaharta's offer. Banks also have an incentive to sell their NPLs because they can amortise losses over five years.

Danaharta has broad powers, giving it an advantage over banks when restructuring loans and realising collateral. For example, a bank must go to court to begin foreclosure proceedings, but Danaharta only needs to give 30 days' notice that it intends to foreclose (Danaharta, 1999). It also can impose conditions on defaulting debtors to facilitate asset restructuring and rehabilitation, and appoint special administrators to manage the affairs of distressed companies (Bank Negara Malaysia, 1999a).

By June 1999, six months ahead of schedule, Danaharta had largely completed its NPL acquisition plan, purchasing around 35 per cent of banking system NPLs at an average 57 per cent discount on face value (Danaharta, 1999). It now manages almost Ringgit 40 billion (US$10.5 billion) of NPLs acquired from 66 financial institutions.[31] By the end of 1999, Danaharta almost will reduce the banking system's NPL ratio to 10 per cent, which the Government believes is manageable (Figure 8.4).

Managing Danaharta's assets

Danaharta's approach to asset management falls somewhere between that of a rapid disposal agency and a warehousing agency, which stores assets until prices recover.[32] Danaharta's strong powers should enable it to add value to assets before it disposes of them; improving economic conditions also should help increase their value.

Danaharta's approach is quite well tailored to Malaysia's circumstances as:

- Malaysia's NPLs are highly concentrated; 70 per cent of NPLs are in only 2 000 to 3 000 accounts each worth more than Ringgit 5 million

- resolving most NPLs requires industry and business restructuring rather than merely renegotiating interest and payment terms.

---

[30] Institutions receive government guaranteed zero coupon bonds that are zero risk weighted in capital adequacy calculations.

[31] This includes Ringgit 17.8 billion in NPLs acquired from private banks and another Ringgit 21.5 billion of NPLs from government-owned Sime and Bumiputera banks which Danaharta manages for the Government.

[32] The US Resolution Trust Corporation and Thailand's Financial Restructuring Agency are rapid disposal agencies. Mexico used a warehousing agency, holding assets from five to ten years until asset values recovered.

Figure 8.4

Gross NPLs Peak, Net NPLs Fall towards 10 per cent
Non-performing Loans in the Banking System, March 1997 to July 1999

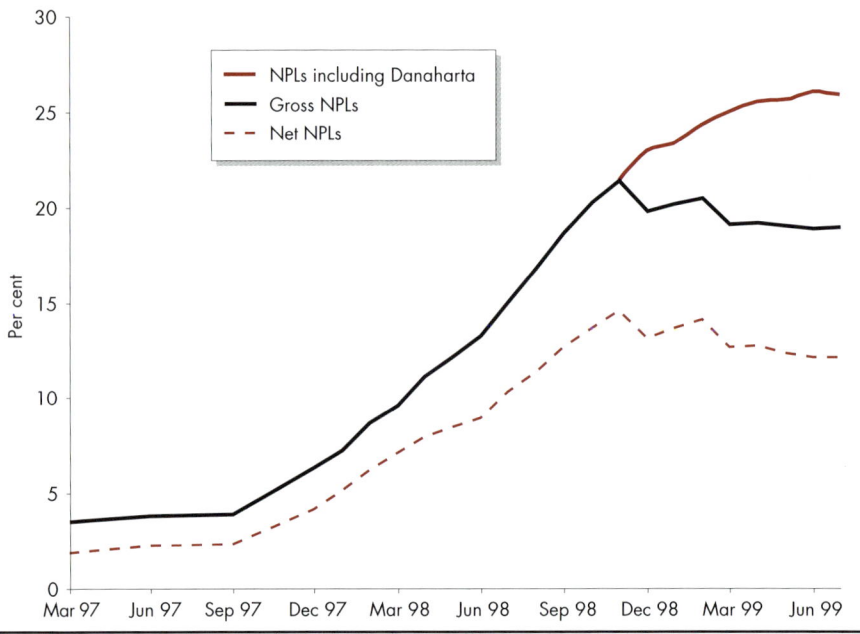

Source: CEIC, 1999; and Bank of America, 1999.

Danaharta started disposing of assets in late 1999 through joint ventures, stock exchange listing, securitisation, asset sales and liquidation (Danaharta, 1999). Subject to foreign ownership limits, foreign companies can bid for NPLs.[33]

Danamodal: Recapitalising the Banking System

Danamodal was established in August 1998 to:

- recapitalise and strengthen the banking industry
- help consolidate and rationalise the banking system to support Malaysia's next phase of economic development (Bank of America, 1999).

By July 1999, Danamodal had injected Ringgit 6.4 billion or 14 per cent of the banking sector's total 1998 tier-1 capital into ten financial institutions. This boosted the banking sector's average capital adequacy to 13 per cent.

As banks also are raising funds from new equity issues, hybrid instruments, domestic and international bond issues, and borrowing, the Government should need significantly less than the estimated Ringgit 16 billion to recapitalise the financial

---

[33] Foreign ownership is limited to 61 per cent in telecommunications, 30 per cent of listed banks and 51 per cent of insurance companies, but manufacturing enterprises can be wholly foreign owned.

sector. Also, in 1999, several banks began repaying capital injections, and some analysts predict further injections could be unnecessary after 2000, if conditions continue to improve.[34]

Danamodal has two years to complete its recapitalisation task. It then will own a significant portfolio of banking sector shares; it plans to sell these through strategic sales and directly to the public on the stock market.

CONSOLIDATING THE FINANCIAL SECTOR

The Malaysian Government and Bank Negara believe banking sector consolidation is a high priority. They anticipate mergers are necessary to allow Malaysian financial institutions to compete with international banks, and avoid future banking system crises and rescues (Bank Negara Malaysia, 1999c). In July 1999, the Government announced an ambitious plan to consolidate the banking sector: by April 2000, the Government had hoped to merge 55 banking institutions including 20 commercial banks, 12 merchant banks and 23 finance companies into six banking groups, each with an anchor bank chosen by the Government to control the group.[35]

Responding to strong objections from the financial sector in October 1999, the Government modified this approach and tight merger timetable (Bank Negara Malaysia, 1999c). The revised plan allows banks and other financial institutions to choose their own merger partners and leader within each merged group; more than six groups will be permitted. However, Bank Negara can intervene to select merger partners if institutions fail to participate in mergers voluntarily. Institutions must notify Bank Negara of their merger groupings by the end of January 2000, and the merger process should be completed by the end of December 2000.

Investment bank Goldman Sachs estimates the consolidation program could slash operating costs by 20 to 25 per cent (Asian Banker Interactive, 1999). However, merged institutions only could realise such savings through staff reductions and branch closures and the Government has indicated it will not allow forced retrenchments. While the process should consolidate Malaysia's banking system, the likely shape of the industry will only become clear in January 2000.

FOREIGN PARTICIPATION

Foreign institutions dominated Malaysia's financial sector until the 1970s, but then their role diminished as their participation was restricted under Malaysia's 'New Economic Policy'. Now the financial system is significantly undercapitalised, and Malaysia is seeking some strategic foreign investment, albeit subject to significant restrictions. Unlike in Indonesia and Korea, the Malaysian banking system is unlikely to open fully to international investment, although World Trade Organisation disciplines may require some opening by 2003.

---

[34] Arab-Malaysian Bank repaid Ringgit 500 million of the Ringgit 1.5 billion it received; Rasheed Hussain Bank repaid Ringgit 500 million of the Ringgit 1.5 billion it received; and the Ringgit 317 million loan to United Merchant Finance was repaid as part of the Ban Hin Lee Bank merger with Southern Bank.

[35] The proposed anchor banks were Maybank, Multi-Purpose Bank, Bumiputera Commerce Bank, Perwira Affin Bank, Public Bank and Southern Bank.

Banking

To allow banks to source funds for recapitalisation, the Government has relaxed the long standing 30 per cent cap on foreign ownership of domestic banks. However, approval is given on a case-by-case basis (Fitch IBCA, 1999). Despite restrictions, foreign banks still hold around 21 per cent of Malaysian deposits and advance 23 per cent of commercial bank loans (Delhaise, 1999).

Foreign banks face several other constraints. Wholly foreign-owned banks face restrictions on their branch network expansion and their use of foreign management personnel.[36] Furthermore, local banks must supply 60 per cent of foreign companies' borrowing requirements in Malaysia.

Insurance

Malaysia has a high level of international participation in its insurance sector. However, contrary to the trend in most other regional economies to liberalise insurance markets, Malaysia's 1996 insurance law forced foreign insurers to sell down their shares in locally licensed companies to 51 per cent of equity. It also introduced a 30 per cent limit on new foreign investment in existing insurers. However, five foreign insurers were granted joint-venture licences in February 1999, allowing them to convert their foreign branches into locally incorporated entities with Malaysian equity participation.[37]

Under its 1998 World Trade Organisation financial services commitments, Malaysia agreed to maintain at least 51 per cent foreign ownership of joint-venture companies, grant six new licences for life reinsurance by 30 June 2005, and allow up to 30 per cent foreign shareholding of two government-owned reinsurance companies.

FUTURE TRENDS AND CHALLENGES

Malaysia has strengthened prudential regulation and supervision, and rapidly progressed in refinancing and restructuring the financial sector. The long term effect of capital controls remains uncertain. However, in late 1999, potential negative effects appeared largely offset by increased market confidence due to Malaysia's ongoing structural reforms, generally sound macroeconomic management and recovering confidence throughout East Asia. Furthermore, in 1999, the fixed exchange rate probably prevented appreciation of the ringgit, assisting exports.

In establishing Danaharta and Danamodal, the Government moved decisively to address the banking system's asset quality problems. Efficiently purchasing large volumes of bank NPLs and injecting public capital into undercapitalised banks significantly reduced the potential for systemic bank failure and allowed lending to resume to support economic activity.

---

[36] Standard Chartered, Hong Kong Shanghai Bank, Overseas Chinese Banking Corporation and United Overseas Bank have the most extensive branch networks (Tan, 1999).

[37] The licencees were Great Eastern Life Assurance Company, Overseas Assurance Corporation, Asia Life Assurance Society, Asia Insurance Company, and Wing On Fire and Marine Insurance Company.

The government driven consolidation of the financial sector is ambitious, but if handled efficiently and fairly, could make the industry more competitive. Recent moves to allow the banks greater flexibility in choosing merger partners were necessary, and well received by the market. Because these consolidated financial groups will own banks, finance companies and merchant banks, the importance of consolidated supervision will increase; Bank Negara already is implementing this. Merging so many financial institutions in such a short time will challenge Malaysian bankers and regulators; difficulties in agreeing on fair valuations are possible, but should be less problematic now voluntary groupings are permitted. Despite these uncertainties, the Malaysian Government's financial system reforms appear to be facilitating the sector's recovery.

THE PHILIPPINES

Massive loan growth, exposure to foreign currency borrowing and the real estate boom came late to the Philippines, and were moderated by an attentive central bank. Pre-crisis reforms to supervision and regulation helped the Philippines survive the Asian financial crisis with its banking system largely intact, although much of the sector is still relatively uncompetitive. After its mid 1980s banking crisis, the Philippines strengthened its banking sector. Consequently, better transparency and accounting practices, a more robust, although far from perfect bankruptcy system, and more highly educated and experienced bankers insulated the Philippines from the worst of the crisis.

PRE-CRISIS EXPERIENCES

Unlike other East Asian countries, the Philippines only experienced high economic growth and substantial capital inflows from 1994.[38] Capital inflows rose with post-1994 economic growth but were not excessive.[39]

After economic crises in 1984-86 and 1991-92, the Government with World Bank and IMF support undertook comprehensive economic reforms. Under the Ramos administration the pace of reform accelerated; major measures included the dismantling of private and public monopolies, international trade, foreign exchange and foreign investment liberalisation, fiscal reform, privatisation and financial sector reforms (East Asia Analytical Unit, 1998). As excessive public sector foreign borrowing had caused several past crises, the Government avoided extensive foreign borrowing after 1994. Many commercial banks also had been exposed to foreign exchange borrowing in 1983-84, making major banks more conservative in the late 1990s boom period (Beltran and Guinigundo, 1999).[40]

---

[38] Real GNP growth rose from 1.6 per cent in 1992 to 7.2 per cent in 1996, with inflation remaining manageable, averaging 8.5 per cent during these years.

[39] Capital inflows rose from US$2.1 billion in 1993 to US$3.6 billion in 1996 (International Monetary Fund, 1999).

[40] Some smaller banks did get into trouble in 1997-98 due to excessive foreign exchange exposure.

Thailand, Malaysia and the Philippines

After 1994, rising capital inflows strengthened the Philippine balance of payments, improved international reserves and allowed increases in capital equipment and infrastructure investment. Foreign capital inflows also stimulated domestic capital market development. However, higher capital inflows made the economy vulnerable to capital flight. Analysts estimated that in early 1997, foreign funds accounted for 15 per cent of stock market capitalisation and 70 per cent of turnover (Beltran and Guinigundo, 1999). Capital inflows also exposed the economy to serious foreign exchange risks, as a near fixed exchange rate and low world interest rates made unhedged foreign borrowing appear a low risk activity.

FINANCIAL SYSTEM STRUCTURE

Like most low income developing economies, banks dominate the financial sector, accounting for around 80 per cent of total assets in 1998. The Philippines has 19 universal commercial banks, 34 ordinary commercial banks, 118 thrift banks and 839 rural banks.[41] Universal and ordinary commercial banks hold 80 per cent of bank assets (Figure 8.5). The Government wholly owns two specialised development banks, the Land Bank of the Philippines and the Development Bank of the Philippines. These also undertake some commercial banking functions.

Figure 8.5

Commercial Banks Dominate the Financial System
Share of Financial System Assets, 1998

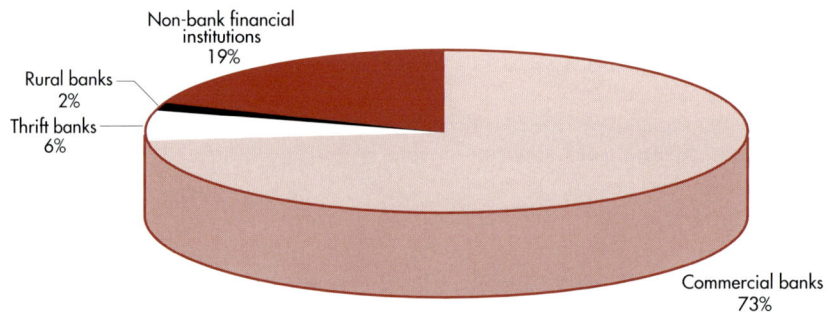

Source: CEIC, 1999.

---

[41] Universal commercial banks, also known as expanded commercial banks, can underwrite securities and own equity in non-financial enterprises, while ordinary commercial banks cannot.

After 1993, a result of liberalisation and an improved business environment, the financial sector grew strongly. However, while deposits and loans grew by around 40 per cent per year in 1996 and 1997, the banking sector remained small. In 1998, its total assets were only US$72 billion, less than those of some Asian banks (CEIC, 1999; and Delhaise, 1999). Financial intermediation deepened rapidly, with the ratio of money in circulation and bank deposits to GDP nearly doubling from 34 per cent in 1991 to 61 per cent in 1997. However this ratio is still much lower than elsewhere in the region.[42]

Banks' market share dominates that of non-bank intermediaries.[43] In mid 1999, the non-bank financial institutions held only 19 per cent of the financial system's assets and 9 per cent of its liabilities (CEIC, 1999). Over the 1990s, non-bank financial institutions actually lost market share to banks.[44]

IMPACT OF THE CRISIS ON FINANCIAL MARKETS

Like elsewhere in the region, capital flight during the financial crisis caused the exchange rate to depreciate substantially and interest rates to rise steeply.[45] The stock market also plummeted. Initially, banks profited from increased interest rates on their loans and the higher peso value of their positive net foreign exchange holdings. However, NPLs rose as high interest rates and unhedged foreign exchange exposures increased corporate bankruptcies.

Previous banking sector reforms shielded the Philippine banking system from the more severe effects of the Asian crisis, allowing it to avoid major bank failures.[46] While the central bank, Bangko Sentral ng Pilipinas, provided emergency liquidity assistance, it was not on the scale of Indonesia or Thailand.[47] The Bangko Sentral ng Pilipinas's most controversial intervention was the temporary (eight month) closure of Orient Commercial Bank in 1998, before it eventually went into receivership. The Bangko Sentral ng Pilipinas decision subsequently led to tighter regulation of capital deficient banks.

---

[42] Using another measure of financial depth, in 1997, the ratio of loans to GDP for the Philippines was 60 to 70 per cent, less than half that of Malaysia (140 to 160 per cent) and Thailand (130 to 150 per cent). Only Indonesia (50 to 60 per cent) had a lower ratio (Delhaise, 1999).

[43] Philippine non-bank institutions include insurance companies, securities companies, financing companies, investment companies, securities dealers and brokers, fund managers, pawnshops, lending investors, non-stock savings and loan associations, building and loans associations, venture capital corporations, cooperatives, and credit unions.

[44] From 1990 to 1998, non-bank financial institution assets grew at an average of 17 per cent while bank assets grew at an average of 21 per cent per year.

[45] The exchange rate bottomed at P 42.66:US$1 in January 1998, down from P 26.38:US$1 in June 1997. The benchmark 91 day Treasury bill peaked at 19.1 per cent in January 1998 up from 10.5 per cent in June 1997.

[46] Since the crisis began, only one small commercial bank, Orient Commercial Bank, seven thrift banks and 18 rural banks have failed. Their combined assets represent less than 1 per cent of the banking system.

[47] From July 1997 to November 1998, 11 banks, excluding rural banks, received emergency liquidity assistance worth P 14.8 billion (US$383 million) or 0.6 per cent of GDP and less than 1 per cent of bank deposits (Beltran and Guingundo, 1999).

Despite generally good prudential controls, the slowing economy, peso depreciation and high interest rates reduced banks' asset quality and profitability in 1997 and 1998. The NPL ratio grew from 4 per cent in June 1997 to 14.4 per cent in May 1999, before falling to 14.3 per cent in July 1999. NPLs are much higher in thrift and rural banks than in commercial banks (Figure 8.6). The worsening ratio of NPLs to total loans also partly reflects tighter prudential standards for loan classification and loss provisioning, making asset quality problems more transparent.[48]

Bank lending decelerated as a result of growing NPLs and weak macroeconomic conditions. Net domestic credit growth slowed to close to zero in late 1998. Depositor confidence in the banking system remained strong, with no major run on deposits. However, thrift and rural banks' share of total deposits fell from 11.9 per cent to 10.3 per cent, suggesting a flight to quality. The deposit share of foreign banks also rose from 4.0 per cent to 7.1 per cent between 1996 and 1998, although this was partly because many foreign-owned banks were newly opened and just starting to mobilise deposits.

Figure 8.6

Commercial Bank NPLs Modest
NPLs by Major Bank Type, 1993-98 (Per cent of Total Loans)

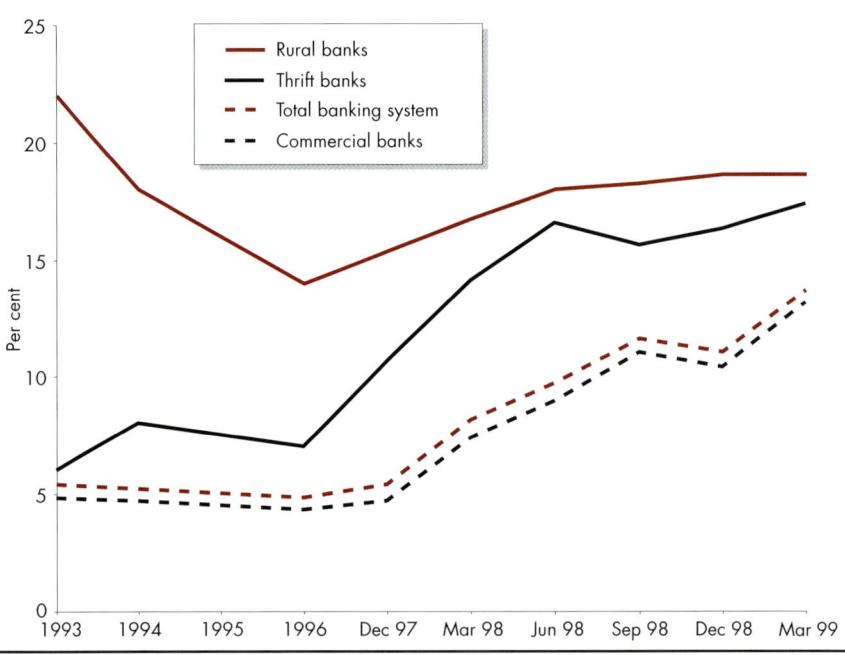

Source: CEIC, 1999.

[48] Bank profitability also fell, with returns on banking system assets falling to 0.37 per cent in June 1998, from 1.66 per cent in 1997, and an average of over 2.3 per cent during 1990-96.

Banks' strong and rising capital adequacy buffered them from rising NPLs. In 1996, Philippine banks were among the most highly capitalised and least leveraged in the region. In mid 1997, their capital adequacy ratios averaged 17.6 per cent, well above the regulatory minimum of 10 per cent and almost double those of Thailand and Korea (Bangko Sentral ng Pilipinas, 1999a). Over 1998, their capital adequacy ratios actually increased to 17.8 per cent; of the commercial banks, only Orient Commercial Bank had a capital adequacy ratio below 10 per cent. However, average capital adequacy levels disguised some significant problems, especially in smaller banks and the 46 per cent government-owned Philippine National Bank.

Fortunately, bank exposure to real estate lending was lower than in other ASEAN economies. Property demand was flat through much of the 1990s and an excess supply had not developed, except in prestige condominiums. Office vacancy rates were only 2 per cent before the crisis. Central bank restrictions on real estate lending encouraged real estate developers to pre-sell projects and tap foreign equity and stock market funds; this reduced bank exposure to this risk (East Asia Analytical Unit, 1998).

PRE-CRISIS FINANCIAL SECTOR REFORMS

After the 1992-93 financial crisis, the Bangko Sentral ng Pilipinas tightened prudential regulations, strengthened the banking system's capital base and reduced exposure to real estate and foreign currency risk. Between 1993 and 1998, the Ramos administration sought to reform further the inefficient and protected financial sector. It lifted restrictions on domestic bank branch networks in 1993, opened the banking and insurance sectors to new entrants in 1994, and expanded the business scope of universal commercial banks (East Asia Analytical Unit, 1998). However, despite these reforms, the banking sector remained small and inefficient, even by regional standards.

POST-CRISIS BANKING REFORMS

After the crisis began, the Bangko Sentral ng Pilipinas progressively increased bank minimum capital requirements to strengthen banks' equity bases and encourage mergers. Over 1999-2000, it will introduce further increases of between 20 and 60 per cent, depending on the type of bank.[49] In June 1997, Bangko Sentral ng Pilipinas lowered ceilings on real estate development lending from 30 per cent to 20 per cent of total loans and reduced the maximum ratio of real estate loans to collateral value from 70 per cent to 60 per cent, further limiting real estate lending exposure.[50] The Bangko Sentral ng Pilipinas also restricted borrowing from bank foreign currency deposit units to finance real estate and other speculative investments. With a few exceptions, like selected infrastructure projects, banks only can lend foreign currency to borrowers like exporters and others with a foreign currency revenue flow, who demonstrate a natural hedge.[51]

---

[49] This requirement applies to existing banks; the central bank did not issue any new bank licences in 1998-99.

[50] In March 1997, when the Government started regular monitoring of banks' real estate exposure, the average exposure was only 11 per cent. In September 1998, only ten commercial banks out of 53 exceeded the 20 per cent ceiling.

[51] In addition, the Bangko Sentral ng Pilipinas requires 30 per cent of foreign currency deposit unit liabilities to be kept in highly liquid assets.

Other post-crisis reforms include progressively introducing a risk based capital adequacy regime and a new loan classification and provisioning system, increasing the general loan to loss provision to 2 per cent from October 1999 and improving disclosure standards.[52] Banks now must publish their NPL ratios and loan loss provisions quarterly. By pressuring banks to increase their capital, these prudential reforms will encourage mergers and attract foreign capital.

FOREIGN CURRENCY DEPOSIT UNITS

Foreign currency deposit units allow Filipinos to deposit and borrow in foreign currencies (largely US dollars). They were first introduced in 1971 to encourage Filipinos to keep their money in the country and counter widespread capital flight. Overseas workers repatriate close to US$6 billion in savings every year; much of this is kept in US dollar savings deposits in Philippine banks (Delhaise, 1999). Throughout the 1970s and 1980s, the Government introduced incentives to increase the attractiveness of these accounts to compensate for lack of confidence in the Philippine economy.

Although foreign currency borrowing and lending poses great risks, as Thailand's and Indonesia's experiences demonstrate, two factors limited the Philippines' exposure to currency fluctuations. Firstly, Bangko Sentral ng Pilipinas regulations ensured most Philippine bank foreign currency lending was to exporters who have a natural hedge, as most of their revenue is in US dollars. In the March quarter in 1997, exporters or export oriented users accounted for 60 per cent of foreign currency deposit unit loans. Some utilities (like private power and water suppliers) which hold these loans also have a natural hedge because they can raise prices in line with currency fluctuations.

Secondly, most Philippine bank foreign currency liabilities are owed to domestic residents. In September 1997, residents held 63 per cent of the Philippine banking sector's total stock of foreign liabilities and 80 per cent of their foreign currency deposit unit liabilities. This contrasts with Thailand where residents held only 1 per cent of the financial sector's foreign exchange liabilities in the first quarter of 1996. Under these conditions, the peso's depreciation merely transferred wealth between domestic residents, with over 60 per cent of foreign exchange losses offset by gains to other residents. This significantly reduced the macroeconomic severity of the crisis. Domestic residents had little reason to withdraw funds from foreign currency deposit units, and domestic banks had no reason to call in loans from these units. Consequently, the Philippines suffered less capital flight than many other regional economies which had high exposure to short term foreign lending and portfolio investments.

Source: East Asia Analytical Unit, 1998.

---

[52] The definition of overdue was amended from six to three months. By 15 March 1999, banks were required to provision for special mention loans (5 per cent), sub-standard loans (25 per cent), doubtful loans (50 per cent), and loss loans (100 per cent). In addition, general loan loss provisions of 2 per cent were required (Bangko Sentral ng Pilipinas, 1998a).

Reforms to Reduce Bank Margins

In the three to four years before the crisis, Philippine banks had the highest profit rates but also the highest cost margins in Asia, implying low competitiveness and inefficiency (Delhaise, 1999). In the 1990s, the spread between borrowing and lending rates ranged from 4.1 to 5.4 percentage points, well above the spreads in Malaysia, the United States and Singapore (Figure 8.7). Philippine banking is quite concentrated, and many analysts believe an interest rate cartel produces the high spreads between borrowing and lending rates, imposing high costs on the economy.[53]

Nevertheless, to prevent growth stagnating, reducing the high intermediation costs of the local banking sector deserves high government priority. Options include encouraging new bank entry, including foreign banks, lowering statutory reserve requirements, abolishing inefficient banking taxes, particularly the documentary stamp tax, removing branching restrictions on foreign banks, abolishing sectoral lending requirements and encouraging bank mergers. In March 1998, the Bangko Sentral ng Pilipinas reduced the banks' statutory reserve requirement by 3 percentage

Figure 8.7

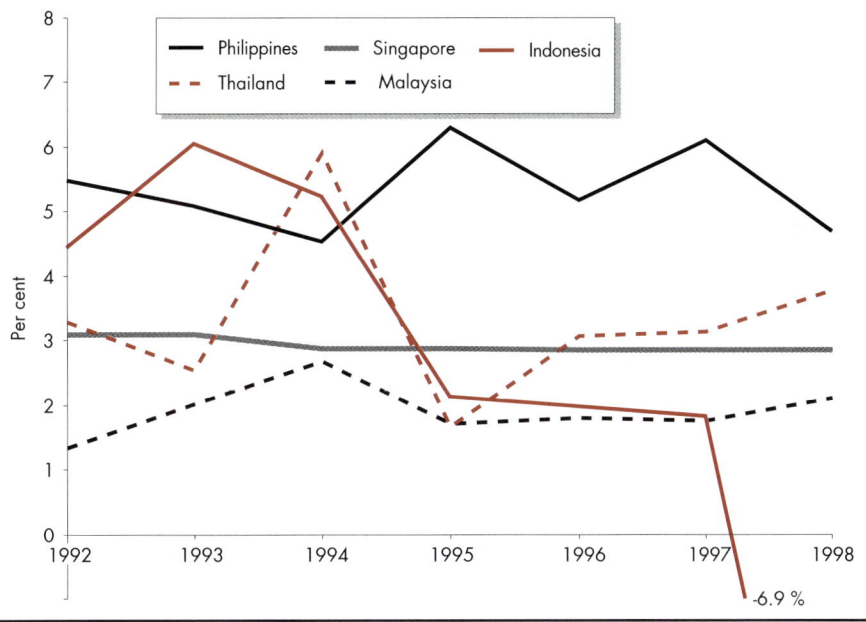

Philippine Interest Rate Spread One of Region's Highest
Regional Lending and Deposit Rate Differentials, 1990-98

Source: CEIC, 1999.

---

[53] However, during the crisis, these high spreads proved an advantage as most Philippine banks could write off NPLs from retained earnings and still maintain high capital adequacy ratios. Bankers claim that inefficient taxes like the documentary stamp tax and high statutory reserve requirements are mainly responsible for high spreads.

points to 10 per cent while raising liquidity reserves by an equal amount to 7 per cent. The move aimed to reduce domestic interest rates by lowering bank intermediation costs.[54] In May 1998, the Bangko Sentral ng Pilipinas increased the proportion of statutory reserve deposits which can earn interest from 25 per cent to 40 per cent.[55] In February 1999, it began to ease banks' compulsory lending to agriculture by allowing development loans and lending to farmer associations and some types of housing in the mandated 25 per cent.

PRUDENTIAL SUPERVISION REFORMS

The Bangko Sentral ng Pilipinas supervises nearly all deposit taking and lending organisations.[56] The Office of the Insurance Commission supervises insurance companies and the Securities Exchange Commission supervises securities firms. The Philippines does not yet have sufficient human resources to set up an independent financial sector regulator outside the Bangko Sentral ng Pilipinas, but the Bangko Sentral ng Pilipinas is consolidating supervision; already, it supervises insurance and securities companies affiliated with banks.[57] Once new banking legislation currently before Congress is passed, the Bangko Sentral ng Pilipinas will introduce consolidated supervision (Government of the Philippines, 1999).

Improving financial supervision was a government priority well before the financial crisis, but since 1997 efforts have increased. In 1993, a new law strengthened the Bangko Sentral ng Pilipinas's capital base and increased its independence, and a new charter shielded it from political interference. Since 1998, Bangko Sentral ng Pilipinas accredited external auditors have had to report any matters adversely affecting the condition or soundness of banks to the Bangko Sentral ng Pilipinas. If they fail to inform the Bangko Sentral ng Pilipinas about bank problems, these auditors will be blacklisted (Bangko Sentral ng Pilipinas, 1999).

Most importantly, the Bangko Sentral ng Pilipinas now has tighter procedures for closing insolvent banks.[58] Supervisors have adequate immunity for their actions, and commercial banks cannot hide behind secrecy provisions. However, the Philippines Insurance Deposit Corporation still is hampered in its role as receiver, insurer and liquidator of troubled banks.

---

[54] Liquid reserves can be kept in short term market yielding government securities, while statutory reserve deposits are held at the Bangko Sentral ng Pilipinas, and 75 per cent receive no return.

[55] The Bangko Sentral ng Pilipinas reduced the statutory reserve deposits requirement by a further 2 percentage points to 8 per cent on 29 May 1998. In an effort to siphon off excess liquidity, the Bangko Sentral ng Pilipinas then increased statutory reserve deposits to 10 per cent from 2 October 1998. Concurrently, it increased the interest rate on the 40 per cent of the banks' balances with the Bangko Sentral ng Pilipinas from 4 per cent to 4.5 per cent.

[56] These include non-bank financial institutions with quasi-banking functions, trust or investment management authority, building and loan associations, non-stock savings and loan associations, trust companies, and non-bank subsidiaries of banks. The Philippine Deposit Insurance Corporation also has some supervisory responsibilities, and is empowered to examine insured institutions, although it extensively uses Bangko Sentral ng Pilipinas supervisory findings.

[57] In June 1995, expanded commercial banks could become majority stockholders of insurance companies.

[58] Steps now enhance exit procedures, including earlier identification of troubled banks, intensified monitoring and inspection of troubled banks, harsher penalties for capital shortfalls, time-bound liquidation procedures, and more restrictive guidelines for the granting emergency loans to banks.

Disclosure Based Supervision

In line with developed economy trends, the Bangko Sentral ng Pilipinas is changing the focus and method of bank supervision, so it can detect early bank distress symptoms and better assess the health of the banking system. A forward looking, risk based framework will replace the current compliance based and checklist driven approach. The Bangko Sentral ng Pilipinas has reoriented examination processes and bank rating methods to assess and manage risks (International Monetary Fund, 1999).

Draft Legislation before Congress

In 2000, Congress should pass important changes to the general banking law and the central bank law, further strengthening Bangko Sentral ng Pilipinas regulatory powers. The changes will enable the Bangko Sentral ng Pilipinas's controlling board, the Monetary Board, to adopt internationally accepted standards for setting risk based capital requirements and defining unsound practices; allow 100 per cent foreign ownership of distressed banks (although foreign owners must reduce their stake to 70 per cent over ten years); tighten bank licensing criteria; strengthen disclosure requirements and restrictions on lending to directors, officers, stockholders and their related interests; and penalise erring directors (Economist Intelligence Unit, 1999). This legislation will raise Philippine prudential standards closer to international best practice.

MERGERS

The Bangko Sentral ng Pilipinas is encouraging mergers among local banks by raising minimum capital requirements. In the largest merger announced to date, Far East Bank and Trust Corporation will merge with Bank of the Philippine Islands, creating the largest bank in the country with assets of P 352 billion (US$8.7 billion). Equitable Banking Corporation and two state run funds bought a controlling stake in the PCI Bank for P 31.9 billion. Several other mergers are being negotiated and many others are expected; for example, Bank of the Philippine Islands and Metropolitan Bank are expected to take over smaller banks (Asian Banker Interactive, 1999). The future banking sector will be significantly more consolidated, and foreign banks will increase their market share.

FOREIGN FINANCIAL INSTITUTION ENTRY

In 1995, for the first time since 1949, the Government issued ten new foreign bank licences, adding to the four foreign banks already operating. It also issued licences to ten foreign insurance companies to compete with the 12 new domestic insurance companies. The new entrants encouraged existing financial institutions to boost their capital base, diversify their products and adopt new technologies.

However, new foreign banks can open only six branches, limiting them to wholesale banking. Further, they can only borrow US$4 dollars of head office capital for every US$1 of domestically held capital, limiting their capacity to expand local lending (La Brooy, 1997). As a result, foreign banks' share of domestic banking has grown only slowly. By 1997, foreign banks had around 20 per cent of the equity of universal commercial banks and 12 per cent of ordinary commercial banks. However, their share of total deposits jumped from 4 per cent to 7 per cent during the financial crisis.

Foreigners now can hold up to 60 per cent equity in an existing local bank. In 1999, the Bangko Sentral ng Pilipinas approved 100 per cent foreign ownership of distressed local banks, although this provision will not be legislated until 2000.[59] Under this provision, Singapore banks acquired two medium sized commercial banks; and foreign banks also acquired smaller thrift banks.[60] However, new foreign owners must reduce their stake to 85 per cent within five years and to 70 per cent within ten years. The new general banking law also will increase foreign participation on bank boards by removing the requirement for two thirds of directors to be Filipino citizens.

In February 1998, the amended financing company law expanded the maximum foreign ownership of finance companies from 40 per cent to 60 per cent. Now finance companies can issue bonds and other capital instruments, as well as provide money market, trust and quasi-banking services (Institute of International Bankers, 1999).

Opportunities for Foreign Financial Institutions

Opportunities will increase once the legislation supports central bank policy to allow greater foreign ownership of local banks. Privatising the Philippines National Bank, which is on the Government's reform agenda, may allow a foreign bank to take a significant shareholding. As competition increases, merger activity should accelerate, and foreign banks may increase their share of the local market by acquiring smaller domestic banks or finance companies. Already, ANZ and CMG Asia have built a significant presence in the Philippines (East Asia Analytical Unit, 1998).

CAPITAL MARKET DEVELOPMENTS

Before the crisis, the Government undertook several reforms to develop capital markets and reduce reliance on bank finance. Most importantly, in 1994, it unified the Manila and Makati stock exchanges, boosting total liquidity. The new Philippine Stock Exchange has stock market trading monitors in regional cities to enhance investor participation outside Metro Manila. The long standing difficulties in settling and clearing government securities soon may be resolved, providing a workable delivery-versus-payment system (*Asiamoney*, April 1999, p. 26). The Government also recently established a central clearing and settlement agency for equity securities, and issued new rules to curb price manipulation and insider trading.[61]

---

[59] Despite the lack of legislative backing, Bangko Sentral ng Pilipinas Governor Rafael Buenaventura has urged Congress to allow 100 per cent foreign ownership of local banks, subject to the proviso that foreign banks own only 30 per cent of total banking system assets (Asian Banker Interactive, 1999).

[60] Development Bank of Singapore acquired a medium sized commercial bank, Bank of Southeast Asia in August 1998 for P 1.2 billion to P 1.5 billion, and United Overseas Bank acquired Westmont Bank of Philippines in July 1999 for P 3 billion. Among the thrift banks, ABN Amro acquired Great Pacific Savings Bank in April 1999, and Royal Canadian Financial Group invested in Prime Savings Bank in February 1999.

[61] For instance, licensed traders cannot directly or indirectly trade their personal account in the exchange. The securities regulator also issued new rules on the dissemination of news tips or rumours by listed companies.

The Philippine bond market is embryonic. The corporate bond market remains much smaller than the government bond market, with around P 50 billion outstanding as against P 750 billion in the government bond market. The 0.75 per cent documentary stamp tax applicable to private debt security trades inhibits the growth of private debt markets and secondary market trading. It also inhibits the emergence of an effective settlement and clearing system for private debt securities.[62] A 20 per cent withholding tax applies to private investors' income from private and government debt securities, further inhibiting secondary market trading.

Securities Regulation

Since 1996, securities regulation reforms have promoted full disclosure and self-regulation, a trend evident in more developed regional markets (See Chapter 5 - *Capital Markets*.) In 1998, the Government granted the Philippines Stock Exchange self-regulatory organisation status. Corporate return processing changed from a merit based to a full disclosure system. Further reforms to the regulatory framework promise a full shift to disclosure based regulation, upgraded prudential standards and improved enforcement.[63]

FUTURE CHALLENGES

One of the Philippines' most important medium term challenges is to reduce the wide gap between bank lending and deposit rates. Increasing international bank competition in domestic banking, including allowing 100 per cent takeovers of non-distressed banks, should help reduce these spreads. Further liberalising and preferably abolishing restrictions on the number of branches foreign banks can operate, removing restrictions on their access to head office capital to underwrite lending, and encouraging further rationalising and merging of small and medium sized banks should increase competition. Similarly, abolishing the documentary stamp tax, reducing the statutory reserve requirement and increasing the proportion of statutory reserves receiving a market rate of return also will reduce spreads.

Other useful measures include abolishing the mandatory credit allocations which force banks to lend 25 per cent of funds to agriculture and agriprocessing, and 10 per cent to small and medium enterprises.[64] These restrictions prevent banks from allocating capital to maximise returns. They also increase default risks by forcing banks to lend to sectors in which they have less experience.[65] The resulting inefficiency widens the spread between lending and deposit rates.

---

[62] To avoid stamp duty, the sale of private debt usually is not followed by a legal transfer of title. Instead a new paper certifies the security has been assigned to a new owner.

[63] The proposed *Securities Regulations and Enforcement Act (House Bill 8015)* will strengthen the regulatory powers of the Securities Exchange Commission, and enshrine disclosure based regulation and self-regulation in the securities industry. In January 1999, the Government transferred control of the Securities Exchange Commission from the Department of Finance to the Office of the President, potentially giving it more autonomy.

[64] These restrictions are circumvented somewhat as lending to large corporations, such as San Miguel which has some food processing activities, may count as lending for agriculture and agri-processing.

[65] To mitigate this problem, the Bankers Association of the Philippines encourages institutions like the Land Bank of the Philippines and the Small Business Guarantee Finance Corporation, which have relevant sectoral expertise, to issue market based securities for banks to buy in lieu of direct lending to these sectors.

The Bangko Sentral ng Pilipinas and Government remain committed to further rationalising the banking industry through mergers and acquisitions. They also appear willing to allow increased foreign presence, although the long term provisions for foreign takeovers remain uncertain. Similarly, the Government is committed to further reducing the Government's stake in the banking system by selling its remaining share in the Philippine National Bank. This bank was severely affected by the crisis, and is likely to be sold to a strategic partner by mid 2000 (Government of Philippines, 1999).

Although reforms to regulation and supervision are ongoing, some still need congressional approval. While adopting risk based and consolidated financial supervision represent major positive developments, the Bangko Sentral ng Pilipinas has yet to implement these new approaches. Enforcing capital adequacy requirements and bank exit policies present further challenges.

PROSPECTS FOR THAILAND, MALAYSIA AND THE PHILIPPINES

Due to structural reforms and stimulatory macroeconomic policies, the financial sectors of Thailand, Malaysia and the Philippines all are recovering from crisis.

Compared to Malaysia's approach, Thailand's less interventionist approach to financial sector restructuring and refinancing probably has lengthened its crisis. While its private sector led approach possibly limited the short term cost of the public bailout, by slowing economic recovery, the ultimate cost of this strategy may be higher than rapid intervention to clear NPLs. Continuing uncertainty, slow corporate and financial restructuring, and weak economic recovery have escalated Thailand's NPLs; as the Government has guaranteed all deposits, higher NPLs will raise the fiscal cost of resolving the financial system's problems.

Despite the large number of smaller financial institutions and their exposure to some highly leveraged corporates, Malaysia's pre-crisis banking system and prudential controls were stronger than many others in the region. Capital controls introduced in 1998 may have given Malaysia useful policy flexibility, but in other regional economies, which did not employ such controls, interest rates also fell and the currency also stablised in late 1998. More importantly, Malaysia continues to make good progress in restructuring and recapitalising its financial system and this is building market confidence.

In the Philippines, major pre-crisis improvements in financial regulation and supervision were central to modernising the financial sector and helping avoid systemic bank failure. The nature of foreign currency liabilities and the late start to the Philippine asset boom also helped the country avoid the worst of the crisis.

The Philippines' financial system has opened gradually to foreign participation. Competition from foreign banks and higher capital requirements are forcing mergers between domestic players. The banking system will emerge from the crisis better regulated with the major players bigger, better capitalised and more competitive than before. In the relatively open foreign investment environment, many opportunities are emerging for foreign financial institutions.

All three economies recognise the importance of improving prudential regulation and supervision, and increasing domestic competition, but the Philippines is the most advanced in recognising the benefits of foreign competition. All three are making progress on enhancing financial market infrastructure and further developing capital markets. In the medium to long term, as these initiatives are effectively implemented, they will enhance these three economies' ability to achieve high levels of sustainable growth.

REFERENCES

AFX-Asia, 1999, AFX-Asia news service, www.indoexchange.com/afx/, last accessed on 25 October.

Asian Banker, 1999, 'Bank Mergers and Acquisitions in Asia (January 1998-July 1999)', *Asian Banker Journal*, issue 19, pp. 51-52.

Asian Banker Interactive, 1999, 'Account Update,' 1 November, subscriber service for *Asian Banker*, www.asianbanker.com.sg, accessed on 1 November.

Bank of America, 1999, 'A Survey of Banking Reform in Asia', Global Markets Group Asia, Hong Kong, July.

Bank Negara Malaysia, 1999a, *Annual Report* 1998, BNM, Kuala Lumpur.

___ 1999b, Press release 'Repatriation of Portfolio Capital', 2 February, www.bnm.gov.my, accessed on 20 September.

___ 1999c, Press release, 21 October, www.bnm.gov.my, accessed on 23 October.

___ 1998, Press release 'Measures to Regain Monetary Independence', 1 September, www.bnm.gov.my, accessed on 16 September.

Bangko Sentral ng Pilipinas, 1999, Press release 'The Commercial Banking System', 3 February, www.bsp.gov.au, accessed on 16 September.

___ 1998a, 'The Philippines: Onward to Recovery', Manila, July.

___ 1998b, Selected Philippine Economic Indicators, August, Manila.

Bank of Thailand, 1998, 'Financial Institutions and Markets in Thailand', Economic Research Department, November, www.bot.or.th/govnr/public/BOT_Homepage/EnglishVersion/index_e.htm accessed on 20 August 1999.

Beltran, G., and Guinigundo, D., 1999, 'Financial Market Developments in the Philippines', Paper presented at the joint East Asia Analytical Unit / National Centre for Development Studies workshop on Financial Sector Reform in Asia, 22 February - 4 March, Canberra.

CEIC, 1999, CEIC Database, Hong Kong, supplied by EconData, Canberra.

Collins, G., 1999, East Asia Analytical Unit interview with General Manager, Bangkok International Banking Facility, National Australia Bank, Bangkok, July.

Danaharta, 1999, 'Operations Report: Half-year Ended 30 June 1999', www.danaharta.com.my, accessed on 28 September.

Delhaise, P., 1999, *Asia in Crisis: the Implosion of the Banking and Finance Systems*, John Wiley and Sons (Asia), Singapore.

East Asia Analytical Unit, 1999, *Korea Rebuilds: from Crisis to Opportunity*, Department of Foreign Affairs and Trade, Canberra.

___ 1998, *The Philippines: beyond the Crisis*, Department of Foreign Affairs and Trade, Canberra.

Economist Intelligence Unit, 1999, 'Philippine Alert', April, Manila.

Finance Committee on Corporate Governance, 1999, 'Report on Corporate Governance', Ministry of Finance, Kuala Lumpur.

Fitch IBCA, 1999, 'Asian Bank Restructuring: Comparative Analysis', April.

Flatters, F., 1999, 'Thailand the IMF and the Economic Crisis: First in, Fast Out?' Paper presented at the Brookings/CIER conference on the Asian Financial Crisis and Taiwan's Role in the Region, April, Washington DC.

Government of the Philippines, 1999, 'Supplementary Memorandum on Economic and Financial Policies', Manila.

Institute of International Bankers, 1999, Global Survey 1998, www.iib.org, accessed on 15 July.

International Monetary Fund, 1999, International Financial Statistics, various issues, Washington DC.

Kawai, M.,1999, 'The Resolution of the East Asian Crisis: Financial and Corporate Sector Restructuring', Paper presented at the international conference Reforms and Recovery in East Asia: the Role of the State and Economic Enterprise, Asia Pacific School of Economics and Management, Australian National University, 21-22 September, Canberra.

La Brooy, M., 1997, East Asia Analytical Unit interview with General Manager, ANZ Philippines, Manila, August.

Ministry of Finance, 1999, *Economic Report 1998/99*, Malaysian Ministry of Finance, Kuala Lumpur.

Nidhirabda, B., and Warr, P., 1999, 'Thailand's Experience with Reform: the Financial Sector', paper for Conference on Reform and Recovery in East Asia: the Role of the State and Economic Enterprise, Australian National University, 21-22 September, Canberra.

Nomura Securities, 1999, 'Thailand Economics: Reform at a Stately Pace', Asia Pacific Research Group, Bangkok, July.

Pakorn, V., 1999, East Asia Analytical Unit interview with Research Director, Thailand Development Research Institute, July.

Standard and Poor's, 1999, Press release on the Thai banking sector, reproduced at *Asian Banker*, www.asianbanker.com.sg, accessed on 23 October.

Tan, P., 1999, East Asia Analytical Unit interview with Vice President, Corporate Finance Analysis and Strategies, Citibank.

Thillainathan R., 1998, 'Reforming Financial Sector and Promoting Capital Market Development in Asia', Paper presented at the PACAP Conference, October.

Tomasic, R., and Little, P., 1997, 'Insolvency Law and Practice in Asia', FT Law and Tax Asia Pacific, Hong Kong.

World Bank, 1999a, World Bank World Tables, supplied by EconData, Canberra.

——— 1999b, 'Thailand Economic Monitor', www.worldbank.or.th/monitor, accessed on 5 November.

——— 1999c, *World Economic Outlook 1999*, Washington DC.

Zeti Akhtar Aziz, 1999, Speech by Deputy Governor, Bank Negara Malaysia at the Hewlett-Packard Sales (Malaysia) Sdn Bhd. Bond Issuance Signing Ceremony, www.bnm.gov.my, accessed on 10 October.

Chapter 9

HONG KONG AND SINGAPORE

While the Asian financial crisis affected both Singapore and Hong Kong, Singapore's more flexible exchange rate regime allowed it to adjust better than Hong Kong's currency board peg. Both cities are undertaking financial market reforms to position themselves to attract more regional and international financial business; this will open new opportunities for foreign financial institutions.

Hong Kong has a generally very open and well regulated financial market; it also is deregulating its banking sector, establishing a market managed compulsory pension fund, and merging its equities and futures exchanges. Singapore's regulatory regime has been more interventionist but its banking reform now is further advanced than Hong Kong's. It also is moving towards a less interventionist approach to supervision and opening its life insurance market. Already, its equity and futures exchanges are merged. While Singapore is liberalising the Central Provident Fund, the fund remains relatively tightly controlled and government dominated.

This chapter reviews the key financial sector reforms in Hong Kong and Singapore since the financial crisis, the impact of the Hong Kong dollar peg on Hong Kong's economy and the implications and opportunities for foreign financial institutions.

HONG KONG

Hong Kong is a leading regional trading and financial service centre. Its finance, insurance, business service and real estate sectors grew rapidly in the 1980s and 1990s, and by 1997 accounted for 25 per cent of GDP.[1]

PRUDENTIAL REGULATION

Unlike most economies, Hong Kong does not have a central bank. Instead, the Hong Kong Monetary Authority conducts certain central bank activities such as prudential supervision of banks, management of foreign reserves and open market operations.[2] The Insurance Authority regulates insurers while the Securities and Futures Commission regulates securities firms and the stock and futures exchanges. Despite global trends towards amalgamating regulators, this option is not actively discussed in Hong Kong yet (Procter, 1999). (See Chapter 3 - *Prudential Reform*.)

Notwithstanding the impending harmonisation of the regulatory approach across the equities and futures markets, a major problem remains the fragmented financial sector regulatory system. For example, regulation of fund managers employed by the new Mandatory Provident Fund will be split between the Securities and Futures Commission (existing fund managers), the Insurance Authority (insurance companies) and the Hong Kong Monetary Authority (banks).

---

[1] This contribution was up from 23 per cent of GDP in 1992.
[2] Three major commercial banks, the Hong Kong Shanghai Banking Corporation, Standard Chartered Bank and the Bank of China, issue bank notes.

BANKING SYSTEM STRUCTURE

Hong Kong's banking system is well capitalised but some interest rate controls and other restrictions on foreign entry persist. However, significant reforms will occur over the next two years; these reforms should improve the environment for foreign banks.

Hong Kong has a three tier banking system consisting of:

- fully licensed banks
- restricted licence banks
- deposit taking companies.[3]

Licensed banks, which operate current and savings accounts and accept deposits of any size and maturity, dominate the system, holding 98 per cent of deposits and making 93 per cent of loans (CEIC, 1999). Foreign banks account for two thirds of deposit taking financial institutions and over half their assets (Figures 9.1 and 9.2). However, two banks incorporated outside Hong Kong, the Bank of China and Hong Kong Shanghai Bank, own the bulk of foreign bank assets.

Figure 9.1

Foreign Banks Dominate in Hong Kong
Foreign and Local Bank Numbers, December 1998

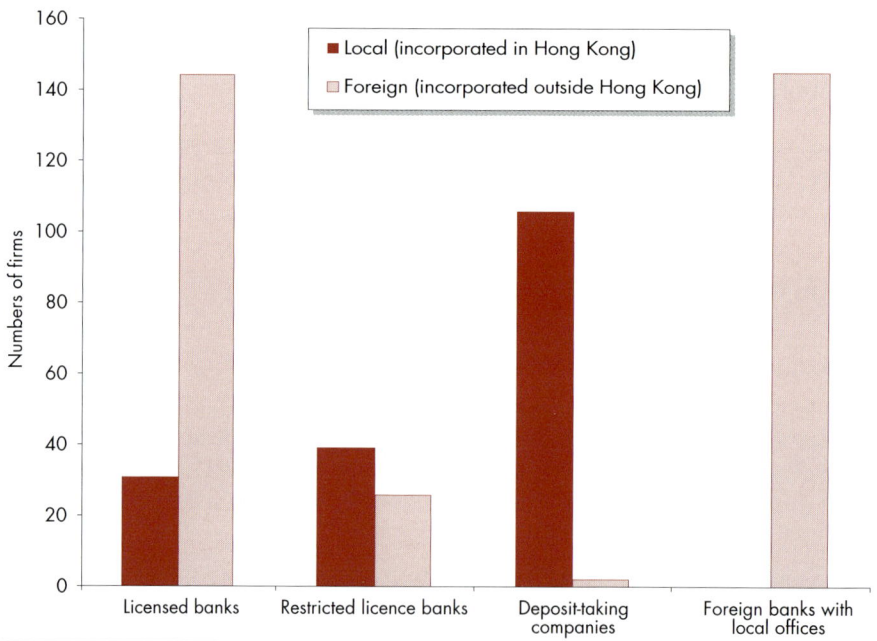

Note: Licensed banks operate current and savings accounts, and accept deposits of any size and maturity. Restricted licence banks undertake merchant banking and capital market activities and may accept call, notice or time deposits of any maturity but in amounts greater than HK$500 000. Deposit taking companies are owned or associated with banks and engage in specialised activities including consumer finance, trade finance and securities business. They are restricted to taking deposits greater than HK$100 000 with an original term to maturity of at least three months.

Source: Hong Kong Monetary Authority, 1999; and CEIC, 1999.

---

[3] The three tiers of banks are defined in a note to Figure 9.1.

Figure 9.2

Foreign Banks Dominate Hong Kong Bank Assets
Foreign and Local Bank Assets, December 1998

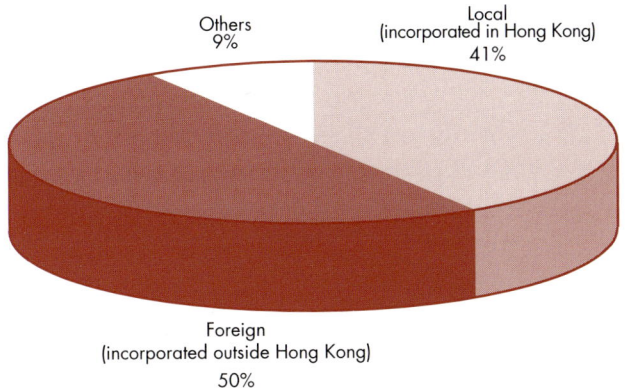

Source: Hong Kong Monetary Authority, 1999; and CEIC, 1999.

Hong Kong has no limits on bank ownership, although retail activities of foreign banks are restricted. Most notably, foreign banks entering after 1978 can have only one branch, although foreign banks in the market before 1978 have unrestricted branching. Also for foreign banks entering since 1978, restrictions apply to the number and situation of ATMs. Furthermore, the interest rate cartel run by the Hong Kong Association of Banks also distorts the market. It imposes maximum interest rates on Hong Kong dollar deposits under HK$500 000 with a term less than seven days. Further, current and savings accounts cannot accrue interest. Approximately HK$387 billion, or 27 per cent of total Hong Kong dollar deposits, are subject to these cartel set interest rates (National Australia Bank, 1999). This cartel protects many small, marginal local banks but also boosts the profits of the three major banks.

HONG KONG'S BANKING REFORMS

As Hong Kong's banking system is generally efficient, adequately provisioned and well regulated, it remained strong during the crisis. Bank capital adequacy ratios average 18 per cent, and no bank's capital adequacy is less than 13 per cent (Carse, 1999). However, as a result of the serious domestic recession in 1998, non-performing loans, NPLs, increased and averaged 9 per cent of outstanding loans by the end of March 1999. NPLs could rise further due to exposure to Chinese lending, though the domestic economy appeared to have bottomed by mid 1999.[4]

---

[4] Exposure of authorised institutions in Hong Kong to enterprises in Guangdong province is US$2.5 billion. However, this figure includes only the exposure of foreign banks that is booked in Hong Kong. Overall bank debt of Guangdong enterprises, including that booked outside Hong Kong, is about US$4 billion and mainland debt, including red chips is US$32 billion or 3 per cent of banking sector assets as at the end of June 1999. This fell from over US$38 billion at the end of 1998. This exposure is spread widely throughout the banking system, although some concentrations exist. However, with the exception of Peregrine, Hong Kong financial institutions had only a limited exposure to South East Asia and Korea (Carse, 1999).

Despite its relative strength, the banking sector is subject to major reform. In response to the crisis, authorities have strengthened prudential supervision by:

- increasing banks' mandatory capital adequacy ratios to 10 per cent
- introducing a standard for interest recognition on NPLs[5]
- requiring local and foreign banks to disclose information on their NPLs.

Moreover, in July 1999, the Hong Kong Monetary Authority submitted its government endorsed response to a consultancy study aimed at enhancing the banking sector's competitiveness. One key reform adopted is to deregulate all remaining interest rate restrictions by July 2001.[6] This will increase competition, reduce interest margins and promote mergers among small local banks and with larger banks. Importantly for foreign banks, the Hong Kong Monetary Authority also recommended removing branching restrictions on foreign banks, with an immediate move from a one building restriction to a three branch limit, and possible full liberalisation after a review in 2001.

The Hong Kong Monetary Authority also signalled a move to two tiers of banks, with restricted licence banks gaining the privileges of fully licensed banks.[7] This should decrease systemic risk, as restricted licence banks will gain access to the real time gross settlement system. (See Chapter 3 - *Prudential Reform*.) It also should benefit foreign banks, which mainly hold restricted banking licences and are thus restricted in the type, maturity and amount of deposits they can accept. On the supervision side, the authorities will develop a more formal risk based supervisory system and continue efforts to improve disclosure requirements; foreign banks will be required to publish information on their Hong Kong activities.

HONG KONG'S CAPITAL MARKET AND PENSION REFORMS

Over the decade before the Asian financial crisis, the Hong Kong Government implemented several financial sector initiatives:

- in 1989, it established the Securities and Futures Commission, to supervise securities markets
- in 1993, the Hong Kong Securities and Futures Commission and Stock Exchange of Hong Kong signed a Memorandum of Regulatory Cooperation with the China Securities Regulatory Commission, Shanghai Securities Exchange and Shenzhen Stock Exchange to facilitate cooperation regarding cross listed securities in Hong Kong and China.[8]

---

[5] Banks must stop accruing interest on uncollateralised NPLs after three months and on all loans overdue for more than a year.

[6] On 1 July 2000, Hong Kong's interest rate rule on time deposits of less than seven days will be dropped, and on 1 July 2001, the interest rate rule on current and savings deposits will be dropped.

[7] The move to two tiers will occur after a review in the second half of 2000.

[8] The memorandum mainly responded to the listing of Chinese stocks (red chips) in Hong Kong, providing limited regulation and disclosure.

Since the financial crisis, the Government generally has accelerated reform, but due to speculative attacks on the Hong Kong dollar in 1997 and 1998, it also has tightened regulations and increased intervention in specific areas. One example of increased intervention is its US$20 billion purchase of equities in August 1998, designed to impose costs on speculators engaged in currency stock 'double play'.[9] From late October 1999, Exchange Fund Investment Limited, the agency managing this portfolio, started selling two thirds of its portfolio through a mutual fund. The remaining one third will be retained as a long term investment, partly to defend the Hong Kong dollar from further attacks (*Australian Financial Review*, 13 October 1999, p. 1).

Securities Market Reforms

In general, securities market volatility did not cause problems during the crisis. Settlement and clearing systems worked well, so firms did not fail (Procter, 1999). However, to ensure Hong Kong keeps abreast of new developments and meets increasing competition from traditional and Internet exchanges, in May 1998, the Securities Review Committee introduced:

- new governance mechanisms for the Hong Kong Stock Exchange, such as a board structure and improved disclosure requirements

- a world best practice 'T plus two' clearing and settlement system[10]

- new listing procedures similar to those in western markets.

Several other policies introduced in 1998 tightened and rationalised regulations to enable Hong Kong to deflect speculative attacks on its currency via the stock and futures markets. For example, large securities purchasers must provide information on their identity to their securities traders. Authorities also tightened regulations on short selling and enforcing T plus two share settlement.[11]

Stock and Futures Exchanges Merger

To enhance Hong Kong's position as a leading financial centre and rationalise stock and futures exchange regulation, the Hong Kong Government has successfully pressured the stock and futures exchanges to demutualise, merge with the clearing houses and by September 2000, list on the stock exchange under a single holding company, the Hong Kong Exchanges and Clearing Corporation.

---

[9] The 'double play' involved short selling Hong Kong dollars and Hong Kong equities. Short selling the Hong Kong dollar raised interest rates, causing equities to fall and creating profit for speculators.

[10] 'T plus two' (T+2) refers to delayed settlement of transactions. In this case, successful buy orders require payment two days after execution. Similarly, successful sell orders require delivery of securities two days after execution. T+2 is currently one of the fastest settlement times in the world. For example, for many years, the Australian Stock Exchange operated under T+5 (days). It moved to T+3 in early 1999.

[11] These regulations were partly a response to 244 brokers who in the first week of September 1998 failed to settle trades valued at almost HK$2 billion. Many of these brokers sought to take advantage of government intervention in the market in August 1998 when it spent around US$20 billion in a share play designed to frustrate speculators, particularly hedge funds, hoping to profit from shorting the equities and currency markets.

Separating the ownership and management of the new exchange, as demutualisation will entail, should remove conflicts of interest, assisting new product and service development. In particular, it should reduce the power of the many small members who often seek to keep out new entrants, maintain the archaic system of fixed minimum commissions and slow the introduction of new technology. Following a two year grace period, new brokers, both domestic and foreign, will be able to trade on the exchange, after paying an admission fee.[12]

Another major rationale of the merger is to harmonise the regulatory approach across equities and futures markets (Carse, 1999). Consolidating the exchanges and clearing houses also will generate economies of scale, particularly in clearing and settlement systems. When the new amalgamated exchange is listed, all members will get shares and only will have influence proportionate to their shareholdings. As existing exchange members will be able to sell their stock without losing trading rights, demutualisation will give small brokerages a chance to raise capital to invest in new technology (Government of Hong Kong, SAR, 1999).

Developing a Regional Bond Market

Although since the financial crisis, corporate bond issues have fallen, the Hong Kong Government is seeking to develop a regional bond market centred on Hong Kong. (See Chapter 5 - *Capital Markets*.) The Government provided a pricing benchmark for corporate bonds by issuing up to ten year Government Exchange Fund Notes on its foreign exchange reserves.[13] While Hong Kong has high quality public and private companies issuing corporate bonds, it currently has little absorptive capacity and issuers need to resort to the United States or Europe. This may change as the Mandatory Provident Fund increases the investment demand for Hong Kong dollar paper (Carse, 1999).

The Government has introduced a book entry system linked to the real time gross settlement system and is trying to link up with Australia and New Zealand to encourage a regional debt market. The Government also is investigating whether it can list regional sovereign bonds issued by Japan's Miyazawa Fund. However, the Hong Kong Monetary Authority has discouraged the Asian Development Bank and World Bank from issuing bonds in Hong Kong because of fear these assets may be used to speculate against the Hong Kong dollar (Carse, 1999).

The Mandatory Provident Fund

In November 2000, Hong Kong will introduce its Mandatory Provident Fund to provide comprehensive, funded pension cover. (See Chapter 6 - *Non-bank Financial Institutions*.) Unlike Singapore's Central Provident Fund, the Mandatory Provident Fund provides extensive choice, with employers free to select their private sector Mandatory Provident Fund provider and employees able to invest account balances in a range of unit trusts and mutual funds. Fierce competition among fund managers should promote financial product innovation and capital market development, enhancing returns for savers.

---

[12] In contrast, under the current system, the only way a new broker can enter is by buying an existing seat on the stock or futures exchange.

[13] Before the crisis, the Government routinely ran a budget surplus, and therefore had no need to issue traditional government bonds.

HONG KONG'S CURRENCY BOARD AND THE PEG

The Hong Kong dollar peg to the US dollar is an important feature of the Hong Kong financial system. Since 1983, Hong Kong has pegged its dollar to the US dollar at a fixed rate of HK$7.80:US$1.[14] The pegged exchange rate means all Hong Kong dollars in circulation are fully backed by US dollars held by the Exchange Fund. Any increase in demand for US dollars draws Hong Kong dollars out of circulation, raising interest rates. Hence, interest rates, money supply and economic activity bear the full burden of adjusting to balance of payments pressures, currency speculation and other shocks.[15]

Peg's Consequences for Financial Sector Competitiveness

When the peg was introduced in 1983, many argued that the Hong Kong dollar was undervalued, and a rate of around HK$6:US$1 was more consistent with fundamentals (Freris, 1991; Obstfeld and Rogoff, 1995; and Scott, 1997). After the peg's introduction, US inflation and interest rates declined; to maintain the peg Hong Kong had to lower its interest rates. The undervalued exchange rate and low interest rates combined to fuel a booming, high inflation economy with real GDP growth averaging 5 per cent between 1987 and 1997, and annual inflation averaging 9 per cent. Between 1991 and 1995, the combination of high inflation and negative real interest rates stimulated strong real estate investment.

Since the onset of the Asian crisis, the high interest rates needed to defend the peg have depressed investment, consumer credit and real estate demand. Weaker demand contributed to the 5.1 per cent GDP decline in 1998 and to the forecast growth of 0.6 per cent in 1999 (CEIC, 1999; and Consensus Economics, 1999).

Following the substantial depreciations of most Asian currencies in 1997 and 1998, the peg caused a significant (8 per cent) real trade weighted appreciation of the Hong Kong dollar by mid 1998, undermining Hong Kong's export and service sector competitiveness.[16] Total merchandise exports declined 7.4 per cent in 1998 compared to around 4 per cent growth in 1996 and 1997 (CEIC, 1999). While this fall partially was due to the Asian crisis, Hong Kong's merchandise exports performed much more poorly than Singapore's.[17] Over the past 15 years, the peg has caused Hong Kong's cost environment to rise well above competitors'. For example, while Hong Kong's property prices have fallen substantially since mid 1997, total occupancy costs remain about double those of Singapore (Jackson, 1999).

---

14   The Hong Kong dollar is actually now pegged at HK$7.75:US$1 but is being moved gradually back to HK$7.8 over the next two years. The exchange rate for bank deposits varies by 1 per cent above and below the pegged rate, as banks charge a commission fee of 1 per cent on transactions initiated by non-bank customers (Scott, 1997).

15   A detailed review of the operations of currency boards appears in Shu-ki, 1998; Williamson, 1995; Obstfeld and Rogoff, 1995; and Caprio et al, 1996.

16   This 8 per cent real trade weighted appreciation was recorded between June 1997 and June 1998 (JP Morgan, 1999). It compares to a 3 per cent depreciation in the real trade weighted value of the Singapore dollar over the same period.

17   By comparison, Singapore's merchandise exports fell only 1 per cent in 1998, after 5 per cent growth in 1996 and 1997. However, due largely to the collapse in Indonesian growth and Malaysian capital controls, Singapore's service exports declined by around 32 per cent in 1998, while Hong Kong's declined by 10 per cent (CEIC, 1999).

Currency stability associated with the peg arguably benefited Hong Kong's financial markets by reducing foreign exchange risk and helping establish domestic currency bond markets. However, as no other major financial centre relies on a fixed exchange rate regime, Hong Kong probably does not need to maintain the peg to retain its role as a regional financial centre.

Future of the Peg

The failure of concerted speculative attacks in October 1997 and throughout 1998 indicates it is very difficult for outsiders to break the peg. As no free floating supply of Hong Kong dollars exists outside Hong Kong, speculators wishing to sell Hong Kong dollars have to borrow them first, then convert them into foreign currency, forcing interest rates up. This happened in October 1997 when speculators started short selling the Hong Kong dollar and banks lending to the hedge funds had to settle two days later.[18] On settlement day (23 October), interest rates were bid up to 280 per cent, inflicting tremendous pressure on banks and speculators.

In the short term, the only events likely to break the peg are if Hong Kong residents lose faith in the peg or if the Hong Kong Government decides the economic pain outweighs the gain. Hong Kong residents show no sign of losing faith in the Hong Kong dollar; during the Asian financial crisis, foreign exchange did not rise significantly as a share of money supply (Figure 9.3).

The Hong Kong Government considers the peg to be a central economic policy plank and has no plans in the foreseeable future for change to a floating exchange rate regime. On the contrary, in 1998 and 1999, it intervened in the stock market to defend the pegged exchange rate; it also introduced several policies to strengthen the peg and ameliorate its adverse economic consequences. Since September 1998, the Government has let domestic banks borrow foreign currency at the pegged exchange rate through a Hong Kong Monetary Authority discount window.[19] During periods of heavy speculative attack, access to the discount window effectively expands available Hong Kong dollar liquidity in the system beyond Hong Kong dollars in circulation, to the full amount of Hong Kong's foreign exchange reserves (US$89 billion). Hence future runs on the Hong Kong dollar should not push up interest rates to the highs of 1997 and 1998, mitigating against previous effects on stock and futures markets and real economic activity.[20]

While confidence in the Government's capacity to maintain the peg remains high and the authorities are wedded to it, the question remains whether the real economy is flexible enough to prevent Hong Kong losing long term competitiveness. If it is not, long term growth may slow, eventually eroding commitment to the peg.

---

[18] Settlement in Hong Kong works to T+2 (days).

[19] Banks will be able to adjust their clearing balances through the discount window by discounting exchange fund paper to obtain liquidity.

[20] The Hong Kong Monetary Authority also extended its convertibility undertaking, which already applies to bank notes, to the clearing balances the licensed banks held with the Hong Kong Monetary Authority. Hence the Hong Kong Monetary Authority undertakes to convert Hong Kong dollars in the banks' clearing accounts to US dollars at a predetermined rate (initially HK$7.75:US$1, then moving to HK$7.80:US$1 over time). In addition, the Hong Kong Monetary Authority now publishes details of its foreign exchange operations on a real time basis, foreign exchange reserves details on a monthly basis and its new Currency Board Committee minutes. The committee now oversees the operation of the currency board system (Carse, 1999).

Figure 9.3

Hong Kong Residents Maintain Faith in the Peg
Ratio of Domestic Money Supply to Foreign Currency in Use

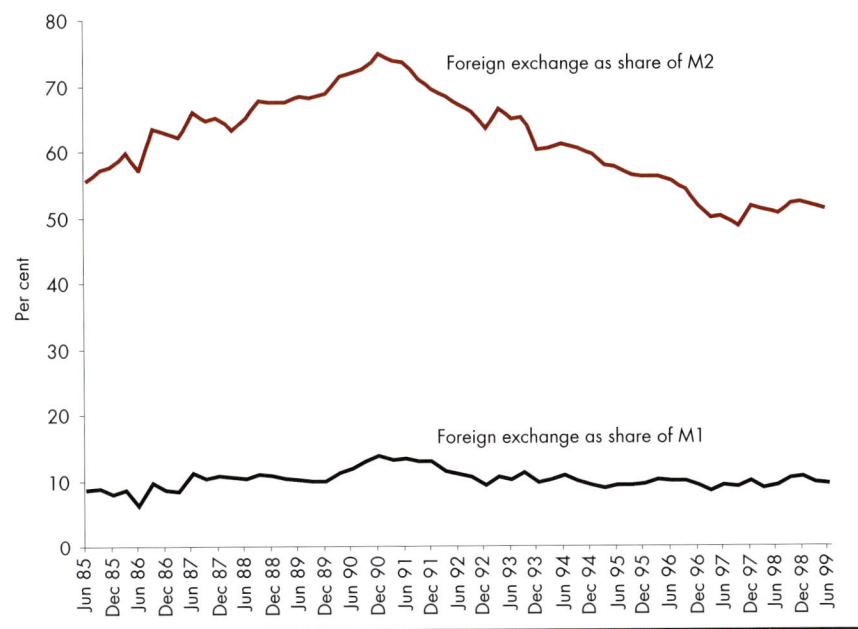

Note: M1 includes currency in circulation and demand deposits. M2 includes M1 plus time deposits. The ratios are the foreign currency portion of M1 or M2 divided by the total value of M1 or M2 respectively.
Source: CEIC, 1999.

Beyond the Peg

Factors other than the peg and regulatory reform also will influence future levels of financial sector activity. For example, in 1998 and 1999, government controls on land releases squeezed supply to protect property developers and owners. This prevented asset prices from fully adjusting during the recession. In August 1998, the Government purchased US$20 billion worth of Hong Kong stocks, preventing stock price adjustment. Any further government intervention in share and property markets would cause major concerns among international market participants.

Since the Guangdong International Investment and Trust Corporation closure in October 1998, the other major risk is financial contagion if Chinese financial institutions and state enterprises fail to repay foreign loans.[21] (See Chapter 12 - *China*.) However, being part of the huge, growing Chinese market offers enormous opportunities for Hong Kong. Many financial sector companies are in Hong Kong primarily because they believe China will continue to reform and grow, providing significant new financial intermediation opportunities (Morgan Stanley Dean Witter, 1999).

---

[21] The Guangdong International Investment and Trust Corporation was one of China's largest trust and investment companies. It was closed in October 1998 with extensive liabilities to both Chinese and foreign creditors.

SINGAPORE

Singapore also is accelerating its financial market reform, partly to protect itself from contagion but mainly to increase its attractiveness as a regional financial sector. These reforms are designed to build on Singapore's strengths: its sound legal environment, transparent and efficient government, and an established position as funds intermediator for neighbouring South East Asian economies.

During the crisis, Singapore retained competitiveness because of its more flexible exchange rate; it also cut labour costs through a 10 percentage point reduction in the employer Central Provident Fund contribution.[22] Singapore's real GDP grew 1.5 per cent in 1998 compared to Hong Kong's contraction of more than 5 per cent. This was despite Singapore's hinterland, Indonesia, Malaysia and Thailand, suffering much more in the crisis than Hong Kong's hinterland, China and Taiwan. Like Hong Kong, Singapore's future depends partly on the growth prospects of its hinterland. As Malaysia, Thailand and Indonesia emerge from the crisis, these prospects should improve.

FINANCIAL SYSTEM STRUCTURE

In 1998, Singapore's business and financial services sector was its single most important economic sector, accounting for 41 per cent of GDP (CEIC, 1999).[23] From 1990 to 1997, this sector's real growth averaged over 9 per cent per year. In 1998, growth dropped to 3 per cent, due principally to slower overall Singaporean and regional economic growth, Malaysia's decision to impose capital controls and Indonesia's economic crisis.

The Monetary Authority of Singapore supervises and regulates all Singapore's financial institutions.[24] By April 1999, Singapore had:

- nine local and 22 wholly foreign-owned banks, offering the full range of banking services
- 13 restricted banks, which can have only one main branch and cannot accept Singapore dollar savings accounts or Singapore dollar fixed deposits of less than S$250 000 from non-bank customers
- 98 offshore banks, largely restricted to the foreign currency deposit business (Monetary Authority of Singapore, 1999a and 1999b).[25]

Singapore has several specialised securities exchanges. With few large conglomerates of its own, Singapore has been forced into tough competition with other regional exchanges to attract foreign companies to list on its exchange or trade financial instruments through Singapore. Recent measures to make listing on Singapore's

---

[22] In January 1999, the employer contribution to the CPF fell from 20 per cent to 10 per cent.
[23] This grew from only 28 per cent in 1992.
[24] The Board of Commissioners of Currency is responsible for currency issue.
[25] They may not accept any interest bearing Singapore dollar deposits from entities other than approved financial institutions and they face a limit of S$300 million on credit facilities extended to resident non-bank customers.

exchanges more attractive include the June 1997 relaxation of fees and listing requirements to promote foreign currency debt and securities trading, and the deregulation of brokerage commissions.

> **SINGAPORE'S SECURITIES EXCHANGES**
>
> - Over 250 local and 37 foreign companies trade on the Singapore Stock Exchange main board.
>
> - Central Limit Order Book, Clob International, provides over-the-counter trading for shares in a further 18 regional companies; this facility included 130 companies until Malaysian companies withdrew following the imposition of capital controls.
>
> - The Stock Exchange of Singapore Dealing and Automated Quotation Market, SESDAQ, provides fully electronic clearing and settlement for a further 65 companies. A dual trading facility is provided with the North American exchange NASDAQ, which specialises in technology stocks.

SINGAPORE'S FINANCIAL MARKET REFORMS

Even before the Asian financial crisis, analysts and the Government recognised Singapore's financial sector needed reforming. Japan's 'big bang' reforms made Tokyo likely to attract more regional financial business while the Monetary Authority of Singapore's strict approach to regulation stifled innovation.[26] Globalisation and technological change could drive the centralisation of operations to one regional financial centre, and cause Singapore to be left behind.

The Asian financial crisis increased the urgency for reform, strengthened government resolve to push it through, and thus accelerated its pace. The speed of liberalisation is sending a clear signal that Singapore's future as a regional financial centre is more important than the health of any individual financial institution (Bhaskaran, 1999). Moreover, since 1998, the Monetary Authority of Singapore has explicitly promoted the financial sector, offering incentives for three years from 1999 and establishing a financial sector promotion department.[27]

Prudential Reforms

Since Deputy Prime Minister Lee Hsien Loong was appointed Chairman of the Monetary Authority of Singapore in January 1998, it has shifted its emphasis from regulation to supervision of the financial sector. The new approach emphasises monitoring compliance, asset quality and the adequacy of risk based management systems rather than 'one size fits all' regulation (Monetary Authority of Singapore,

---

[26] For details on Japan's 'big bang' reforms, see Chapter 11 - *Japan*.

[27] The Monetary Authority of Singapore has a pipeline of 100 new financial sector investments it hopes will emerge over the next three years, including multinational firms setting up their own finance operations and expanding existing business (Monetary Authority of Singapore, 1998).

1999c). To complement this new approach, the Monetary Authority of Singapore has made disclosure standards for local banks consistent with international accounting standards. For example, banks now must disclose the market value of investments, NPL figures, and past and future provisions (Monetary Authority of Singapore, 1999c). The new system should give stronger institutions the flexibility to develop and innovate without lowering prudential standards.

Securities Reforms

Important changes in securities markets include:

- the Singapore International Monetary Exchange's February 1998 approval to list a Singapore stock index and regional equity and interest rate products[28] and its April 1999 alliance with the Chicago Mercantile Exchange and the Paris Bourse allowing all three exchanges cross-exchange trading privileges for electronically traded products[29]

- brokerage rate deregulation over two to three years, with the removal in 1999 of the 1 per cent fixed commission for institutional brokers

- the Corporate Finance Committee's October 1998 recommendation that Singapore's securities markets move from merit based to disclosure based regulation[30]

- the merger from 1 December 1999 of the Stock Exchange of Singapore and the Singapore International Monetary Exchange.

Capital Market and Insurance Reforms

Debt market developments include:

- explicit official encouragement of statutory boards and government linked corporations to issue bonds

- issue of a ten year government bond to extend the benchmark yield curve for pricing corporate bonds

- promotion of asset-backed securitisation, including through a series of measures currently being developed by the Monetary Authority of Singapore.

In the insurance industry, Deputy Prime Minister Lee announced in August 1999 the closed door policy for new life insurance entrants would end, and a broad ranging insurance industry review would be completed by December 1999 (Lee, 1999).[31]

---

[28] Singaporean, Thai and Hong Kong stock index products were launched in 1998.

[29] This alliance is called the GLOBEX alliance. Exchanges from Montreal and Brazil have subsequently joined the alliance. (See Chapter 5 - *Capital Markets*.)

[30] The Government agreed with all the committees' specific recommendations, including imposing a legal obligation to disclose information. To complement the move to a disclosure based regime, securities regulation was consolidated under a single regulator, the Monetary Authority of Singapore, with the Stock Exchange of Singapore focusing on the adequacy of disclosure, supervising its members and conducting market surveillance. (See Chapter 3 - *Prudential Reform*.)

[31] Singapore's insurance market is currently closed to new entrants, although both foreign and local companies are in the market. (See Chapter 6 - *Non-bank Financial Institutions*.)

Financial Market Corporate Governance Reforms

To improve corporate governance, in the May 1999 reform package, the Monetary Authority of Singapore required all banks to choose a nominating committee from their board, with its composition subject to Monetary Authority of Singapore approval.[32] The nominating committee will decide appointments and reappointments to the board and other top bank posts, helping to clear 'dead wood' from bank boards by preventing the reappointment of non-performing board members.

Internationalisation of the Singapore Dollar

The Government has resisted fully internationalising the Singapore dollar and removing all capital account controls because trade is so important to Singapore's economy and the Government wants to maintain a competitive exchange rate.[33] However, to increase Singapore's attractiveness as a financial centre, the Monetary Authority of Singapore has somewhat increased Singapore dollar internationalisation by:

- easing requirements for foreign entities listing Singapore dollar denominated shares and bonds, even if proceeds are used outside Singapore
- giving offshore banks more flexibility to undertake Singapore dollar wholesale business and allowing them to engage in Singapore dollar denominated swaps.[34]

SINGAPORE'S BANKING SECTOR FOREIGN INVESTMENT REFORMS

In May 1999, a broad ranging reform liberalised access rules for foreign banks and equity limits for foreign shareholdings in local banks (Monetary Authority of Singapore, 1999b). In the wholesale business, the Government issued eight more restricted bank licences.[35] The lending limit for offshore banks increased to S$1 billion from the current S$300 million limit and they now also are allowed to accept Singapore dollar funds from non-bank customers via swap transactions (Monetary Authority of Singapore, 1999b). The Government also issued eight more qualifying offshore bank licences, including one to National Australia Bank (Asian Banker Interactive, 1999). In retail banking, the Government added a new category of foreign bank licence for 'qualifying foreign banks'.[36] Between 1999 and 2001, six qualifying foreign banks will be able to establish up to five branches and off-premise

---

[32] Nominating committees are accepted internationally as a means of improving corporate governance. Many US companies, including Citigroup and First Union, have nominating committees with similar functions to those in Singapore. The UK *Cadbury Report on Corporate Governance* also recommended UK corporates establish nominating committees (Monetary Authority of Singapore, 1999b).

[33] In 1998, the value of imports plus exports was 2.5 times that of GDP (CEIC, 1999). The only other Asian economy with a ratio close to this is Hong Kong, where the ratio was also 2.5 (CEIC, 1999).

[34] This was done in the May 1999 reform package.

[35] Restricted banks can engage in wholesale Singapore dollar business. Four of these licences were effective 20 October 1999 and four more will be effective 1 October 2000 (Asian Banker Interactive, 1999).

[36] This new category, qualifying foreign bank, is added to the existing categories of full, restricted and offshore foreign banks.

ATMs in up to ten locations. They also can share their ATM network. The first four qualifying foreign banks were announced on 20 October 1998, with applications reopening for the remaining two licences in January 2000.[37]

While these reforms will increase competitive pressure on local banks, they are far from full scale liberalisation. If a qualifying foreign bank already has more than five branches (as MayBank, Standard Chartered and Hong Kong Shanghai Bank do) branches will be capped at that number, although up to five off-premise ATMs will be allowed.[38] Moreover, even if qualifying foreign banks can negotiate a commercial arrangement to share ATMs, their network would be small compared to the networks of the Development Bank of Singapore (with 951 outlets) and the other local banks (with around 900 outlets) (Kim Eng Securities, 1999).[39]

Overall, the Government does not want foreign banks' share of the resident deposit base, currently 38 per cent, to rise above 50 per cent (Monetary Authority of Singapore, 1999b). Therefore although liberalisation will continue, it is likely to remain tightly controlled.

While the Government abolished the formal 40 per cent limit on foreign ownership of Singaporean banks in May 1999, outright foreign bank takeovers are unlikely because:

- boards must have a majority of Singapore citizens and permanent residents (although the authorities point out permanent residency is not difficult to achieve)

- Monetary Authority of Singapore statements indicate it would not approve takeovers of local banks (*Straits Times*, 18 May 1999, p. 1).

However, abolishing foreign ownership limits has ended the dual market for Singaporean bank shares, making it easier to value stakes in Singaporean banks.[40] Along with the recent decision to permit financial holding companies, this reform should encourage foreign and domestic bank mergers and alliances. One such alliance already has occurred, with Allied Irish Bank buying a 25 per cent stake in Keppel Tat Lee Bank.

CENTRAL PROVIDENT FUND REFORMS

A further ongoing reform is liberalisation of the Central Provident Fund. In September 1998, the Government approved an additional 24 fund management companies offering unit trust products to eligible Central Provident Fund contributors.[41] In addition, the Central Provident Fund through the Government of Singapore Investment Corporation, announced plans to place another S$25 billion

---

[37] The first four qualifying foreign bank licences issued were to ABN Amro, Banque Nationale de Paris, Citibank and Standard Chartered Bank (Asian Banker Interactive, 1999).

[38] MayBank, Standard Chartered and Hong Kong Shanghai Bank are currently full foreign banks.

[39] All Singaporean banks except the Development Bank of Singapore share their ATM network.

[40] The dual market caused valuation problems as strong demand from foreign institutions for Singaporean banks caused foreign tranche share values to exceed local tranche shares.

[41] Eligible contributors must have Central Provident Fund balances above a set minimum. The September 1998 approvals follow 22 original approvals between May 1987 and May 1998.

with private fund managers over the next three years. However, compared to public pension schemes in Hong Kong, Japan and Australia, the Central Provident Fund remains tightly controlled; employees can only invest in the Central Provident Fund or its approved products, and most funds are still managed by two government-owned companies. (See Chapter 6 - *Non-bank Financial Institutions*.)

SINGAPORE'S FUTURE TRENDS AND OPPORTUNITIES

As a result of its ongoing reform process, Singapore has increased significantly its financial market flexibility and efficiency, increasing its attractiveness as an Asian financial centre.

In the banking sector, increasing local and foreign competition will accelerate the restructuring process, encouraging mergers and alliances. In 1998, the Development Bank of Singapore took over the Post Office Savings Bank. The May 1999 package increased the pressure for mergers among the Overseas Chinese Banking Corporation, Overseas Union Bank and Union Overseas Bank. The Government believes Singapore cannot sustain more than two big local banks (Monetary Authority of Singapore, 1999b). The Development Bank of Singapore seems certain to be one of these banks, with the market increasingly viewing Overseas Chinese Banking Corporation as the other (Kim Eng Securities, 1999).

Local banks also are likely to make greater efforts to rationalise staff numbers; this should be easier as the macroeconomic situation improves. With real estate prices high, competitive pressures also will force branch network consolidation and the use of price incentives to encourage telephone and Internet banking. Fee income also is likely to increase over time, moving towards full cost recovery for services such as ATMs and cheques.

Banks also are likely to boost profits by returning to core bank business, reversing the diversification into many unrelated businesses. For example, Keppel Group in an effort to maintain control of Keppel Tat Lee Bank, has unwound complex cross-shareholdings and rationalised its structure (ABN Amro, 1999).

For the reasons discussed above, Singapore's banks are unlikely to experience full foreign takeovers. However, foreign involvement must grow if Singapore is to develop internationally competitive banks. Use of foreign management expertise is an increasingly common approach.[42] Because they would give Singaporean banks access to world class risk management and marketing skills, mergers and alliances with foreign banks also are likely to become increasingly common. Such arrangements may be attractive to foreign banks because of their potential to yield major efficiency gains in a sound legal environment. Abolishing the dual market for bank shares and legalising holding companies should assist this process.

Singapore's relatively sound legal framework and ongoing reform of its securities laws should ensure continued growth in Singapore's bond and equity markets. (See Chapter 5 - *Capital Markets*.) In funds management, pressure will increase for greater competition to maximise returns from Singapore's large savings pool. (See Chapter 6 - *Non-bank Financial Institutions*.)

---

[42] For example, Overseas Chinese Banking Corporation hired Alex Au, the ex head of Hang Seng Bank in Hong Kong as its CEO, while John Olds from JP Morgan now heads the Development Bank of Singapore.

IMPLICATIONS FOR HONG KONG AND SINGAPORE

Singapore has come through the financial crisis in better shape than Hong Kong, partly because of its flexible exchange rate. Hong Kong and Singapore both are undertaking major financial market reforms to improve their growth prospects and position themselves to attract more regional financial centre business. Similar patterns in their reform programs include improving market access for foreign banks, amalgamating equities and futures exchanges, and increasing emphasis on bond market development. While starting from behind, some analysts believe Singapore's recent reforms are helping it close the competitive gap on Hong Kong.

Looking to the future, the operating environment of Hong Kong's Mandatory Provident Fund is considerably more liberal than that of Singapore's Central Provident Fund, offering employers a choice of providers, and employees a choice of unit trusts and mutual funds. The greater competition inherent in the Mandatory Provident Fund is likely to stimulate Hong Kong's funds management industry and the range of financial products it offers, enhancing Hong Kong's role as a regional funds management centre.

REFERENCES

ABN Amro, 1999, 'Singapore: Frogs on Logs', ABN Amro Research Report, Singapore, May.

Asian Banker Interactive, 1999, 'The Monetary Authority of Singapore (MAS) Announces 4 Foreign Banks Named Qualifying Full Banks (QFBs), 8 Additional Restricted Bank Licences and 8 Qualifying Offshore Banks (QOBs)', 20 October, subscriber service for The Asian Banker, www.asianbanker.com.sg, accessed on 21 October.

Bhaskaran, M., 1999, East Asia Analytical Unit interview with the Managing Director, Group Head of Research, SG Securities (Singapore) Pte. Ltd., Singapore, May.

Caprio, G., Dooley, M., Leipziger, D. and Walsh, C., 1996, 'The Lender of Last Resort Function under a Currency Board: the Case of Argentina', Policy Research Department, World Bank, Working Paper 1 648, Washington DC, September.

Carse, D., 1999, East Asia Analytical Unit interview with Deputy Chief Executive, Hong Kong Monetary Authority, Hong Kong, May.

CEIC, 1999, CEIC Database, Hong Kong, supplied by EconData, Canberra.

Consensus Economics, 1999, 'Asia Pacific Consensus Forecasts: September 1999', Consensus Economics, London, September.

Freris, A., 1991, *The Financial Markets of Hong Kong*, Routledge, London.

Government of Hong Kong Special Administrative Region, 1999, 'Policy Paper on Securities and Futures Market Reform', March, www.hksfc.org/eng/index.htm, accessed on 29 June.

Hong Kong Monetary Authority, 1999, Data on bank assets supplied to the East Asia Analytical Unit, July.

Jackson, D., 1999, 'Asia Pacific Property Trends', Colliers Jardine, Sydney.

JP Morgan, 1999, 'Monthly Average for OECD and Emerging Market Currencies', www.jpmorgan.com/MarketDataInd/Forex/currIndex.html, accessed on 1 September.

Kim Eng Securities, 1999, 'The Singapore Big Bang: No Pain No Gain', Singapore, 19 May.

Lee, Hsien Loong, 1999b, 'Life Insurance in the 21st Century', Speech presented at the 19th Pacific Insurance Conference, Singapore, 16 August.

Monetary Authority of Singapore, 1999a, 'Fact Sheet: Commercial Banking in Singapore', 17 May, www.mas.gov.sg/newspeeches, accessed on 17 May.

___ 1999b, Press statement 'Liberalising Commercial Banking and Upgrading Local Banks', 17 May, www.mas.gov.sg/speeches, accessed on 17 May.

___ 1999c, *'Supervision of Financial Institutions'*, www.mas.gov.sg/singfinsec/singfinsec_supervisionoffininst-c.html, accessed on 19 October.

___ 1998, 'Singapore Presses Ahead with Financial Sector Reforms, Financial Hub Singapore', Financial Sector Promotion Department, MAS, Singapore.

Morgan Stanley Dean Witter, 1999, Information provided to East Asia Analytical Unit, August.

National Australia Bank, 1999, 'Economic Comment: Hong Kong', International Economics Department, Melbourne, 15 January.

Obstfeld, M. and Rogoff, K., 1995, 'The Mirage of Fixed Exchange Rates', *Journal of Economic Perspectives*, vol. 9, no. 4, pp. 73-96.

Procter, A., 1999, East Asia Analytical Unit interview with Executive Director, Securities and Exchange Commission, Hong Kong, May.

Scott, R., 1997, 'Pegged Exchange Rate Systems of Macau and Hong Kong', *Multinational Finance Journal*, vol. 1, no. 2, June, pp. 153-68.

Shu-ki, Tsang, 1998, 'Two Essays on Hong Kong's Currency Board', BRC papers on China, Business Research Centre, Hong Kong Baptist University.

Williamson, J., 1995, 'What Role for Currency Boards?', Institute for International Economics, www.iie.com/pa40.htm, accessed on 27 November 1998.

Chapter 10

TAIWAN

Taiwan's financial sector has experienced problems, but by regional standards, remains relatively healthy. Key factors assisting the financial sector's relatively good performance include Taiwan's sound macroeconomic management, high foreign exchange reserves, generally prudent banking regulation and practices, and the preponderance of small and medium enterprises with low debt to asset ratios. Nevertheless, Taiwan's financial market reform is ongoing and still faces many challenges.

As in many East Asian economies, banks dominate Taiwan's financial sector. However, unlike most of East Asia, many banks are wholly or partly government owned. In addition, the government-owned postal savings system is a major competitor with the banks. In part due to banking sector shortcomings, corporate bonds issues and the number of listed firms on equity markets are growing rapidly.

This chapter first examines Taiwan's performance in the Asian crisis. It then assesses major developments in Taiwan's financial sector, including regulatory system structure and issues in banking, non-bank financial institutions and capital markets. It analyses the impact of recent financial market reforms and examines foreign involvement in Taiwan's financial sector. Finally, it highlights potential opportunities for foreign financial institutions and service suppliers, and remaining priority reforms.

FINANCIAL SECTOR PERFORMANCE IN THE CRISIS

At the macroeconomic level, Taiwan remained very resilient to the Asian financial crisis. Real GDP grew 6.8 per cent in 1997, 4.8 per cent in 1998 and 4.3 per cent through the year to March 1999. It avoided a major depreciation of its exchange rate; the nominal NT$:US$ exchange rate depreciated only 14 per cent in the two years to July 1999, and the real trade weighted exchange rate depreciated only 1.6 per cent (JP Morgan, 1999). Taiwan's good economic performance was mainly due to its sound macroeconomic management and strong financial sector. It had a balanced budget, low inflation and high foreign reserves for much of the 1980s and 1990s. Taiwan also has a high savings ratio, an excess of savings over investment and a significant current account surplus (Figure 10.1).[1]

---

[1] However, if the trends of the last decade continue, Taiwan's savings and current account performance could become increasingly problematical.

Figure 10.1

Strong Savings and Current Account Performance
Savings, Investment and Current Account Performance as a Per cent of GDP

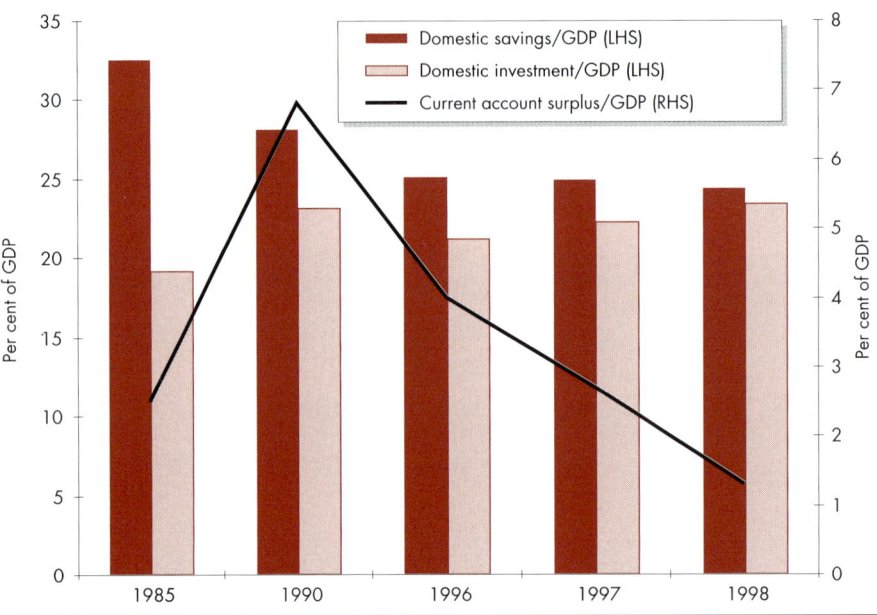

Source: Barclays Economics Department, 1998; and Asian Development Bank, 1999.

Taiwan is not heavily dependent on volatile foreign capital inflows. Unlike some East Asian economies with high savings rates, in the lead up to the crisis the banking and corporate sectors were financed primarily from domestic savings. This made Taiwan less susceptible to external shocks. At the end of 1997, domestic banks' foreign borrowing and other liabilities were only 3.5 per cent of total liabilities (Central Bank of China, 1999c). While over 80 per cent of Taiwan's US$28 billion external debt was short term, short term foreign debt equalled only 27 per cent of foreign exchange reserves. Furthermore, total 1997 foreign debt was only 4 per cent of GDP (Bank of International Settlements, 1999; and CEIC, 1999).

One of the main reasons for this low exposure to foreign debt was the low or negative differential between Taiwanese and US interest rates. This contrasts with the large excess of domestic over US interest rates in economies like Thailand, Korea and Indonesia (Figure 10.2). Furthermore, as Taiwanese banks were slow to lend internationally, they had a low exposure to corporate clients in Asian economies in crisis.

Figure 10.2

Low US-Taiwan Interest Rate Differential
Interest Rate Differentials between the United States and Taiwan, Thailand and Indonesia

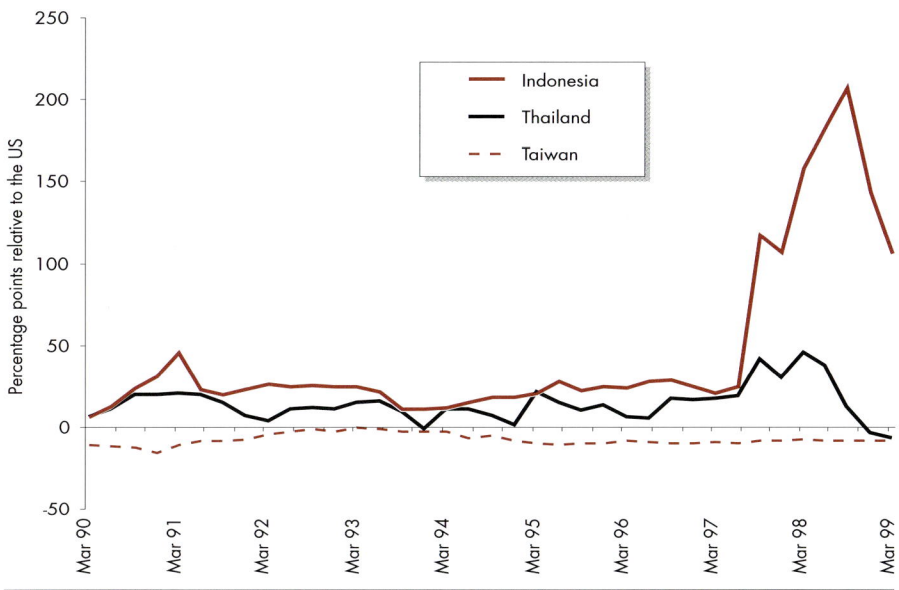

Note: Thai and Indonesian interest rates are money market rates (International Monetary Fund, 1999); US data is a commercial paper rate (International Monetary Fund, 1999); and the Taiwanese interest rate is a commercial paper rate (CEIC, 1999).
Source: CEIC, 1999; and International Monetary Fund, 1999.

At the micro level, the Asian financial crisis inevitably generated some negative spillover effects for Taiwan's financial markets. For example, in November 1998, Taichung Business Bank failed while two bill finance companies nearly collapsed and were taken over by banks. Also, the governing Nationalist Party-owned Central Investment Holding Company rescued the troubled Pan Asia Bank, acquiring a major shareholding.

However, unlike in East Asian crisis economies, most financial institutions employed prudent lending policies. Officially, shares backed only 2 per cent of bank loans, and banks financed up to only 60 per cent of a share's face value.[2] Similarly, banks only extend mortgages for up to 70 per cent of the purchase price of assets, and all real estate loans are fully secured (Yen, 1998).

In common with much of East Asia, Taiwan's property market is oversupplied and financial institution exposure to property lending is second only to Hong Kong's (Goldstein, 1998). While smaller credit cooperatives are experiencing difficulties from the weak property market, the conservatism of Taiwanese banks shielded them from major non-performing loan, NPL, problems.

---

[2] It is difficult to know banks' total lending for share purchases as both home mortgage loans and credit cards can be used for share purchases without banks' knowledge.

Taiwan's corporate structure also contributed to its strong performance. Small to medium sized enterprises are relatively important in Taiwan and tend to have low debt leveraging. Taiwanese firms' heavy dependence on reinvested profits, owners' savings and informal finance kept their average debt to equity ratio at 30 per cent in 1998. This ratio is substantially lower than every East Asian economy except Hong Kong, and ten to fifteen times less than Korean enterprises' (*Economist*, 7 November 1998, p. 15; and East Asia Analytical Unit, 1999). In the 1990s, large corporations increasingly raised funds through the stock market; this reduced their exposure to interest rate increases imposed to defend the Taiwanese dollar from speculation.

THE REGULATORY SYSTEM

Taiwan's financial sector regulatory system is highly fragmented. Bank supervision is split between the Ministry of Finance and Central Bank of China. The Securities and Futures Commission regulates securities markets; the Department of Insurance regulates insurance companies; and the Central Deposit Insurance Corporation can inspect the records of all institutions participating in the voluntary deposit insurance scheme, except the new private banks, and may refuse or cancel insurance.[3]

This fragmented regulatory structure creates problems: two different agencies supervise banks; and with the trend towards universal banking, financial institutions sometimes must deal with several different regulators.

Recent and Prospective Reforms

Recognising the problems flowing from Taiwan's fragmented regulatory structure and the worldwide trend to consolidate supervision, the authorities announced that by 1 January 2000, they will establish a new financial services regulator to monitor the banking, securities and insurance sectors (*Australian*, 28 May 1999, p. 27). To reduce scope for political interference, the section of the agency responsible for executing policy will be funded from fees collected from supervised institutions rather than from a budget subject to legislative approval (*Taipei Times*, 6 September 1999, p. 17).

In addition to this proposed consolidation of regulatory power, the government has reformed significantly other regulatory arrangements. In particular:

- the revised banking law passed in March 1999 gives the Ministry of Finance more power to intervene in banks facing difficulties. For example, it may suspend a bank's licence, dismiss key bank personnel and take over a bank

- in 1999, Taiwan also introduced a new law compelling all financial institutions to take out deposit insurance. Institutions with overdue loan ratios above 8 per cent are excluded from the scheme and will be shut down or merged after a three year grace period.[4]

---

[3] At the end of 1998, 87 per cent of private sector institutions and 56 per cent of government-owned ones participated in the deposit insurance scheme (Central Deposit Insurance Corporation, 1999).

[4] 'Overdue loans' and 'non-performing loans' have some minor differences. For a discussion, see Fitch IBCA, 1999a.

Transparency Issues

To complement these reforms, financial reporting and accounting standards should be raised to reach international levels. For example, some banks, such as the Bank of Taiwan and the International Commercial Bank of China do not disclose their NPLs. While the Finance Ministry and the Central Bank of China release other individual bank's NPL figures, analysts query whether regulators can adequately verify the NPL information provided by the banks.

THE BANKING SYSTEM

With only 21 million people, Taiwan has 50 domestic and 46 foreign banks, making overbanking a major problem. In addition, 60 credit cooperatives, 314 farmers' and fisherman's credit unions and the postal savings system compete with the banking system for deposits (Tradeport, 1998). The combined assets of Taiwan's top three banks, Bank of Taiwan, Land Bank of Taiwan and Taiwan Cooperative Bank account for only 26 per cent of total domestic bank assets (Bureau of Monetary Affairs, 1999). The relatively small size of Taiwan's banks may inhibit their future domestic and international competitiveness.

Taiwan's banking system is dominated by wholly and partially privatised former state owned banks (Figure 10.3).[5] Wholly private domestic banks control approximately 38 per cent of banking assets and foreign banks control a further 5 per cent.

The New Private Banks

In 1991, banking reform advanced significantly when the government granted licences to 16 new private banks. The new private banks compete successfully with the dominant government-owned and partially privatised banks, offering more competitive interest rates and improved products and services. However, in recent years, these new banks have experienced some NPL problems due to their acquisitions of troubled credit cooperatives, related party lending, and rapid real estate and construction lending growth (Figure 10.4). Generally, the new banks' large NT$10 billion (US$313 million) minimum capital requirement provides a buffer against loan losses and a good platform for growth. However, problems exist at particular institutions, most notably Pan Asia Bank, where the overdue loan ratio was 10.2 per cent in April 1999 (Fitch IBCA, 1999a).

Large business conglomerates own many of these new private banks and related party lending can be a serious problem. For example, before the Asian crisis, most of Pan Asia Bank's assets were short term loans to companies related to Taiwan's troubled Everfortune Group, which owned 35 per cent of Pan Asia Bank (*Far Eastern Economic Review*, 28 January 1999, p. 53).

---

[5] In Chang Hwa Bank, government equity now is down to around 28 per cent. In Hua Nan Commercial Bank and First Commercial Bank, government equity still is around 40 per cent (Cutler, 1999a).

Taiwan

Figure 10.3
Government-owned Banks Still Important
Assets and Numbers of Taiwan's Banks, December 1998

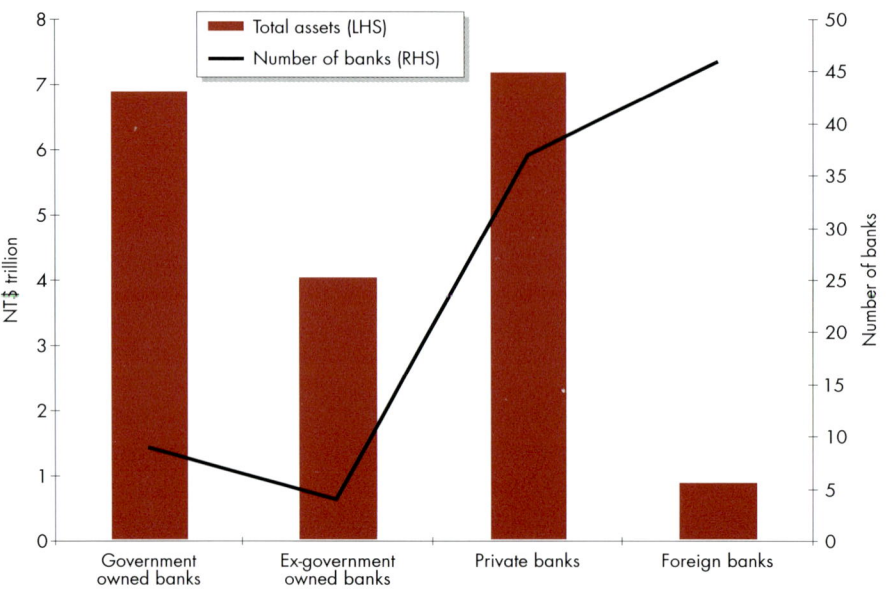

Source: Bureau of Monetary Affairs, 1999; and Taiwan Economic Data Centre, 1999.

Moreover, while private bank NPL problems presently are less severe than in the government-owned and partially privatised banks, the loan portfolios of new commercial banks remain vulnerable to declines in economic activity or rises in interest rates. Many private bank clients either were refused loans from government banks or already had loans from them which have prior claims on collateral.

Government Bank Privatisations

From 1949 to 1991, except for a few pre-1949 private banks, banking was reserved for government-owned institutions. In the 1991 financial market reforms, the government announced the privatisation of First Commercial Bank, Hua Nan Commercial Bank, Chang Hwa Commercial Bank and the Medium Business Bank of Taiwan. This was achieved by selling share tranches until the banks had majority private ownership. Moreover, Taiwan's three largest government banks will incorporate by December 1999 as a first step towards privatisation (*Taipei Times*, 4 August 1999, p. 18). Privatisation progress, while slow, is significant. Based on total assets, the partly privatised banks are among Taiwan's largest, and majority private shareholding should increase their independence and strengthen bank competition.[6]

---

[6] Based on assets at the end of December 1998, First Commercial Bank, Hua Nan Commercial Bank, Chang Hwa Commercial Bank and the Medium Business Bank of Taiwan are the fourth, fifth, sixth and seventh biggest banks in Taiwan, controlling 22 per cent of bank assets (Bureau of Monetary Affairs, 1999).

Enforcement of prudential regulations limiting the ownership of banks by individuals or companies to 15 per cent has been weak.[7] It is important diversified corporate groups are unable to purchase privatising banks and improperly divert funds to group loans. Another concern is that partially or even fully privatised banks may remain under informal government influence, as occurred after Korea privatised its banks in the 1980s (East Asia Analytical Unit, 1999). Full privatisation would reduce but not remove this possibility.

TAIWAN'S BANKS DURING THE CRISIS

The Taiwanese banking system has a reputation for conservative lending practices and generally is subject to tight prudential regulation. In 1989, the government required banks to maintain a capital adequacy ratio of 8 per cent. Until December 1998, Taiwan's measure of capital adequacy was not fully consistent with the Bank for International Settlements' definition, but this requirement nevertheless ensured Taiwanese banks were reasonably well capitalised.[8] Consequently, local banks dealt well with domestic financial market volatility during the increase in cross strait tension in 1996, and in 1997 and 1998 during the Asian financial crisis (Kuo and Liu, 1998, p. 8). Bank capital adequacy ratios remained high throughout the crisis. At the end of 1998, older banks had an average capital adequacy ratio of 11.6 per cent and the new private sector banks had an average ratio of 10.3 per cent (Central Bank of China, 1999a).

As a result of most banks' prudent lending practices and no major crashes in property or currency markets, average bank NPL ratios are only around 5.2 per cent. However, NPL ratios are rising, and among the business banks average 8 per cent (Figure 10.4). Taiwan's older, government-owned banks have higher NPL ratios than the new banks. However, unlike the new banks, typically old banks have large hidden reserves in long term equity investments which can be used to cover write-offs.[9] Looking forward, NPL ratios are likely to increase further because some problem corporate loans are yet to be recorded as non-performing, and small and medium enterprises increasingly face difficulties in accessing credit (Fitch IBCA, 1999a). Taiwanese banks also are dealing with the aftermath of the 21 September 1999 earthquake. Analysts estimate rising NPLs from businesses made insolvent by earthquake inflicted losses will force banks to write off around 40 per cent of their loan loss reserves; as these reserves are rebuilt, bank profitability will suffer (Cutler, 1999b).

---

[7] Everfortune group's 35 per cent ownership of the private Pan Asia Bank before the crisis is an example of weak enforcement of this regulation.

[8] The main changes made in 1998 were to incorporate market risk in calculating risk weighted assets, specify loan loss reserves and deduct long term investments. Overall, the Ministry of Finance estimates that the new method for calculating capital adequacy reduces average capital adequacy ratios, measured using the previous definition, by between 1 and 1.5 percentage points (Fitch IBCA, 1998).

[9] A range of measures, such as tax concessions, a cut in banks' reserve requirement ratio and changes in legal procedures have been introduced to speed up the process of writing off bad loans. However, given the relatively small size of Taiwan's NPL problem, these measures probably are not critical to the future shape of the financial sector.

Figure 10.4

Most Banks Have Modest NPL Problems
NPLs by Type of Bank, December 1997 to September 1998, Per cent of Outstanding Loans

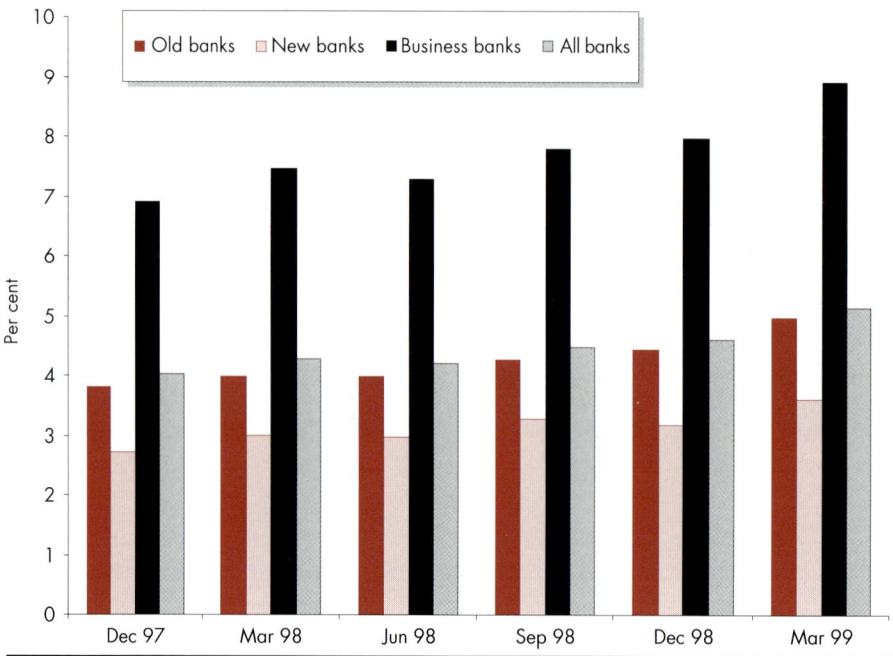

Note: 'Old banks' were established before 1991 and mainly are government owned or formerly government owned. The 16 'new banks' were granted licences in 1991. 'Business banks' initially were established to lend to small and medium sized enterprises but progressively have branched out into lending to consumers and larger corporates.
Source: Fitch IBCA, 1999a.

BANKS' WIDER BUSINESS SCOPE

From the mid to late 1990s, government reforms significantly broadened banks' business scope. From 1993, banks could engage in securities brokering and underwriting, and issue short term debt instruments. From 1994, banks could trade in derivatives, privately deal in bonds and provide fee-based consultancy services (Kuei, 1999). Under banking law amendments approved in March 1999, commercial banks also can issue bank debentures, invest in stock market shares and unlisted venture capital firms, and operate securities and trust services.[10] These reforms will further the progression of commercial banks to universal banks, help raise their capital adequacy levels and improve their ability to provide long term funding.

---

[10] Most of these recent liberalising moves also apply to foreign banks.

BANK RATIONALISATION

Some rationalisation of government-owned or partly government-owned banks is likely by 2000 or 2001. No firm plans exist but the government has asked three large state owned banks, Bank of Taiwan, the Cooperative Bank of Taiwan and the Land Bank of Taiwan to incorporate by the end of 1999; this will open up various merger options (*Taipei Times*, 4 August 1999, p. 18).[11] The big three commercial banks, Chang Hwa Bank, First Commercial Bank and Hua Nan Commercial Bank which still have some government equity, also could merge (*Taipei Times*, 28 July 1999, p. 19).

Rationalising the new commercial banks will be more difficult. The main barrier is that the large business groups owning many of these banks are unwilling to cede control; bank ownership offers prestige and access to capital. However, given the large number of banks and their variable asset quality, depositor differentiation and pressure for mergers could increase in the medium to long term. The government also is considering tax incentives to encourage consolidation of Taiwan's smaller financial institutions, including farmers' and fisherman's associations and credit cooperatives.[12]

Bank dominance within the financial sector is likely to grow as a result of this consolidation process; a draft law stipulates new institutions formed by mergers between banks and other financial institutions will become banks.[13] However, this process would further increase the number of banks, and such mergers may worsen banks' NPL problems and credit ratings.

FOREIGN BANK OPERATIONS

While foreign banks have been in Taiwan since 1959, reforms in 1994 better equipped them to compete with domestic banks.[14] Between 1994 and 1997, foreign bank numbers increased from 37 to 45. Their assets grew by 47 per cent, although they fell by 10 per cent in 1998 (Figure 10.5).

New reforms approved in March 1999 allow foreign banks to issue bank debentures, invest in real estate and operate securities businesses. However, before opening new branches, foreign banks still face complex procedures, which inhibit their growth (American Chamber of Commerce and the European Council for Commerce and Trade, 1999).

---

[11] As detailed earlier, incorporation is also a necessary precondition for privatisation. Possible rationalisation options include merging some or all of these banks. Merging all three banks would create a bank in the top 30 in the world, by assets (*Taipei Times*, 4 August 1999, p. 18).

[12] For example, preferential tax treatment and subsidies would encourage mergers among the credit departments of farmers' and fisherman's associations.

[13] Other financial institutions include credit departments of farmers' and fisherman's associations, bill finance firms and investment trust firms.

[14] After 1994, foreign banks could engage in retail and corporate deposit taking and lending, trade financing, foreign exchange dealing and trust business.

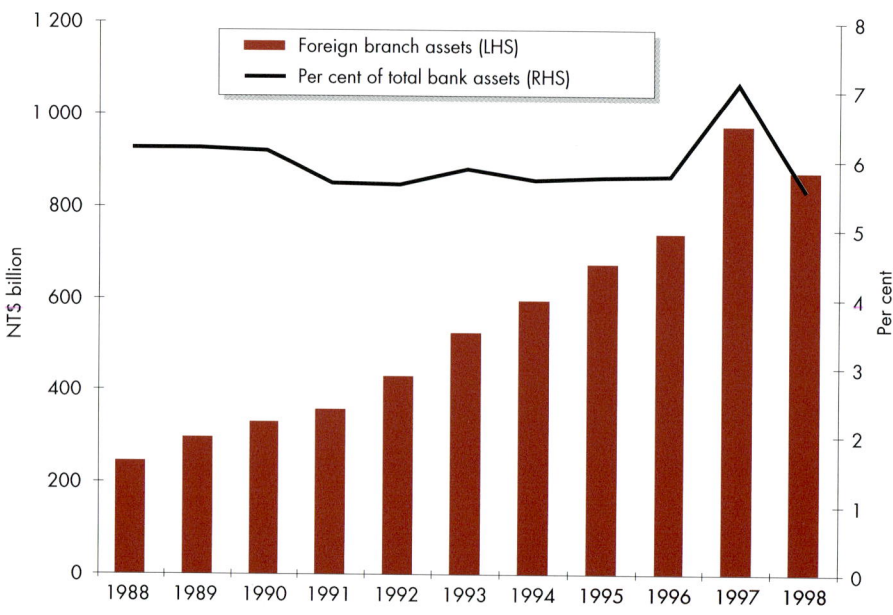

Figure 10.5

Foreign Bank Assets Growing Rapidly to 1997

Assets of Foreign Bank Branches

Source: Taiwan Economic Data Centre, 1998.

Most foreign banks focus on treasury business, trade financing and providing services to clients from their home economy. Citibank, Standard Chartered and Hong Kong Shanghai Banking Corporation also are active in the retail market, particularly the credit card business (IBCA, 1997). Stimulated by heavy foreign stock purchases in 1999, custodial business is a recent growth area.[15] Major fee opportunities lie in service fees, foreign currency exchange fees and a range of related businesses including settling stocks and collecting dividends (*China Post*, 26 April 1999).

Australia does not have a strong presence in the Taiwanese banking sector. Only two banks have branch offices, ANZ Bank and National Australia Bank.

---

[15] This business essentially involves providing banking services for foreign portfolio investors in Taiwan. Four foreign banks, Hong Kong Shanghai Banking Corporation, Citibank, Chase Manhattan and Standard Chartered and one local bank, Central Trust of China dominate it.

> **ANZ TAIWAN**
>
> The ANZ Bank's Taiwan presence dates back to 1980 when Grindlays Bank obtained branch status. ANZ acquired Grindlays in 1984, gaining a direct presence in the market. The Taipei branch office provides a full range of personal, commercial and corporate banking services. Retail banking includes both domestic and foreign currency transactions, including providing residential property loans in Australia and New Zealand.
>
> The branch provides a wide range of corporate and commercial banking services, including commercial paper guarantees and performance bonds, as well as trade finance facilities. Treasury services include spot and forward foreign currency dealing and domestic money market transactions.
>
> ANZ Taipei also offers introductory services and advice for customers wishing to do business in Taipei.
>
> Source: ANZ Bank, 1999.

Potential Foreign Bank Opportunities

In May 1999, the Ministry of Finance proposed raising the maximum foreign ownership of local banks to 50 per cent, up from the existing threshold of 15 per cent applying to any domestic or foreign group.[16] If this proposal becomes law, foreign banks could gain a foothold in Taiwan's core banking industry. However, major risks involve continued government participation and overbanking. These factors depress spreads and increase the danger banks will undertake poor quality lending to increase their market share.

NON-BANK FINANCIAL INSTITUTIONS

Of the non-bank financial institutions that compete with banks in taking deposits, the four most important are the postal savings system, insurance companies, pension funds and the farmers' and fisherman's associations and credit cooperatives.

The Postal Savings System

While Taiwan's post office network provides cheap and extensive branch access, in recent years, the postal savings system has become a relatively less attractive savings option.[17] Postal savings lending is subject to considerable government direction; this reduces its rate of return. For example, in late 1998 and early 1999, the government used postal savings funds to intervene in support of the stock and property markets

---

[16] The 15 per cent limit will continue to apply to domestic companies or company groups. The limit is designed to prevent major shareholders from manipulating a bank and make related party lending more difficult. However, significant problems remain with enforcing this law; in particular, over time, companies and company groups often manage to move their shareholdings above the limit.

[17] Postal savings system assets were around NT$2.6 trillion in 1998, up more than 250 per cent over the last decade, but over this decade, its assets have fallen from 27 per cent to only 17 per cent of total bank assets.

(Fitch IBCA, 1999a; and 1999b).[18] Institutions like the government Long Term Funding Committee also allocate postal savings to infrastructure and utility investments (East Asian Executive Reports, 1997). As in Japan, if left largely unreformed Taiwan's postal savings system is likely to stunt rates of return on savings. Because it is state owned, involves implicit government subsidies to savers and is an important store of savings, it also impedes the viability of privately run financial institutions. (See Chapter 11 - Japan.)

Insurance

Amendments to the insurance law in 1992 liberalised the market, permitting new entrants including foreign firms, and eased restrictions on investment strategies. Life insurance firms now can invest in a wider range of domestic securities but can only put up to 5 per cent of total funds in foreign security markets. The life insurance sector, with total assets of NT$1.8 trillion in 1997, is far larger than the separate non-life sector (Taiwan Economic Data Centre, 1999).

Foreign insurance company participation

Foreign insurance companies' market share quadrupled between 1990 and 1997, although since 1993, few new foreign firms have entered Taiwan (Figure 10.6). US companies permitted access under 1980s bilateral agreements dominate foreign-owned insurance firms.

Pension Funds

Taiwan's major pension fund is the public Labor Retirement Fund. The government-owned Central Trust of China acts as custodian for this fund; it prohibits private investment management companies from managing these funds and employees from withdrawing contributions for individual investments. Rates of return at around 6 per cent per year are seen by some analysts as low, with investment in stock market stabilisation funds also causing controversy (*China Post*, 7 May 1999, p. 13 and *Taipei Times*, 30 July 1999, p. 18). Reform of Taiwan's pension system now is on the agenda, although few firm decisions have been made and momentum is likely to be slowed by the earthquake of 21 September 1999 (*China Post*, 7 May 1999, p. 13).

Farmers' and Fisherman's Associations and Credit Cooperatives

Taiwan's 314 farmers' and fisherman's associations and credit cooperatives account for only around 6 per cent of total financial sector lending (*Taipei Times*, 28 July 1999, p. 19). However, many of these institutions have NPL problems and their large numbers contribute significantly to Taiwan's overbanking problem; the government

---

[18] In November 1998, the Government announced a US$8 billion stock stabilisation fund to support share prices in the period leading up to the 5 December mayoral and legislative assembly elections (Fitch IBCA, 1999b, p. 1). In early 1999, the Government introduced a US$31 billion package to help soak up the excess supply of apartments (Fitch IBCA, 1999a, p. 3).

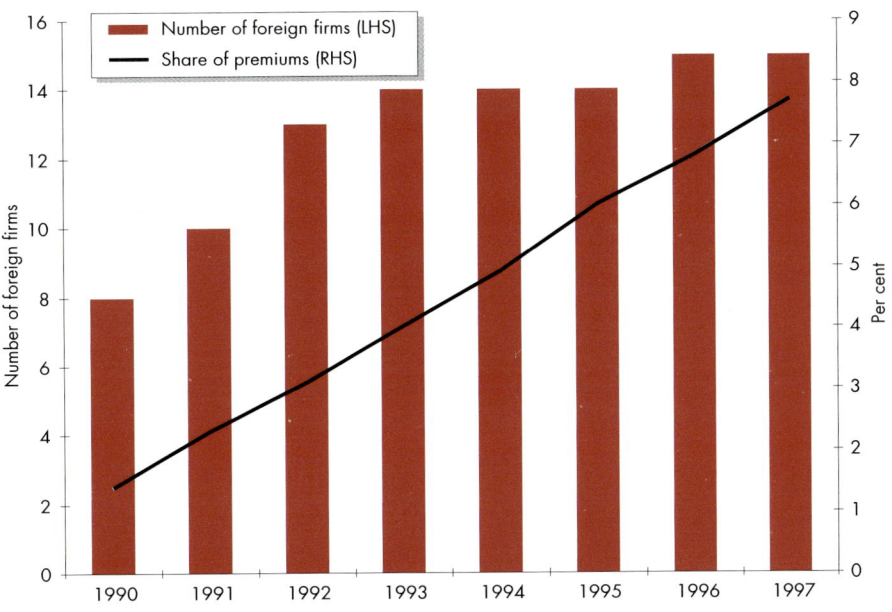

Figure 10.6

Foreign Presence in Insurance Grew Rapidly
Number and Market Share of Foreign Insurance Companies

Source: Council for Economic Planning and Development, 1998.

is encouraging consolidation and allowing some bank takeovers.[19] Another option is to liquidate the weakest institutions and merge the remainder into a few regional agricultural banks (*Taipei Times*, 24 July 1999, p. 17).

THE INFORMAL FINANCIAL SECTOR

Taiwan also has an important informal or 'curb' financial sector. It developed during the long pre-deregulation period when state banks rationed credit to preferred large private and public sector companies. In the decade to 1995, the informal financial sector still provided 30 to 40 per cent of small and medium sized enterprises' funding (Smith, 1999). At its simplest level, the informal market pools and lends funds among associates and family members. At a more organised level, rotating credit clubs or *huis* advance credit to club members.[20] Firms also take deposits from employees, and pawnbrokers and moneylenders make loans against post-dated cheques. The more formal level of this market includes underground banks and

---

[19] Some of these cooperatives have NPL levels above 20 per cent. The Government has encouraged consolidation with tax incentives and by indicating it will withdraw operating licences from credit unions and cooperatives unable to achieve capital adequacy ratios of 8 per cent by 2002 (Smith, 1999).

[20] A large 1985 Ministry of Justice survey indicated 85 per cent of the population had participated in *huis* (Shea, 1995, p. 134).

community savings and credit associations.[21] While the informal sector remains important, its role is likely to continue declining as ongoing financial sector liberalisation yields greater choice and flexibility among financial products offered by licensed financial institutions.

CAPITAL MARKETS

In Taiwan's active equity market, the number of listed firms is increasing steadily. Some money market instruments also are growing rapidly, although the corporate bond market remains small.

Stock Market

Taiwan's stock market is important to overall financial sector health; banks are exposed to the stock market by their own shareholdings, by loans collateralised by shares and through customers borrowing to purchase shares. Over the past ten years, the stock exchange's market capitalisation and listed firm numbers have increased dramatically, reflecting price rises over time and the exchange's increasing importance as a source of corporate funds (Figure 10.7).[22]

However, around another 500 Taiwanese firms are large enough to list but choose not to do so (Naughton, 1999). As in other East Asian economies, many large family controlled firms are reluctant to dilute ownership or disclose the information on corporate activities which listing entails.[23]

In 1998, the Taiwan stock exchange had the world's highest turnover ratio, 323 per cent; a typical developed country's ratio is below 100 per cent (International Finance Corporation, 1999).[24] This high liquidity largely reflects the dominance of speculative retail investors in the market.[25]

Foreign Investor Access

The securities market first started opening to foreign institutional investors in 1990. Initially the annual quota for qualified foreign institutional investors was set at NT$400 million, rising to NT$600 million in 1996. In April 1999, the government raised the cap on a single foreign investment in an individual stock from 15 per cent to 50 per cent of total stock, and on total foreign investment in an individual stock from 30 per cent to 50 per cent (*China Post*, 1 May 1999, p. 12). By 2001, the 50 per cent foreign ownership ceiling will be removed completely (*Asiamoney* Supplement, July/August 1999, p. 1).

---

[21] Instalment credit companies, financial leasing companies and credit unions also form part of this sector as they are unregulated and unlicensed.

[22] The increased capitalisation is due to both rising market values of listed stocks and the steady flow of new listings; these continued in 1998 despite a 22 per cent fall in the benchmark stock exchange index. The Taiwan stock exchange is formally called the Taiwan Stock Exchange Corporation, TSEC.

[23] It often is feared that this information will assist competitors or tax authorities.

[24] The turnover ratio, the ratio of total trading volume for the year to market capitalisation, is widely used to measure liquidity. The ratio indicates how many times the average share changes hands in a given period.

[25] In 1997, Taiwanese individuals accounted for 90 per cent of trading volume.

Figure 10.7

New Listings Rising Continuously
Market Capitalisation and New Listings on the Taiwanese Stock Exchange

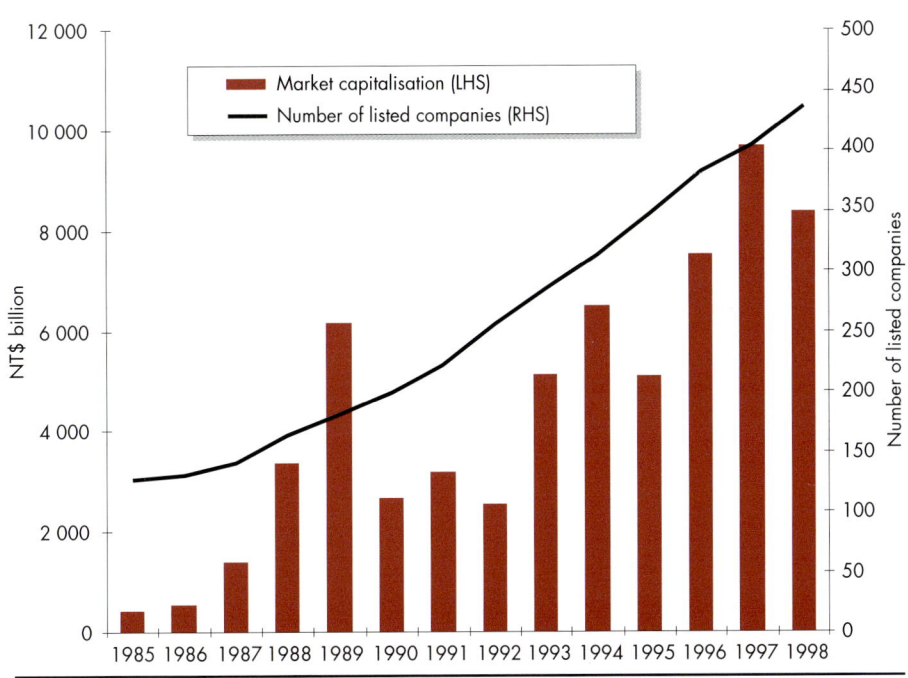

Source: CEIC, 1999.

As restrictions eased, foreigners' share holdings increased from 0.5 per cent of share market capitalisation in 1993 to 2.6 per cent in 1997 (Taiwan Stock Exchange Corporation, 1998b). In the first half of 1999, foreign investors purchased NT$186.3 billion (US$5.8 billion) of Taiwanese stocks (CEIC, 1999). This was the largest amount on record for a half year period, although still only 1.3 per cent of total turnover (CEIC, 1999).

However, compared to Thailand and Korea, significant restrictions on foreign participation remain. Most notably, qualified foreign institutional investors still face quotas on their individual investments of NT$600 million per year. Furthermore, they must invest within six months of gaining approval even if market conditions are inappropriate (*Asiamoney* Supplement, July/August 1999, p.12).

Money Market

Taiwan's money market only started to grow in the 1990s, driven by interest rate liberalisation in the late 1980s and increasingly active bill finance companies (Emery, 1991).[26] Commercial paper and negotiable certificates of deposit dominate

---

[26] Bill finance companies are intermediaries in Taiwanese money markets, buying and selling on their own account and on behalf of clients. They also act as underwriters of commercial paper.

the market, which is mainly a secondary financing source for larger private sector firms (Figure 10.8).[27] In the 1990s, the commercial paper and equity markets' rapid growth increased pressure on Taiwan's banks to retain their larger corporate customers. This pressure is likely to increase in future.

Figure 10.8

Commercial Paper Market Growing Rapidly
Taiwanese Money Market Instruments

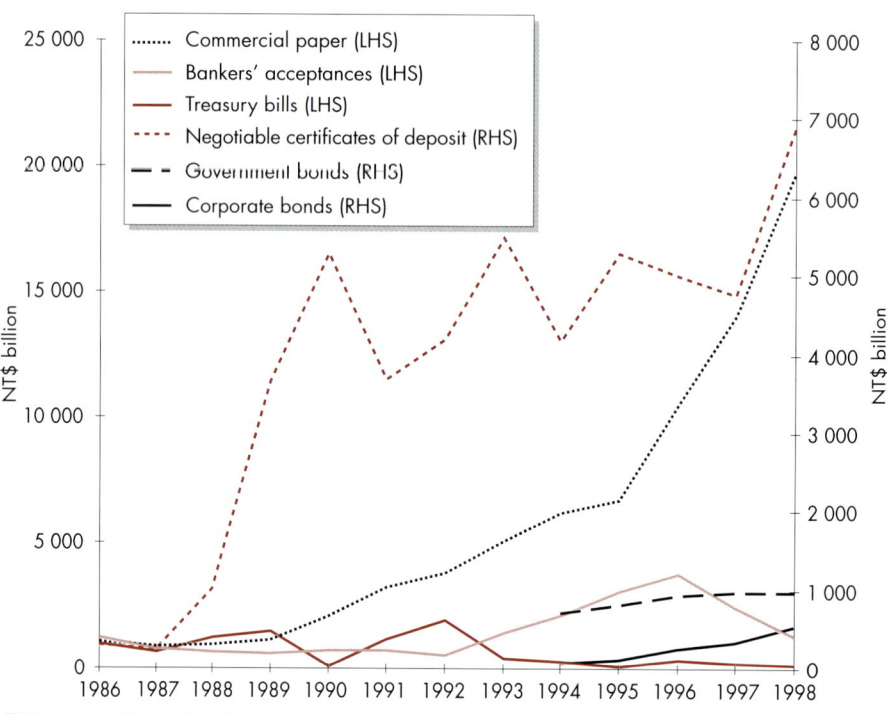

Note: Corporate bonds are long term, fixed-obligation debt securities a company issues. Commercial paper is short term, unsecured debt securities issued at a discount. Treasury bills are short term, discounted government debt securities issued for 90 or 180 days. Bankers' acceptances allow banks to advance credit to customers without necessarily advancing funds. The instrument is a bill of exchange drawn by a customer and 'accepted' by a bank, in effect guaranteeing to honour payment of the bill at a future date. Negotiable certificates of deposits are negotiable time deposits with banks, acknowledged by the issue of a certificate that can be negotiated in the money market. Typically, banks issue them either directly to customers or through bill finance companies.

Source: CEIC, 1999.

---

[27] Because of their longer term to maturity, government and corporate bonds typically are not considered money market instruments. They are included in Figure 10.8 for convenience and to indicate the scale of bond markets.

Bond Market

government infrastructure financing raised outstanding government bonds from NT$710 billion in 1994 to NT$969 billion in 1998 (US$22 billion to US$30 billion) (Figure 10.8). Expanding secondary market trading of government bonds and spreading government bond issues to better cover each maturity level would boost the corporate bond market. Introducing hedging facilities such as interest rate futures, also would help develop the bond market (*Asiamoney*, April 1999, p. 28).

Taiwan's corporate bond market is relatively small but has grown extremely rapidly, with outstanding bonds up from NT$70 billion in 1994, to NT$324 billion in 1997 and NT$532 billion in 1998 (US$17 billion) (Figure 10.8). In 1998, the surge in outstanding corporate bonds reflected the increased currency risk in raising foreign denominated funds and the weaker share market. A decline in local long term interest rates and a requirement for enterprises issuing unsecured corporate bonds to provide credit ratings from 1999 also stimulated growth (Central Bank of China, 1999b).

Banks and insurance companies are the main bond holders. Corporate bond holdings remain small compared to commercial paper holdings which have a shorter maturity. This bias reflects market concerns about long term financial market stability and corporate reluctance to disclose financial data. Secondary market trading of corporate bonds remains minimal because of tax barriers. (See Chapter 5 - *Capital Markets*.)

Supranational bond issues also have grown rapidly, with issues up from NT$2.6 billion in 1995 to NT$63 billion in 1998. Institutions such as the Asian Development Bank and the European Bank for Reconstruction and Development drove this market's growth by floating supranational issues to tap the liquid and relatively low cost local market.[28] The government strongly encourages supranational issues, providing domestic and foreign investors with tax incentives.[29]

The Futures Exchange

The futures exchange, the Taiwan International Mercantile Exchange, TAIMEX, is another significant development providing Taiwanese corporates with a potentially valuable risk hedging institution. Officially launched in April 1998, by late 1999 its only product was a stock index.[30] Because the Singapore Stock Exchange and Chicago Mercantile Exchange launched rival Taiwanese stock index futures in 1998, TAIMEX needs to build up domestic and international investor participation to compete with them. To provide a comprehensive risk hedging service, it also will ultimately need to offer interest rate and currency derivatives. Its ability to offer liquid interest rate derivatives is enhanced by the growing pool of government bonds on issue.

---

[28] Issuers typically float bonds in NT dollars and swap the proceeds into US dollars.
[29] For example, it waives the 0.1 per cent transaction tax for supranational issue investors.
[30] This product is the Taiwan Stock Exchange Capitalisation Weighted Stock Index Future.

> **TAIWAN'S ASIA PACIFIC REGIONAL OPERATIONS CENTRE PLAN**
>
> The Asia Pacific Regional Operations Centre plan approved in 1995, was designed to transform Taiwan into a regional centre for multinational manufacturing, telecommunications, air and sea transport, financial services and media companies. Promotion of this centre helped to drive deregulation, including in the financial sector. However, since mid 1997, the government has scaled down the plan as it relates to multinational financial institutions and focused on developing Taiwan's attractiveness as a manufacturing centre and telecommunications hub.
>
> Source: Smith, 1999.

Opportunities for Foreign Participation in Capital Markets

Two emerging areas of opportunity for international financial institutions are Taiwanese equity and derivative markets. Further growth in equity markets is likely now Taiwan has liberalised substantially its rules governing foreign participation. Investment banking services, particularly the initial public offer market, also provide considerable potential. While the number of listed firms has grown rapidly over recent years, many more firms could list as the corporate and financial sectors become more modern and transparent.

Taiwan's fledgling derivatives market also provides opportunities for foreign financial institutions, which often have longer experience in this market than local players. The launch of the futures exchange is likely to considerably expand derivative use, as stock index volumes grow and the exchange launches new products. With ongoing financial market liberalisation, growth opportunities also exist in insurance and banking.

FUTURE CHALLENGES

While Taiwan's basically sound macroeconomic and financial sector policies insulated it from the Asian crisis, to maintain its position Taiwan must address many pressing policy challenges, including:

- fully privatising state owned banks
- reducing the influence of large conglomerates on Taiwan's banks
- ensuring privatised banks are independent of government influence
- significantly restructuring, and possibly privatising, the postal savings system
- lifting financial reporting and accounting standards to international levels
- continuing to open the financial sector to foreign competition
- continuing to liberalise restrictions on capital controls, most notably requirements to approve of inward and outward direct investments and remaining restrictions on share ownership.

Maintaining the momentum of financial sector reform will be an important challenge. Improving regional economic prospects may weaken the resolve to press ahead with this reform; the ruling party also may be reluctant to cede further control of the financial system to the private sector until after the March 2000 presidential election. However, the government is fully aware of the importance of continuing reform to insulate Taiwan from future financial instability.

CONCLUSIONS

Taiwan's banking system has come through the Asian financial crisis relatively well and its equity, commercial paper and corporate bond markets are developing rapidly. It still has many important reform challenges: improving prudential enforcement and transparency; privatising its government-owned banking and postal savings systems; and further liberalising and opening financial markets to international competition. However, ongoing reforms in banking, insurance and capital markets provide significant opportunities for local and foreign financial institutions.

REFERENCES

American Chamber of Commerce and the European Council for Commerce and Trade, 1999, 'Taiwan Financial System: Challenges and Opportunities, Market Structure, Risk Management and Profitability', Joint paper by the Banking Committees of the American Chamber of Commerce and the European Council for Commerce and Trade, Taipei, March.

ANZ Bank, 1999, Information supplied to the East Asia Analytical Unit, August.

Asian Development Bank, 1999, Economic and Financial Statistics, Taipei, www.internotes.asiandevbank.org/notes/tap/TAPNACT.htm, accessed on 10 August.

Bank for International Settlements, 1999, 'Joint BIS-IMF-OECD-World Bank Statistics on External Debt', www.bis.org/publ/index.htm, accessed on 10 August.

Barclays Economics Department, 1998, *Country Report: Taiwan*, London, November.

Bureau of Monetary Affairs, 1999, Unpublished Statistics on 'Assets of Taiwanese Banks', Bureau of Monetary Affairs, Ministry of Finance, Taiwan.

CEIC, 1999, CEIC Database, Hong Kong, supplied by EconData Canberra.

Central Bank of China, 1999a, 'The Quarterly Publication on Taiwan's Banking Sector Performance' (in Chinese), Bank Examination Division, Taipei.

___ 1999b, *The Central Bank of China: Annual Report 1998*, Taipei.

___ 1999c, 'Financial Statistics Taiwan District', gopher://cbisco.cbc.gov.tw:70/00/eng/ecod/fs/s199809, accessed on 10 September.

Central Deposit Insurance Corporation, 1999, 'Statistics', www.cdic.gov.tw/e876.html, accessed on 10 August.

Council for Economic Planning and Development, 1998, 'Essential Economic Indicators', cepd.spring.org.tw/English/Statistic/, accessed on 10 September.

Cutler, P., 1999a, East Asia Analytical Unit personal communication with Director, Fitch IBCA, 28 May.

___ 1999b, East Asia Analytical Unit personal communication with Director, Fitch IBCA, 20 October.

East Asia Analytical Unit, 1999, *Korea Rebuilds: from Crisis to Opportunity*, Department of Foreign Affairs and Trade, Canberra.

East Asian Executive Reports, 1997, 'Taiwan Long Term Funding System', Washington DC, 15 April.

Emery, R., 1991, *The Money Markets of Deepening Asia*, Praeger, New York.

Fitch IBCA, 1999a, 'Taiwan's Banks: in for a Bumpy Ride', June.

___ 1999b, 'Taiwan's Banks: Battening Down', February.

___ 1998, 'Taiwan's Banks: in the Eye of the Storm', July.

Goldstein, M., 1998, *The Asian Financial Crisis: Causes, Cures and Systemic Implications*, Institute for International Economics, Washington DC.

IBCA, 1997, 'Taiwan Banking System', Brisbane, May.

International Finance Corporation, 1999, *Emerging Stock Markets Factbook 1988*, IFC, Washington DC.

International Monetary Fund, 1999, *International Financial Statistics*, IMF, Washington DC.

JP Morgan, 1999, 'Currency Indices', www.jpmorgan.com/market/dataind/forex/currindex.html, accessed on 10 August.

Kuo, Shirley W.Y. and Liu, Christina Y., 1998, 'Taiwan', in McLeod, R. and Garnaut, R. (eds), *East Asia in Crisis: from Being a Miracle to Needing One*, Routledge, London.

Kuei, Hsien-Nung., 1999, East Asia Analytical Unit interview with Secretary General, Bureau of Monetary Affairs, Ministry of Finance, Taipei.

Naughton, T., 1999, 'The Role of Stock Markets in the Asian Pacific Emerging Economies', *Asian-Pacific Economic Literature*, vol. 13, no. 1, May, pp. 22-35.

Shea, Jia-Dong, 1995, 'Financial Development and Policies in Taipei, China', in Zahid, S.N. (ed.), *Financial Sector Development in Asia: Country Studies*, Asian Development Bank, Manila.

Smith, H., 1999, 'The State, Banking and Corporate Relationships: Korea and Taiwan', Paper presented to international conference on Reform and Recovery in East Asia: The Role of the State and Economic Enterprise, Australian National University, 21-22 September, Canberra.

Taiwan Economic Data Centre, www.edu.tw/moecc/rs/pkg/tedc.htm, accessed on 10 August.

Taiwan Stock Exchange Corporation, 1998a, *Taiwan Stock Exchange Statistical Data 1997*, TSEC, Taipei.

___ 1998b, *1998 Stock Exchange Factbook*, TSEC, Taipei.

Tradeport, 1998, 'Taiwan Economic Trends and Outlook', www.tradeport.org/ts/countries/taiwan/trends.shtml, accessed on 12 December.

Yen, T.T., 1998, 'The Impact of the Asian Financial Crisis on the Taiwan Economy,' Paper presented at SEACEN Seminar on Financial Crisis in the Asian Region, Kuala Lumpur, June.

Taiwan

Chapter 11

JAPAN

Japan is the world's second largest economy, its largest exporter of capital and Asia's largest financial market. The health of the Japanese economy is very important to Asia, and as Australia's largest trading partner, highly significant to Australia.

Throughout the 1990s, serious problems have burdened Japan's financial sector, compounding concerns over the economy's long term growth potential. However, a major financial sector transformation now is underway; poor profitability and serious efforts to undertake reforms and resolve non-performing loan, NPL, problems drive it. Key influences include significant corporate restructuring, growing pressures on the main bank system, greater disparities between strong and weak financial institutions, and increasing involvement of foreign financial institutions in the Japanese market. However, serious challenges remain, including needing to continue to resolve NPL problems in weaker banks and insurance companies, locking in the credibility of Japan's new supervisory arrangements and reforming the postal savings system, which absorbs about 20 per cent of Japanese household savings.

This chapter analyses recent key financial sector reforms, the scale of NPL problems and progress in resolving them. It also assesses pressures on the banking and life insurance sectors, and restructuring that is underway. Finally, it examines foreign financial institutions' prospects, and major future trends and challenges.

FINANCIAL SECTOR DEVELOPMENTS

Since the mid 1990s, the regulatory structure of Japan's financial sector has changed substantially. Patterns of savings and financing also continue to change gradually.

Regulatory Changes

Major financial sector supervisory reforms include establishing the Financial Reconstruction Commission and the Financial Supervisory Agency, focusing the Bank of Japan on implementing monetary policy and supervising the payments system, and substantially reducing the Ministry of Finance's power in financial sector supervision.[1] Since it was established in December 1998, a cabinet minister has chaired the Financial Reconstruction Commission, which now heads Japan's regulatory structure. A commission secretariat oversees public capital injections into banks and, in conjunction with the Deposit Insurance Corporation, disposes of failed institutions. The Financial Supervisory Agency, established in mid 1998, supervises banks and other financial institutions. The Ministry of Finance's Financial System

---

[1] The Bank of Japan law, effective since April 1998, contains a range of measures to enhance the bank's independence and transparency in running monetary policy. For example, minutes of monetary policy meetings now are published promptly. The Bank of Japan retains an ongoing responsibility for maintaining financial system order and, as such, retains the right to examine banks.

Planning Bureau retains broad policy responsibility for financial system stability. However, from 2000, the Financial Supervisory Agency will assume this responsibility also and be renamed the Financial Agency.[2]

Consolidating financial sector supervision in independent institutions separate from ministries of finance and central banks is in line with many developed economies' reforms. Separation helps overcome goal confusion and conflicts of interest, for example in implementing monetary policy, and consolidation enables more consistent supervision of universal financial institutions. (See Chapter 3 - *Prudential Reform*.)

Changing Savings and Financing Patterns

Banks remain the single most important savings vehicle for Japanese households (Figure 11.1). While life insurance's importance increased from 1989 to 1996, the sector's serious problems have caused a significant exodus of funds since then. Although the importance of shares waned as a savings vehicle due to the equity market's prolonged weakness, recent equity market strength could reverse this trend. Postal savings continue to be very important; their savings' share grew in the mid 1990s due to problems in the private banking system.

Figure 11.1

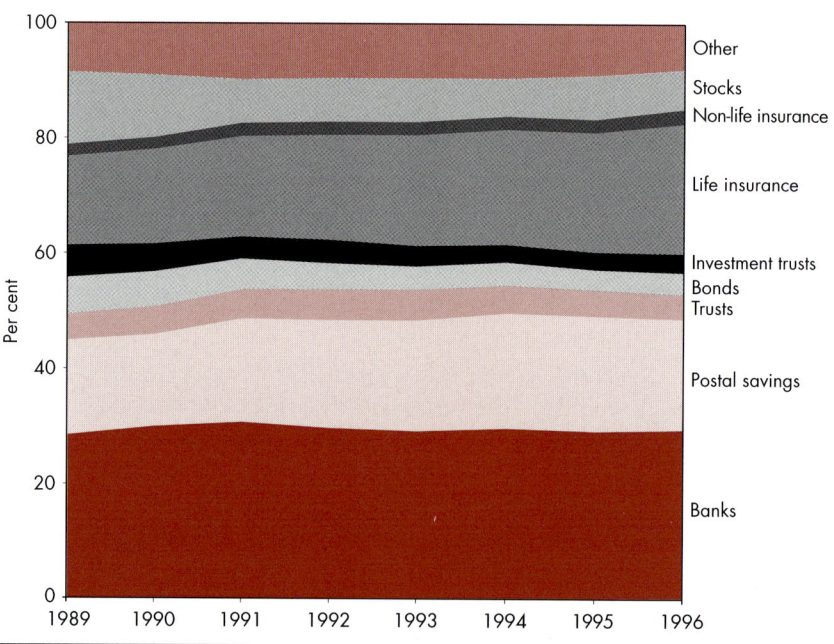

Banks and Life Insurance the Major Savings Vehicles
Major Personal Savings Vehicles, Per cent

Note: Other includes deposits with credit associations and cooperatives, agricultural and fishery cooperatives, labour credit associations and personal subscriptions to local government bonds.
Source: Bank of Japan, 1996.

---

[2] The long term regulatory structure is not entirely clear as the Financial Reconstruction Commission will be wound up at the end of March 2001, or thereabouts.

Patterns of corporate financing also are changing. In the second half of the 1980s, eligibility requirements for bond and stock issues were relaxed, significantly increasing their importance in corporate funding. In the 1990s, equity market weakness reduced the corporate financing role of shares, with bond issues also growing more slowly (Figure 11.2). The importance of private banks was not eroded. However, in the new regulatory environment, banks will face more competition from other financial institutions; sustained equity market recovery will increase this pressure.

MAJOR FINANCIAL SECTOR REFORMS

Japan has been liberalising its financial sector since the early 1980s. It:

- started to liberalise interest rates in 1985 and all rates were liberalised by 1994

- relaxed eligibility requirements for firms wishing to issue bonds and stocks during the 1980s and early 1990s

- relaxed regulations preventing banks and securities companies from entering each other's lines of business from 1992 (East Asia Analytical Unit, 1997).

Figure 11.2

Securities Market Financing Peaked in 1995
Corporate Financing Shares, Per cent, 1980-96

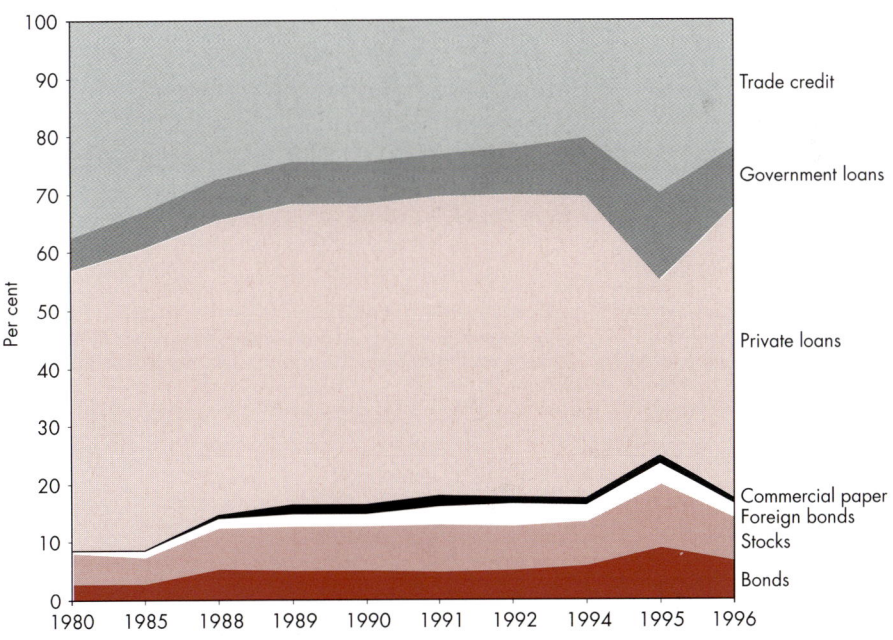

Note: Private loans are loans from private financial institutions while government loans are loans from government financial institutions.

Source: Data for 1981-84 and 1986-87 are not available. Yoshino, 1995, updated by East Asia Analytical Unit.

In November 1996, then Prime Minister Hashimoto accelerated this reform agenda by announcing the 'big bang' financial sector reforms; these were designed to make Japanese financial markets internationally competitive and promote Tokyo as a world financial centre. A key element of these reforms is progressively to remove barriers between different types of financial institutions. By 2001, banks, insurance companies and securities firms all will be allowed to operate in each other's areas of business.

MAJOR BIG BANG INITIATIVES AND TIMETABLE

Fiscal year[3] 1997
- Securities houses can establish bank-type accounts for customers and handle unlisted stocks

Fiscal year 1998
- Companies and individuals can undertake foreign exchange transactions without government authorisation
- Banks can sell their own investment trust products over the counter
- Ban on financial holding companies lifted
- Firms can enter securities broking without government licences
- Securities houses can expand their asset management services
- Loans can be transformed into asset-backed securities

Fiscal year 1999
- Securities houses can set their own commissions on securities trading
- Financial assets are assessed at market rather than book value, and accounting practices are brought to international standards
- Controls on banks' securities subsidiaries are removed
- Banks can issue straight bonds[4]
- Insurance firms can establish banking and securities subsidiaries

By fiscal year 2001
- Banks and securities houses will be allowed to enter the insurance sector
- Remaining restrictions on pension fund allocation will be removed

Source: OECD, 1997.

---

[3] The Japanese fiscal year runs from 1 April to 31 March.
[4] A straight bond is a simple debt contract between an investor and a firm.

The big bang package is being implemented on schedule. For example, in December 1997, authorities scrapped the ban on financial holding companies and liberalised foreign exchange controls.[5] From June 1998, banks could sell investment trusts over the counter and freely enter the securities business. These far-reaching reforms and Japan's bad loan problems together are stimulating a major restructuring of Japan's financial sector.

In July 1997, in addition to the big bang reforms the Ministry of Finance revoked restrictions on new bank branch numbers and locations, and bank and ATM operating hours. In June 1998, it increased insider trading penalties, permitted off-exchange equities trading and consolidated the ordinances interpreting financial laws and providing administrative guidance (OECD, 1998). From December 1998, the brokerage and insurance sectors created investor and policy holder protection funds.

NON-PERFORMING LOANS

Japan's NPL problem developed well before the Asian financial crisis, originating in the 'bubble economy' period of the late 1980s and early 1990s. At that time, lending to real estate companies and small businesses increased rapidly, inflating asset prices (East Asia Analytical Unit, 1997). When the asset price bubble burst, the NPLs of banks, non-bank financial institutions and life insurance companies all increased significantly, but rather than writing off NPLs and attempting to collect collateral, many financial institutions rolled over loans and under-reported NPLs to shield the true extent of their problems.

Government NPL and Bank Restructuring Policies

Until the late 1990s, the Government believed the banks could grow out of their problems, so it focused on resolving the problems of politically sensitive non-bank financial institutions, like the *jusen* (mortgage companies) and agricultural cooperatives.[6] After the Government suffered a political backlash for committing public funds to the *jusen, it* remained reluctant to intervene in resolving the banks' problems or injecting public funds. However, in late 1997, as major financial institutions, such as Hokkaido Takushoku Bank and Yamaichi Securities collapsed, the Government increasingly promoted bank NPL workouts. By October 1998, it had allocated ¥60 trillion in public funds to restructure the financial sector including:

- ¥17 trillion to nationalise failed banks and protect their depositors

- ¥18 trillion to purchase preferred and ordinary shares to recapitalise undercapitalised banks[7]

---

[5] Liberalising foreign exchange controls saved traders an estimated ¥175 billion per year in commission fees by allowing them to net their foreign exchange transactions and put them through a wider range of institutions (OECD, 1998). This reform also allowed residents to hold foreign currency accounts abroad.

[6] For example, in 1996, the Government brokered a complex deal involving significant public funds to liquidate the *jusen* and bail out agricultural cooperatives.

[7] Preferred shares have preference over common stock in paying dividends and liquidating assets but do not carry voting rights.

- ¥25 trillion to purchase preferred shares in 'healthy' banks, with capital adequacy ratios over 8 per cent, thereby increasing their liquidity and willingness to lend.

In December 1998 and January 1999, authorities imposed conditions on major banks' access to capital injections (Financial Reconstruction Commission, 1999a). Participating banks had to reduce staff and non-staff expenses, and increase their provisioning.[8] Moreover, the Government required weaker banks to offer higher dividends on their preferred bank shares and demonstrate stronger restructuring initiatives. All but three of the 17 major banks applied for public funds and received ¥7.5 trillion.[9] In fiscal year 1999, the banks also attempted to raise about ¥2 trillion by new equity and bond issues; Bank of Tokyo-Mitsubishi is the most successful fundraiser in Japan and abroad.

The authorities also have improved significantly arrangements for purchasing NPLs. In April 1999, the Resolution and Collection Organisation took responsibility for NPL purchase and disposal from the Housing Loan Administration Corporation, established to take over the seven failed *jusen's* business, and the Resolution and Collection Bank, which managed failed bank and credit cooperative NPLs.[10] Unlike its predecessors, the Resolution and Collection Organisation purchases NPLs from both healthy and distressed institutions. This enables solvent banks to move debt off their balance sheets and recommence normal lending activities.

The predecessors of the Resolution and Collection Organisation did not perform well. From its inception in 1996 to September 1998, the Housing Loan Administration Corporation liquidated only about 20 per cent of its NPL portfolio. Similarly, despite buying its NPLs at only 20 to 30 per cent of their face value, the Resolution and Collection Organisation had sold only 19 per cent of its inventory by April 1998 (International Monetary Fund, 1998). A more transparent pricing formula based on expected future cash flows was needed to improve asset sales, increase market confidence and reduce political interference (International Monetary Fund, 1998).

SCALE OF NPLS

While still subject to some risks, major banks' NPLs now are well on the way to resolution.[11] However, smaller regional banks and life insurance companies still have major problems; the Government recognises it must resolve these to restore confidence in the financial sector.

---

[8] Banks must provision 100 per cent of the unsecured portion of loans to bankrupt borrowers, 70 per cent of the unsecured portion of high risk loans and 15 per cent of loans deemed potentially at risk. This is double or triple previous provisioning.

[9] Bank of Tokyo-Mitsubishi and Nippon Trust and Banking did not apply for funds, while Yasuda Trust and Banking will receive funds through Fuji Bank.

[10] Originally the Resolution Collection Bank and its predecessor, the Tokyo Kyodo Bank, were established to manage the assets of failed credit cooperatives such as Cosmo and Kizu.

[11] Japan has 17 major banks. One is a long term credit bank; the rest are either trust or city banks.

Major Banks

As at 31 March 1999, according to official figures, the 17 largest city and trust banks still had ¥21.4 trillion (US$194 billion) in NPLs, almost 7 per cent of outstanding loans (Figure 11.3). Against these NPLs, the banks hold ¥7.5 trillion in public capital, ¥10.4 trillion in loan loss reserves and a substantial level of realisable collateral. Consequently, the Minister for Financial Reconstruction considers the current stock of NPLs resolved, and many analysts broadly agree with this assessment.

However, concerns remain about whether banks have fully disclosed their NPLs. For example, in March 1999, major banks applying for public funds from the Financial Reconstruction Commission revealed they rated as 'normal' around 40 per cent of their loans to bankrupt companies (HSBC Securities, 1999).[12] Moreover, NPL problems could increase further if share and real estate prices fall, economic activity

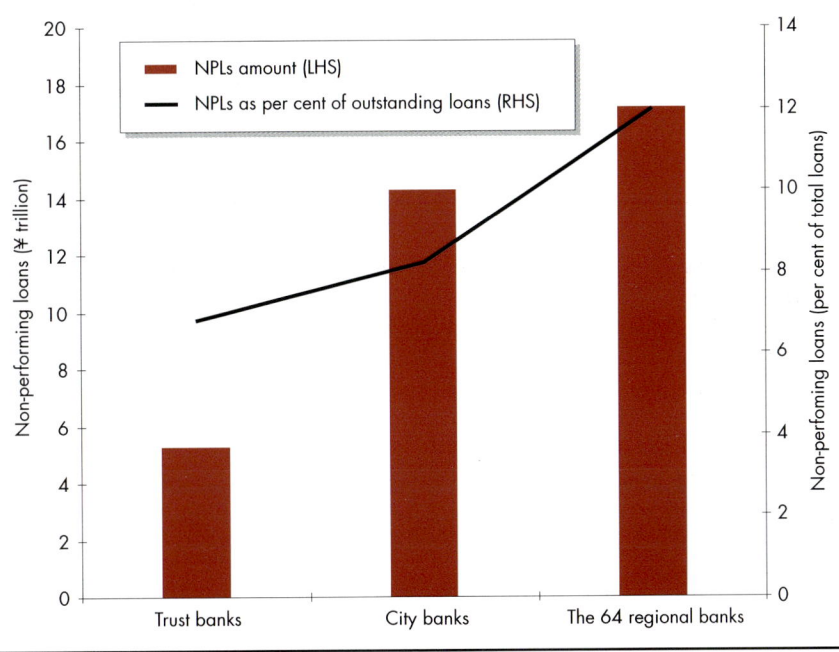

Figure 11.3

Regional Bank NPLs Are Highest
Banks' Non-performing Loans, March 1999

Source: HSBC Securities, 1999; and Financial Supervisory Agency, 1999a.

---

[12] Another concern with the NPL figures is that of the ¥21.4 trillion, the amount of loans classified as 'at risk' (3.9 per cent) is greater than the amount classified as 'requiring special attention' (1.4 per cent), a lower risk category. This is most unusual; the value of loans 'requiring special attention' should be greater than the value of loans 'at risk' (HSBC Securities, 1999, p. 16).

remains weak or Japanese banks incur more losses in Asia.[13] To date, most banks have provisioned against expected losses from NPLs rather than liquidating them and removing them from their balance sheets; this practice exacerbates the risk of future NPL problems. However, enabling the Resolution and Collection Organisation to purchase NPLs from both healthy and failed institutions should encourage NPL liquidation. Tax incentives to write off loans, and since 1998, the capacity to move loans off balance sheets via securitisation also should speed this process.[14] (See Chapter 4 - Banking.)

Regional Banks

In December 1998, after auditing Japan's major city banks, the Financial Supervisory Agency focused its attention on Japan's 64 regional banks and 60 secondary regional banks. In the three months to June 1999, the Financial Supervisory Agency declared three secondary regional banks insolvent. In March 1999, a self assessment by the 64 regional banks put NPLs at ¥22.7 trillion, 11.8 per cent of total credits (Figure 11.3). While these figures surpass major banks' NPLs, they still may be an underestimate; June 1999 audits for fiscal year 1997 of the 64 regional banks showed NPLs were ¥2 trillion higher than these banks declared in March 1998 (Financial Supervisory Agency, 1999b).[15] Furthermore, the regional banks are less well provisioned to write off these NPLs; their 1997 bad debt reserve ratio averaged only 40 per cent, compared to 52 per cent for the major city banks (*Nikkei Weekly*, 28 June 1998, p. 12).

Government policies on bank recapitalisation of regional banks are broadly similar to those applied to the 15 major banks (Financial Reconstruction Commission, 1999b). The ratings agency, Moody's, believes many small, severely undercapitalised regional banks ultimately risk liquidation; larger regional banks are likely to receive government support because of their perceived importance to local economies (*Australian*, 27 August 1999, p. 23).

Life Insurance

After bank deposits, life insurance is Japan's second most important savings vehicle (Figure 11.1). The life insurance sector also has extensive NPL problems but in late 1999, their true size was unknown. Official data on the state of insurers is scarce but in May 1999, the Financial Supervisory Agency began the first stage of a comprehensive audit of the sector, starting with the five largest life insurers.

---

[13] As at the end of June 1998, Japanese banks had ¥27 trillion in outstanding loans to Asia, representing around 7.5 per cent of major banks' total loans. A significant proportion were experiencing difficulties, particularly those which lent to Indonesia and Thailand.

[14] In 1998, taxes were adjusted to permit deductions for losses incurred from debt write-off arrangements and legislation passed to encourage securitisation of assets, including bad loans (International Monetary Fund, 1998).

[15] According to the banks, NPLs were ¥15.2 trillion, compared to the Financial Supervisory Agency's figure of ¥17.2 trillion (Financial Supervisory Agency, 1999b). Similarly, secondary regional banks self assessed NPLs as of September 1998 were ¥5.4 trillion, compared to the Financial Supervisory Agency's figure of ¥6.6 trillion (Financial Supervisory Agency, 1999c).

For fiscal year 1998, the seven main life insurance companies officially admitted to NPLs of ¥978 billion (US$10 billion) (*Nikkei Weekly*, 14 June 1999, p. 8). However, one analysis estimates life insurers' investment losses are as high as 10 to 18 per cent of assets, or ¥19 trillion to ¥34 trillion (US$172 billion to US$309 billion), up to 50 per cent more than the banks (*Economist*, 19 April 1999, p. 88). Low asset quality compounds problems caused by the gap between guaranteed returns and actual yields; low equity prices and interest rates often reduce yields on market instruments to levels below minimum yields guaranteed to policy holders.[16] In fiscal year 1998, for the seven major life insurers this negative yield gap reached ¥1.3 trillion (*Nikkei Weekly*, 14 June 1999, p. 8). In the two years to December 1998, low returns and increased risk perceptions caused life insurance policy holders to cash in 11 per cent of contracts by value (Figure 11.4).

Figure 11.4

Life Insurance Contracts Drop Dramatically
Outstanding Japanese Life Insurance Contracts, 1992-98

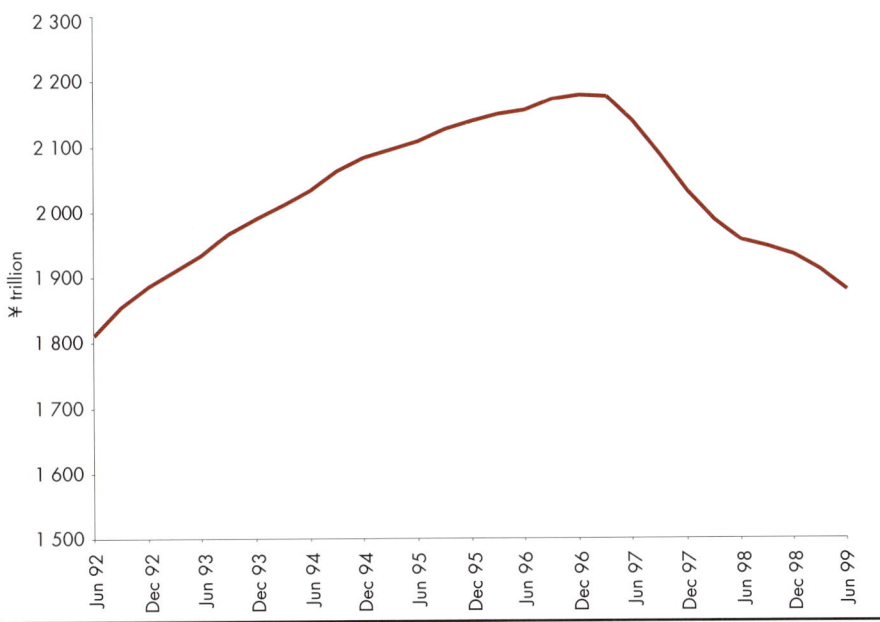

Source: CEIC, 1999.

[16] For example, in fiscal year 1998, the yield on Nippon Life's investments was 1.6 per cent while its average guaranteed payout was 4.1 per cent. In April 1996, the requirement that life insurers guarantee a minimum return of 4.5 per cent per year was lowered to 2.5 per cent per year (East Asia Analytical Unit, 1997). However, a large proportion of insurance policies still carry guaranteed returns of around 5 per cent (International Monetary Fund, 1998).

Since 1997, two life insurance companies, Nissan Mutual Life and Toho Mutual Life have collapsed. Many commentators believe more failures are likely as the Financial Supervisory Agency proceeds to audit and act against companies found to be below the statutory minimum 200 per cent solvency margin.[17] These failures could exhaust the industry's safety net, and some combination of public funds and reductions in guaranteed yields will be needed to rescue the industry (*Nikkei Weekly*, 7 June 1999, p. 12).[18]

STRUCTURAL CHANGE IN BANKING AND INSURANCE

Continued poor profitability, NPL problems and financial market desegmentation combine to drive far reaching structural change in Japan's banking and insurance industries. Consequently, downsizing, mergers, alliances and a growing role for foreign financial institutions are occurring and more can be expected.

Banking

Staff downsizing has been underway for several years. However, previously staff often were merely transferred to subsidiaries. Since 1998, the conditionality attached to public fund injections has boosted downsizing. Major banks receiving public funds agreed to reduce staff by 122 800 (13.9 per cent) between March 1999 and March 2003 (Financial Supervisory Agency, 1999d). Branch network rationalisation also is ongoing, with examples including Fuji, Sumitomo and Sakura Bank announcements in late 1998 (*Daily Yomiuri*, 30 October and 4 November 1998).

Banks also are consolidating their operations by withdrawing from international business. Weaker banks like Mitsui Trust and Banking and Daiwa Bank have abandoned their international operations altogether to avoid the higher required capital adequacy standards and to focus on domestic activities (*Nikkei Weekly*, 2 November 1998, p. 12).[19] However, Bank of Tokyo-Mitsubishi is maintaining all its overseas branches while Fuji, Sanwa and Sakura Banks have substantially reduced overseas operations but are still maintaining a global presence (*Nikkei Weekly*, 14 December 1998, p. 13).

Mergers and alliances also can enhance efficiency. The 1996 merger of Bank of Tokyo and Mitsubishi Bank was the first major merger.[20] The resulting Tokyo-Mitsubishi Bank now is one of Japan's strongest banks; it was one of only two banks which did not seek public capital injections in 1999. The conditionality attached to banks accessing public funds gave further impetus to mergers. After a series of relatively small scale alliances, such as that between Toyo Trust and Sanwa

---

[17] The solvency margin is the ratio of capital and unrealised profit to a weighted measure of risky assets. Since April 1999, life insurers have had to disclose this ratio, and if it falls below 200 per cent, the Financial Supervisory Agency may order them to close.

[18] An industry funded safety net was set up in December 1998 and has ¥400 billion in assets. However, Toho's liabilities alone exceeded its assets by ¥200 billion (*Nikkei Weekly*, 7 June 1999, p. 12).

[19] Purely domestic banks require capital adequacy ratios of only 4 per cent: those with international networks require 8 per cent capital adequacy ratios.

[20] The merged bank capitalised on the two institutions' complementary expertise. Before the merger, the Bank of Tokyo had a good reputation in international financial transactions, while Mitsubishi Bank was strong in domestic lending (East Asia Analytical Unit, 1997).

Bank in early 1999, Japan's next major merger, of Dai-Ichi Kangyo Bank, Fuji Bank and Industrial Bank of Japan, was announced in August 1999.[21] The proposed merger, to be completed by 2002, would create the world's largest financial institution. More importantly, it targets major cost areas. For example, within five years the merger will reduce joint domestic branch numbers by around 150 and the joint workforce by 6 000 people.[22] The merger also will enable the new bank to make major new information technology investments (Fuji Bank, 1999). In October 1999, a further large merger was announced between Sumitomo and Sakura Banks, to be completed by April 2002.

However, public funds could be wasted if mergers lack a sound commercial rationale. For example, some analysts question the commercial rationale of merging two weak trust banks, Mitsui Trust and Banking and Chuo Trust and Banking, believing trust banks and commercial banks have more synergies (*Nikkei Weekly*, 25 January 1999, p. 1).

Life Insurance

The same factors, NPL problems, poor profitability and removal of barriers between financial sectors also are driving structural change in the life insurance industry. From fiscal year 1999, insurers can enter the banking and securities sector; from 2001, banks and securities companies should be able to offer insurance products.[23]

These pressures are increasing alliances with foreign financial institutions and between Japanese insurers.[24] The most notable example of the latter is the comprehensive alliance between Taiyo Mutual Life Insurance and Daido Mutual Life Insurance, to enhance their life insurance business; many previous alliances targeted non-core businesses.[25]

The Government will submit a bill to permit demutualisation to the Diet in the first half of 2000. This reform should generate further structural change in life insurance, as companies switch from unlisted mutual organisations to listed companies which must supply information to shareholders. Listing also allows insurers to raise fresh equity capital and facilitates mergers.[26]

---

[21] The Toyo-Sanwa alliance, which includes the merger of Sanwa Trust and Banking, a wholly-owned subsidiary of Sanwa and Toyo, is seen as commercially astute, as major commercial banks like Sanwa have difficulty establishing trust banking subsidiaries because they lack experience in global portfolio management (*Nikkei Weekly*, 25 January 1999, p. 1)

[22] However most of these job cuts already had been pledged as part of the conditionality for public fund injections (*Far Eastern Economic Review*, 2 September 1999, p. 38).

[23] While it is part of the scheduled 'big bang' reforms, no final decision has been made on whether banks will be able to sell insurance products.

[24] These alliances are discussed later in the chapter.

[25] Life insurers typically team up with banks and other non-insurance financial institutions in pension and investment trusts (*Nikkei Weekly*, 25 January 1999, p. 3).

[26] As a result of their problems, life insurers also are becoming more active holders of corporate shares. Previously, they gave unconditional discretionary power to company chairmen of companies in which they held shares, but now Nippon Life, Dai-Ichi Mutual Life and Sumitomo Life have guidelines for exercising their voting rights at annual general meetings (*Nikkei Weekly*, 14 June 1999, p. 12). However, it remains to be seen how much actual practice will change.

Japan

Mergers and Alliances

Ongoing big bang reforms will maintain the pressure for mergers across the financial services industry. Progressive dismantling of financial sector barriers is producing a spate of mergers and alliances (Table 11.1). For example, declining distinctions between commercial and investment banking reduces the rationale for separate institutions in these business areas.[27] In August 1999, the Diet passed a bill permitting the exchange of shares between merging companies, further encouraging mergers.

Table 11.1
Alliances Gather Pace
Major Financial Institution Alliances and Mergers, 1998-99

	Participating firms	Joint activity
May 1998	Industrial Bank of Japan and Nomura Securities	Two joint ventures in derivatives and asset management
	Fuji Bank, Yasuda Trust and Banking, Yasuda Fire and Marine Insurance and Yasuda Mutual Life Insurance	Investment trust fund joint venture
June 1998	Nikko Securities Company and Travelers Group	Wholesale securities service joint venture
July 1998	Mitsui Trust and Banking and Prudential Insurance	Investment trust fund joint venture
	Sumitomo Bank and Daiwa Securities	Comprehensive alliance in wholesale securities, derivatives and asset management
September 1998	Bank of Tokyo-Mitsubishi, Mitsubishi Trust and Banking, Meiji Life Insurance and Tokio Marine and Fire Insurance	Comprehensive alliance in investment trusts, securities, insurance and pension fund management
	Tokai Bank and Asahi Bank	Comprehensive alliance to focus on domestic retail service
October 1998	Dai-Ichi Kangyo Bank and JP Morgan	Investment trust joint venture
	Sumitomo Trust, Sumitomo Bank and Daiwa Securities	Comprehensive alliances in wholesale capital markets
	Industrial Bank of Japan and Dai-ichi Mutual Life Insurance Company	Comprehensive alliance in all financial services
January 1999	Mitsui Trust and Banking and Chuo Trust and Banking	Merger of two trust banks
	Sanwa Bank and Toyo Trust and Banking	Strategic alliance including forming a fixed contribution pension fund
August 1999	Industrial Bank of Japan, Fuji Bank and Dai-Ichi Kangyo Bank	Full merger by mid 2002 via a holding company structure
	Sanwa Bank and Morgan Stanley Dean Witter	Comprehensive alliance for sale of investment trusts
October 1999	Sumitomo and Sakura Banks	Merger by April 2002

Source: *Nihon Keizai Shimbun,* 5 October 1998; *Nikkei Weekly,* 25 January 1999, p. 1; *Nikkei Weekly,* 6 September 1999, p. 1; and Fuji Bank, 1999.

---

[27] For example, from 1999, commercial banks can issue corporate debt more freely.

Japan

THE GROWING FOREIGN PRESENCE

Since 1994, approvals for foreign direct investment in Japan's banking and insurance industry have increased approximately five fold (Figure 11.5). Despite Japan's poor economic performance, approvals particularly surged in 1998 when they were worth more than in the six previous years combined. This surge reflected the weak yen, new opportunities emerging from big bang reforms and financial sector weakness. Approvals growth also reflects increasing government recognition of foreign financial institutions' valuable role in upgrading practices and products.

Many foreign and domestic institutions find alliances mutually beneficial. While Japanese firms have well established marketing networks and corporate clientele, they often lack product variety, state-of-the-art technology and risk management skills that major foreign players can provide. The unpopularity of full takeovers also may be due to concerns about undisclosed NPLs.

Figure 11.5

Foreign Investment in Banking and Insurance Surges
Foreign Direct Investment Approvals in Banking and Insurance (US$ million)

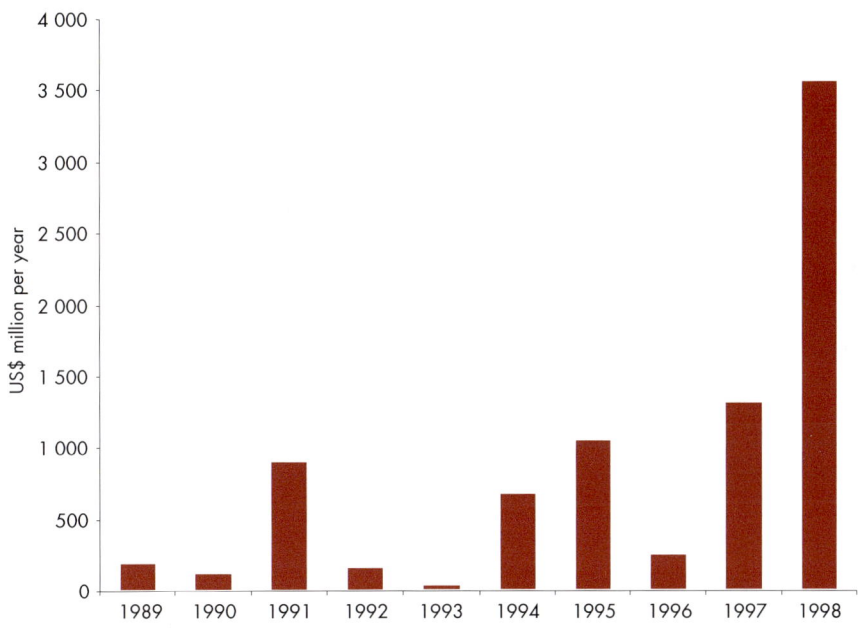

Source: Ministry of Finance, 1999.

INDUSTRY LEVEL FOREIGN PARTICIPATION TRENDS

Foreign financial institutions are increasingly prominent in the securities industry, pension funds management, life insurance and banking.

The Securities Industry

In August 1997, the 21 foreign securities firms on the Tokyo Stock Exchange together had a larger share of securities trade than Japan's four largest securities firms together (Suzuki, 1998). Japanese securities companies have been hit hard by deregulated brokerage commissions and banks' capacity to underwrite various bonds and sell mutual funds and increasingly accept foreign partners.[28] In July 1998, Merrill Lynch commenced retail business with 33 branches and 2 000 employees taken over from the defunct Yamaichi Securities. In June 1998, the Travelers Group effectively took over Nikko Securities' investment banking and international operations. Nikko's corporate business and research operations will become a joint venture with Salomon Smith Barney, a unit of Travelers.[29]

Pension Fund Management

Foreign firms also are increasingly active in pension fund management. To boost returns and asset security, pension funds are moving funds out of life insurance into investment adviser managed funds; many of these are foreign owned. Foreign firms offer superior risk management systems and a consequent ability to obtain greater returns. Foreign companies now manage around 8 per cent of Japanese pension fund assets (OECD, 1998). Future prospects for investment advisory companies are very strong; in April 1999, regulations restricting to 50 per cent the proportion of funds that could be placed with investment advisory firms were abolished. From 2001, pension funds will not need to invest 50 per cent of their funds in government bonds and other safe assets (OECD, 1998; and Takahara and Tanaka, 1996).

Foreign companies are even making inroads into managing public pension funds. For example, in fiscal year 1997, the Ministry of Health and Welfare's pension fund manager, one of the world's largest, Pension Service Public Welfare Corporation, increased funds under foreign management by about 6 per cent to ¥3.2 trillion (US$29 billion). This increase in foreign funds management represented around half of its new business that year.

---

[28] Like banks, securities firms also are reducing staff numbers and closing overseas branches. For example, in mid 1998, Nomura Securities announced a worldwide staff cut of between 1 000 and 2 000 people, and closure of 20 overseas offices. Nomura, Daiwa and Nikko Securities, the three biggest securities houses, also are shifting their business emphasis from commissions to asset accumulation (*Nikkei Weekly*, 25 January 1999, p. 16).

[29] While Nikko will hold 51 per cent of the venture, Salomon Smith Barney will run it. Travelers also will take over up to 25 per cent in Nikko. In October 1998, Travelers Group merged with Citicorp to form Citigroup, the world's largest financial group.

Life Insurance

In the life insurance sector, foreign companies also benefit from domestic insurers' profitability and NPL problems. In the year to September 1998, the value of outstanding policies at Japan's seven big life insurers fell 4 per cent to ¥1 149 trillion, while from a small base, the five biggest foreign insurers expanded contracts by 10 per cent (Figure 11.6).[30] Foreign life insurers are succeeding by:

- emphasising specialised niche products rather than generic products
- offering a consulting style approach with well trained sales people rather than untrained 'insurance ladies'
- marketing actively and directly (Austrade, 1999).[31]

Figure 11.6

Foreign Insurers' Business Growing
Major Foreign Life Insurers' Outstanding Contracts and Growth, Year to September 1998

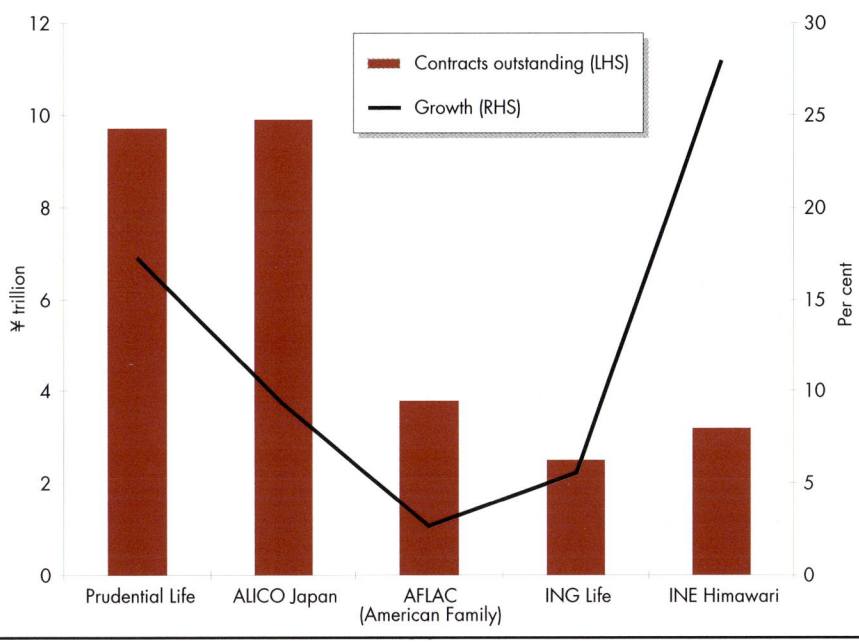

Note: INA Himawari is a foreign insurance company. (INA stands for Insurance Company of North America.)
Source: *Diamond Weekly*, 1999.

---

[30] The big seven Japanese insurance companies are Nippon Life, Dai-ichi Life, Sumitomo Life, Meiji Life, Asahi Life, Yasuda Life and Mitsui Life.

[31] Some newer Japanese life insurers, such as Sony Life Insurance, also use similar strategies to expand market share from low bases.

Japan

Several foreign financial institutions are taking over or forming alliances with Japan's troubled life insurers. Most notably, in early 1998, GE Capital bought Toho Mutual Life's offices, sales and marketing functions, giving GE access to Toho's customers and its workforce of 7 000 (*Far Eastern Economic Review*, 6 May 1999, p. 11).[32] Although Toho Life subsequently went bankrupt, GE Capital has not been adversely affected because it bought only selected parts of the company.[33]

Banking

While Japanese banks dominate retail and commercial banking, from a low base foreign banks gradually are increasing their presence. Over the two years to late 1998, domestic banking system problems raised foreign banks' deposit share to 2 per cent or almost ¥10 trillion (US$90 billion). However, by June 1999, increasing confidence in the solvency of major domestic banks caused foreign banks' deposit share to contract to 1.4 per cent (Figure 11.7). Since mid 1997, foreign banks' share of domestic lending has been more stable at around 2 per cent (Figure 11.7).

Figure 11.7

Growth in Foreign Banks' Deposit Share

Share of Foreign Banks in Domestic Lending and Deposits, 1985-98

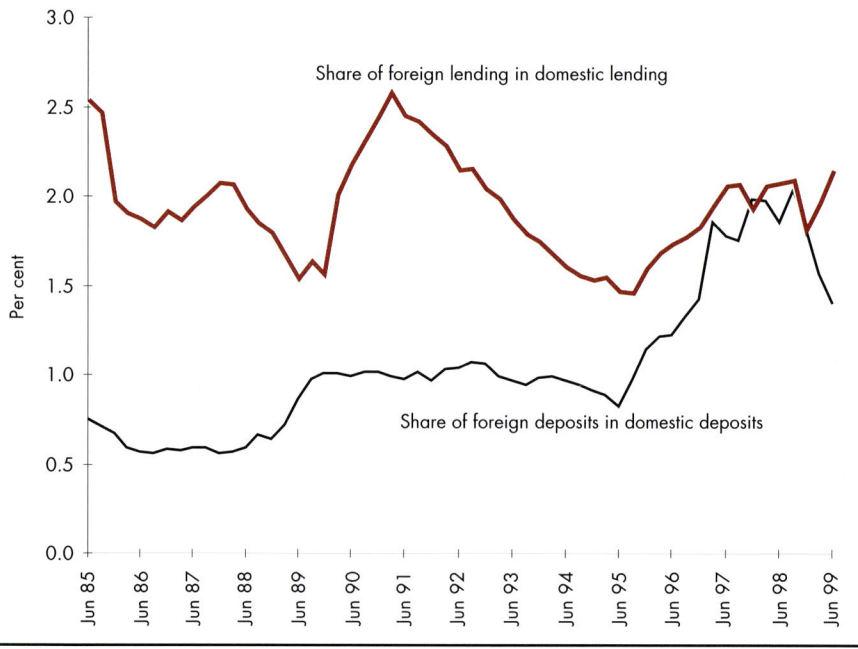

Source: CEIC, 1999.

---

[32] Toho kept its existing insurance policies and received cash and a 10 per cent stake in the new firm, GE Edison Life.

[33] In another deal, Meiji Life allied itself with Dresdner Bank (OECD, 1998).

Domestic and foreign banks are forming alliances too.[34] Although no formal foreign ownership restrictions exist, foreign banks are yet to acquire domestic banks partly due to concerns about possible undisclosed NPLs. However, in late 1999, a US investment company, Ripplewood Investment Holdings, obtained priority rights to negotiate with the Government to purchase the nationalised Long Term Credit Bank of Japan. If the purchase proceeds, several major foreign banks are expected to take a stake in Ripplewood's investment and cooperate with the Long Term Credit Bank to boost earnings (*Nikkei Weekly*, 27 September, p. 12).

AUSTRALIA'S PRESENCE IN JAPAN'S FINANCIAL SECTOR

While Australian financial institutions have not participated in any large, high profile mergers and alliances, they increasingly are active in Japan's financial sector.[35] In May 1999, Macquarie Bank announced a joint venture with Industrial Bank of Japan to undertake derivatives trading. In September 1999, the Commonwealth Bank took advantage of falling financial market barriers and established a registered securities company, Commonwealth Securities. By diversifying its Japanese operations from banking to securities, the Commonwealth Bank will help develop its financial market business (Commonwealth Securities, 1999).[36] Both AMP and Sydney Reinsurance, a subsidiary of QBE, set up offices in Tokyo in 1998-99. According to Austrade, good opportunities exist for Australian firms in asset management and financial information technology.

FACTORS PROMOTING FOREIGN FINANCIAL INSTITUTIONS

Desegmentation of financial markets and growing strains on the main bank system help foreign financial institutions penetrate Japanese financial markets.

Desegmentation of Financial Markets

Financial market desegmentation, the removal of regulatory barriers between financial sectors like banking, securities and insurance, increases the opportunities available to foreign financial institutions entering the market. For example, some Japanese banks have met the lifting of restrictions on their trading in trusts in 1998 and 1999 by negotiating with foreign service providers, who often are more experienced in managing new trust-related products. Dai-ichi Kangyo Bank and an affiliate of JP Morgan established a company to market investment trusts, while Mitsui Trust and Banking established a joint venture with Prudential Insurance to develop and manage investment trusts (Kamata et al, 1999).

---

34 For example, Fuji Bank and Goldman Sachs are selling mutual funds jointly, while Sakura Trust and Banking and Chase Manhattan Bank have allied their custody and overseas securities trading operations (OECD, 1998; and Kamata et al, 1999). Chase Manhattan will conduct Sakura Trust's overseas securities transactions and settlements.

35 The four major Australian banks have been in Japan for over 20 years. They focus on niche capital and financial market business, particularly Japanese capital flows into Australian and New Zealand debt products.

36 For more detail on Commonwealth Securities' operation, see Chapter 4 - *Banking*.

> **MACQUARIE BANK IN EQUITY DERIVATIVES ALLIANCE WITH INDUSTRIAL BANK OF JAPAN**
>
> In May 1999, Macquarie Bank entered an alliance with the Industrial Bank of Japan, IBJ, to take advantage of the October 1999 full deregulation of Japan's equity derivatives markets.
>
> Macquarie has successfully entered derivatives markets in Australia, Hong Kong and South Africa. IBJ Securities Company Limited, IBJS, a wholly-owned subsidiary of IBJ, was one of the first Japanese securities companies granted an over-the-counter derivatives licence and is establishing a full service equities brokering operation. The 50-50 joint venture will trade and issue products including listed and over-the-counter options, convertible bonds, equity swaps, warrants and other tailored equity products for wholesale and retail clients in Japan, Europe and other markets.
>
> Macquarie provides derivative pricing models and risk management systems to the business. Initially, it will manage the market risk component of equity derivative products issued and traded by the alliance on its balance sheet.
>
> This alliance allows Macquarie to use its equity derivatives expertise to develop a business with one of Japan's leading banks. The Industrial Bank of Japan's announced merger with Fuji Bank and Dai-Ichi Kangyo Bank has not distracted it from its joint venture with Macquarie and ultimately the merger should positively affect Macquarie's operation.
>
> Source: Macquarie Bank, 1999.

The 'Main Bank' System's Decline

Under Japan's traditional 'main bank system', a firm's 'main bank' would meet most of the firm's financial needs, take an equity stake in the firm, participate in its management, and organise debt workouts if necessary. This role inhibited foreign banks from penetrating the local market. However, the current decline of the main bank system should help foreign financial institutions expand their business with Japanese companies.[37]

In the past, major firms' increasing use of the corporate bond market was the chief cause of the main bank system's gradual decline (East Asia Analytical Unit, 1997).[38] One new driver is more stringent supervision, which forces banks to resolve NPLs, sell collateral on bad loans and reassess risk more generally. This new tougher approach is likely to reduce the benefits of firm loyalty to one bank. The Financial Supervisory Agency also wants banks to reduce their corporate shareholdings to reduce the riskiness of bank assets (Hale, 1999).

---

[37] The main bank system (Aoki et al, 1994) contrasts with the western system of corporate governance where shareholder discipline is more important.

[38] The gradual weakening of the main bank system also significantly affects corporate governance (see East Asia Analytical Unit, 1997).

The growing importance of market forces, including new mergers, also strains main bank arrangements. When Nikko Securities established an alliance with Citigroup, this tested relations with its main bank Tokyo-Mitsubishi.[39] Moreover, due to their size, mega banks emerging from the recent major mergers may attract customers from other corporate groups, further loosening main bank ties. Even mergers outside the financial sector can undermine main bank relationships. For example, in the strategic capital alliance between Nissan Motor Company and Renault, Nikko Salomon Smith Barney was appointed financial adviser in preference to Nissan's two main banks, Industrial Bank of Japan and Fuji Bank (*Nikkei Weekly*, 21 June 1999, p. 8).

LIKELY FUTURE TRENDS

The growing role of market forces in Japan's financial sector is increasing disparities between strong and weak financial institutions, making further consolidation likely. Strong financial institutions can enter new markets as desegmentation permits, offer new financial products, invest in new technology and use securitisation to free up their capital. These advantages increasingly should allow them to undercut smaller, weaker competitors. Domestic and foreign financial institutions also will continue to form alliances and joint ventures. Hence merger and acquisition activity is likely to increase. Recent legislation allowing the exchange of shares between merging companies will make holding companies more attractive and accelerate merger activity.[40]

Fewer cross-shareholdings, increasingly vocal institutional investors and a realisation asset prices will not rise continually should drive an increasing focus on profitability and shareholder value. This trend will favour foreign financial institutions accustomed to this market discipline, encourage further merger and acquisition activity, and improve customer focus, efficiency and financial product availability.

Use of corporate bond markets probably will become more important as economic recovery continues and large corporations search for cheaper funding sources. Ministry of Finance efforts to increase the range of maturities at which government bonds are issued will increase the government bond yield curve's usefulness as a pricing benchmark, stimulating the corporate bond market.[41]

Like the United States and Australia in the last decade, Japan's financial institutions increasingly will emphasise best practice risk assessment and credit allocation.

---

[39] These problems were evident before June 1998 when Nikko Securities agreed to merge with Travelers Group. The strains increased when Travelers merged with Citicorp to form Citigroup in October (*Nikkei Weekly*, 14 December 1998, p. 1). Contrary to initial expectations, Bank of Tokyo-Mitsubishi formed its strengthened investment banking arm without Nikko (*Nikkei Weekly*, 14 December 1998, p. 1).

[40] While holding companies have been permitted since fiscal year 1998, an outstanding restraining factor is the inability of subsidiaries to consolidate their tax liability.

[41] At present, ten year bonds dominate government bond issues. In early 1999, an advisory body to the Ministry of Finance recommended issuing five year government bonds; the Ministry of Finance apparently supports such a move (*Nikkei Weekly*, 26 April 1999, p. 15).

FUTURE CHALLENGES

To ensure future financial sector health, Japan's priorities include maintaining a firm and efficient supervisory regime, reforming the postal savings system and pursuing a broad based microeconomic reform program. The latter is required to restore growth to a sustainable level consistent with financial sector health.

Maintaining Vigilant Supervision

Japan has significantly improved its supervisory regime with consolidated supervision, tightened provisioning guidelines and a new procedure to improve inspection systems. The Financial Supervisory Agency's audits also increase confidence in the tighter supervisory regime, and after the next budget, the agency will be fully independent.[42]

Nonetheless, to ensure long term financial system stability, regulators must continue to build credibility and keep pace with the expanding range of financial products, rapidly changing financial sector practices and complex organisational structures. A culture recognising the need for ongoing reform is important.

Reforming the Postal Savings System

Reform of Japan's rather anachronistic postal savings system is very slow. The system was established to encourage savings and fund development projects in the post war reconstruction phase, and could have been phased out as Japan's economy matured. However, in the 1990s, the system's share of savings increased because it provided a 'safe haven' during the private bank crisis (Figure 11.1). In addition, the postal savings system does not impose many of the deposit fees incurred by private bank depositors, such as deposit insurance premiums. Preferential treatment for the postal savings system discourages growth of an efficient profit oriented private banking system.[43]

Funds deposited in the postal savings system are channelled into government investment projects and provide a subsidised finance source for government corporations.[44] The rate of return on postal saving funds is low; the difference between average returns and funding costs was only 0.14 per cent in fiscal year 1997 (Ministry of Finance, 1998). If Japan is to increase the rate of return on its savings and have a competitive financial sector, market forces should play a greater role in allocating this vast pool of assets more efficiently.

---

[42] A June 1999 audit of 64 regional banks found ¥2 trillion worth of loans misclassified as fully performing, while a December 1998 audit of 17 major banks found ¥5.4 trillion worth of loans misclassified as fully performing (Financial Supervisory Agency, 1998).

[43] Depositors will indicate the popularity of postal savings in 2000 and 2001 as ¥62.9 trillion in postal term savings mature. These deposits, worth more than ¥100 trillion including principal and interest payments due at maturity, were invested for ten years in 1990 and 1991 when interest rates peaked at 6.3 per cent (*Nikkei Weekly*, 24 May 1999, p. 13).

[44] Approximately 53 per cent of assets go to government related institutions or local public organisations (Ministry of Finance, 1998).

Improving Economic Growth

Financial sector recovery requires improvement in Japan's macroeconomic performance. While bank recapitalisation should assist economic recovery by improving confidence and expanding bank lending, financial sector restructuring and reform alone will not restore sustainable economic growth.[45] Indeed, the fiscal costs of recapitalisation and recent stimulus packages may drive up long term bond rates and generate an expectation of future tax liabilities, restraining consumption and credit demand (McKibbin, 1997).[46]

The OECD estimates that without further structural reform, Japan's potential rate of sustainable output growth could fall from 1.5 per cent per year to 1 per cent over the next decade, then to 0.5 to 0.75 per cent (OECD, 1998).[47] Such projections underline the importance of further broad based microeconomic reform. Key areas in need of reform include land use laws, agriculture and the electricity and telecommunications industries (OECD, 1998).

CONCLUSIONS

Japan finally is making significant progress in eliminating banks' NPLs, although problems remain among the regional banks and life insurance companies. Japan's financial markets are changing rapidly, driven by poor profitability, NPL resolution efforts, ongoing reform and foreign participation. These changes present foreign financial firms with opportunities to expand and develop in the Japanese market.

However, even after NPL problems are resolved, financial sector reforms must continue to ensure long term economic health and vigour. Furthermore, to achieve Japan's long term growth potential and a solid base for further financial sector development, accelerated structural reforms also are needed in other sectors.

---

[45] Given the risks associated with lending to the Japanese corporate sector in an environment of weak economic growth and widespread restructuring, banks may be slow to increase lending to companies, even after they recapitalise.

[46] The increase in long term bond rates from 0.9 per cent in October 1998 to 2.1 per cent in February 1999 was attributed largely to increased market realisation of the fiscal costs of bank recapitalisation.

[47] The main factors driving this decline in potential output growth are the labour force reduction flowing from population aging, the deceleration in capital stock growth and a slowing trend in total factor productivity growth (OECD, 1998).

REFERENCES

Aoki, M., Patrick, H. and Sheard, P., 1994, 'The Japanese Main Bank System: an Introductory Overview', EDI Working Papers, Economic Development Institute of the World Bank, pp. 94-102.

Austrade, 1999, 'The Changing Japanese Insurance Sector: Opportunities for Australian Companies', Australian Trade Commission, March.

Bank of Japan, 1996, *Economic Statistics Annual*, Bank of Japan, Tokyo.

CEIC, 1999, CEIC Database, Hong Kong, supplied by EconData, Canberra.

Commonwealth Securities, 1999, Information supplied to East Asia Analytical Unit, September.

Diamond Weekly, 1999, 'Safety Ranking of Life Insurance Companies', Special Supplement, vol. 3, March, pp. 10-20.

East Asia Analytical Unit, 1997, 'Finance' in East Asia Analytical Unit, *A New Japan? Change in Asia's Megamarket*, Department of Foreign Affairs and Trade, Canberra.

Financial Reconstruction Commission, 1999a, 'The Viewpoint on the Write-Offs and Allowances in Association with the Capital Injection', 25 January, www.frc.go.jp/news, accessed on 6 August.

____ 1999b, 'Basic Policies for Capital Injections for Regional Financial Institutions', 10 June, www.frc.go.jp/news, accessed on 28 September.

Financial Supervisory Agency, 1999a, 'The Status of Risk Management Loans Held by All Banks in Japan (as at the end of March, 1999)', 22 June, www.fsa.jo.jp/news, accessed on 9 July.

____ 1999b, 'Results of Inspection of the Regional Banks (64 Banks)', 22 June, www.fsa.jo.jp/news, accessed on 9 July.

____ 1999c, 'Results of Inspection of the Regional Banks II (56 Banks)', 22 June, www.fsa.jo.jp/news, accessed on 9 September.

____ 1999d, Information supplied to the Australian Embassy, Tokyo, July.

____ 1998, 'Results of Inspection on the Major Banks (17 Banks)', 25 December 1998, www.fsa.go.jp/news, accessed on 9 July 1999.

Fuji Bank, 1999, Press release 'The Dai-Ichi Kangyo Bank, Limited, The Fuji Bank, Limited and The Industrial Bank of Japan, Limited to Get Consolidated to Form a New Financial Services Group', 20 August, www.fujibank.co.jp/eng/fb/news, accessed on 13 September.

Hale, D, 1999, 'The Outlook for Japan: Will She Become a Capitalist Country?', 8 March, The Zurich Group, Chicago.

HSBC Securities, 1999, 'The Bad Debt Situation: Almost Home?', HSBC Securities, Tokyo.

Kamata, Y., Mizobuchi, A., and Maeda, S., 1999, 'Financial Services Industry Response to Deregulation in Japan', *NRI Quarterly*, Spring, pp. 48-71.

International Monetary Fund, 1999, *IMF Survey*, vol. 28, no. 8, pp. 121-22.

___ 1998, *International Capital Markets: Developments, Prospects and Key Issues*, IMF, Washington DC.

Macquarie Bank, 1999, Information supplied to East Asia Analytical Unit, September.

McKibbin, W., 1997, 'The Macroeconomic Experience of Japan since 1990: an Empirical Investigation', Brookings Discussion Papers, no. 131, Washington DC, June.

Ministry of Finance, 1999, 'Inward Direct Investment by Industry', www.mof.go.jp/english, accessed on 9 July.

___ 1998 , *FILP Report 1998 (Fiscal Investment and Loan Program)*, Finance Bureau, Tokyo, October.

OECD, 1998, 'OECD Economic Surveys: Japan', November, Paris.

References1997, 'OECD Economic Surveys: Japan', November, Paris.

Suzuki, Y., 1998, 'Strategy toward the Big Bang: the Industrial Bank of Japan's Approach', Center of Japanese Economy and Business Occasional Paper Series no. 35, Columbia University.

Takahara, N., and Tanaka, H., 1996, 'Improving Japan's Corporate Pension Plan System', *NRI Quarterly*, vol. 5, no. 2, pp. 60-79.

Yoshino, N., 1995, 'Changing Behavior of Private Banks and Corporations and Monetary Policy in Japan' in Sawamoto, K., Nakajima. Z. and Taguchi, H. (eds), *Financial Stability in a Changing Environment*, Bank of Japan and St Martin's Press, New York.

Chapter 12

CHINA

By late 1999, the Asian financial crisis had only modestly affected China's economic performance. The non-convertibility of the Chinese renminbi, China's large foreign exchange reserves, its modest commercial foreign debt, government measures to stimulate domestic demand and the renminbi's relative undervaluation in 1997, all insulated China from contagion.

Although China's financial sector will take many years to become efficient and commercially oriented, financial sector reform now is receiving high priority and making encouraging progress. Most analysts anticipate China will avoid a financial sector crisis like those many other East Asian economies suffered in 1997 and 1998; government ownership of much of the sector and its willingness to support the banks will be important in this regard. However, over the next two to three years, it is important financial sector reform continues to be a high priority, significant public funds are injected to write off non-performing loans, NPLs, and several crucial financial sector policy decisions are sound and well implemented.

This chapter reviews major recent reforms and developments in the prudential framework, banks, non-bank financial institutions and capital markets. It then draws conclusions regarding likely future developments and prospects for foreign financial institutions.

Lessons from the Asian Crisis

Despite its reasonably mild impact on China to date, the Asian financial crisis provided China with some clear lessons. The crisis highlighted the damaging economic consequences of weak prudential controls and an unreformed financial sector. China's financial sector suffers from many weaknesses that caused the Asian crisis. These include government directed lending (to state owned enterprises at the expense of the more efficient non-state sector), a weak prudential and legal framework, limited financial sector disclosure and restricted foreign competition. These factors have generated a serious NPL problem in the dominant state owned banking sector. Indeed, China's NPLs are higher than in some economies more severely affected by the crisis.

In November 1997, financial sector reform accelerated after most of the top Chinese leadership participated in a major financial sector conference.[1] In early 1998, the Government announced an ambitious financial sector reform program to:

- introduce a stringent new loan classification system in line with international standards

- give banks the authority to independently evaluate projects and allocate credit on a commercial basis

---

[1] Although the Chinese Government commenced financial sector reform in 1984, this issue received relatively low priority until 1993, when repeated economic overheating convinced decision makers monetary policy and banking reform was needed. Even then, slow state owned enterprise reform frustrated efforts to transform banks into commercially oriented institutions.

- improve banks' risk management capacity through staff training
- abandon the centralised credit plan and instead manage banks' credit expansion via asset liability and capital adequacy ratios
- increase bank and non-bank financial institution capital adequacy ratios to the Bank for International Settlements' benchmark of 8 per cent
- ensure state owned banks reach the new capital adequacy ratio by writing off more NPLs and injecting public funds to recapitalise them
- adopt tougher accounting standards in financial institutions (Capital Intelligence, 1999).

In addition, the Government is reforming and widening the securities market; strengthening prudential supervision of banks, non-bank financial institutions and the stock market; and improving the institutional capacity of the central bank, the People's Bank of China, PBOC.

Foreign Exchange Regime

Despite the approximately 8 per cent real trade weighted appreciation of the renminbi since the crisis began, the Chinese Government has resisted pressure to devalue. With foreign exchange reserves of over US$140 billion rising, and a continuing current account surplus, there was little rationale for a devaluation. While export growth slackened and briefly became negative, this mainly was because China's Asian export markets were in serious recession. With justification, the Government judged renminbi devaluation could cause a further round of devaluations in volatile Asian currency markets, eroding the benefits of any renminbi devaluation and inflicting considerable economic damage on its Asian neighbours and export markets.

However, as pegged exchange rate regimes were a major contributor to the Asian financial crisis, once Asian currency markets stabilise, the PBOC might increase the flexibility of the exchange rate regime. Public statements issued in 1999 stressing the market-determined nature of the renminbi rate give limited support to a relaxation of arrangements in the future. However, until the Government advances other aspects of financial reform, including removing interest rate and capital controls (reforms which depend on completing state enterprise and banking reforms), a strong case can be made for China retaining its present foreign exchange arrangements.

STRUCTURE OF CHINA'S FINANCIAL SECTOR

China's huge population, high savings rate, growing incomes and ongoing liberalisation are producing rapid financial sector growth. In 1999, four large state owned commercial banks dominated China's financial sector (Figure 12.1) but the sector also included:

- three policy banks, which make loans consistent with government trade, agriculture and infrastructure development policies
- 98 domestically-owned commercial banks, including 20 state owned nationwide and joint-venture banks and 78 new city banks

- 173 entities representing foreign banks
- 41 500 rural credit cooperatives
- 3 240 urban cooperatives
- 239 trust and investment companies, and various other non-bank financial institutions, NBFIs, including leasing and finance companies (Figure 12.2).

Despite recent stock market growth, bank loans still provide most capital raised by Chinese enterprises (Figure 12.3).

Figure 12.1

State Owned Commercial Banks Dominate Lending
Asset Distribution of Chinese Financial Institutions, December 1998

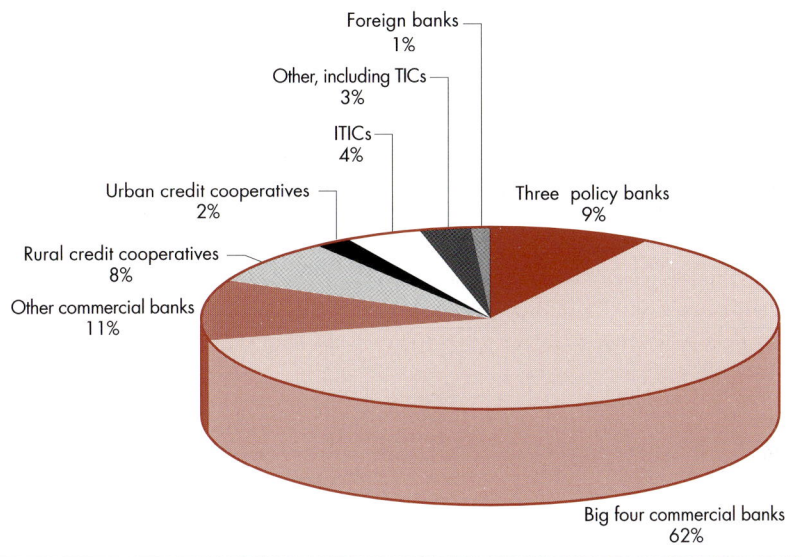

Note: TICs are trust and investment companies; ITICs are international trust and investment companies.
Source: People's Bank of China, 1999a.

Figure 12.2

Financial Sector Diversifying but Banks Still Dominate
Structure of China's Financial System, 1998

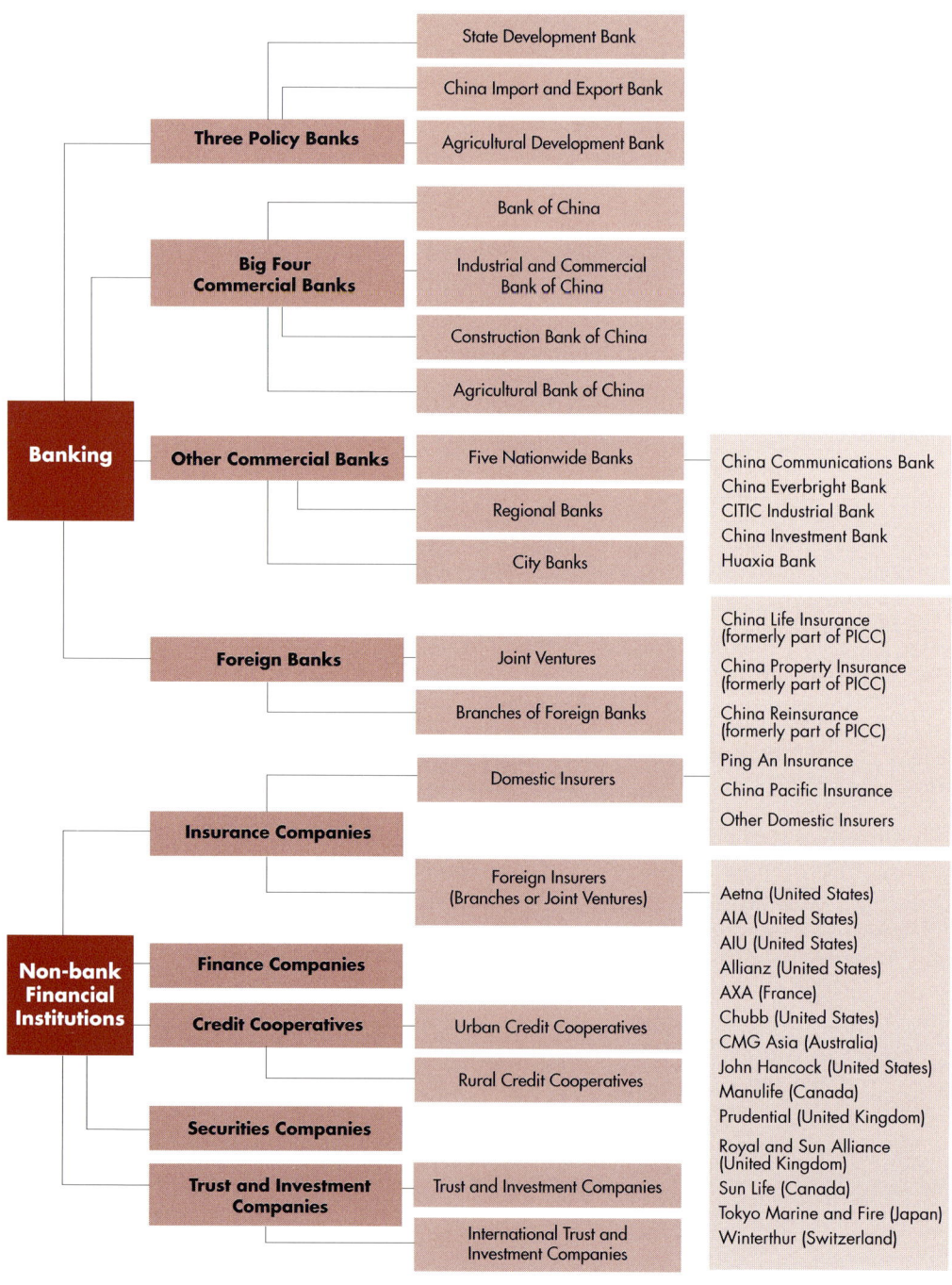

Source: China Online, 1999.

THE PEOPLE'S BANK OF CHINA

The PBOC heads the regulatory framework covering all these financial institutions. After 1949, the PBOC became China's only bank and issued the official currency. Nationalised banks came under its authority. Although the Government designated the PBOC as China's central bank in 1984, only in 1995 did the central bank law formally legislate the PBOC's authority to supervise and regulate the financial sector and determine monetary policy.[2] The central bank law specifically forbids the PBOC from lending to the Government, removing a major source of previous inflation episodes.

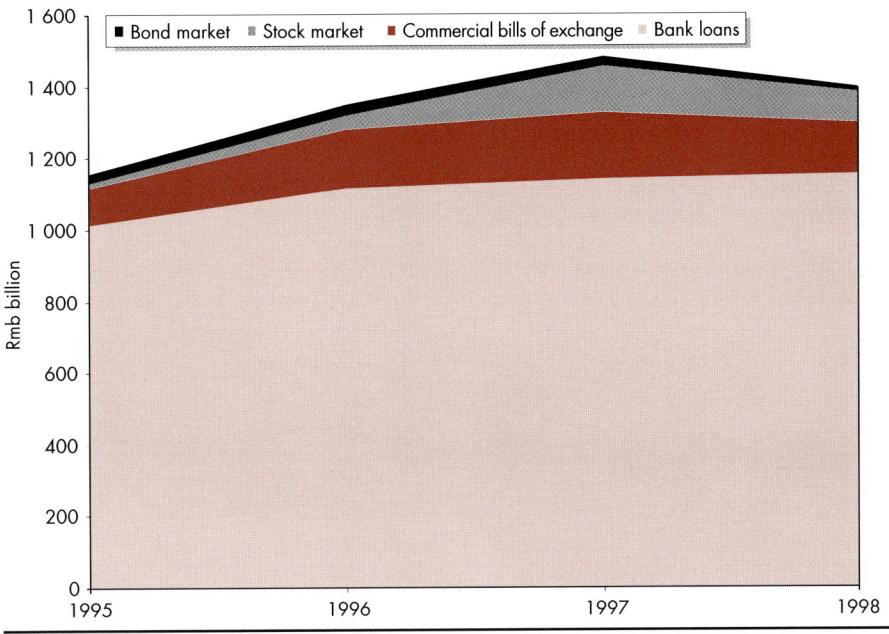

Figure 12.3

Bank Lending Dominates Stocks and Bonds
Enterprise Capital Raising, 1995-98

Source: Moody's Investor Service, 1999.

---

[2] The 1995 law also gave the PBOC other standard central bank responsibilities, such as issuing currency, providing last resort lending, acting as the Government's treasury, arranging payments and managing the Government's foreign exchange reserves.

To implement monetary policy, the PBOC can determine interest rates and levels of central bank lending to commercial banks, set banks' reserve deposit requirements, undertake open market operations (buying and selling government bonds) and manage foreign exchange reserves.³ As well, the PBOC is the prudential supervisor of:

- four major state commercial banks
- three policy lending banks
- nationwide and other commercial banks
- non-bank financial institutions, including domestic and international trust and investment companies, finance companies, and rural and urban credit cooperatives.

However, the PBOC no longer is responsible for the securities and insurance industries; the China Securities Regulatory Commission and the China Insurance Regulatory Commission now supervise these.

The Government's November 1998 decision to restructure the PBOC branch network along the lines of the US federal reserve system should enhance significantly PBOC independence and effectiveness. Previously, the PBOC had major branches in 27 provinces and four autonomous regions. Now it operates monetary and supervision policy from only nine supra-regional offices, controlled directly by PBOC headquarters in Beijing. Consequently it should be less vulnerable to provincial government pressure on provincial branches to expand bank credit limits to fund favoured local projects.⁴

The PBOC also is upgrading its prudential control system. In early 1998, the PBOC announced it would implement the Bank for International Settlements' 25 core principles, considered the minimum standard of prudent financial supervision. In addition, the PBOC's training institute will upgrade the skills of 30 000 supervisory staff in 1999 (Capital Intelligence, 1999).

Prudential, Lending and Interest Rate Reforms

In January 1998, the Government replaced the banks' long standing credit allocation system with reference guidelines based on capital adequacy and deposit to loan ratios.⁵ This system gives banks more freedom to determine lending volumes and allocations among provinces, sectors and businesses. Although the Government still indicates its sectoral lending priorities, banks now must allocate credit predominantly by assessing potential risks and returns, and borrowers' capacity to repay. Bank managers and loan officers are held responsible for new NPLs.⁶

---

3   While the State Council is ultimately responsible for key monetary policy decisions, the 1995 law guaranteed the PBOC a high degree of monetary policy independence from other levels of government and individuals, most importantly provincial governments and central government ministries (East Asia Analytical Unit, 1997).

4   Now regional and provincial branch PBOC managers are appointed by and report to Beijing; previously provincial managers were appointed by and reported to provincial governments.

5   This reform also reflected the broader range of monetary policy instruments now available to the PBOC, including increasing use of banks' required reserve ratios, benchmark interest rates, rediscounting, lending to commercial banks and open market operations to control the monetary base (East Asia Analytical Unit, 1997).

6   Nevertheless, some reports during 1999 suggest the Government has not always adhered strictly to this non-interventionist policy on bank lending.

Moreover, by 2000, banks must reach the minimum Bank for International Settlements' capital adequacy ratio (capital to risk weighted assets) of 8 per cent, a maximum loan to deposit ratio of 75 per cent and a minimum liquid asset ratio of 25 per cent.[7]

In mid 1996, the Government began to reform interest rates by removing controls on short term and interbank interest rates (East Asia Analytical Unit, 1997). However, the State Council through the PBOC, effectively controls other interest rates. More thorough interest rate deregulation would enable rates to better reflect the demand and supply of capital, and individual lenders' risk premiums.[8]

The 1995 Commercial Bank Law

The PBOC also enforces the 1995 commercial bank law, which with the central bank law sets the legal framework for China's banking system. The commercial bank law requires banks to operate as independent commercial entities responsible for their own profits and losses.[9] Despite the 1998 reforms, the major commercial banks still can be pressured to provide 'social' loans to unviable state owned enterprises, and therefore are not totally free to act as commercial banks. However, this pressure is less than in the past and likely to diminish further.

Accounting Standards

China's financial accounting and disclosure standards are well below international standards.[10] In early 1998, in parallel with reforming the supervisory system, the Government undertook to introduce international accounting standards for banks and financial institutions, although no date yet has been set for achieving this.[11]

THE FOUR STATE OWNED COMMERCIAL BANKS

Bank lending provides about 83 per cent of enterprises' external finance. Four major state owned commercial banks dominate bank lending (Figure 12.1) (Moody's Investor Services, 1999). In 1998, the Industrial and Commerce Bank of China, the Bank of China, the China Construction Bank and the Agricultural Bank of China, had 1.7 million employees, over 150 000 branches and total assets of US$1.15 trillion (Figure 12.4). All rank them among the world's 60 largest banks (Moody's Investor Services, 1999; and Capital Intelligence, 1999).

---

[7] However, banks only can meet these targets if the Government recapitalises the banks by purchasing their NPLs.

[8] To reflect the creditworthiness of customers, banks can charge up to 20 to 25 per cent above or below the fixed rate, although in times of slow growth and poor business performance like 1999, this flexibility probably does not compensate for lending risks, and may restrict credit growth. Some analysts point out that many state owned enterprise borrowers are not very interest rate sensitive because they do not expect to repay borrowed funds and therefore are keen to borrow at any rate.

[9] It also protects the legal rights of depositors and banks, strengthens prudential supervision requirements and requires banks to improve loan asset quality, internal management and credit allocation operations.

[10] However, practices of the Bank of China and some second tier banks like Everbright, CITIC Industrial Bank are better than average. Only Bank of China, Everbright and Minsheng Banks use internationally recognised accountants to audit their accounts.

[11] The Government has placed a high priority on improving accounting standards and is establishing several new training institutes for this purpose. Certifying accountants is a Ministry of Finance responsibility (Feng, 1999).

China

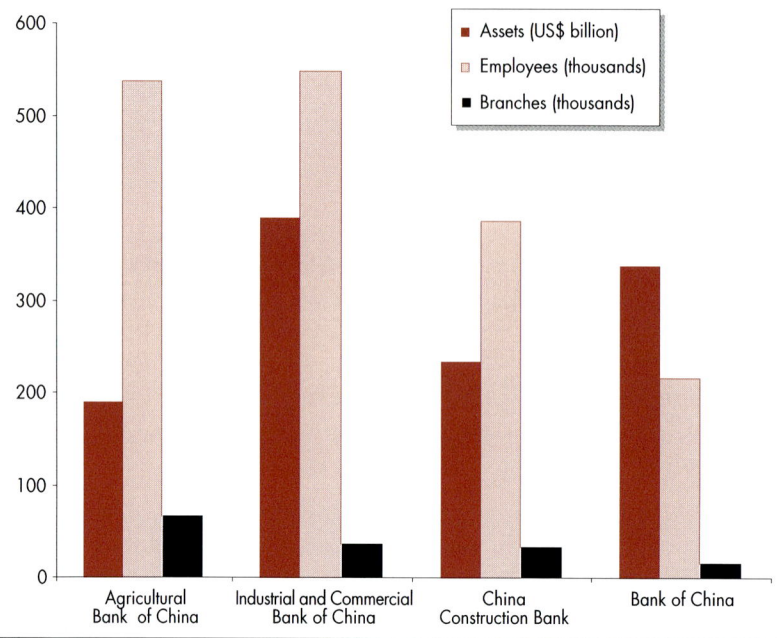

Figure 12.4

Four Big Commercial Banks Have Huge Assets
Assets, Employees and Branch Network of the Four Major State Commercial Banks, December 1998

Note: Employees and branches are 1997 values.
Source: *Almanac of China's Finance and Banking*, 1998; Moody's Investor Services, 1999; and Capital Intelligence, 1999.

These banks increasingly compete for enterprise and household business across all sectors, reducing their sectoral exposure risk. However, only the Bank of China has extensive overseas operations and it undertakes most foreign exchange business. If these banks can resolve their NPL problem, streamline staff and branch numbers, and improve operational and credit allocation efficiency, eventually their size should be a strong competitive advantage (Morgan Stanley Dean Witter, 1998a).

From 1994 to 1998, the other commercial banks grew faster than the four state commercial banks, although from much lower bases (Figure 12.5). Net foreign liabilities of the large state commercial banks contracted after 1995 due to tighter prudential controls, helping protect China from financial crisis contagion in 1997 and 1998. However, the net foreign liabilities of smaller commercial banks continued to accumulate rapidly until 1998.

Figure 12.5

New Commercial Bank Growth Outpaces Big Four
Annual Asset Growth Rates of State and Other Commercial Banks, 1994-98, Per cent

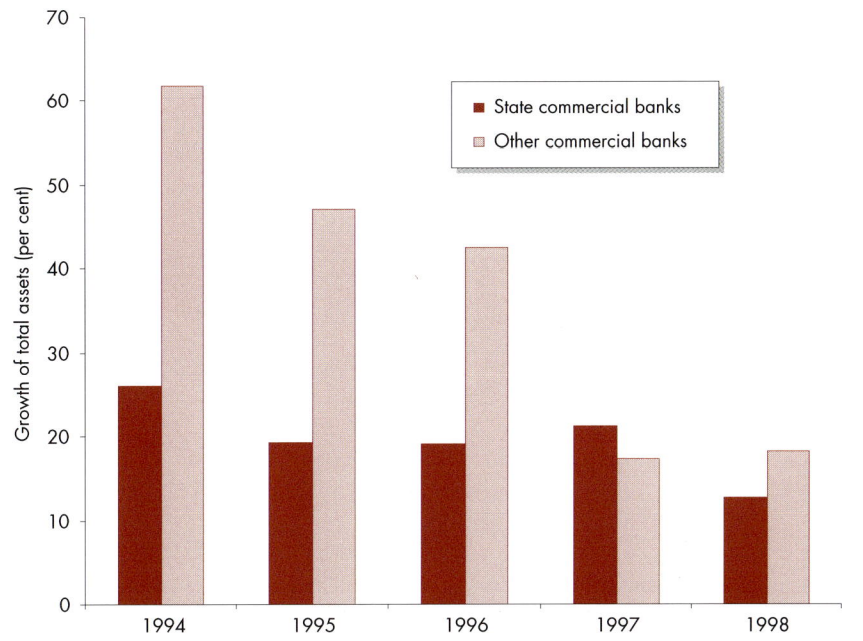

Source: People's Bank of China, 1999a, pp. 20-23.

KEY COMMERCIAL BANK WEAKNESSES

Due to limited bank and enterprise reform in the 1980s and 1990s, banks failed to develop into commercial institutions able to evaluate credit risk. Instead, for many years they allocated loans in response to central and provincial government directives, lending large sums to non-viable enterprises and acquiring many NPLs.

Weak Human Resources and Management Systems

The quality of bank staff generally is poor, particularly among older staff and in non-urban areas. Bank pay scales do little to attract high quality officers. Banks also are weak in loan classification, income and expenditure accounting, risk and asset management practices, and loan loss provisioning. Most banks' accounting and disclosure standards are poor, allowing banks to underestimate their NPLs and overstate their profits and capital base (Capital Intelligence, 1999).

Early 1998 government reforms clearly indicated bankers are responsible for their lending decisions; senior managers' careers now depend more on not creating new NPLs. However, without good credit assessment skills and relationships with private sector lenders, bank managers apparently have become very cautious about *any* new lending. Consequently, bank liquidity rose in 1999, exacerbating the slowdown in economic activity.

State Owned Enterprise Borrowing

China's partially reformed state owned enterprises receive about 63 per cent of all bank lending, and inadequate incentives fail to restrict their demand for credit or enforce loan repayment. Therefore state owned enterprises mainly cause bank NPLs. Concerns about the social consequences of bankrupting numerous unviable state owned enterprises, low enterprise profitability and the Government's 1998 fiscal stimulus package generally impede the Government's aim of making the banks fully commercial entities.

State owned enterprise reform therefore is a key to solving the banks' NPL problems. An important government approach to solving the state enterprise problem is 'grasping the big, enlivening the small', *zhuada fangxiao*, (East Asia Analytical Unit, 1997).[12] While the Government placed some constraints on releasing small and medium sized enterprises from state ownership in 1998, this process proceeded quite rapidly in 1999 (Heytens, 1999). Eventually this *de facto* privatisation should solve the property rights problem of about half the state owned enterprise sector, by value of output.[13]

However, most remaining state owned enterprises are not subject to market discipline and are more likely to try to maximise workers' incomes than returns for their state owners (Meng and Perkins, 1999). Many state enterprise managers are not convinced they will have to repay loans, so they seek new loans for non-viable projects or even to pay wages. This behaviour will cease only when lenders can acquire defaulting borrowers' assets and managers' careers suffer if their enterprises default. Recent proposed state owned enterprise reforms attempt to deal with such management deficiencies.

Limited Lending to Non-state Sector

Only about 37 per cent of bank loans are extended to the private non-state sector although it produces over 70 per cent of output.[14] Although recent changes to the constitution have improved the status of the private sector and in early 1998, the Government announced commercial banks would increase their lending to non-state enterprises, in practice, Chinese banks' loan officers are inexperienced in assessing credit risk. They are less secure lending to the private sector than to the state sector, as they still believe loans to the latter carry implicit government guarantees.

---

[12] In early 1998, in his first press conference as Premier, Zhu Rongji announced while 40 per cent of state owned enterprises make losses, many of these enterprises are very small. However, 500 very large state owned enterprises provide 85 per cent of state profits and enterprise taxes, and only 10 per cent of state owned enterprises in this category make losses (*China Daily*, 20 March 1998; and *South China Morning Post*, 20 March 1998).

[13] In 1998, the Government issued a directive requiring local governments to follow strict guidelines when disposing of state owned enterprises, to prevent abuses and the sale of state assets for below their true value. However, the Government sold 10 000 small and medium sized state owned enterprises in 1997, 20 000 in 1998 and anecdotal evidence suggests this increased sales pace has continued (Heytens, 1999).

[14] The Bank of China, the main banker of Sino-foreign joint ventures, believes 50 per cent of its loans are advanced to the private sector (Geng, 1999).

To help overcome banks' reluctance to lend to non-state enterprises, the Government is promoting credit guarantee companies to guarantee bank loans to small and medium sized enterprises. By mid 1999, two were operating, including a joint venture initiated by the International Finance Corporation and Fitch IBCA (Geng, 1999). In a potentially important move in late 1999, the State Economic and Trade Commission announced each province would soon establish credit guarantee funds on a pilot basis to encourage lending to small and medium sized enterprises. Provinces will establish funds at three administrative levels, with reguarantee facilities at the provincial level. Funds will come from local fiscal allocations including allocated properties, membership fees and charges for credit guarantees (*China Daily*, 17 June, 1999, p. 1).

BANK MANAGEMENT REFORMS

In 1998 and 1999, the banks commenced considerable internal reform and reorganisation. To improve lending quality, the four specialised commercial banks, followed the PBOC and introduced vertical authority chains. Bank headquarters rather than provincial governments now appoint provincial and local branch managers (Geng, 1999). Bank managers can use more commercial criteria to determine staff levels and branching structures. To cut costs, banks plan to reduce staff numbers by 10 to 30 per cent and rationalise branch structures.[15] Moreover, banks now are beginning to use consistent lending criteria across all their branches.

While lack of systematic reporting produces poor bank disclosure and little financial data, the Government is trying to overcome this problem.[16] Banks increasingly hire new graduates from business universities in Beijing and Shanghai such as the China Europe International Business School, and provide in-house training to develop staff capacity. In addition to expanding lending to non-state enterprises, banks recently have been urged to do more mortgage and consumer credit lending.

NON-PERFORMING LOANS

The major weakness in China's financial system is the high level of bank NPLs. The unrecoverable portion of bank NPLs may exceed their capital, making them technically insolvent (Lardy, 1998a). In a privately-owned banking system, this situation could precipitate a major bank run requiring the government to guarantee bank deposits and/or nationalise insolvent banks, as in Korea, Thailand and Indonesia in 1997 and 1998. However, China's central and provincial governments own all but one commercial bank. As depositors believe the Government will stand behind these banks, the prospect of a major bank run in China is very small (Ma, 1999; Li, 1999; and Woo, 1998). Nevertheless, until banks are recapitalised,

---

[15] For example, China Construction Bank plans to increase branching in the coastal areas because it believes this will be profitable. Greater commercial orientation could significantly shift regional lending patterns to wealthier coastal provinces.

[16] While most branches still operate with considerable autonomy, in 1998, the PBOC instructed banks to audit regularly their branches' accounts. This had not occurred previously. With World Bank and IMF assistance, banks are investing in computer technology to consolidate electronic reporting (Krumm, 1999; and Heytens, 1999).

their NPLs are written off and the flow of potential new bad loans is staunched, the banking system will remain a potential source of systemic risk. While recapitalisation will be expensive, until the banks are reformed, they will continue to impose a heavy cost on the Chinese economy by misallocating China's scarce savings.[17]

The New Loan Classification System

The true level of NPLs will not be known until the Government announces the results of audits using the new loan classification process. China's new five tiers of loan classifications announced in March 1998 will lift the system closer to international standards and significantly improve transparency. New loan classifications are:

- normal loans, where borrowers fulfil contractual agreements and make repayments

- special mention loans, where borrowers could repay but are at risk of not fulfilling their requirements

- sub-standard loans, where cash flows from borrowers' business operations cannot cover interest and principal servicing

- idle loans, where borrowers have not repaid interest or principal for over 12 months

- loss loans, where the bank cannot recover any of the loan after all legal procedures have been pursued (*Hong Kong Economic Times*, 30 and 31 March 1998; and *South China Morning Post*, 14 March, 1998).

The Government is considering strengthening some of these provisions, including reducing the period before loans are considered overdue from 12 to six months, then eventually three months. In 1998, the major banks trialed this classification system in Guangdong province, and by the end of 1999, they will have implemented it in all provinces.[18]

The PBOC also may require banks to lift their general provisioning against bad loans from 1 per cent to 1.5 per cent of loans, and introduce specific provisions against each of the four impaired loan categories.[19]

---

[17] One analysis estimates losses due to inefficient bank lending practices over the last decade could have been as high as 2.3 per cent of GDP per year (Woo, 1998).

[18] Implementing the new classifications forced banks to upgrade their limited credit assessment and monitoring system capacities, requiring a major training effort. Many major accounting firms, like PricewaterhouseCoopers, Deloittes, Lehman Brothers, Morgan Stanley and Goldman Sachs are helping the banks implement the loan classification system (Ziegler, 1999).

[19] The current proposal is for banks to make provisions equal to 5 to 7 per cent of special mention loans, 20 to 30 per cent of sub-standard loans, 50 per cent of idle loans and 100 per cent of loss loans.

NPLs Cost Estimates

Using the old classification system, in 1998, the Governor of the PBOC estimated about 25 per cent of outstanding loans were overdue, doubtful and bad loans (*Hong Kong Economic Times*, 18 October 1998).[20] Based on the new tougher standard, NPLs could be considerably higher. If in December 1998, NPLs were 25 to 30 per cent of deposits in deposit taking banks, they would have totalled Rmb 2.2 trillion to Rmb 2.6 trillion, of which 25 to 50 per cent may have to be written off. Hence the NPL write-off could range from Rmb 540 million to Rmb 1.3 billion (US$65 billion to US$156 billion) or from 7 to 16 per cent of 1998 GDP (People's Bank of China, 1999a). As the net capital in the banking system was only Rmb 621 billion in December 1998 (People's Bank of China, 1999a), these write-offs would be from 87 to 210 per cent of the banking system's current capital value.

The Government could assume fiscal responsibility for the write-off. Assuming NPLs are around 30 per cent of total loans, public debt still would only rise to approximately 40 per cent of GDP over the next eight to ten years (given China's quasi public debt was only 25 per cent of its GDP in 1998). While this is well within developed country levels, the Chinese Government's debt servicing capacity is lower than that of many other countries as its revenue to GDP ratio is only around 12 per cent.

ASSET MANAGEMENT COMPANIES

Probably the most important development resulting from the early 1998 reform package was the Government's decision to establish four asset management companies, AMCs, to buy NPLs from the four major banks. The Ministry of Finance established Xinda at the China Construction Bank in April 1999. In October 1999, the Agriculture Bank of China established Great Wall Asset Management Company; Bank of China established Dongfang Asset Management Company; and Industrial and Commercial Bank of China set up China Huarong Asset Management Company (Reuters, 16 and 18 October 1999).[21] Shanghai's municipal government also has established its own AMC to buy NPLs from several local banks and the Shanghai branch of the Industrial and Commercial Bank (Reuters, 15 October 1999).

The AMCs will use government funded bonds to purchase, at face value, NPLs from the banks.[22] The AMCs will attempt to maximise asset recovery by selling collateral backing the loans, via debt to equity swaps, securitising and auctioning NPLs, and restructuring debts. AMC purchased assets will be sold to both foreign and domestic investors (Wang, 1999).

---

[20] One 1996 estimate put overdue loans of the four largest state banks at 12 per cent, doubtful loans at 8 per cent and unrecoverable loans at 2 per cent (Lardy, 1998a citing Tang Xiong, 1996). The China Construction Bank believes its NPLs are about 25 per cent of outstanding loans (Wang, 1999).

[21] All AMCs have registered capital of Rmb 10 billion.

[22] The Government has not yet decided how many of the banks' NPLs the AMCs will purchase. However, they will buy only non-loss NPLs extended by major banks before 1995. The banks will be paid in long term government bonds which they will have to hold till maturity. The 1995 cut off was chosen because in that year, the new banking law theoretically gave non-policy banks the right to act as commercial entities and refuse to undertake social loans.

While the Government is yet to finalise funding arrangements, it probably will fund interest payments on these AMC issued bonds, and ultimately cover the significant gap between purchased NPLs' face and recovery values. To ensure NPLs do not reappear, the chief executive officers of the four major banks will sign 'governance contracts' with the Ministry of Finance and the PBOC taking responsibility for future NPL losses and agreeing to meet best practice performance targets. Once the major banks sell their NPLs, they will be expected to focus on commercial banking; future NPL sales will not be possible. China's AMC model is based on those used to successfully resolve NPL problems in the United States, Scandinavia and Korea.

XINDA AMC

Xinda was established in April 1999 with senior management staff drawn from the China Construction Bank. While Xinda works closely with the China Construction Bank, it is independent from it, answering to the Ministry of Finance. Xinda hopes to attract outside experts, including Chinese nationals living abroad, to its middle management.

In its first three years, Xinda will focus on resolving the NPLs of small companies, and subsequently tackle larger companies. Xinda and other AMCs will not undertake large scale closures of defaulting enterprises; rather they will help arrange debt restructuring for viable businesses. If Xinda accepts a debt to equity swap, it will outsource the enterprise's restructuring; this could provide opportunities for foreign management advisory firms. If the company's performance improves, Xinda will on-sell its equity to other owners. Hopeless cases will be bankrupted.

NPL recovery rates are not expected to be high. Major constraints will include:

- resistance from local governments seeking to protect local employment
- lack of a comprehensive social safety net for displaced workers, although Xinda recognises this is the Government's responsibility, not the AMC's
- the weak legal and administrative framework, including an inadequate foreclosure law that is strongly biased against creditors
- lack of accounting, enterprise restructuring and evaluation expertise within Xinda; to address this, Xinda is seeking international assistance.

Xinda recognises its efforts must accompany continuing bank and state owned enterprise reform. The banks must tighten credit controls and monitoring, increase their use of feasibility studies, enhance organisational reform and close excess branches.

Source: Wang, 1999.

DEPOSIT INSURANCE SCHEME

The Government also wants to introduce a deposit insurance scheme, although details and timing still are unclear. Currently, the Government provides *de facto* deposit insurance by prioritising small and medium sized depositors during liquidation and reimbursing depositors even if proceeds are inadequate. However, this protection exposes the Government to huge unfunded contingent liabilities from poorly managed rural and urban cooperatives and some regional banks. Instead the Government believes a contributory deposit insurance scheme should fund these obligations.

Details of the proposed deposit insurance scheme are not yet decided but:

- an independent institution, eventually funded by risk adjusted premiums paid by member institutions, would operate the scheme
- probably only small and medium sized deposits would be covered.

Initially the Government would establish separate funds for banks, credit cooperatives and other major non-bank financial institutions, but eventually they would be amalgamated into a single fund.

However, international financial institutions believe the Government should overhaul insolvent financial institutions before a deposit insurance scheme is introduced.

THE STATE POLICY BANKS

In 1994, to remove commercial banks from policy lending and expand funding sources for public works, the Government established three policy banks.[23] The China Development Bank lends for major state infrastructure projects; China Export and Import Bank provides long term trade finance for machinery and equipment imports; and China Agricultural Development Bank finances state crop purchases.

In 1998, policy bank assets of Rmb 1.5 trillion were less than 9 per cent of commercial bank assets (Figure 12.1). Long term bonds account for 88 per cent of total policy bank liabilities (Figure 12.6) (*Almanac of China's Finance and Banking*, 1997). Since 1995, the China Development Bank has issued yen, Yankee and global bonds in international markets; a US$500 million issue in May 1999 was the first by any Asian issuer since the Asian crisis (Cai, 1999).

---

[23] However, as the commercial banks have to purchase bonds issued by the policy banks, they indirectly continue to shoulder policy lending obligations.

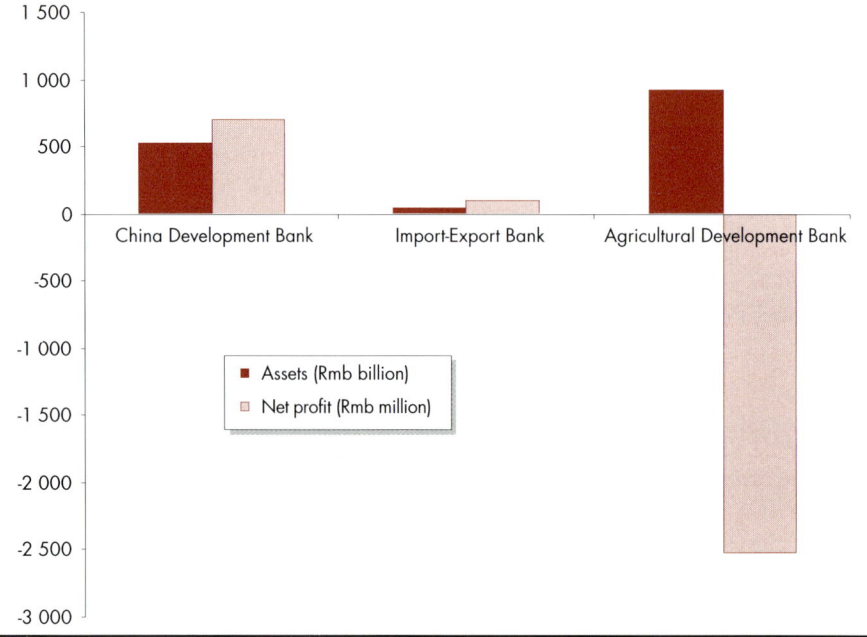

Figure 12.6

Largest Policy Bank Is Least Profitable
Asset Base and Profitability of Policy Banks, 1998

Note: Agricultural Development Bank data are 1997.
Source: Moody's Investor Services, 1999.

Policy banks also are undergoing reform. In 1998, the China Development Bank followed the PBOC and commercial banks in re-centralising credit allocation decisions in Beijing, and centrally appointing local managers (Cai, 1999). Policy banks also must maintain a capital adequacy ratio of 8 per cent.[24]

OTHER COMMERCIAL BANKS

Other smaller commercial banks hold only 11 per cent of total financial institution assets but are growing much more rapidly than the four big commercial banks (Figures 12.1 and 12.5).[25] The five main nationwide banks are medium sized and were nationalised in 1949 or established in the late 1980s, mainly by major state owned conglomerates.[26] These banks have much slimmer staffing and branching profiles than the four big commercial banks; together they have 1.6 per cent of the staff and 0.25 per cent of the branches of the four major banks, but hold 17 per cent of the assets.

---

[24] If policy banks' capital adequacy approaches this level, they must cease lending as the Ministry of Finance cannot replenish their capital base (Cai, 1999).

[25] At the end of 1997, other commercial banks had assets of Rmb 744 billion (US$90 billion) and in 1996, had 3 748 offices and branches, employing 85 505 officers. In 1996 alone, they established 11 new branches, 20 sub-branches and 108 business offices. By contrast, in 1996, the four state commercial banks merged or terminated 6 000 branches (Morgan Stanley Dean Witter, 1998a).

[26] They are the Bank of Communications, CITIC Industrial Bank, Hua Xia Bank, Everbright Bank and China Merchants' Bank.

In addition, China has seven smaller, regionally based banks, including China Minsheng Bank, China's first majority privately-owned local bank. Furthermore, since 1986, Chinese and foreign investors have established eight joint-venture banks to undertake merchant and investment banking and trade financing.

These twelve smaller commercial banks are better placed than the four major banks to build new relationships with the private sector and foreign banks, conduct business more freely, have cleaner balance sheets and have better growth and earnings prospects (Morgan Stanley Dean Witter, 1998a). Some, like CITIB and Everbright are more entrepreneurial, attempting to reach international standards of credit control and accounting transparency. Nevertheless, while many have diversified state owners, almost all still are wholly state owned entities. Many provide directed and connected lending, have weak management and personnel skills, were highly exposed to the 1990s property bubble and, for new banks, have relatively high levels of NPLs. The Hainan Development Bank's closure in 1997 was China's first since 1949.

> **HAINAN DEVELOPMENT BANK CLOSURE**
>
> Established in 1993, the Hainan Development Bank was the first profit-driven bank in China. In June 1998, the PBOC ordered the bank to close. Despite the PBOC injecting Rmb 4 billion, the Hainan Development Bank still was unable to repay its debts of Rmb 14.2 billion, even though its assets were listed as Rmb 13.8 billion. Its poor management and risk control had allowed many of its 70 trust and investment companies to invest in Hainan's volatile real estate market; subsequently, these companies were unable to repay their loans. (*Far Eastern Economic Review*, 16 July 1998, pp. 66-69). In addition, the Government directed the bank to absorb several insolvent urban credit cooperatives before its collapse.

While these smaller banks are disadvantaged vis-a-vis the four state commercial banks due to their small deposit share and limited branch networks, they are a positive force in the Chinese financial sector, often providing better customer service and seeking out viable non-state borrowers.[27]

City Banks

By the end of 1997, the Government had approved 152 city banks, mostly by amalgamating urban credit cooperatives. By 1997, 71 city banks were operating, up from 18 in 1996, and 15 more were preparing to open (*Almanac of China's Finance and Banking*, 1998). Some of these banks may prove useful joint-venture partners for foreign banks.

---

[27] As they cannot exceed the PBOC set 75 per cent loan to deposit ratio, the pace of deposit growth constrains them. The commercial bank law stipulates commercial banks must have minimum registered capital of Rmb 1 billion.

> **SHANGHAI CITY COOPERATIVE BANK**
>
> One of China's best new banks is Shanghai City Cooperative Bank. The International Finance Corporation, IFC, of the World Bank Group plans to invest US$22 million in it, or 5 per cent of equity. The IFC sought its equity investment after the Government asked it to help merge urban credit cooperatives into banks. Premier Zhu Rongji approved IFC's shareholding in 1998. The IFC recognises a very professional group of Shanghaiese managers operates the bank; it is one of a few in China to receive technical assistance from IFC.
>
> While the bank has low NPLs, it is exposed to the Shanghai property bubble. The bank plans to gain international standing, with accounts accepted by the big five accounting firms.
>
> Source: Mackenzie, 1999.

FOREIGN BANKS

China first allowed foreign bank entry in 1982 and by September 1999, 52 foreign banks operated 162 branches throughout China (People's Bank of China, 1999b).[28] ANZ Bank is the only Australian bank with a (foreign currency) banking licence, with branches in Shanghai and Beijing.[29]

While by December 1998, foreign banks' combined assets were only 3 per cent of total bank assets, or US$41.2 billion, they held 16 per cent of financial institutions' foreign exchange assets and undertook 24 per cent of foreign exchange lending (Capital Intelligence, 1999; and People's Bank of China, 1999a).

Between 1991 and 1997, foreign bank lending increased 12 fold, averaging a 47 per cent increase per year, and peaking in December 1997. However, the Asian crisis and growing risk perceptions after the closure of Guangdong International Trust and Investment Company, GITIC caused foreign banks to reduce their Chinese assets and liabilities by approximately 10 per cent since mid 1998 (Figure 12.7).

---

[28] In general, foreign banks must have at least two years' business experience in China as a representative office before they can apply for a licence or establish a branch. The minimum capital requirement for a foreign bank branch is Rmb 300 million and for a joint venture is Rmb 200 million (*Almanac of China's Finance and Banking*, 1998, pp. 363-68). Japanese, US and Hong Kong financial institutions have the greatest presence. Standard Chartered has the largest foreign bank presence with eight branches and eight representative offices.

[29] Commonwealth Bank, Westpac and National Australia Bank have representative offices.

Figure 12.7
Foreign Bank Assets and Liabilities Fall in 1998
Aggregate Balance Sheet of Foreign-funded Banks and Finance Companies, US$ million

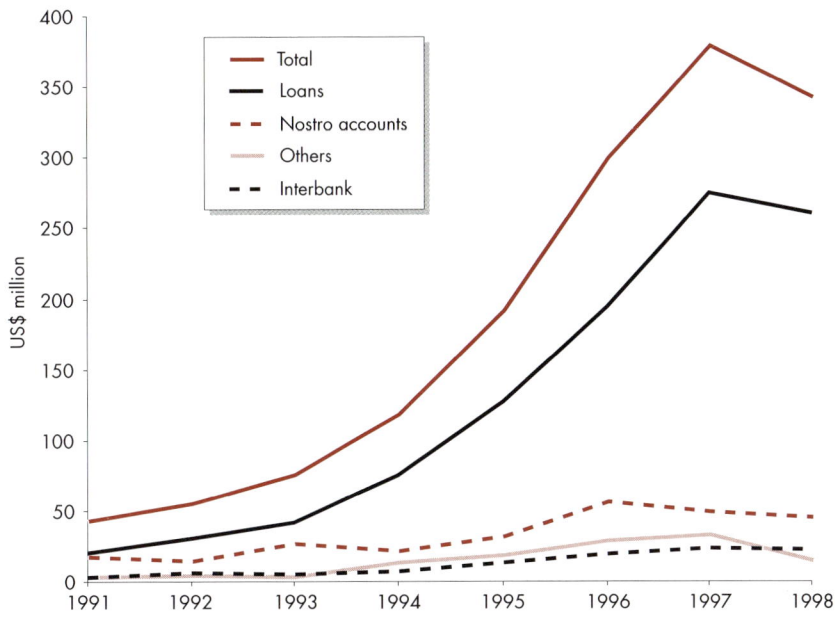

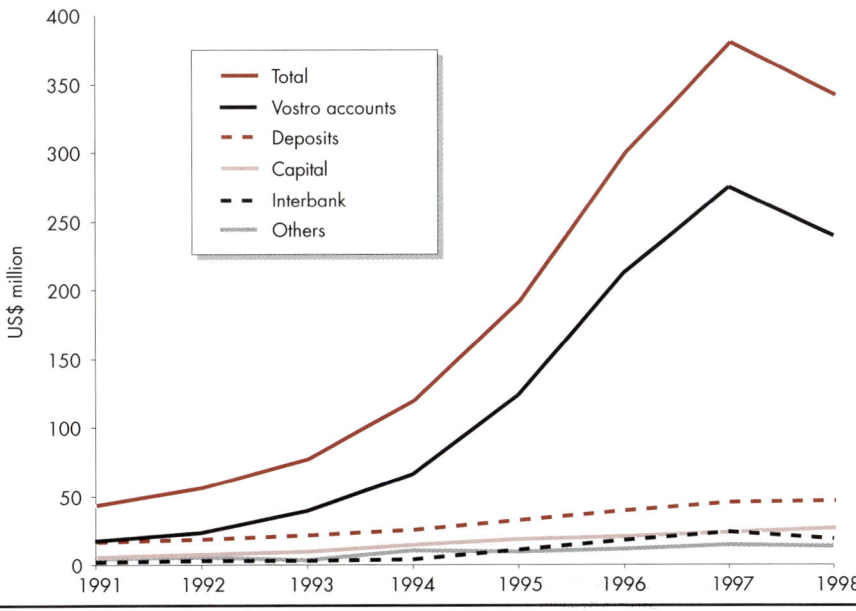

Note: Nostro and vostro accounts refer to financial relationships between the foreign bank and its overseas owner. Interbank assets and liabilities include deposits and lending between banks.
Source: People's Bank of China, 1999b.

The Chinese operations of most foreign banks generate low profits. Most can accept only foreign currency deposits from foreign-funded enterprises and foreign residents; therefore, their deposit base is weak. Parent bank credit largely funds foreign banks' foreign currency loans, but these loans can be extended only to foreign-funded enterprises to invest in fixed assets and finance trade.

However, in 1998 and 1999, a booming business area for foreign banks was to provide letters of credit to guarantee foreign companies' renminbi borrowing from Chinese banks.[30] Because many local banks lack credit allocation experience, they often will not make such loans without foreign bank guarantees, even though borrowers include reputable multinationals (Brown, 1999).

Renminbi Business

Because state owned banks may not survive unrestricted competition from foreign banks, the Government heavily constrains foreign banks' renminbi operations. In April 1997, the Government issued the first nine foreign banks licences to allow limited renminbi business in Pudong, Shanghai. By October 1998, it had granted eight more licences, including some to operate in Shenzhen.

However, foreign banks with renminbi licences only can:

- accept renminbi deposits from registered foreign-invested enterprises and foreign nationals in Shanghai (or Shenzhen)
- lend renminbi to state owned enterprises with foreign currency dealing relationships, registered foreign-invested enterprises in Shanghai (or Shenzhen), and foreign nationals and people from Hong Kong, Macau and Taiwan
- issue guarantees and settle payments
- invest in government treasuries and bonds.[31]

Constraints on deposit raising ability and small branch networks restrict lending.[32] Heavily restricted operations mean few, if any, renminbi licencees make significant profits. In 1998, Royal Bank of Canada handed in its renminbi currency banking licence because of difficulties involved in meeting licence conditions and poor profitability projections.

---

[30] Foreign companies operating in China sought renminbi loans to hedge their renminbi investments in China. For a fee of about 1 per cent of the loan, foreign banks provide letters of credit guaranteeing loans advanced by Chinese state owned banks.

[31] In addition, licencees can only lend renminbi up to 30 per cent of their foreign currency lending and cannot deal in forward contracts.

[32] While licence holders can borrow renminbi from the interbank market, its interest rates are very high, its liquidity is low and its borrowing is short term. In contrast, most bank lending is longer term.

NON-BANK FINANCIAL INSTITUTIONS

Chinese banks' dominance of the financial sector is extreme even by Asian standards; non-bank financial institutions, NBFIs, play a minor role. (See Chapter 4 - *Banking*.) In the past, state owned commercial banks nearly monopolised savings; controls on stock market listings, bond issues and foreign and domestic firms entering sectors like insurance stifled NBFI growth.

However, as controls gradually ease and prudential supervision improves, the role of NBFIs should increase significantly. The Government now acknowledges NBFIs are important in intermediating China's savings and can provide many services state owned enterprises previously supplied.[33] Recognition of the insurance industry's important potential contribution may well have spurred China to include the complete opening of this sector in its World Trade Organisation offer (Li, 1999). NBFI competition also could encourage banking reform, offering customers more efficient personal financial services and the non-state sector better access to loans.

However, poor management and corruption have caused several NBFIs to fail, including domestic and international trust and investment corporations, and rural cooperatives; this could undermine depositor confidence. Most domestic NBFIs are state or collectively owned, and managers usually do not bear the consequences of their poor decisions. Without improved prudential controls, the danger of financial abuse, excessive NPLs and the threat of closure could seriously constrain the sector's potential growth.

At present the three main NBFIs are:

- insurance companies, which over the past ten years have been licensed to compete with the former monopoly provider
- trust and investment companies, which expanded rapidly following bank, enterprise and provincial fiscal reforms in the 1980s and 1990s
- credit cooperatives, which were encouraged after 1949 as collective financial institutions.

INSURANCE COMPANIES

Over the decade to 1997, growth in China's gross insurance premiums averaged 32 per cent per year (Morgan Stanley Dean Witter, 1998b). Industry liberalisation, rapid income growth, increased life expectancy and state owned enterprise efforts to quit their social security provider role drove this rapid growth. By the end of 1998, the total premium income of all domestic insurance companies reached Rmb 124.73 billion (US$15.08 billion), up 15.5 per cent from 1997. Life insurance represented 55 per cent of total premiums (*China Online*, 1999). While the insurance to GDP ratio grew from 0.56 in 1990 to 1.45 in 1997, it remains low compared to other countries, indicating significant growth potential. (See Chapter 6 - *Non-bank Financial Institutions*.)

---

[33] For example, credit cooperatives can provide mortgage finance to develop the private housing market while the insurance industry can provide pension, life, health and accident insurance as well as long term financing for infrastructure projects (Fleisher et al, 1996).

China

Three companies, covering life, general and reinsurance business, created in 1996 from the former state owned monopoly provider, People's Insurance Company of China, PICC, dominate the insurance market (Figure 12.8).[34] The three companies, which only became fully independent in 1998, still hold almost 70 per cent the market. Ping An and China Pacific are other major domestic players. The five largest domestic insurance companies operate in a more favourable regulatory environment than foreign insurers; several can engage in both life and general insurance markets and the PBOC consults them about premium rates. New domestic and foreign insurance companies must operate in either life or property and casualty insurance, not both.

In November 1998, the China Insurance Regulatory Commission replaced the PBOC as the insurance industry's regulator. Foreign participants in the industry regard the commission favourably as it efficiently resolves many regulatory and prudential problems and prevents illicit activities (Wedding, 1999; and Brent, 1999). However, regulations require insurers to invest premiums in fixed rate bank deposits or government bonds, but also to pay policy holders at above prevailing interest rates. This undermines the industry's profitability and growth.

Figure 12.8

Five Companies Dominate Premium Writing
Estimated Gross Premium Market Shares, 1997

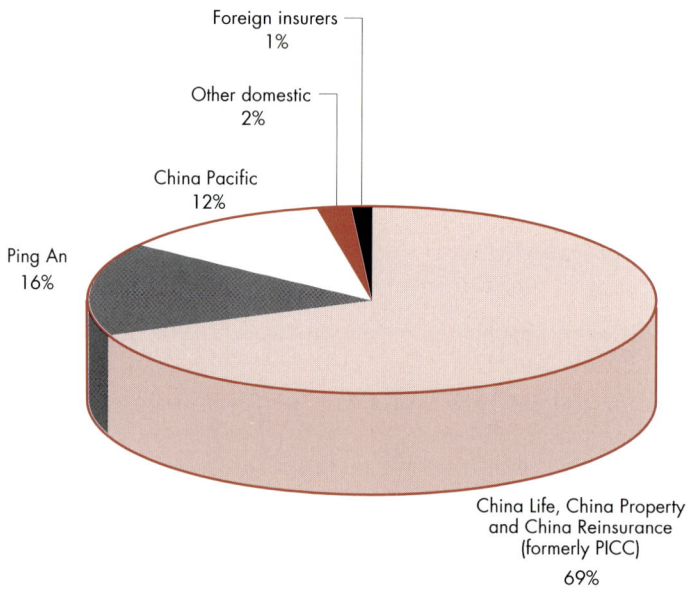

Source: Morgan Stanley Dean Witter, 1998b.

---

[34] In 1998, the three companies were removed from the PICC holding company structure and renamed China Life Insurance, China Property Insurance and China Reinsurance.

PING AN INSURANCE

Established in 1988, Ping An is China's second biggest insurer. It provides a more efficient, cost effective service than the PICC; this enabled it to increase its market share from 0.3 per cent in 1990 to 16 per cent by 1997. Its gross premiums increased from Rmb 59 million to Rmb 17 650 million over the same period, averaging an annual growth rate of 126 per cent.

Lack of a national distribution network constrains Ping An's growth. Hence to diversify its operations, it has developed joint businesses with ten foreign companies. It cooperates with Morgan Stanley and Goldman Sachs on financial strategies; with Lincoln National in life reinsurance and group life reinsurance; with Munich Reinsurance; with Nippon Life for training; and with Taiwan Ming Tai in property insurance.

Source: Morgan Stanley Dean Witter, 1998b.

Foreign-funded Insurance Companies

By the end of 1998, the Government had issued licences to nine foreign insurance companies from eight countries, operating 35 branches; a further 104 foreign insurers had representative offices. In the first half of 1998, the Government issued three additional licences to foreign insurance companies, including Australia's CMG Asia (Ministry of Foreign Trade and Economic Cooperation, 1998).

COLONIAL GROUP IN CHINA

In 1994, as China's financial market opened, CMG Asia, established its first representative office in Beijing, then a second office in Shanghai in 1995. In April 1998, CMG Asia became the first Australian insurer and eighth international life insurer to be offered a licence to establish a life insurance business in Shanghai. In September 1999, it agreed with China Life Insurance Company, China's largest life insurer, to establish this joint-venture business.

CMG Asia manages and partly owns CMG CH China Investments Limited which invests exclusively in Chinese equities listed on the Shanghai and Shenzhen stock exchanges. A Beijing based partnership, CMG Mahon (China) Investment Management Limited, undertakes direct equity investments in Chinese enterprises.

CMG Asia actively supports central and provincial government initiatives to develop China's financial markets. For example, in 1999, CMG Asia jointly sponsored a major review of China's pension system in collaboration with other international insurers and lead government agencies. Other projects provide training assistance and advice on insurance, actuarial and regulatory matters, and business procedures and practices. CMG Asia also cooperates with Australian government initiatives in developing China's financial system. (See Chapter 14 - *Implications*.)

Source: Colonial Mutual Group Asia, 1999.

However, the Government limits direct foreign participation in China's insurance market. Most foreign insurers can operate only in one city, Shanghai, Beijing or Guangzhou, and their business scope is restricted to either life or property and casualty insurance. They cannot sell life insurance on a group basis and must form joint ventures with local insurance companies. In 1997, foreign insurance companies had 8 per cent of the life insurance market and less than 1 per cent of China's total insurance market (China Online, 1999).

However, as part of its World Trade Organisation negotiations, China offered to open the domestic insurance industry to foreign competition over the next five to six years.

> **CHINA WORLD TRADE ORGANISATION ACCESSION: FINANCIAL SERVICES**
>
> China made substantial market access commitments in the financial services sector as part of its in-principle agreement on World Trade Organisation accession reached with Australia in May 1999.
>
> China agreed to:
>
> - liberalise business operating conditions, using more transparent and commercial criteria in approving licences
>
> - phase out discriminatory restrictions on the range of financial services foreign suppliers can provide
>
> - phase out limitations on foreign equity participation in the financial services sector, including removing onerous joint-venture requirements and phasing out internal branch restrictions
>
> - eliminate geographic limits on establishments.
>
> A final multilateral outcome on the liberalisation of China's financial services will depend on full agreement being reached with all of China's World Trade Organisation partners. While China has reached agreement with Japan, China needs to settle with the United States, European Union, Canada and others. When agreement is reached with these partners, China's offers of market access also will be available to Australian industry on a most favoured nation basis.
>
> Source: Department of Foreign Affairs and Trade, 1999.

TRUST AND INVESTMENT COMPANIES

In the 1980s and 1990s, central and provincial governments established trust and investment companies, TICs, and international trust and investment companies, ITICs, to mobilise domestic and international resources to undertake investment projects. Together they hold about 4 per cent of financial sector assets (Figure 12.1). TIC business supposedly is confined to local currency business in China, while ITICs borrow and invest overseas, and hold both renminbi and foreign currency accounts. However, in the past decade, TICs and ITICs have expanded their business beyond their original briefs, accepting deposits and engaging in stock exchange and real estate speculation in China and abroad.[35]

---

[35] As a result of 1995 reforms giving banks more freedom to undertake investments, many banks established TIC and ITIC subsidiaries, commonly called window companies.

Recent ITIC and TIC performance deteriorated because of these speculative activities, compounded by mismanagement, poor internal controls, fraud, weak supervision and falling mainland Chinese and Hong Kong real estate and share prices. TICs and ITICs now are barred from engaging in securities business and competing with banks for deposits; their overseas activities also are under close scrutiny. They no longer can borrow abroad or invest in real estate and insurance, and many have been restructured, merged or closed.[36] Consequently, many are being forced to explore new business options including investment banking (Morgan Stanley Dean Witter, 1998b).

THE GITIC CLOSURE

GITIC was one of China's largest ITICs and the Guangdong Government's largest financial institution. GITIC was established in 1980, and its history reflects that of many other ITICs, if on a larger scale.[37] In January 1999, the Government officially declared GITIC bankrupt and injected Rmb 20 billion into GITIC assets so more than 25 000 individual Chinese depositors and creditors could have their deposits repaid. However, overseas creditors were not given priority in repayment, even if their loans were registered with the State Administration of Foreign Exchange. Foreign creditors reacted negatively to this announcement.

Many foreign creditors believe the GITIC closure raises fundamental questions about the credibility of major Chinese institutions, including provincial governments and the quality of audited accounts.[38]

Since GITIC, foreign investors have been uncertain about how to assess Chinese enterprises' credit risk. Poor accounting standards, inadequate transparency and foreclosure laws, and a generally weak legal framework make it difficult to undertake normal commercial risk-based lending. While most foreign bankers agree lending will continue at some level, because China is 'too big to ignore', many are cutting back their exposure to China. This particularly applies to ITICs and other financial institutions, as foreign bankers consider it too difficult to assess their loan portfolios.

---

[36] In 1996, then Vice Premier Zhu Rongji closed 130 ITICs; in 1997, the China Agribusiness Trust and Development Corporation failed; and in June 1998, China Venturetech Investment Corporation was closed. In February 1999, five other ITICs of national banks were closed mainly due to lack of business and bank restructuring plans (*South China Morning Post*, 3 February 1999; and Reuters, 2 February 1999).

[37] GITIC's initial startup capital of Rmb 200 million grew 100 fold between 1980 and 1995. By 1996, it had total assets of Rmb 21.4 billion and a net profit of Rmb 160 million. However, its profit dropped by 80 per cent in the first half of 1998. Of the Rmb 36.2 billion in liabilities, Rmb 15.9 billion was owed to foreign creditors, with another Rmb 14.7 billion in contingent liability guarantees to foreign companies (*South China Morning Post*, 11 January 1999).

[38] Although the Government indicated in 1994 that provincial government letters of comfort to ITICs' creditors had no legal standing, many of GITIC's foreign creditors believed its foreign borrowing carried an implicit government guarantee. They maintain the Guangdong Government encouraged them in this belief. The 1997 audited accounts of GITIC showed assets of US$2.7 billion: in January 1999, assets were given as US$2.5 billion but by April 1999, they were only US$700 000. Creditors were seriously concerned by this lack of transparency and were unsure if asset stripping had occurred or if accounts were faulty.

Following the October 1998 closures of GITIC, and Guangdong Development Enterprises, a window company incorporated in Hong Kong, the Government has further tightened ITIC accounting and reporting procedures, and strengthened prudential control.

The run of ITIC closures led to concerns about the ability of other ITICs to repay their estimated US$6.8 billion in foreign debt (*Hong Kong Economic Times*, 21 October 1998). Both Moody's and Standard and Poors downgraded ITIC credit ratings. At a central bank conference in October 1998, the Government indicated all 242 ITICs had bad loans and needed to rectify their internal operations by March 1999. It subsequently announced plans to restructure the whole sector, reducing ITIC numbers from 240 to 40 institutions. Foreign investors were warned not to lend money to bankrupt institutions and new loans have been delayed.

CREDIT COOPERATIVES

China's largest NBFIs are urban and rural credit cooperatives; in 1998, they held 10 per cent of financial sector assets (Figure 12.1).[39] Urban credit cooperatives provide finance to urban non-state enterprises including town and village enterprises, urban collectives and private and individual enterprises. Rural credit cooperatives have four times more assets and account for about 20 per cent of household deposits, often providing rural communities with their only financial services.[40]

In the 1990s, poor management, declining profitability of township and village enterprises, controlled interest rates, high operating costs and occasional fraud undermined cooperatives' performance. Hence, since 1994, the Government has attempted to restructure cooperatives, merging many weaker institutions with stronger ones to create city banks and county level rural credit cooperatives, and strengthen their prudential supervision.[41] However, the sector remains weak and, if defaults became more widespread, is a potential local source of social instability.[42]

CAPITAL MARKETS

Developing deeper and more flexible capital markets so firms can directly tap them for funds is an important means of increasing China's growth potential and would help reduce the banks' near monopoly on savings and corporate funding options. The Shanghai and Shenzhen securities markets trade government and finance bonds, corporate shares and small volumes of corporate bonds. However, China's relatively undeveloped capital markets do not yet provide credible alternative savings vehicles for savers or reliable sources of enterprise financing. Nonetheless, the Government

---

[39] By the end of 1998, urban credit cooperatives had around 3 200 offices employing nearly 145 000 officers and assets of Rmb 392 billion (US$47 billion) (*Almanac of Finance and Banking*, 1998; and Capital Intelligence, 1999).

[40] By the third quarter of 1998, rural credit cooperatives had assets of Rmb 1 054 billion (US$127 billion), 49 692 offices and 648 613 officers.

[41] In 1996, to strengthen prudential supervision, rural credit cooperatives ceased their administrative relationship with the Agricultural Bank of China and were placed under PBOC control.

[42] For example, to accelerate its campaign to strengthen the cooperative sector, the Government closed 12 small credit cooperatives in the city of Beihai, Guangxi in October 1998 (*South China Morning Post*, 30 October 1998).

recognises capital market development will improve corporate governance, so capital market reform is on the agenda. Introduction of the new securities law in mid 1999 is an important development for capital market growth.

STOCK MARKETS

Stock market turnover and capitalisation have grown rapidly since the mid 1990s, particularly in Shanghai (Figure 12.9) However, per capita capitalisation is still small compared to many economies.[43] After an Asian crisis induced downturn in 1998, new listings expanded again after mid 1999 with passage of the new securities law and government policies to promote stock market investment.

While non-state enterprises listed on the stock exchange for the first time in 1999, listing procedures lack transparency.[44] Because the Government fears excessive new listings will depress prices, State Council sets a listing quota for each province.

Figure 12.9

Strong Growth in Share Markets since Mid 1990s
Turnover and Market Capitalisation of Shenzen and Shanghai Stock Exchanges, 1995-99

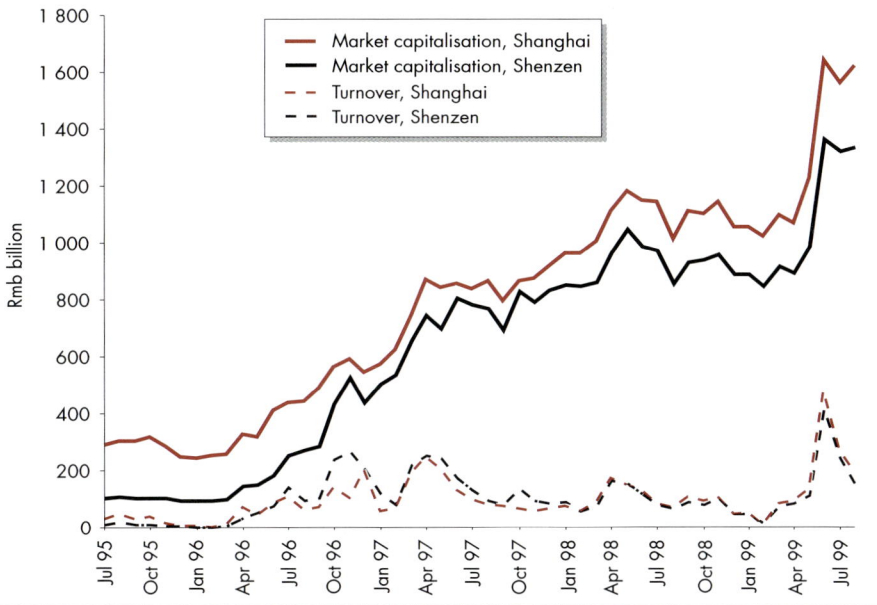

Source: CEIC, 1999.

[43] In December 1997, market capitalisation reached 10.5 per cent of GDP, up from only 7.2 per cent in December 1996. At the end of 1998, 865 companies were listed (*Almanac of China's Finance and Banking*, 1998, p. 63). (See Figure 5.3 in Chapter 5 - *Capital Markets*.)

[44] The new securities law implemented in mid 1999 supposedly formalises criteria by which new firms may list, reducing government discretion. However, the Government will vet and ration listings for the foreseeable future (Yan, 1999).

However, listing enterprises can make huge financial gains, so listed firms can be required to subsidise loss making companies in return for being allowed to list. Sometimes loss makers can list to get funds to solve problems, although this is not supposed to occur.

Shares in Chinese enterprises are not freely traded but segmented into three categories:

- A-shares are ordinary shares denominated in renminbi and traded only by domestic legal entities, enterprises and individuals
- B-shares are settled in foreign currencies only by foreign investors, including Chinese in Hong Kong, Macau and Taiwan
- H-shares are issued in Hong Kong by mainland Chinese registered enterprises; in addition a few shares are listed in New York and other international exchanges.

This segmentation prevents foreign sentiment about the state of China's economy being transmitted through the share market to the renminbi. B-share sellers cannot quit the market until they find a foreign buyer willing to pay foreign currency for their shares (Lardy, 1998b). However, this isolation results in a shallow and volatile market for B-shares (Figure 12.10). Hence local individual investors have fuelled most of the growth in the two local exchanges.

Figure 12.10

Turnover in B-shares Plunged in Late 1997
Turnover in B-shares in Shanghai and Shenzen, 1995-99

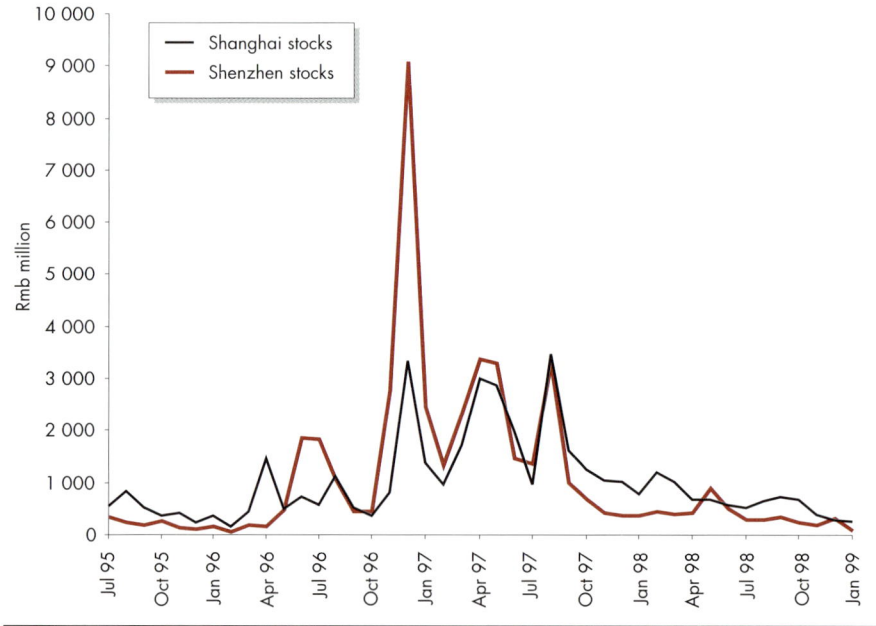

Source: CEIC, 1999.

Security Market Regulation

Once fully implemented, the new security law, effective since 1 July 1999 will move China closer to international best practice, providing a sound legal basis for future capital market development. The law was passed after nearly ten years of debate, reflecting a new political consensus that shareholding companies have a legitimate role in the economy (Chan, 1999). The new law:

- establishes one national organisation, China Securities Regulatory Commission, CSRC, responsible for all capital market regulation

- applies standard disclosure and other criteria to all listing enterprises

- requires listed securities be traded in approved securities exchanges, and cleared and settled through approved clearing houses

- requires all stock market intermediaries be licensed under specified standards, including meeting minimum capital requirements and maintaining an 8 per cent capital adequacy ratio

- places responsibility for due diligence with company officers and all professionals involved in disclosure

- forbids insider trading and market manipulation[45]

- grants the regulator power to investigate possible breaches, but ensures decisions must be supported and are subject to court review.[46]

The China Securities Regulatory Commission will find implementing these regulations challenging, but the new unified structure will assist in this task (Heytens, 1999).[47]

BOND MARKETS

Through 1998 and 1999, government bond issues grew rapidly, driven by the Government's large fiscal stimulus package, which was financed by domestic bond issues. By the end of 1998, outstanding government bonds reached around Rmb 900 billion (US$108 billion); new bond issues in 1999 should exceed Rmb 400 billion, up from around Rmb 250 billion in 1998. The increasing volume and maturity range of government bonds will deepen and develop the bond market,

---

[45] The new securities law defines insider trading but while the CSRC set up a body to investigate this in 1998, it is still deciding how to monitor insider trading. The CSRC started prosecutions in 1998 but penalties are light by western standards, where jail terms are the norm. If convicted, offending Chinese securities companies face losing their licence for up to a year, while individuals face being banned from securities trading for life. The Shanghai office of CSRC had made no prosecutions by mid 1999 (Yan, 1999).

[46] In addition, re-centralising local and provincial security company control and management, and province and central government stock management committees should reduce market manipulation and insider trading (State Information Centre, 1998).

[47] By replacing the previous overlapping sets of regulations with a separate and unified regulatory authority, enforcement should be easier (Heytens, 1999). In July 1999, CSRC took over provincial securities administrations, including the Shanghai Securities and Futures Regulatory Office. Since July, the CSRC has been able to prosecute offenders under the securities law and sentence them to up to five years' imprisonment (Yan, 1999).

providing benchmark yields for corporate bonds.[48] China established an interbank bond market in 1997 to allow secondary trading in long term government securities, including treasury bonds, central bank bonds and bonds issued by the policy banks.[49]

Compared to the government bond market, China's corporate bond market is relatively small. In 1998, new corporate bond issues were only Rmb 15 billion, 6 per cent of government bond issues. Corporate bonds also are much less important than share issues in funding enterprises (Figure 12.11). Government regulations tightly control corporate bond issues and mainly limit them to selected large, state owned enterprises and utilities.[50] Institutional investors are prohibited from holding and trading corporate bonds; this also restricts the market's growth (Cai, 1999).

Figure 12.11

Corporate Bonds Lag Behind Shares' Growth
Enterprise Shares and Corporate Bonds Issued 1995-98

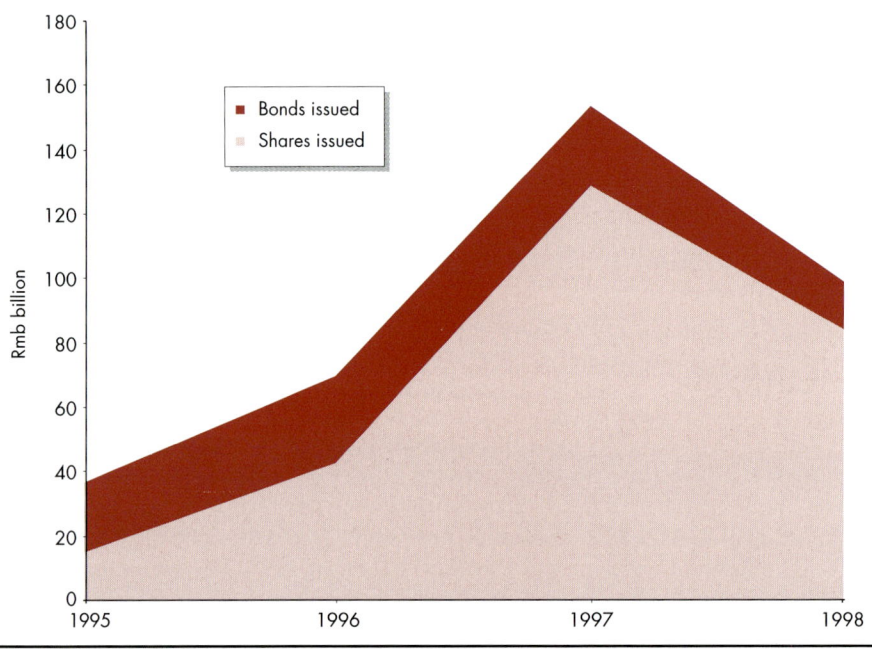

Source: Moody's Investor Services, 1999.

[48] However, many recently issued bonds are non-marketable or held by buyers to maturity, constraining liquidity. In 1996, the Government auctioned bonds, but since then, the numbers of marketable securities has fallen.

[49] The Central Bond Registration and Settlement Company manages the interbank market (China Online, 1998).

[50] Issuers in 1999 included the Ministry of Railways, Three Gorges Dam Company, and Hongqiao Airport. In the past, smaller state owned enterprises issued bonds to their employees to raise funds, but recently, the Government restricted such issues due to concerns about abuse. Private enterprises are not yet permitted to issue bonds.

PROSPECTS FOR FOREIGN FINANCIAL INSTITUTIONS

The Government wants to protect domestic financial institutions from unconstrained foreign competition until state owned enterprises are successfully reformed and local financial institutions can compete. However, it is continuing financial sector liberalisation, and opening up to foreign financial institutions will proceed at a pace consistent with the economy's needs and domestic firms' capacity to compete. In terms of the opportunities it will give international financial institutions, financial market opening is an important part of China's ongoing World Trade Organisation accession negotiations. Insurance and banking are the major areas of international interest at present, but pension fund management, home mortgage securitisation, loan syndication and related legal, debt workout, accounting and financial services are all areas of high potential financial service export growth as financial markets continue to open. For example, Macquarie Bank has initiated an innovative home mortgage securitisation project with China Construction Bank. (See Chapter 5 - *Capital Markets*.)

Until full liberalisation, financial sector joint ventures are likely to continue to be important. By strengthening domestic institutions via knowledge and experience transfer, joint ventures should increase the pace of reform.

CONCLUSIONS

The major Chinese financial institutions are burdened by high NPL ratios, excess and relatively low calibre staff, and weak management systems. As well, risk assessment and disclosure still are major problems.

Nevertheless, financial sector reform now is a high priority and is underway. The Government is strengthening prudential regulation and supervision, and allowing increased domestic and foreign competition. Joint ventures are introducing new skills and systems. Most importantly, the Government has acknowledged it must fund a write-off of at least some bank NPLs. As these issues are resolved, opening of China's financial markets should make more headway.

REFERENCES

Almanac of China's Finance and Banking, 1998, English edition, Almanac of China's Finance and Banking Editor Board, Beijing.

___ 1997, English edition, Almanac of China's Finance and Banking Editor Board, Beijing.

Brent, C., 1999, East Asia Analytical Unit interview with Chief Representative, Colonial Mutual Group, Beijing Representative Office, Beijing, June.

Brown, L., 1999, East Asia Analytical Unit interview with Chief Executive, Standard Chartered Bank, Shanghai, May.

Cai Zhiwei, 1999, East Asia Analytical Unit interview with Chief Economist, Department of International Finance, China Development Bank, Beijing, May.

Capital Intelligence, 1999, 'People's Republic of China: National Banking Environment', Cyprus.

Chan, K., 1999, East Asia Analytical Unit interview with Head of Greater China Economic Research, Nomura International, Hong Kong, May.

CEIC, 1999, CEIC Database, Hong Kong, supplied by EconData, Canberra.

China Online, 1999, 'China's Financial Services Industry', www.chinaonline.com, accessed on 10 October.

___ 1998, 'The Central Bond Registration and Settlement Company', www.chinaonline.com.

Colonial Mutual Group Asia, 1999, Information supplied to the East Asia Analytical Unit by Colonial Mutual Group, CMG Asia, Melbourne, August.

Department of Foreign Affairs and Trade, 1999, China's World Trade Organisation Accession, Trade Negotiations Division, Canberra.

East Asia Analytical Unit, 1997, *China Embraces the Market - Achievements, Constraints and Opportunities*, Department of Foreign Affairs and Trade, Canberra.

Feng, Yushu, 1999, East Asia Analytical Unit interview with the Adviser, International Division, Ministry of Finance, Beijing, May.

Fleisher, B., Yong, Yin and Hills, S., 1996, *The Role of Housing Privatization and Labor-Market Reform in China's Dual Economy*, Department of Economics, Ohio State University, Columbus.

Geng, Qun, 1999, East Asia Analytical Unit interview with Director, Institute of International Finance, Bank of China, Beijing, May.

Heytens, P., 1999, East Asia Analytical Unit interview with Deputy Resident Representative, International Monetary Fund, Beijing, May.

Krumm, K., 1999, East Asia Analytical Unit interview with Lead Economist for China, The World Bank Resident Mission, Beijing, June.

Lardy, N.R., 1998a, *China's Unfinished Revolution*, Brookings Institution Press, Washington DC.

___ 1998b, 'China and the Asian Contagion', *Foreign Affairs*, vol. 77, no. 4, July/August, pp. 78-88.

Li, Kui-Wai, 1999, East Asia Analytical Unit interview with Associate Professor, Department of Economics and Finance, City University of Hong Kong, Hong Kong, May.

Ma, Guonan, 1999, East Asia Analytical Unit interview with Vice President, Merrill Lynch (Asia Pacific) Limited, Hong Kong, May.

Mackenzie, D., 1999, East Asia Analytical Unit interview with Chief of Mission, International Finance Corporation Resident Mission in the People's Republic of China, Beijing, May.

Meng, Xin and Perkins, F.C., 1999, 'Wage Determination Differences between Chinese State and Non-state Firms', *Asian Economic Journal*, vol. 12, no. 3, pp. 295-316.

Ministry of Foreign Trade and Economic Cooperation, 1998, *Foreign Trade Research* (in Chinese), vol. 19, no. 1091, 1 July, Beijing.

Moody's Investor Services, 1999, 'Banking System Outlook: China', New York.

Morgan Stanley Dean Witter, 1998a, 'Financial System Reform: the Journey Has Just Begun', *China: Financial Services*, 2 February, Hong Kong, p. 11.

___ 1998b, 'China Finance Workshop', *China: Financial Services*, 9 March, Hong Kong, p. 2.

People's Bank of China, 1999a, *Quarterly Statistical Bulletin*, various issues.

___ 1999b, *China Financial Outlook 1998*, Beijing.

State Information Centre, 1998, *Finance Express* (in Chinese), no. 119-121, 16, 23 and 30 October, Beijing.

Wang, Haijun, 1999, East Asia Analytical Unit interview with Director International Division, Xinda Asset Management Company, Beijing, May.

Wedding, I., 1999, East Asia Analytical Unit interview with Chief Representative Beijing, AMP, Beijing, June.

Woo, Wing-Thye, 1998, 'China', Country Profile in Sachs, J. and Woo, Wing-Thye (eds), *Asian Competitiveness Report*, prepared for the World Economic Summit at Davos.

Yan, Xu, 1999, East Asia Analytical Unit interview with Deputy Director of New Issues Department, Shanghai Securities and Futures Regulatory Office, China Securities Regulatory Commission, May.

Ziegler, D., 1999, East Asia Analytical Unit interview with Chief Correspondent, *Economist*, Beijing, May.

China

Chapter 13

KOREA

Highly leveraged firms, a banking sector inexperienced in managing risk and poor prudential regulation and supervision mainly caused Korea's 1997-98 financial crisis. A lack of transparency in government foreign exchange management and corporate accounting disguised these problems, exacerbating the crisis. During the mid 1990s boom, easy access to bank finance resulted in the *chaebol*, Korea's corporate conglomerates, over borrowing and over investing, and financial institutions seeking short term foreign borrowing to fund reckless lending. By December 1997, the financial system faced collapse, necessitating prompt government and IMF action. Consequently, significant financial sector reform was one of the Government's key policy responses to the crisis.[1]

This chapter examines the causes of Korea's financial sector weakness and analyses how major market opening and regulatory reforms have strengthened the sector. It examines the structure of the reshaped financial system, measures to liberalise and deepen capital markets, foreign financial institutions' prospects in this new environment, and the outlook for ongoing financial sector recovery and reform.

PRE-CRISIS FINANCIAL MARKET MANAGEMENT

Except for the serious 1980 crisis, official financial sector intervention and protection did not constrain Korea's expanding industrial capacity until the mid 1990s.[2] However, government intervention eventually undermined the financial sector's market orientation, maturation and ultimately, its viability.

Despite some piecemeal reforms in the 1980s, financial market opening did not begin in earnest until 1993. Until the early 1990s, the Government strictly regulated interest rates and directly allocated credit. High domestic entry barriers, a virtual prohibition on foreign financial institution entry and strict market segmentation limited the sector's initiative, profitability and flexibility. Even in 1993, the Government's reform plan involved only gradually opening financial markets over the next ten years. The Government liberalised short term capital inflows but continued to restrict longer term financial inflows. Furthermore, financial liberalisation occurred without the Government simultaneously strengthening prudential standards or improving enforcement.

---

[1] This chapter draws extensively on Chapter 8 - *Financial Market Management and Reform* in the East Asia Analytical Unit's recent report on the Korean economy, *Korea Rebuilds: from Crisis to Opportunity*, 1999.

[2] Real GDP grew by an average annual rate of around 9 per cent in 1961-91, with per capita income doubling every seven years.

Implicit government guarantees that banks would not fail created pervasive moral hazard problems, encouraging financial institutions to take excessive risks, particularly in lending to the *chaebol*.[3] Korea's over exposure to short term external debt made it particularly vulnerable to cyclical shocks and changes in market expectations.

In this environment, contagion from South East Asia's financial crisis, yen depreciation, falling terms of trade and bankruptcies among leading *chaebol* triggered Korea's crisis. From mid 1997, international creditors began to reduce their exposure to Korean financial institutions, refusing to roll over short term loans amid growing concerns about the soundness of major corporates and the financial system. *Chaebol* bankruptcies weakened the balance sheets of financial institutions. Many corporates and financial institutions, like the merchant banks, had high unhedged exposure to foreign borrowing. Eventually, with rapidly shrinking reserves, the market lost confidence in the Korean Government's capacity to contain the financial crisis and effectively manage the economy. Non-performing loan, NPL, levels rose rapidly, reducing banks' capital adequacy to below acceptable levels and threatening systemic stability.

POST-CRISIS FINANCIAL SECTOR REFORM

In December 1997, the new Kim Dae-jung Government's first priority was to avoid systemic collapse by guaranteeing depositors' investments, closing and merging unviable institutions, purchasing their NPLs and recapitalising financial institutions. As part of the IMF stabilisation package, the Government also upgraded prudential standards and passed financial sector reform legislation that throughout 1997 had stalled in the National Assembly. These reform bills significantly liberalised Korea's financial sector, lifting most of the legislative framework to international standards.

In early 1998, the Government established a new Financial Supervisory Commission to oversee financial sector restructuring and take over responsibility for prudential supervision from the Bank of Korea. The Government also revamped the Korea Asset Management Corporation and Korea Deposit Insurance Corporation to clean up financial institution balance sheets and help them recapitalise.

To minimise the burden on taxpayers and moral hazard risk, the Government's fiscal support for distressed institutions depended on their plans to restructure, cut costs and recapitalise. Shareholders, management and employees all shared the financial burden and responsibility of restructuring.

The Government recognised foreign participation would assist recapitalisation, financial institution efficiency and corporate governance. From April 1998, it allowed 100 per cent foreign ownership of banks and hostile takeovers of financial institutions.[4]

---

[3] The Government averted periodic bankruptcy of large enterprises by directing banks to provide relief loans or reschedule debt. To avert bank insolvency, the Bank of Korea compensated commercial banks for some losses through subsidised rediscounts. Implicit government guarantees that banks would not be allowed to fail meant banks took lending risks, while a generous deposit insurance scheme effectively removed the need for depositors to monitor the health of their banks (Smith, 1998).

[4] The general banking law was revised to ease limits on non-residents' bank shareholdings. See *Prospects for Foreign Financial Institutions* later in this chapter.

> **KEY REFINANCING AND REFORM MEASURES**
>
> *Recapitalising NPLs*: since December 1997, the Korean Government has mobilised Won 64 trillion to recapitalise and resolve NPLs held by weak but potentially viable financial institutions.
>
> *Improving financial supervision*: the Financial Supervisory Commission raised capital adequacy ratios and NPL categorisation to international standards. It took over the responsibilities and staff of several supervisory institutions, and can implement standard 'prompt corrective action' when necessary.[5]
>
> *Improving the credit system and culture*: banks established specialised credit rating units, and credit extension generally now depends on debt servicing capacity. Banks will not be bailed out if they fail to meet capital requirements.
>
> *Developing capital markets and infrastructure*: improving the government bond issuing system has deepened the bond market and helped develop benchmark interest rates in the financial market. New initiatives such as mutual funds will deepen the capital market.
>
> *Opening financial markets to international competition*: the Government removed virtually all restrictions on international entry into Korean banking, insurance, funds management and securities industries; this should improve significantly the sector's long term efficiency.
>
> Source: Ministry of Finance and Economy, 1999a.

BANK RESTRUCTURING

Since introducing the IMF stabilisation package in December 1997, the Korean Government has taken major steps to restructure the banking system. Before the crisis, Korea had 33 banking organisations, including 26 commercial banks that accounted for more than half the financial sector's total assets (Table 13.1). Within a month of introducing the IMF package, the Government had injected public funds to nationalise two commercial banks, Korea First and Seoul Banks, and closed 16 merchant banks.

In early 1998, the Government began to restructure the remaining banks using transparent criteria, including bank capital adequacy ratios. The Financial Supervisory Commission required all commercial banks to prepare rehabilitation plans, including plans for capital enhancement. Then after reviewing these plans in mid 1998, it ordered five more commercial banks to close. Relatively sound banks took over the assets and liabilities of the closed banks through purchase and assumption, assisted by more public capital injections.[6] Other undercapitalised

---

[5] A prompt corrective action system imposes a series of obligatory corrective measures on unsound financial institutions.

[6] The acquiring banks were selected because they were financially sound (with a capital adequacy ratio of 10 per cent or higher), could re-capitalise the acquired bank through equity issues and alliances with foreign strategic partners, and could improve the management of the target bank.

Table 13.1

Significant Progress in Financial Restructuring

Post-crisis Status of Korea's Bank and Non-bank Financial Institutions

	Share of total assets December 1997 (per cent)	Total institutions December 1997	Resolution			Total institutions August 1999
			Licences revoked	Merged	Liquidated	
Commercial banks	54	26a	5	5	-	16b
Merchant banks	9	30	17	2	-	11
Insurance companies	12	50	4	1	-	45
Securities companies	4	36	5	-	1	32c
Investment trust companies	11	31	2	-	5	24
Leasing companies	4	25	-	-	5	22c
Mutual savings	4	231	25	5	-	201
Credit unions	2	1 666	72	44	59	1 499c
Total	100	2 095	130	57	70	1 850

Note: a Excludes trust accounts.

b Four of these banks have been nationalised, Seoul Bank, Korea First Bank, Hanvit Bank and Chohung Bank.

c Two new leasing companies, two securities companies and eight credit unions were established over the period.

Source: Financial Supervisory Commission, 1999.

banks were merged or acquired; staff were laid off; and branches closed. Restructuring resulted in three important commercial bank mergers in 1998 and further mergers continued throughout 1999.[7]

NON-BANK FINANCIAL INSTITUTION RESTRUCTURING

The Government takes a similar approach to restructuring non-bank financial institutions, strictly applying prompt corrective action procedures. It first encourages majority shareholders' rehabilitation efforts but where institutions are non-viable because liabilities exceed assets or losses are excessive, they are liquidated or sold to third parties (Ministry of Finance and Economy, 1998).

[7] As part of the process, in September 1998, Boram Bank announced a merger with Hana Bank, the first merger between two viable banking institutions. Then Kookmin Bank and Korea Long Term Credit Bank also announced a voluntary merger. Of the four big banks, the Commercial Bank of Korea and Hanil Bank merged in early 1999 (becoming the Hanvit Bank). Of the other two large banks, Chohung had to rehabilitate itself through either foreign capital participation or merger. In December 1998, Chohung, Kangwon and Hyundai International Merchant Banks agreed to merge and create a new bank by March 1999. Subsequently, Chungbuk Bank was added as a merger partner. The Financial Supervisory Commission also ordered the Korea Exchange Bank to increase its capitalisation while continuing to look for merger opportunities.

By August 1999, the Government had closed or suspended over 250 bank and non-bank financial institutions, including 19 merchant banks, five insurance companies, six securities firms, 30 mutual savings and finance companies, and 175 credit unions (Table 13.1).

Insurance Companies

At the end of 1997, Korea had 33 domestic and foreign life insurance companies and 14 non-life companies. In August 1998, the Government closed four non-viable life insurance companies, and in March 1999, named other weak companies that had to close or merge. Sixteen insurers are being rehabilitated.[8] A new international auction will be held for Korea Life Insurance, Korea's third largest insurer.[9]

In March 1999, the Government extended to insurance, banking regulations on capital adequacy, loan classification, provisioning of large exposures, connected lending and disclosure. The Government aimed to complete insurer restructuring by mid 1999 but investor concerns about possibly hidden liabilities in insurance company balance sheets delayed this timetable.

Other Non-bank Financial Institutions

Securities, investment trusts, investment management, leasing, mutual savings, credit unions and finance companies also suffered major crisis induced losses and required financial restructuring. The Government plans to complete the restructuring of all non-bank financial institutions, except investment trust companies, by July 2000. A measure already taken includes introducing capital adequacy requirements for securities firms, similar to those for banks and other non-bank financial institutions. The Financial Supervisory Commission determined eight of Korea's 34 securities companies were unsound; it liquidated six and the rest are being rehabilitated.

The Government initially planned to restructure domestic investment trust companies from July 2000. However, it may accelerate the timetable because many of these companies are heavily exposed to the Daewoo group's financial problems.

COST OF FINANCIAL SECTOR RESTRUCTURING

The Government will use public funds equal to around 16 per cent of 1998 GDP to purchase NPLs, and recapitalise and restructure weak institutions.[10] Along with fiscal expansion to stimulate the economy, this recapitalisation will raise national debt from the pre-crisis level of 18 per cent to around 48 per cent of GDP in 2002. However, the Government and IMF believe this debt level is manageable because Korea's public debt burden was low at the start of the crisis.

[8] Korea Deposit Insurance Corporation will inject Won 1.2 trillion to recapitalise Seoul Guarantee Insurance.

[9] The Financial Supervisory Commission had earlier disqualified four 'first round' contenders, including foreign bidders. In addition, the Financial Supervisory Commission will accept bids from domestic and foreign investors for five other ailing insurance companies.

[10] The fiscal cost of dealing with NPLs depends on the pace of economic recovery, interest rates, Korea Asset Management Corporation's discount on the face value of NPLs, the time Korea Asset Management Corporation holds the impaired assets and their final selling price. Recouping recapitalisation costs will depend on how long it takes to re-privatise commercial banks, through government sales of its shares in nationalised banks.

By the end of 1998, the Government had spent Won 58 trillion (US$48 billion) or 14 per cent of 1998 GDP on purchasing NPLs, recapitalising financial institutions and honouring deposit insurance. By early 1999, the Government estimated it would need to spend between Won 64 trillion and Won 74 trillion (US$53 billion and US$62 billion) to complete financial sector restructuring.[11]

The Government aims to recoup the costs of purchasing NPLs and recapitalising financial institutions by selling collateralised assets and divesting itself of financial institution equity. Nonetheless, interest on the bonds issued to finance the financial sector's rescue still could cost the Government an average Won 10 trillion to Won 12 trillion per year, or 1.8 to 2 per cent of 1998 GDP.[12] If NPL disposal and recapitalisation costs are higher than expected, which is possible following Daewoo's dismantling, the Government could mobilise additional funds by selling assets held by the Korea Asset Management Corporation[13] and issuing asset-backed securities. The Korea Deposit Insurance Corporation also could dispose of acquired equities and bond issues.

PRUDENTIAL REGULATION AND SUPERVISION REFORM

In the 1990s, Korea's prudential regulation and supervision systems failed to keep pace with economic growth and the liberalisation and globalisation of Korea's financial markets. As financial institutions' loan portfolios weakened, monitoring guidelines and procedures were inadequate. Before the financial crisis, Korean financial institutions had serious currency and maturity mismatches in their external liabilities and domestic assets. They also were excessively exposed to individual borrowers, particularly the heavily leveraged *chaebol* whose financial viability had been in doubt since 1996.

In May 1998, the Government brought Korea's financial sector prudential regulations in line with international best practice, detailed in the Basle Committee's *Principles for Effective Bank Supervision*. The Government's new best practice accounting and disclosure standards started operating on 1 January 1999.[14]

Prudential reforms included:

- stricter review of financial institutions' capital adequacy, which was raised to the Bank for International Settlements' standard of 8 per cent

- tighter exposure control, including mandatory guidelines for maturity matching and country exposure

---

[11] According to government estimates, this should purchase around Won 70 trillion to Won 80 trillion of NPLs, assuming the purchase price is around 45 per cent of the nominal book value, and provide funds for recapitalisation and deposit insurance of around Won 32.5 trillion.

[12] The 1998 budget estimated interest costs associated with financial restructuring would be Won 3.6 trillion, while the draft 1999 budget estimated this cost at Won 7.7 trillion, 1.8 per cent of projected GDP. At a 12 per cent interest rate, annual interest costs could increase to Won 12 trillion by 2003 (2 per cent of GDP) before public funds associated with financial restructuring are fully recovered.

[13] The Korea Asset Management Corporation plans to sell US$13.3 billion of NPLs in 1999. It plans to dispose of 98 per cent of purchased NPLs by 2003 (Korea Asset Management Corporation, 1999).

[14] Provisions also covered rules on connected lending, inter-subsidiary cross guarantees, foreign exchange liquidity and exposures, and the treatment of trust accounts.

- tougher loan classification and provisioning guidelines[15]
- stronger prompt corrective action for distressed institutions[16]
- stronger in-house risk management systems
- a more transparent accounting system with tighter accounting practices and disclosure rules meeting international standards
- enforced liquidity management of foreign exchange risk
- more transparent treatment of trust accounts (Financial Supervisory Commission, 1998).

The Government also relaxed or abolished many restrictions on financial businesses to encourage competition and managerial innovation. However, some important restrictions and regulations continue to constrain financial sector competition and growth (AMCHAM, 1999).

CAPITAL MARKET DEVELOPMENTS

Deepening the equity, bond and money markets is central to overall financial market reform and restructuring. Liberalising and deepening capital markets will increase Korea's access to foreign capital and new financial sector technology, providing more financial instruments to diversify or absorb risks.

Capital Market Liberalisation

In 1998 and 1999, major reforms affecting capital markets included:

- liberalising foreign direct investment and eliminating the ceiling on foreign equity ownership[17]
- permitting hostile mergers and acquisitions by foreign investors
- abolishing all interest rate ceilings
- allowing unrestricted investment by foreigners in local bonds and short term money market instruments
- fully liberalising foreign exchange transactions.

---

[15] Since January 1999, loan classification has reflected the actual ability of borrowers to repay, and not past history. In addition, from July 1998, loans in arrears for 90 days have been classified as 'sub-standard'.

[16] Supervisors apply prompt corrective action measures to financial institutions that fall below required capital adequacy levels. It covers improvements in management personnel and organisation, including changes in senior management, capital reduction, restriction of profit dividends, merger or purchase and assumption, closure of institutions, sale of risky assets and subsidiaries, among other measures. (See Chapter 3 - *Prudential Reform*.)

[17] The *Foreign Investment Promotion Act, 1998*, abolishes restrictions on foreigners owning land and simplifies and makes more transparent administrative procedures for foreign direct investment. In addition, the Government provided tax exemptions and subsidies to make foreign direct investment more attractive.

> **MEASURES TO SUPPORT CAPITAL ACCOUNT LIBERALISATION**
>
> To fully liberalise international capital movements, the Government has:
>
> - liberalised foreign exchange transactions in two stages, starting in April 1999 when it liberalised corporate overseas borrowing and permitted a futures market. Foreign exchange buyers no longer need to submit real demand documents and can remit profits without restriction. Foreign bank branches in Korea can undertake more foreign exchange business
>
> - announced the second stage of reform to be effective from December 2000. This will liberalise all remaining capital account transactions
>
> - established an information network to provide up-to-date information 24 hours per day on worldwide financial transactions directly or indirectly involving the Korean won
>
> - established an International Financial Centre to closely monitor activities in the international financial market
>
> - implemented an early warning system to help identify early symptoms of financial market instability and alert authorities.
>
> Source: Ministry of Finance and Economy, 1999a.

Capital Market Deepening

Before the crisis, capital markets were relatively underdeveloped. Corporates traditionally relied on bank debt to fund investment, although the *chaebol* also issued corporate bonds. The government debt market was shallow and illiquid as the Korean Government typically ran budget surpluses throughout the 1990s.

Since the crisis, this situation has changed significantly. High interest rates, the bank credit crunch and government directives have forced the *chaebol* to reduce their bank debt; increasingly they resort to equity and bond markets to raise funds. At the same time, the Government increased public bond sales to fund its rising budget deficit, and financial and corporate restructuring. Privatising state owned enterprises also increases bond and equity market activity. Foreign financial institutions are participating in the rapidly expanding debt market. The resulting equity, bond and money market deepening should raise the efficiency and soundness of Korea's financial system, and improve the balance of corporate finance.

STOCK MARKET DEVELOPMENTS

Korea's stock market capitalisation should expand rapidly in the next few years as corporates reduce excessive reliance on bank credit and lower their debt to equity ratios by issuing more stock. Strong stock market activity in late 1998 was due to improved market sentiment about Korean economic prospects, removal of most restrictions on foreign share ownership and corporates' need to reduce debt to equity ratios. By the end of 1998, stock market capitalisation was Won 137.8 trillion, and had reached Won 270 trillion by September 1999, up 280 per cent on its end 1997 level (Korea Stock Exchange, 1999a). Almost 100 million shares were traded on an average day in 1998, but this rose to an average of over 260 million in the first nine months of 1999.[18]

Before the crisis, stock exchange infrastructure for trading, clearing and settlement was reasonably good, but supervision was not optimal. Since the crisis, the Government has strengthened prudential oversight and reduced illegal activities. In 1998, the Financial Supervisory Commission absorbed the Securities Supervision Board, and now regulates stock traders and the 700 listed companies. In addition, as one of East Asia's few self regulating exchanges, the Korea Stock Exchange monitors the activities of its members to prevent insider trading (Kim, 1998).[19] This task was made easier by the stock exchange's complete computerisation in 1997.[20] (See Chapter 5 - *Capital Markets*.)

FUTURES AND OPTIONS MARKETS

Since 1997, futures and options markets have expanded much more rapidly than the share market (Figure 13.1). In 1996, the Korea Stock Exchange introduced stock price index futures and, in July 1997, stock price index options to improve the robustness of the derivatives market and market liquidity.[21] In 1998, Won 408 trillion of futures and options were traded, more than double the value of equity transactions (Figure 13.1). In 1998, the average daily futures' trading volume was 61 000 contracts, making it the world's second largest futures market after the US S&P 500 index futures market (Korea Stock Exchange, 1999a; and Samsung Economic Research Institute, 1999a). The futures stock index market was so successful it actually expanded during the financial crisis, providing an alternative to stock investments.

Another positive development for managing corporate and financial sector risk was the April 1999 opening of the Korea Futures Exchange in Pusan, Korea's second largest city. It offers Korea's first full scale derivatives trading, with initial trading in US dollar futures and options, certificates of deposit (three month interest) futures and gold futures.[22] In the second half of 1999, the exchange listed three year government bond futures to deepen the market and increase liquidity. These should be popular as the volume of marketed government bonds has increased significantly since early 1998. From 2000, the exchange also plans to list foreign futures products and allow its products to be listed on foreign exchanges.

....

[18] During the worst of the crisis in mid 1998, average daily trading was down from the normal level of US$500 million to US$200 million (Kim, 1998).

[19] Insider trading is common in developing country markets, but while its incidence has probably not increased in recent years, more is now being detected and dealt with, due to improved surveillance and ethical standards in the financial industry. As the Financial Supervisory Commission has the legal right to prosecute offenders, the Korea Stock Exchange refers suspicious behaviour to it for further investigation and possible prosecution (Kim, 1998).

[20] Several members also offer Internet access to clients.

[21] The underlying asset is the KOSPI 200, a composite index of market-leading companies; their market value covers 70 per cent of the market.

[22] The *Futures Trading Act, 1996* requires stock price index futures currently traded on the Korean Stock Exchange to be transferred to the new futures exchange, when it is established. The Korean Stock Exchange is resisting this move because of its heavy investment in the index futures market.

Figure 13.1
Futures Market Buoyant
Korean Stock and Futures Markets Transactions (Won trillion)

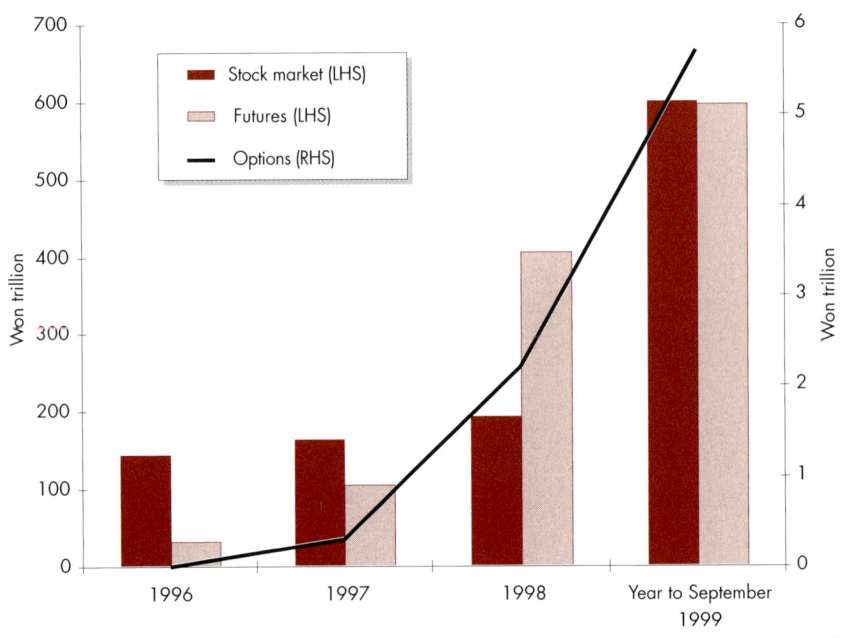

Source: Korea Stock Exchange, 1999b.

Compared to other Asian financial centres, Korea is a late starter in developing derivatives markets and the associated skills. However, with the rapidly growing stock index futures market, the successful futures exchange in Pusan and the more open financial market and upgraded regulatory environment, Korea should rapidly catch up with other centres.

BOND MARKETS

Continuing bank recapitalisation costs drive the rapidly expanding public bond market. A government priority is to further develop the long term corporate bond market to deepen and strengthen Korea's corporate finance profile.

Public Bond Market

In 1998, as a result of the crisis, the Government issued Won 22.1 trillion new bonds, up from just Won 6.8 trillion in 1997. Government bond issues should rise to Won 29.5 trillion in 1999, and the amount outstanding should reach Won 67.6 trillion, or 14.4 per cent of GDP (Ministry of Finance and Economy, 1999b). In July 1999, the Ministry of Finance and Economy introduced a primary dealer system to expand government bond demand.[23] The system will help create a competitive auction market for bonds, and with the focus on three year maturity issues, it is establishing a benchmark yield rate to value corporate bonds (Figure 13.2). To further assist development of the corporate bond market it is necessary to increase the maturity range of government bond issues, thus generating a benchmark yield curve.

Corporate Bond Market

While government bonds are increasingly important, corporate bonds dominate bond trading (Figure 13.3) and the *chaebol* dominate the corporate bond market.[24] In 1998, the bank lending crunch and continued market confidence in the top five *chaebol* maintained an active corporate bond market. New corporate bond issues rose over Won 57 trillion, up 65 per cent on 1997 (Korea Stock Exchange, 1999a). Total corporate bond trading reached Won 374 trillion in 1998, up 174 per cent on 1997.[25] More than 90 per cent of corporate bonds have three year maturities.

Figure 13.2

Three Year Treasury Bond Rate Sets the Benchmark since 1998
Korean Bond Rates (Per cent)

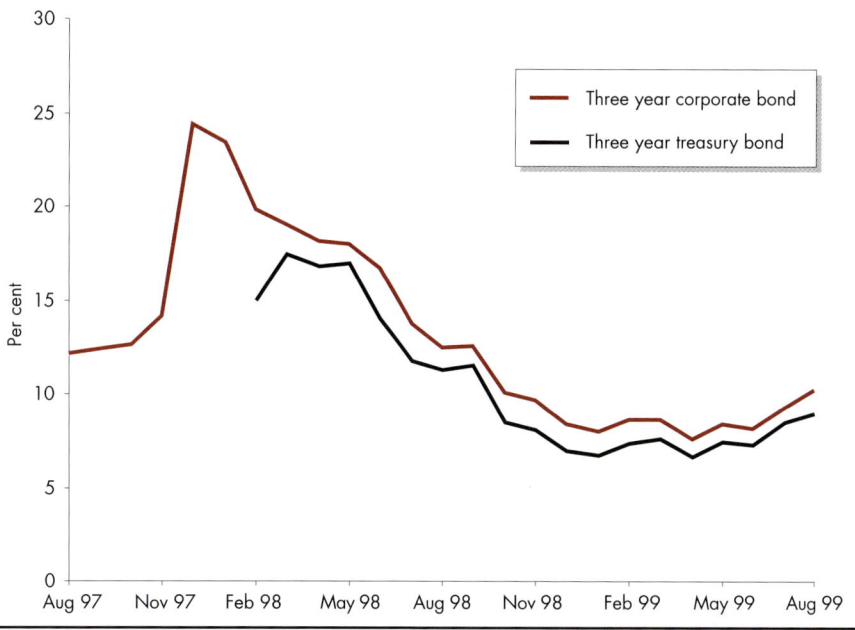

Source: CEIC, 1999; and Korea Stock Exchange, 1999b.

[23] The Government has listed 24 financial institutions (12 commercial banks, 11 securities companies and a merchant bank) as government primary bond dealers.

[24] In 1998, small and medium sized enterprises accounted for just 1.3 per cent of total corporate bond issues.

[25] Corporate bond issues rose a further 38.3 per cent in the first five months of 1999.

Figure 13.3

Corporates Dominate Bond Market
Bond Markets by Trading Volume (Won trillion)

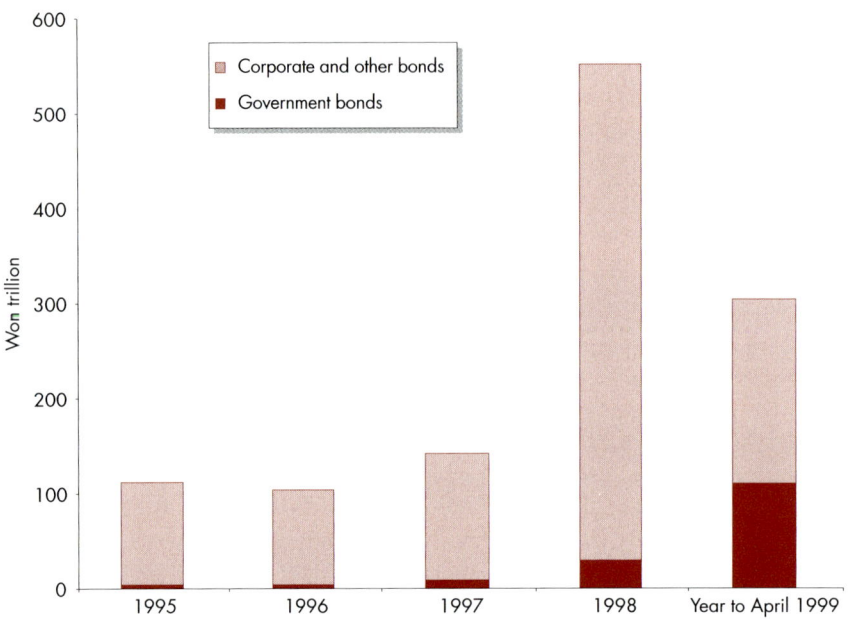

Source: Ministry of Finance and Economy, 1999b.

To strengthen corporate bond markets, the Government needs to tighten corporate bond issue disclosure requirements, introduce 'marking to market' among bond funds and facilitate the development of credit rating agencies.[26] In a far sighted move, the Government opened the credit rating market to foreign competition. Ratings will become more important as non-guaranteed bond issues grow, because they need a credit rating to be listed. (See Chapter 5 - *Capital Markets*.)

Although bond markets are expanding rapidly, to increase their depth and robustness, the Government also needs to encourage an efficiently priced and liquid secondary bond market. Privatising state enterprises, financing large budget deficits and continuing bank rationalisation and market orientation will provide major opportunities to deepen bond markets and introduce more investment instruments. Foreign financial institutions can play a significant role in this process.

---

[26] In the past, many corporate bonds were issued without a rating, but carried bank guarantees. The bank guarantees made the bonds attractive to investors, but increased the banks' off-balance sheet risks. 'Marking to market' is the practice of marking down the value of a financial instrument to the current market value.

Asset-backed Securities

Since 1998, the Government has used asset-backed securities to raise funds and dispose of restructured assets.[27] In 1998 and 1999, the Korean Asset Management Corporation employed asset-backed securitisation to sell nearly Won 600 billion of collateralised NPLs to foreign investors.[28] Corporations and financial institutions plan to enter this market but are constrained because no local asset-backed securities market exists. Secondary trading in such instruments would help price risk and better distribute it across domestic financial markets (AMCHAM, 1999). Wider use of asset-backed securities also will accelerate corporate and financial institution restructuring, improving their capital structures and reducing the cost of new finance.[29]

Bond Markets and Investment Trust Companies

When Daewoo's severe financial problems were exposed in July 1999, the Government became concerned a massive redemption of Daewoo bonds in late 1999 could threaten the viability of investment trust companies and destabilise financial markets.[30] Hence, to stabilise bond and other financial markets, the Government established a Won 20 trillion market stabilisation fund; it will help stabilise interest rates and provide liquidity to the market, if needed (Ministry of Finance and Economy, 1999c).[31] Other key steps that would help stabilise the bond market include requiring bond holdings to be valued at current market rates and establishing a framework for sharing losses from a major *chaebol* bankruptcy.

FINANCIAL SECTOR CONSOLIDATION

Crisis related reform, technological change and increased foreign competition are stimulating significant financial sector consolidation. In line with global trends, regulatory reforms are dissolving divisions between Korean banks, securities companies, insurance providers and other financial institutions. Financial institutions are fewer but larger. For example, commercial bank numbers eventually could fall from 16 in August 1999 to around ten to twelve (Samsung Economic Research Institute, 1999a).

---

[27] Asset securitisation converts various assets, such as real assets, accounts receivable and mortgages into cash flows by issuing asset-backed securities based on those assets. Passage of the *Asset Securitisation Act, 1998*, formalised this market in Korea.

[28] Of the Won 20 trillion in NPLs the Korea Asset Management Corporation purchased, the Government plans to dispose of around 98 per cent over five years by issuing asset-backed securities. Through this method, the Korea Asset Management Corporation expects to recover over 90 per cent of bad debts purchased (KAMCO, 1999).

[29] Asset-backed securities carry very high ratings (usually AAA) and consequently carry little spread. In addition, when a corporation issues asset-backed securities, it does not raise the debt ratio. Financial institutions can enhance their capital adequacy ratios by issuing asset-backed securities, which are less risky assets.

[30] Investment trust companies hold around Won 200 trillion in bond linked funds, including Won 25 trillion in Daewoo bonds.

[31] The Market Stabilisation Fund will provide liquidity by buying corporate bonds that investment trust companies need to sell if depositors rush to redeem their investments. In November 1999, investors will be able to redeem up to 80 per cent of Daewoo bonds held by investment trust companies, and up to 95 per cent by February 2000.

As part of this rationalisation, a three tier banking system is developing: a few mega banks have resulted from large bank mergers; several medium sized banks supply retail banking, housing finance and other niche markets; and some small regional banks operate in specific regions (Bank of Korea, 1998). Mega banks probably will move towards universal banking, offering the full range of financial products from banking to insurance.[32] The merged banks and the two nationalised banks, one of which has been sold and the other still for sale to foreign investors, probably will form the core of Korea's future banking industry.[33]

The revised savings protection law also encourages bank restructuring. From 2001, the Government will not protect bank deposits over Won 20 million (US$16 250). With the lower limit on depositor protection, savings should flow to stronger and more credible banks, possibly forcing more bank mergers.

While it remains too early to assess the impact of recent bank mergers on efficiency, already banks have strengthened the quality of balance sheets, improved internal management and risk management systems, reduced employment, closed unprofitable branches and scrutinised other costs. In future, pressure from shareholders, including the Government, supervisory authorities and rating agencies, and increased foreign and domestic competition should force domestic banks to improve efficiency, lending policies and profitability.[34]

PROSPECTS FOR FOREIGN FINANCIAL INSTITUTIONS

In a reshaped Korean finance industry, foreign investors will play an important role. In 1998, most banks attempted to rebuild their capital base, improve their financial structures and upgrade management expertise and performance by attracting foreign investment. By mid 1999, with growing foreign confidence in the Korean economy, a few banks had succeeded. Furthermore, planned foreign equity participation will produce more joint-venture banks.

To create a joint-venture bank, a single foreign investor must hold at least 25 per cent equity and participate in management. Before 1997, only KorAm Bank, with Bank America sharing ownership, was classified as a joint-venture bank. In 1998, Korea Exchange Bank, with Germany's Commerzbank holding about a 29 per cent share, became the second foreign joint-venture bank. In late April 1999,

---

[32] Initially, the most common structure is likely to be a parent commercial bank with other financial institutions, such as investment banks and insurance firms, as subsidiaries. These structures already exist or are developing in Korea. The next stage could involve establishing financial holding companies; these were long banned in Korea and only recently have been legalised on a limited scale. Financial holding companies could operate commercial banks, and other financial institutions under their umbrella as independent corporations. With true universal banking, single institutions would emerge with many diverse financial businesses as divisions under a single company structure (Samsung Economic Research Institute, 1999a).

[33] The new Hanvit Bank is now Korea's largest bank with assets of over Won 100 trillion. Kookmin Bank, through merger and acquisition, is another mega bank with assets of nearly Won 100 trillion. Korea's third largest bank is likely to emerge from the merger of the Chohung, Kangwon, Chungbuk and Hyundai International Merchant Banks.

[34] The Financial Supervisory Commission now makes its financial assistance conditional on banks achieving, by the end of 2000, at least a 1 per cent return on assets, a 15 per cent return on equity and a capital adequacy ratio over 10 per cent.

Kookmin Bank announced that US investment bank, Goldman Sachs, would invest US$500 million to take an 18 per cent stake in the bank. Housing and Commercial Bank has majority foreign share ownership, so also is foreign owned.[35]

Foreign ownership of the banking sector also will increase with the sales of Korea First and Seoul Banks to overseas interests. In September 1999, following lengthy negotiations, Newbridge Capital reached agreement with the Korean Government to purchase a 51 per cent stake in Korea First Bank for Won 500 billion (US$420 million) and to assume management control.[36] The successful sale of Korea First Bank to foreign investors, raises to five the number of foreign joint-venture banks. Although the similarly protracted sale negotiations of Seoul Bank to the Hong Kong Shanghai Banking Corporation collapsed in September, the Government still plans to sell Seoul Bank if a suitable foreign buyer is found.[37]

Foreign banks' market share has increased commensurately. The deposit share of wholly foreign-owned bank branches grew from 1.8 per cent at the end of 1997 to 2.5 per cent in 1998,[38] but if domestic banks with a majority of foreign shareholders are included, foreign banks' market share increases to over 20 per cent (Samsung Economic Research Institute, 1999b). Inclusion of joint-venture banks raises this share higher again.

While the amended banking law makes foreign investment in Korean banks, particularly mergers and acquisitions, much easier, other regulations still limit the participation of wholly foreign-owned banks. For example, local branches of foreign banks must be separately capitalised and prudential controls on lending limits are based on foreign banks' local branch capital rather than their global capital. However the Bank for International Settlements' core principles allow regulation according to branch rather than global capital, and similar regulations apply in Germany, France, Singapore, Hong Kong and Taiwan.[39] Australia allows foreign

---

[35] Housing and Commercial Bank is the first non-joint-venture bank in which foreign investors have acquired a stake of over 60 per cent purely through stock investment. By March 1999, foreign investors owned 60.5 per cent of the bank's shares, up from 39 per cent in May 1998, just before foreign investment restrictions were lifted. The bank is preparing for foreign shareholders to exert increasing direct and indirect influence over bank management (*Korea Herald*, 26 and 27 January 1999, and 23 March 1999).

[36] The Government in return agreed to guarantee NPLs that might accrue over the next two years. It also agreed to allow a three year guarantee to cover NPLs extended to the Daewoo Group, to which Korea First is the lead banker and major creditor.

[37] In February 1999, the Government announced it intended to sell 70 per cent of Seoul Bank to the Hong Kong Shanghai Banking Corporation for around US$700 million, but the sale collapsed due to a dispute over asset valuation. In the interim, to enable Seoul Bank to continue operations, the Government has injected a further Won 4.5 trillion, bringing its total capital contribution to Won 7 trillion.

[38] Citibank accounted for much of the increase. One of the most profitable banks in Korea, Citibank is acquiring 50 branch offices from cash-strapped domestic banks to expand its previous network of 11 branches.

[39] In addressing the issue of global capital, the Assistant Governor to the Financial Supervisory Service stated Korea would be guided by Basle Committee decisions and international trends. If all members of the Basle Committee agree to recognise global capital in operating foreign banks within their respective markets, Korea would follow suit (Oh, 1999).

banks to choose whether to adopt local branch or global capital criteria. However, in Korea, other burdensome regulations undermine foreign and domestic bank efficiency and profitability.[40]

Foreign investors also are pursuing opportunities in the non-bank financial sector and funds management. A number of US and European insurance firms have expressed interest in Korean insurers.[41] Since Korea opened its investment trust and mutual fund management business to foreigners, four global asset management companies, Templeton, Rothschild, State Street Global Advisers and Scudder Kemper, have applied to operate mutual funds in local stock and bond markets. Nevertheless, some foreign mutual fund managers complain that arbitrary requirements for paid in capital, qualified experts and association membership limit foreign participation in this market (AMCHAM, 1999).

Although many problems remain, in the medium term, the greatly expanded participation of foreign institutions in Korea's financial sector should significantly change deep-rooted corporate practices. To compete for depositors and borrowers, domestic financial institutions will introduce modern management practices, financial structures and stricter lending criteria. Sound credit analysis increasingly will replace lending based on corporate links or political and bureaucratic directives. Already, banks have removed much of management's previous discretionary lending authority and most have established credit appraisal committees to assess potential borrowers before providing large scale loans (Bank of Korea, 1998). However, greater foreign participation will ensure these gains are consolidated and expanded in the future.

FINANCIAL SECTOR'S LONG TERM RECOVERY PROSPECTS

Since the Government introduced the IMF stabilisation package and passed financial reform legislation in December 1997, Korea's financial sector has restructured dramatically. The Government is overcoming decades of entrenched resistance to financial modernisation and liberalisation, and enacting a best practice institutional and regulatory framework, demonstrating strong commitment to financial system reform (OECD, 1998).

At the end of 1998, the Government rather optimistically announced financial restructuring was mostly completed, and financial institutions should resume normal lending operations in 1999. However, the Daewoo restructuring introduced major strains, and all existing banks and investment trust companies may not survive, at least in their present form. Furthermore, the capacity and willingness of banks to make lending decisions on a fully commercial basis and enforce necessary corporate workouts and bankruptcies is yet to be fully tested.

---

[40] For example, foreign banks are held to strict monthly lending ratios for small and medium sized enterprises, constraining their operations and inefficiently allocating and pricing credit services. Although limits on spot positions in the foreign exchange market were eliminated, regulations limiting overbought and oversold foreign exchange positions still constrain foreign banks' ability to provide sophisticated currency risk management services (AMCHAM, 1999).

[41] For example, Hartford Insurance acquired Kumho Life Insurance Company. US giant, Metropolitan Life Insurance Company, MetLife is expected to invest in Daehan Life. Following the December 1998 review of the insurance sector, the Financial Supervisory Commission began proceedings to sell six undercapitalised Korean life insurance companies to foreign investors.

Government intervention in the banking sector and associated moral hazard and commercial risks concern some foreign and local investors. As the Government still owns 90 per cent of one major commercial bank and holds significant shares in many others, it may revert to direct controls. For example, some analysts believe government ownership still could influence First Korea Bank's role in the Daewoo debt workout (*Far Eastern Economic Review*, 26 August 1999, p. 13). However, bank nationalisation contains the fiscal costs of restructuring and prevents systemic collapse, and therefore is inevitable in the short term.

Furthermore, the Government is committed to re-privatising banks as soon as practical. Government divestiture will allow bank managers to develop and assert independent commercial skills. The Government, and particularly the Financial Supervisory Commission has worked hard to convince managers, borrowers, depositors, shareholders and domestic and foreign investors, that the transition towards a competitive, soundly regulated financial system is irreversible and crucial to full recovery. It is unlikely to reverse its position.

The Government wants the finance industry to be one of next century's strategic industries. This vision requires a substantial injection of public funds to recapitalise banks, and foreign competition to stimulate real changes in bank management and business practices. This will require continued commitment to reform, including strictly enforcing new tightened prudential controls, revoking unnecessary financial sector controls, lowering financial market entry barriers, and allowing the market driven exit of non-viable financial institutions. Furthermore, to operate a financial system according to market principles with transparent decision making and disclosure will require a major change in corporate culture; this may take several years to achieve. The competition, efficiency and governance benchmarks foreign financial institutions provide should significantly accelerate this process.

REFERENCES

AMCHAM, American Chamber of Commerce in Korea, 1999, 'Improving the Korean Business Climate - Recommendations from American Business', www.amchamkorea.org/Trade.htm, accessed on 15 October.

Bank of Korea, 1998, 'Bank Restructuring in Korea', Banking Department, Seoul, December.

CEIC, 1999, CEIC Database, Hong Kong, supplied by EconData, Canberra.

East Asia Analytical Unit, 1999, *Korea Rebuilds: from Crisis to Opportunity*, Department of Foreign Affairs and Trade, Canberra.

Financial Supervisory Commission, 1999, Information supplied to the East Asia Analytical Unit on the current status of financial reform.

___ 1998, 'Update on Progress of Strengthening Prudential Supervision and Regulation', FSC Note, Seoul.

Kim, Joe-Il, 1998, East Asia Analytical Unit interview with Director International Division, Korea Stock Exchange, Seoul, June.

Korea Asset Management Corporation, KAMCO, 1999, 'Kamco Profile', www.kamco.or.kr/eng/main1.htm, accessed on 8 September.

Korea Stock Exchange, 1999a, 'Review of the Korean Securities Market in 1998', www.kse.or.kr, accessed on 20 March.

___ 1999b, *Key Statistics for Listed Stocks*, KSE, Seoul, www.kse.or.kr/eng/, accessed on 19 October.

Ministry of Finance and Economy, 1999a, 'New International Financial Architecture - Korea's Perspective', Financial Cooperation Division, www.mofe.go.kr/mofe/eng/e_index.htm, accessed on 12 October.

___ 1999b, 'The Korean Government Bond Market', Treasury Division, Seoul, www.mofe.go.kr/mofe/eng/e_index.htm, accessed on 19 October.

___ 1999c, 'Policy Directions to Stabilise Financial Markets', Foreign Press and Public Relations Division, Seoul, www.mofe.go.kr/mofe/eng/e_index.htm, accessed on 12 October.

___ 1998, *Challenge and Chance, Korea's Response to the New Economic Reality*, MOFE, Seoul.

OECD, 1998, *OECD Economic Surveys: Korea* 1997-98, OECD, Paris.

Oh, Kap Soo, 1999, 'Experience and Future Direction of Structural Reform in Korea', Presentation by the Assistant Governor of the Financial Supervisory Commission to the American Chamber of Commerce, Seoul, 7 April.

Samsung Economic Research Institute, 1999a, *Korean Economic Trends*, 'Prospects for the Re-formation of the Korean Financial Industry after Its Restructuring', 29 May, www.seri-samsung.org/english/ket/ket.html, accessed on 9 July.

―― 1999b, 'Korean Economic Trends, the Advancement of Foreign Capital into the Domestic Financial Industry and Its Effects', 18 September, www.seri-samsung.org/english/ket/ket.html, accessed on 9 October.

Smith, H., 1998, 'South Korea', in McLeod, R. and Garnaut, R. (eds), *East Asia in Crisis: from Being a Miracle to Needing One*, Routledge, London.

Korea

Chapter 14

IMPLICATIONS FOR AUSTRALIA

The Asian financial crisis is one of the most serious economic events since the Great Depression. The major crisis-induced economic contraction and trade dislocation increased regional governments' recognition of the importance of financial sector health, and is driving widespread financial sector reform. If this reform momentum is maintained, it should lay the groundwork for a new period of sustained regional economic growth. However, many other factors also are shaping change in regional financial markets, including global trends towards consolidation, universal banking, regulatory reform, technological change and new financial products.

These global trends and crisis-induced reforms are expanding opportunities in many regional economies for Australian financial institutions and service providers. Australia's good economic performance throughout the crisis and greater international recognition of Australia's advanced regulatory framework make Australia attractive as a regional financial centre and should increase its financial service exports. The crisis also highlighted the need for economic governance assistance in bilateral development cooperation programs and the crucial contribution of the international financial institutions.

IMPLICATIONS FOR GOVERNMENT

The financial crisis severely affected regional economies, emphasising the importance of ongoing vigilance to ensure Australia maintains a world best practice financial sector regulatory framework, and continues microeconomic reform. For example, if trends to directly access capital markets, use Internet based financial services and segment banking into deposit taking and funds management accelerate in the next five to ten years, they may warrant further review of Australia's prudential framework.

The considerable liberalisation in East Asian financial markets since the crisis, the projected growth of these markets, and ongoing technological and regulatory changes in world financial markets, underline the importance to Australia of the World Trade Organisation mandated negotiations on financial services starting January 2000. Analysis in this report and consultation with the Australian financial sector indicate key negotiation priorities include more operating licences for Australian financial service providers, more transparent licensing criteria, fewer restrictions on the form of commercial establishment, higher levels of foreign equity participation, greater freedom for companies to employ their own personnel and more flexibility in the type of products foreign firms can offer. These negotiations also offer an opportunity for regional economies to gain credit for liberalisation already underway, and to proceed with further orderly liberalisation.

As weak economic governance significantly contributed to the financial crisis, development assistance to improve regional economies' capacity in this area can help avert future crises. Building on existing Australian assistance for economic and corporate governance, Australia's Prime Minister announced an A$50 million Economic and Financial Management Initiative at the November 1998 Kuala Lumpur APEC Leaders' Meeting. This program includes advising and training regional government officials in fiscal management, public policy formulation, prudential control, central bank and state owned enterprise reform, and legal framework development (AusAID, 1999a). By late 1999, AusAID had spent or committed A$40 million of these funds (AusAID, 1999b).

Australia also has contributed to improving international coordination and targeting of economic governance cooperation in the region. As part of its contribution to APEC's response to the crisis, Australia funded an economic governance survey (Centre for International Economics, 1998). The survey provided a stocktake of international assistance efforts in developing East Asia, and identified areas of potential economic governance assistance. The survey has since been used by Australia and the broader international community to help frame their assistance efforts.

Australia's strong regulatory framework and economic management means Australian government institutions can provide advice and expertise on economic and corporate governance, and financial market management; consequently they are working with many regional governments in these areas. Assistance includes improving fiscal transparency, statistical collection, banking supervision and securities regulation. For example:

- the Australian Bureau of Statistics provides technical support and skill transfer to strengthen the quality and timeliness of Thai macroeconomic statistics and Indonesian Bureau of Statistics information

- the Australian Auditor General's Office assisted the Thai Government Audit Office to introduce performance based auditing

- the Australian Prudential Regulatory Authority helped train Bank of Thailand officials in financial institution supervision and develop prudential regulations

- the Reserve Bank of Australia assisted the Bank of Thailand with its IT requirements

- the Attorney General's Department trained Indonesian government officials in insolvency and corporations law

- the Australian Stock Exchange seconded officials to the Stock Exchange of Thailand to draw up guidelines to improve good governance (AusAID, 1999b).

In addition, through the Treasury and Reserve Bank, Australia is active in reforming the international financial architecture. Australia is one of only four non-G7 economies in the Financial Stability Forum, the main institution currently examining international financial architecture reforms. Australia also is a member of the newly formed G20, established by the G7 to address international financial architecture issues.[1]

---

[1] Australia also has contributed to this debate through the Executive Board and Interim Committee of the IMF.

Australia's technical advice and training assistance to East Asia already contributes significantly to improving economic and legal governance, and is a significant part of Australia's overall development assistance program.[2] The new Economic and Financial Management Initiative complements this work. Given the region's enormous need for improved economic governance and Australia's relevant capacity in this area, valuable future assistance could include:

- strengthening key institutions involved in prudential supervision and regulation
- improving state financial institution performance and advising on privatisation
- training and advising on commercial law reform
- training to improve corporate governance.

Increasing cooperation between the Australian Government, Australian financial institutions and private sector organisations also would promote economic reform in regional economies (Taskforce on International Financial Reform, 1998). Such an initiative is an A$300 000 project funded by AusAID and the insurance companies, AXA and CMG Asia, in conjunction with the Australian Prudential Regulatory Authority and Australian Securities Investment, to provide practical training on world best practice insurance industry regulation. The training program will bring together about 24 senior level life insurance supervisory and regulatory officials from around the region in March 2000.

An ongoing challenge for the Australian Government is to ensure that assistance to improve regional economic governance meets the practical needs of regional prudential regulators, and augments programs offered by the international financial institutions and other bilateral donors.

IMPLICATIONS FOR AUSTRALIAN BUSINESS

The financial crisis has profound implications for Australian business. Many regional governments have undertaken reforms that opened financial sectors more rapidly and completely than was believed possible before 1997. However, the crisis also has increased actual and perceived investment risks. Regional governments have different levels of commitment to economic reform, causing regional economies' short term economic performance and market perceptions of long term growth potential to diverge significantly.

Across the region, opportunities are opening in banking, capital markets and non-bank financial institutions, and for financial service providers. For some larger Australian financial institutions, acquisitions are the most obvious opportunity

---

[2]   For example, during his visit to Indonesia in early July 1998, Mr Downer announced a package of 60 additional Australian tertiary scholarships for study related to economic reform. The Australia-IMF Scholarship Program for Asia is a five year project with total funding of A$1.6 million, which aims to train government and central bank officials in macroeconomic management. Selected scholars attend well structured and relevant graduate economics courses in the Economics of Development Program at the National Centre for Development Studies at the Australian National University. AusAID also funds many specific training courses. For example, in early 1999, AusAID provided over A$400 000 to support two training courses run by the Mekong Regional Law Centre in Bangkok to develop regional commercial law expertise. Australia also has an A$20 million project over four years to build institutional capacity and strengthen operational skills in key Chinese economic policy and foreign trade ministries.

Implications

flowing from the financial crisis. However, since the crisis began, foreign financial institutions have learnt how important it is to allocate, before purchase, responsibility for new and existing non-performing loans. Since January 1998, around 18 foreign financial institutions have acquired full or part equity stakes in East Asian banks.

Australian financial institutions also can increase their presence in the region by taking over selected activities of regional institutions or forming partnerships to undertake specific activities. This approach may suit smaller Australian institutions and investors uncertain if the local entity has disclosed all its business problems. Such a strategy limits risk exposure and can maximise leverage from the Australian financial institution's skills and technology. For example, Macquarie Bank is involved in derivatives joint ventures with large Japanese and Korean banks, and with China Construction Bank in a securitisation joint venture.

As East Asian banks strive to become more competitive, their increased demand for outsourced financial and technical services provides many opportunities for Australian financial, technological, accounting and legal service providers. In mid 1999, US firm, First Data Corporation, announced it would establish a regional credit card account processing centre in Australia for clients in Australia and East Asia. American Express is pursuing similar opportunities in the region.

Taiwan and Korea are opening their capital markets to foreign equity investment, creating growing opportunities for stockbroking, funds management and related services. The Thai and Japanese securities industries also are undergoing major restructuring and foreign presence is rising significantly. Another area offering opportunities is the sale of software to assist financial institutions with risk management and regulators with enforcement of tightened market regulations. Australian Computershare's sales of the real time surveillance system, SMARTS to exchanges in Hong Kong and Jakarta is an example of the latter.

Growing recognition of the importance of well managed pension schemes to fund the retirement of Asia's aging population should create further opportunities for Australian fund managers and life insurers. More liberal rules on eligibility requirements of fund managers and investable instruments will generate these opportunities.

The trend towards consolidated supervision, and fewer barriers between banks and non-bank financial institutions, should open new business areas for both foreign bank and non-bank financial institutions. For example, to establish their banking presence, some foreign financial institutions have purchased finance company platforms in Thailand and Malaysia. Similarly, to enter China, some foreign banks may seek partners from among better managed urban credit cooperatives and city banks. These same trends also may offer firms already in Asia opportunities to reconfigure their operations.

IMPLICATIONS OF AUSTRALIA'S FINANCIAL MARKET PERFORMANCE

The strength of Australia's economy, financial institutions and regulatory system throughout the financial crisis, and a stream of new government initiatives have boosted Australia's attractiveness as a regional financial centre. Lessons learned by Australia from its late 1980s banking crisis also apply to regional governments dealing with the aftermath of the Asian financial crisis. Consequently, many Australian public institutions and private firms are helping regional governments strengthen their financial markets.

Economic Strengths

In 1997 and 1998, Australia's economic growth was strong, with real GDP growing 4.1 per cent in 1997 and 4.8 per cent in 1998. Unemployment fell; exports held up well; and inflation remained low. However, the current account deficit widened due in part to growing imports, mainly from Asia and the United States.

Financial Market Strength

The crisis showed Australia has first class financial institutions. Partly stimulated by a banking crisis in the late 1980s and early 1990s, Australian banks are highly focused on risk measurement and management. For example, Australian banks have long maintained credit bureaus to separate credit management from credit origination, and manage credit risk at the group level. More recently, banks have established independent risk management groups to assess all risks that bank groups face (Gruen et al, 1998).

Australia's capital markets also are world class. In 1998, Global Securities Consulting Services rated Australia one of the world's top three equities markets for settlement services and operational risk (Lee-Tulliss, 1998). Australia is building on its well established domestic government bond market, with rapidly growing markets for corporate bonds and for foreigners who raise funds in Australia's domestic debt markets.[3] Australia also has a large and active securitisation market, with issues growing from zero in 1983 to A$16 billion in 1998 (*Asiamoney*, May 1999, p. 17).

Regulatory Strength

Following several decades of ongoing reform, Australia's regulatory framework is world best practice. In 1997, the Government accepted the recommendations of its most recent Financial System Inquiry.[4] These reforms saw consolidated prudential regulation of all deposit taking institutions, including banks, building societies, credit unions, life and general insurance companies and superannuation funds, under

---

[3] In 1998 and 1999, issuers included the Asian Development Bank, the German Development Bank, German Development Agency and Nordic Investment Bank (*Asiamoney* Supplement, July/August 1999, pp. 14-19).

[4] The Financial System Inquiry headed by Stan Wallace, with a Secretariat provided by the Australian Treasury, was the first major inquiry into the Australian financial system since the Campbell Committee Inquiry in 1981.

a single new institution, the Australian Prudential Regulation Authority, APRA.[5] Consolidation facilitates coherent regulation of financial institutions with activities in many financial markets and sectors. Many regional governments are adopting similar models.[6]

The other major reform resulting from the Financial System Inquiry was to consolidate responsibility for securities market supervision into a single regulator, the Australian Securities and Investment Commission, ASIC. This initiative overcame regulatory gaps under previous arrangements, and also ensures Australian financial markets will remain well regulated as corporate fundraising shifts from financial sector intermediaries to capital markets, where disclosure regulation is critical.

AUSTRALIA AS A REGIONAL FINANCIAL CENTRE

These prudential framework and financial market strengths enhance Sydney's attractiveness as a regional financial centre. In 1998, to promote Australia's regional financial centre role and initiate policy reforms to enhance this objective, the Government appointed a Minister for Financial Services and Regulation.[7] In mid 1999, the Government introduced a number of tax measures to enhance the operation of offshore banking arrangements and further support the development of funds management and corporate debt markets. These measures included:

- expanding the offshore banking unit regime, taxing at a concessional rate of 10 per cent non-capital gains income from financial transactions between offshore borrowers and lenders[8]

- exempting Australian issued corporate bonds from interest withholding tax.

In addition, in 1999, the Government announced a significant rationalisation of personal, company and other taxation regimes. Major changes include introducing a broad based value added (goods and services) tax, lowering personal tax rates, halving capital gains tax rates, lowering the company tax rate from 36 to 30 per cent and progressively abolishing many state financial transaction taxes.[9]

---

[5] The consolidation of prudential regulation occurred in two stages, 1 July 1998 when the regulatory agencies consolidated and 1 July 1999 when the state based institutions came under the consolidated regulatory umbrella.

[6] For example, Korea and Japan already have moved to consolidated supervision; Indonesia has announced it will do so in 2003; and Thailand and Taiwan are considering such a system.

[7] As part of this promotion strategy the Government also established a Sydney based Centre for Global Finance within the Treasury Department and a Committee of Regulators to ensure financial market regulations do not impair Australia's capacity to compete as a regional financial centre. The committee is chaired by Treasury and includes the Reserve Bank of Australia, the Australian Prudential Regulation Authority, the Australian Securities and Investments Commission, the Australian Competition and Consumer Commission, and the Australian Tax Office.

[8] This is well below the proposed new corporate income tax rate of 30 per cent. In 1999, the concession was broadened from banks and authorised foreign exchange dealers to cover fund managers, life insurance companies, custodial service operators and gold bullion traders (Hockey, 1999a). This scheme competes with Singapore's much larger concession scheme and Hong Kong's very low tax rates, and is crucial in attracting international business.

[9] Except for the company and capital gains tax rate reductions, all these tax changes are legislated. The company and capital gains tax reductions are part of a reform of business taxation and yet to be legislated. The new tax rates generally will be introduced over the next two years, with the goods and services tax effective from 1 July 2000.

Recent Progress

A number of financial institutions already are relocating regional operations to Australia. For example:

- in 1994, Chase Manhattan Corporation, one of the largest banking companies in the United States centralised its bullion operations in Sydney; in 1998 it added global custody and regional headquarters functions (*Dow Jones News*, 9 February 1998)

- in October 1998, Citibank chose Sydney as the site for its Asia Pacific regional processing centre, with 1.5 million transactions handled per year (*Australian Financial Review*, 8 October 1998)

- in December 1998, Deutsche Bank announced the establishment of its Deutsche Asset Management regional headquarters in Sydney; the Sydney office now is responsible for the bank's asset management businesses in Australia and most of East Asia

- in October 1998, Hong Kong Shanghai Banking Corporation announced the regional headquarters of its A$102 billion asset management arm would be based in Melbourne (*Australian Financial Review*, 20 October 1999)

- in September 1999, Merrill Lynch announced the move of 11 of its biggest international funds to Australia (Australian Associated Press, 21 September 1999).

Australia's strong legal, accounting and advisory skills in the workforce, best practice regulatory system, great diversity of Asian and other foreign language skills, lower cost structures than in Hong Kong and Singapore, and offshore banking unit regulation, all contribute to making Australia an attractive destination for regional financial business.

FUTURE PROSPECTS

Because of the crisis, most regional governments have strengthened significantly their prudential regimes and progressively are dealing with non-performing loans and undercapitalised financial institutions. In late 1999, due to these reforms and macroeconomic stimulus policies, virtually all regional economies were recovering from the financial crisis.

In the long term, upgraded bankruptcy laws, prudential control and disclosure requirements should strengthen East Asian economies and enable more sustainable growth. As most East Asian financial markets now are more open to international competition, major global trends in world financial markets will challenge, but ultimately strengthen, these markets.

Consequently, to enhance their future market position and long run profitability, Australian financial institutions and service providers need to capitalise on the wide-ranging reforms and crisis-driven commercial opportunities the region offers. As inadequate legal and disclosure regimes increase the risk of direct acquisitions, strategic alliances and joint ventures may offer safer strategies in some cases. Australian financial service providers also can expand their regional market, as regional financial institutions and capital markets seek to upgrade technologies and skills, and restructure non-performing loans.

Implications

The Australian Government is developing a sound policy framework to attract international financial business and build Australia's status as a regional financial centre. Australia's core prudential and economic strengths enhance its prospects in achieving this objective. The Government considers cooperative efforts within the region to strengthen the financial architecture will have positive spin-offs in expanding the region's share of the global financial services market.

REFERENCES

AusAID, 1999a, 'Australia's Economic and Financial Management Initiative for APEC: 1998-2001', September, AusAID, Canberra.

___ 1999b, Information supplied to East Asia Analytical Unit, October.

Centre for International Economics, 1998, 'APEC Economic Governance Capacity Building Survey', report prepared for the Australian Government as an Australian initiative as part of APEC's response to the East Asian financial crisis, October, Centre for International Economics, Canberra.

Gruen, D., Gray, B., and Stevens, G., 1998, 'Australia', in McLeod, R. and Garnaut, R. (eds), *East Asia in Crisis: from Being a Miracle to Needing One*, Routledge, London, pp. 207-26.

Hockey, J., 1999, Press release by the Minister for Financial Services and Regulation 'Financial Hub Plan Gets Tax Boost', 29 June.

Lee-Tullis, J. (ed.), 1998, 'The 1998 Review of Emerging Markets', Global Securities Consulting Services, London.

Taskforce on International Financial Reform, 1998, 'Report of the Taskforce on International Financial Reform, Commonwealth of Australia', Australian Government Publishing Service, Canberra.

Implications

INDEX

A

ABN Amro, 93, 95, 168
accountability and transparency, 34, 57
    accounting standards, 109-10, 178-9, 291
    see also corporate governance; disclosure
acquisitions, see mergers and acquisitions
American Express, 96
ANZ Bank, 93, 168, 249
appreciation, see exchange rates
Argentina, 32, 76, 81
Asia Pacific Regional Operations Centre plan, 256
asset management companies, 81-3
    China, 297-8
    Korea, 83, 331
    Malaysia, 82, 83, 201-2
    Thailand, 190-1
ATMs, 89, 93, 265
Australia, 49, 87, 88, 339-47
    bonds, 117, 122
    deposit insurance, 71
    derivatives (traded futures and options), 126, 127, 128, 129, 134
    exports to Asia, 14-15
    monetary policy objectives, 38
    payments system, 68
    supervision, 57, 59
Australia: equity markets, 105, 106, 115
    corporate governance requirements, 110
    demutualisation, 113, 114
    disclosure rules, 109
    market surveillance, 111-12
automated systems, see technology
AXA China Region, 152

B

bank business, unbundling of, 87, 89
    Japan, 263-5, 277
    Taiwan, 246
Bank Mandiri, 93, 166
bank reserves and reserve ratios, 52, 53, 211-12
banking, 75-101, 50-62
    credit growth, 48
    deposit insurance schemes, 69-72
    incentives for foreign borrowing, 26
    lending, 28-31, 32-3, 40-1
    see also asset management companies; non-performing loans; see also under name of country
banking technologies, see technology
bankruptcy laws, 65-7, 187-8, 198
Barings incident, 132
Basle Capital Accord, 50, 51
benchmark yield curves, 121-2, 329
bond markets, 116-25
    see also under name of country
Britain, 58, 68, 105, 115

C

capital, 21-45, 49
    payments system, 67-9
    life insurance markets, 147-8
    see also recapitalisation
capital adequacy standards, 50-1, 52, 209, 245
capital markets, 61, 103-38
    see also bond markets; derivatives; equities markets
Chile, 76, 81
China, 285-317
    accounting standards, 109, 291
    bonds, 116-17, 289, 313-14
    capital markets, 310-14
    credit cooperatives, 142, 143, 287, 310
    derivatives (traded futures and options), 128, 129
    exchange rate regime, 286
    gross domestic product (GDP), 31, 37, 117, 297
    insurance, 144-6, 147, 288, 305-8
    pension schemes, 151, 153
    private capital inflows, 30-1
    short term foreign debt, 41
    trust and investment companies, 287, 308-10
China: banking, 286-304
    closures, 85, 301
    electronic, 89
    foreign, 32, 288, 302-4
    lending, 1996, 31
    non-performing loans (NPLs), 285, 290, 295-7
    reserve ratios, 53
    securitisation, 92
China: equity markets, 114, 289, 311-13, 314
    accounting standards, 109
    market capitalisation, 104, 106, 107, 311
    participants, 108, 312
China: prudential and financial reform, 285-6, 289-91, 295-9
    bankruptcy law, 66
    insurance, 306
    payments system, 68, 69
    reserve ratios, 53
    security market, 313
    supervision, 56, 57, 59
Citibank, 93
closures of financial institutions, 85
    China, 85, 301, 309
    Indonesia, 85, 163, 165
    Philippines, 207
CMG Asia (Colonial Group), 95, 149, 307
Columbia, 76
Commonwealth Bank of Australia, 90
Compendium of Standards, 34
contract performance (derivatives), 131-2
corporate bankruptcies, 65-7, 187-8, 198
corporate bonds, see bond markets
corporate finance, 263, 326
corporate governance, 27, 63-5, 110, 339-41

Indonesia, 27, 63, 110, 178
Singapore, 233
corporate stock market participants, 107-8
corporate structure, 242
costs of derivatives trading, effects of regulation on, 132
costs of recapitalisation, see recapitalisation
costs of reinsurance, 148
credit cards, 89
credit growth, 48
credit ratings, 26-7, 122
currencies, see exchange rates
current account balances, 25, 184, 240

D

Danaharta, 83, 201-2
Danamodal, 84, 202-3
demutualisation, 113-14, 225-6, 271
deposit insurance schemes, 69-72, 299
deregulation of financial markets, 88, 90
derivatives (futures and options), 125-34
    see also under name of country
Development Bank of Singapore, 95
disclosure, 61-2, 109-10
    Philippines, 210, 213
    Taiwan, 243
downsizing, 270

E

Economic and Financial Management Initiative, 340
economic governance, 339-41
    see also corporate governance
electronic banking, 88, 89, 93
electronic disclosure, 109
electronic trading, 106, 111-12, 113, 115, 123, 133, 134
employees, 93
    Chinese banks, 291, 292, 293
    Japanese banks, 270
entry barriers, 49
equity markets, 23-4, 104-15
    see also under name of country
European Union banks, 33
excessive forbearance, 54-5
exchange rates, 22-3, 37-8
    China, 286
    Hong Kong, 227-9
    Indonesia, 22, 37, 38, 159-60
    Malaysia, 22, 199
    Taiwan, 37, 239
    Thailand, 22, 38, 185
exchange-traded markets, 125-34
exports, 22-3, 227
    Australian, to Asia, 14-15
exposure limits, 52, 53-4

F

family ownership/control, 54, 95, 108, 252
fees and charges, 87, 89
financial infrastructure reform, see prudential and financial infrastructure reform
Financial Stability Forum, 34, 35

First Data Resources Australia, 97
forbearance, 54-5
foreign banks, 32-3, 40-1, 93-9
    see also under name of host country
foreign bond investors, 124
foreign borrowing, 25–6
foreign currency debt ratings, 26-7
foreign currency deposit units (Philippines), 209, 210
foreign direct investment flows, 28-31, 200
foreign derivatives investors, 133-4
foreign exchange, see exchange rates
foreign ownership restrictions, 94, 111, 133-4, 312
foreign participation, 93-9, 341-2
    China, 302-4, 306, 307-8, 315
    Hong Kong, 95
    Indonesia, 168-9, 174
    Japan, 273-9
    Korea, 332-4
    Malaysia, 203-4
    Philippines, 213-14
    Taiwan, 247-9, 250, 251, 252-3, 256
    Singapore, 233-4
    Thailand, 95, 96, 186, 188
futures and options (derivatives), 125-34
    see also under name of country

G

G20, 34
GE Capital, 96, 168
Germany, 26, 105, 115
GITIC, 309
government bonds, see bond markets
gross domestic product (GDP), 36-7
    current account balance as proportion of, 25
    government bonds outstanding as proportion of, 117
    private capital inflows as percentage of, 31
    recapitalisation costs, 80
    see also under name of country
guarantee funds, 131

H

Hainan Development Bank, 301
harmonisation of rating standards, 122
highly leveraged institutions (hedge funds), 35
Hong Kong, 221-9, 236
    Australian exports to, 14-15
    bonds, 121-2, 123, 124, 116-19, 226
    derivatives (traded futures and options), 128, 129, 133, 225-6
    gross domestic product (GDP), 37, 117, 227
    life insurance, 144-6, 147
    pension schemes, 150, 151, 152, 153
    real estate investment, 23, 91, 227
Hong Kong: banking, 77, 222-4
    deposit insurance, 70, 71
    foreign, 93, 95, 99, 222-3, 224
    non-performing loans (NPLs), 78, 95, 223-4
    securitisation, 91
Hong Kong: equity markets, 224-6, 229
    accounting standards, 109
    listed companies, 113

market capitalisation, 104, 105, 106, 107
stock prices boom, 24
technology, 106, 112
Hong Kong: prudential and financial infrastructure reform, 36, 49, 221, 223-6
   bankruptcy laws, 66, 67
   deposit insurance, 70, 71
   payments system, 68, 69
   supervision, 57, 59, 61
Hong Kong Shanghai Bank, 93

I

IMF, 34, 42-3
implications for Australia, 339-47
incentives for foreign borrowing, 26
independence of supervisory authorities, 55-7, 177, 212
India, 57
Indonesia, 159-81
   accounting standards, 110, 178-9
   bonds, 118, 119, 120, 121, 122, 171-2
   corporate governance, 110, 178
   current account deficits, 25
   derivatives (traded futures and options), 128
   exchange rates, 22, 37, 38, 159-60
   exports, 23
   foreign currency debt ratings, 1996-97, 27
   gross domestic product (GDP), 25, 31, 37, 81, 159, 161
   insurance, 144-7, 173-4
   interest rates, 24-5, 26, 160, 211, 241
   pension schemes, 150, 153
   private capital inflows, 30-1
   real estate investment, 23, 52
   short term foreign debt, 31, 32, 40
Indonesia: banking, 52, 76, 161-9, 174-7
   closures, 85, 163, 165
   capital adequacy standards, 50, 93, 175
   corporate governance, 27, 63
   deposit insurance, 71
   exposure limits, 52, 53-4
   foreign, 32, 93, 96, 99, 165
   lending, 31, 32, 161
   non-performing loans (NPLs), 78, 79, 82, 159, 161
   recapitalisation, 80, 81 84, 165, 166-7
Indonesia: equity markets, 161, 170-1
   accounting standards, 110
   enforcement, 112, 113
   foreign ownership restrictions, 111
   listed companies, 113, 171
   market capitalisation, 104, 105, 106, 107, 171
   participants, 107, 108
   stock prices boom, 24
Indonesia: prudential and financial infrastructure reform, 36, 49, 164-70, 174-9
   bankruptcy laws, 65-6
   capital adequacy standards, 50, 93, 175
   corporate governance, 27, 63, 110, 178
   deposit insurance, 71
   exposure limits, 52, 53-4
   IMF package, 42-3
   payments system, 68
   pre-crisis, 25, 162, 163
   supervision, 54, 56, 57, 59, 175-7

Indonesian Bank Restructuring Agency (IBRA), 53-4, 165
Indonesian Debt Restructuring Agency, 170
information disclosure, *see* disclosure
insolvency laws, 65-7, 187-8, 198
Institute for Financial Stability, 56
institutional arrangements, and supervision, 58-61
institutional investors, 108
insurance, 88, 90, 143-9
   Australian exports to Asia, 14
   see also under name of country
interest rates, 24-5, 26, 49, 211
   China, 291
   Hong Kong, 227
   Indonesia, 24-5, 26, 160, 211, 241
   Japan, 26, 263
   Malaysia, 200, 211
   Taiwan, 240-1
   Thailand, 26, 211, 241
international banks, 32-3, 40-1, 93-9
   see also foreign participation; *see also under name of host country*
international financial architecture, 34-6
International Monetary Fund (IMF), 34, 42-3
Internet, 109
   banking, 88, 89
investment, 23-4, 28-31, 103-38

J

Jakarta Initiative, 169
Japan, 261-83
   Australian exports to, 14-15
   bonds, 116-19, 121, 123, 262, 263, 264
   credit cooperatives, 140, 142
   depreciation of yen, 38
   derivatives (traded futures and options), 127, 128, 129, 133, 278
   gross domestic product (GDP), 37, 81, 117
   interest rates, 26, 263
   pension schemes, 150, 152, 153, 154, 274
   postal savings system, 262, 280
Japan: banking, 76, 77, 261, 264-8, 277-9, 281
   asset management companies, 81
   capital adequacy standards, 50
   closures, 85
   deposit insurance, 71, 72
   foreign, 93, 96, 276-7
   international lending source, 33
   mergers and alliances (structural change), 270-1, 272
   nationalisation, 84, 265
   non-performing loans (NPLs), 82, 265-70
   recapitalisation, 81, 84, 86, 265-6
   as savings vehicle, 262
   securitisation, 91
Japan: equity markets, 114, 262, 263, 264, 274, 277
   accounting standards, 110
   listed companies, 113
   market capitalisation, 104, 105, 106, 107
Japan: insurance, 143, 144-7, 264, 271
   foreign companies, 275-6
   non-performing loans (NPLs), 268-70
   as saving vehicle, 262

Japan: prudential and financial infrastructure reform, 36, 49, 261-2, 263-6, 280
    bankruptcy laws, 66
    capital adequacy standards, 50
    deposit insurance, 71, 72
    payments system, 68
    supervision, 54, 59, 56

K

Korea, 319-37
    bonds, 116-19, 122, 124, 328-31
    current account deficits, 25
    derivatives (traded futures and options), 126, 128, 129, 327-8
    exchange rates, 22, 37
    exports, 23
    foreign currency debt ratings, 1996-97, 27
    gross domestic product (GDP), 25, 31, 37, 81, 117
    interest rates, 24-5, 26
    private capital inflows, 30-1
    short term foreign debt, 31, 32, 40
Korea: banking, 76, 321-2
    asset management company, 83, 331
    capital adequacy standards, 50, 51
    closures, 85
    deposit insurance, 70, 71, 72
    foreign, 32, 98, 320, 332-4
    incentives for foreign borrowing, 26
    lending, 31, 32
    mergers, 85, 86, 98
    nationalisation, 84-5
    non-performing loans (NPLs), 78-9, 82, 324, 331
    recapitalisation, 80, 81, 84, 86
    securitisation, 91
Korea: equity markets, 326-7, 328
    accounting standards, 110
    corporate governance requirements, 110
    disclosure, 109
    enforcement, 112
    foreign ownership restrictions, 111
    listed companies, 113
    market capitalisation, 104, 105, 106, 107, 326-7
    market surveillance, 112
    stock prices boom, 24
Korea: non-bank financial institutions, 143, 322-3
    insurance, 144-7, 148, 322, 323, 334
    investment trust companies, 322, 331
    merchant banks, 141, 142
    pension schemes, 150, 153
Korea: prudential and financial infrastructure reform, 36, 49, 143, 319-25
    bankruptcy laws, 65, 66
    capital adequacy standards, 50, 51
    corporate governance, 63, 64-5, 110
    deposit insurance, 70, 71, 72
    disclosure, 61
    IMF package, 42-3
    payments system, 68
    supervision, 55, 56, 57, 60, 320
Korean Asset Management Corporation, 83, 331

L

Latin America, 76, 139-40
legal infrastructure reform, 65-7
    China, 289, 291
    Indonesia, 174-5, 177-8
    Japan, 271, 272
    Korea, 55, 320
    Malaysia, 66, 198
    Philippines, 212, 213, 214
    Taiwan, 67, 242
    Thailand, 185-6, 187-8
life insurance, see insurance
liquidity, 52, 53
    bond market makers, 123
listed companies, 107, 109-10, 112-13
    Indonesia, 113, 171
    Taiwan, 113, 253
loan loss allowances, 52
    Philippines, 52, 209, 210
    Taiwan, 243

M

Macquarie Bank, 92, 278
Malaysia, 195-205, 216-17
    bonds, 117-19, 122, 123, 199
    capital market reform, 198-200
    current account deficits, 25
    derivatives (traded futures and options), 114, 128, 130, 133
    exchange rates, 22, 199
    exports, 23
    finance companies, 140, 142, 198
    foreign currency debt ratings, 1996-97, 27
    gross domestic product (GDP), 25, 37, 81, 117
    insurance, 144-6, 204
    interest rates, 211
    pension schemes, 149, 150, 153, 154
    private capital inflows, 30-1
    real estate investment, 23, 52
    short term foreign debt, 31, 32, 40
Malaysia: banking, 52, 76, 196-7
    asset management company, 82, 83, 201-2
    deposit insurance, 71
    family ownership, 95
    foreign, 32, 204
    lending, 31, 32
    liquidity requirements, 52, 53
    mergers, 85-6, 90, 203
    non-performing loans (NPLs), 78, 79, 82, 197, 200-2
    recapitalisation, 81, 202-3
Malaysia: equity markets, 114, 115, 196, 198-9
    corporate governance requirements, 110
    foreign ownership restrictions, 111
    information disclosure, 109
    listed companies, 113
    market capitalisation, 104, 105, 106, 107
    market surveillance, 112
    settlement system, 111
    stock prices boom, 24

Malaysia: prudential and financial infrastructure reform, 36, 49, 52, 197-200
    bankruptcy laws, 66, 198
    corporate governance, 27, 63-4
    deposit insurance, 71
    liquidity requirements, 52, 53
    payments system, 68
    supervision, 57, 60
margining, 131
market capitalisation, 104-6, 107, 114
market fairness regulation (derivatives), 132
market liberalisation, see prudential and financial infrastructure reforms
market prospects, 14-15, 341-2
    see also foreign participation
market sentiment, 26-7
market surveillance and settlement, 111-12, 123
mergers and acquisitions, 85-6, 90, 91, 95–6, 114-15
    Hong Kong, 95, 225-6
    Indonesia, 164-6, 168
    Japan, 270-2, 274, 277-8, 279
    Korea, 98, 322
    Malaysia, 85-6, 90, 203
    Philippines, 98, 213
    Taiwan, 247
    Thailand, 86, 95, 98, 192
    see also foreign participation
Mexico, 32, 76
monetary policy, 38, 289-90
Moody's, 122

N

nationalisation, 84-5, 165, 166, 191-3
New Zealand, 62, 68, 87
non-bank financial institutions, 139-57
    see also under name of country
non-performing loans (NPLs), 50, 77-86
    China, 285, 290, 295-7
    Hong Kong, 78, 95, 223-4
    Indonesia, 78, 79, 82, 159, 161
    Japan, 82, 265-70
    Korea, 78-9, 82, 324, 331
    Malaysia, 78, 79, 82, 197, 200-2
    Philippines, 78, 208-9, 210
    Taiwan, 78, 243, 244, 245-6, 250
    Thailand, 78, 79, 82, 95, 186, 190-1
North American Securities Dealing and Automated Quotation System (NASDAQ), 105, 114, 115

O

occupational pension schemes, see pension schemes
offshore financial centres, 35
outsourcing, 87, 96-7
over-the-counter markets, 116, 127, 128
overseas banks, 32-3, 40-1, 93-9
    see also foreign participation and under name of host country
ownership/control, 54, 95, 108, 252
    restrictions, 94, 111, 133-4, 312
    see also mergers and acquisition

P

Panin Bank, 168
past due loan definitions, 52
payments system, 67-9
pension schemes, 139-40, 149-54, 342
    see also under name of country
People's Bank of China, 289-91
Philippines, 205-17
    bonds, 120, 121, 122, 123, 214
    current account deficits, 25
    derivatives (traded futures and options), 128, 130
    exchange rates, 22, 37, 38
    exports, 23
    finance companies, 140, 207, 214
    foreign currency debt ratings, 1996-97, 27
    gross domestic product (GDP), 25, 31, 37, 207
    insurance, 144-7, 148, 212
    interest rates, 26, 211
    pension schemes, 150, 153, 154
    private capital inflows, 30-1
    real estate investment, 52, 209
    short term foreign debt, 31, 32, 40
Philippines: banking, 52, 205, 206-13, 215-16
    deposit insurance, 71
    family ownership, 95
    foreign, 32, 93, 98, 208, 213-14
    incentives for foreign borrowing, 26
    lending, 31, 32
    mergers and acquisitions, 98, 213
    non-performing loans (NPLs), 78, 208-9, 210
    reserve ratios, 52, 53
Philippines: equity markets, 212, 214, 215
    accounting standards, 109
    enforcement, 112
    listed companies, 113
    market capitalisation, 104, 105, 106, 107, 114
    stock prices boom, 24
Philippines: prudential and financial infrastructure reform, 49, 52, 205, 207, 209-13
    deposit insurance, 71
    disclosure, 61
    reserve ratios, 52, 53
    payments system, 68
    securities market, 215
    supervision, 57, 60, 212-13
Ping An Insurance, 306, 307
political interference, 54
portfolio investment, 28-31
powers of supervisors, 55
price limits (derivatives), 132
prices of equities, 23-4
private capital flows, 27-31
private sector involvement in crisis management, 35-6
private sector pension schemes, see pension schemes
privatisation, 49
    Indonesia, 166
    Philippines, 214
    Taiwan, 244-5
    Thailand, 192

Index

prudential and financial framework, 65-7
  bond markets, 119-20
  derivatives markets, 131-2
  international, 34-6
  non-bank financial institutions, 140-3
prudential and financial infrastructure reform, 36-8, 47-74, 88, 90
  banking, 81-6
  capital inflows and, 36-7
  IMF packages, 42-3
  non-bank financial institutions, 142-3, 153-4
  sequencing of, 25, 48
  stock exchanges, 108-15
  see also under name of country
public bond markets, *see* bond markets
public capital injections, *see* recapitalisation
public pension schemes, *see* pension schemes

R

real estate investment, 23, 52, 53
  Hong Kong, 23, 91, 227
  Philippines, 52, 209
  Taiwan, 23, 241
recapitalisation, 80-1, 84
  China, 297-8
  Indonesia, 80, 81 84, 165, 166-7
  Japan, 81, 84, 86, 265-6
  Korea, 80, 81, 323-4
  Malaysia, 81, 202-3
  Thailand, 80, 81, 84, 86, 188-90
reforms, *see* prudential and financial reforms
regional financial centre, Australia as, 344-5
regulation, *see* prudential and financial framework
reinsurance costs, 148
Republic of Korea, *see* Korea
reserves and reserve ratios, 52, 53, 211-12
resource misallocation, 23-4
risk based supervision, 61
risk management instruments, *see* derivatives
RTGS systems, 67-9

S

savings, 239-40, 262
securities markets, *see* equities markets
securitisation, 87, 91-2, 199
settlement and market surveillance, 111-12, 123
Shanghai City Cooperative Bank, 302
share markets, *see* securities markets
short term foreign borrowing/debt, 31, 32, 35, 40-1
  Taiwan, 240
  Thailand, 31, 32, 40, 184
Singapore, 230-6
  Australian exports to, 14-15
  bonds, 116-18, 120, 123, 124, 232
  derivatives (traded futures and options), 115, 127, 128, 130, 133, 134
  gross domestic product (GDP), 37, 117, 230
  insurance, 144-6, 148, 232
  interest rates, 211
  pension schemes, 149, 150, 152, 153, 234-5
  real estate investment, 23

Singapore: banking, 77, 89, 230, 235
  capital adequacy standards, 50
  deposit insurance, 71
  family ownership, 95
  foreign, 233-4
  non-performing loans (NPLs), 78
Singapore: equity markets, 109, 113, 115, 230-1, 232
  market capitalisation, 104, 105, 106, 107, 114
Singapore: prudential and financial infrastructure reform, 36, 49, 231-5
  bankruptcy laws, 66, 67
  capital adequacy standards, 50
  deposit insurance, 71
  payments system, 68
  supervision, 57, 60, 61, 231-2
Singapore dollar, internationalisation of, 233
single borrower limits, 52, 54
skills of supervisors, 56
SMARTS, 112
South Korea, *see* Korea
Standard and Poor's, 27, 122
Standard Chartered Bank, 168
stock markets, *see* equity markets
supervision, 27, 54-62
  see also under name of country

T

Taiwan, 239-59
  bonds, 117, 120, 121, 122, 118, 255
  credit cooperatives, 140, 142, 250-1
  derivatives (traded futures and options), 128, 255
  exchange rates, 37, 239
  gross domestic product (GDP), 37, 239, 117
  insurance, 144-7, 242, 250, 251
  money market, 253-4
  pension schemes, 150, 250
  postal savings system, 249-50
Taiwan: banking, 71, 76, 240-1, 242-9
  non-performing loans (NPLs), 78, 243, 244, 245-6, 250
Taiwan: equity markets, 109, 112, 113, 252-3
  market capitalisation, 104, 105, 107, 253
Taiwan: prudential and financial infrastructure reform, 36, 49, 242-3
  bankruptcy laws, 67
  deposit insurance, 71
  supervision, 57, 60
taxation regimes, 120
technology, 88, 89, 93
  bond markets, 123
  derivatives trading, 133, 134
  stock exchanges, 106, 109, 111-12, 113, 115
Thailand, 183-95, 216-17
  bonds, 116-19, 120, 122, 194
  current account deficit, 25, 184
  exchange rates, 22, 38, 185
  exports, 23
  foreign currency debt ratings, 1996-97, 27
  gross domestic product (GDP), 25, 31, 37, 81, 117, 184, 190, 195
  interest rates, 26, 211, 241

354

private capital inflows, 30-1
real estate investment, 23, 52
short term foreign debt, 31, 32, 40, 184
Thailand: banking, 52, 76, 185-7, 188-94
    capital adequacy standards, 50-1, 52
    closures, 85
    foreign, 32, 93, 95, 96, 98, 186
    incentives for foreign borrowing, 26
    lending, 31, 32: limits, 52, 54
    mergers and acquisitions, 86, 90, 95, 98, 192
    non-performing loans (NPLs), 78, 79, 82, 95, 186, 190-1
    recapitalisation, 80, 81, 84, 86, 188-90
Thailand: equity markets, 110, 112-13, 194
    foreign ownership, 111, 186
    market capitalisation, 104, 105, 106, 107
    stock prices boom, 24
Thailand: non-bank financial institutions, 141, 142, 185, 186, 241
    closures, 85, 193
    insurance, 144-7, 195
    pension schemes, 150, 152, 153
Thailand: prudential and financial infrastructure reform, 36, 49, 52, 185-8
    capital adequacy standards, 50-1, 52
    corporate governance, 63, 65
    IMF package, 42-3
    lending limits, 52, 54
    payments system, 68
    supervision, 56, 57, 60, 193-4
Toronto International Leadership Centre for Financial Sector Supervision, 56
trading halts (derivatives), 132
training, 56, 93
transparency and accountability, 34, 57, 109-10, 178-9, 291
    see also corporate governance; disclosure
treasury bonds, *see* bond markets

U

United Kingdom, 58, 68, 105, 115
United States
    banking, 76, 77, 87, 88: deposit insurance, 70, 71
    capital markets, 106, 117, 133
    interest rates, 26

V

Venezuela, 76
Vietnam, 93, 96

W

World Trade Organisation, 308

X

    Xinda AMC, 298

Y

    yield curves, 121-2, 329
    'yield gaps' (life insurance), 147

Index

ALSO BY THE EAST ASIA ANALYTICAL UNIT

Australia and North-East Asia in the 1990s: Accelerating Change
Published February 1992 (ISBN 0 644 24376 7), 318 pages, A$15

Korea to the Year 2000: Implications for Australia
Published November 1992 (ISBN 0 644 27819 5), 150 pages, A$10

Grain in China
Published December 1992 (ISBN 0 644 25813 6), 150 pages, A$10

Southern China in Transition
Published December 1992 (ISBN 0 644 25814 4), 150 pages, A$10

Australia's Business Challenge: South-East Asia in the 1990s
Published December 1992 (ISBN 0 644 25852 7), 380 pages, A$15

Changing Tack: Australian Investment in South-East Asia
Published March 1994 (ISBN 0 644 33075 9), 110 pages, A$10

ASEAN Free Trade Area: Trading Bloc or Building Block?
Published April 1994 (ISBN 0 644 33325 1), 180 pages, A$10

India's Economy at the Midnight Hour: Australia's India Strategy
Published April 1994 (ISBN 0 644 33328 6), 260 pages, A$15

Expanding Horizons: Australia and Indonesia into the 21st Century
Published June 1994 (ISBN 0 644 33514 9), 350 pages, A$10

Subsistence To Supermarket: Food and Agricultural Transformation in South-East Asia
Published August 1994 (ISBN 0 644 35093 8), 376 pages, A$10

Overseas Chinese Business Networks in Asia
Published August 1995 (ISBN 0 642 22960 0), 362 pages, A$20

Growth Triangles of South East Asia
Published November 1995 (ISBN 0 642 23571 6), 136 pages, only available online.

Iron and Steel in China and Australia
Published November 1995 (ISBN 0 642 24404 9), 110 pages, A$10

Pacific Russia: Risks and Rewards
Published April 1996 (ISBN 0 642 24521 5), 119 pages, A$10

Asia's Global Powers: China-Japan Relations in the 21st Century
Published April 1996 (ISBN 0 642 24525 8), 158 pages, A$10

China Embraces the Market: Achievements, Constraints and Opportunities
Published April 1997 (ISBN 0 642 26952 1), 448 pages, A$20

A New Japan? Change in Asia's Megamarket
Published June 1997 (ISBN 0 642 27131 3), 512 pages, A$20

The New Aseans - Vietnam, Burma, Cambodia and Laos
Published June 1997 (ISBN 0642 27148 8), 380 pages, $20

The Philippines - Beyond the Crisis
Published May 1998 (ISBN 0 642 30521 8), 380 pages, $30

Asia's Infrastructure in the Crisis - Harnessing Private Enterprise
Published December 1998 (ISBN 0 642 50149 1), 230 pages, $30

Korea Rebuilds - From Crisis to Opportunity
Published May 1999 (ISBN 0 642 47624 1), 260 pages, $35

Forthcoming Titles

Thailand: Recovery Prospects and Opportunities, February 2000

The Arabian Peninsula and Iran: Australia's Trade and Investment Prospects, June 2000

Reports can be obtained from:

Jane Monico
Market Information and Analysis Unit
Department of Foreign Affairs and Trade
RG Casey Building, John McEwen Crescent
Barton ACT 0221
Australia

Telephone: 61 2 6261 3114   Facsimile: 61 2 6261 3321

Email: jane.monico@dfat.gov.au

Internet: www.dfat.gov.au/eaau
(provides access to executive summaries, briefing papers and an order form)